A GUIDE TO THE
REPTILES
OF SOUTHERN AFRICA

A GUIDE TO THE
REPTILES
OF SOUTHERN AFRICA

Graham Alexander
Johan Marais

ACKNOWLEDGEMENTS

Most importantly, we thank our families for putting up with us while we wrote this book. Griffen, Josh and Amy Alexander kept us sane, and Natasha Alexander provided sustained support. Riaana Uys also had to cope with a present but rather distant partner at times, and Melissa Marais renamed herself 'Annie the orphan' for obvious reasons. Helen and Peter Emery are thanked for providing free accommodation at 'The Pink Slipper and Smoking Lounge' during our frequent visits to Struik Publishers in Cape Town.

We owe a debt of gratitude to Aaron Bauer, Paul Moler, Marius Burger, Rose Sephton-Poultney and Bryan Maritz for reading and commenting on sections of the text. You made an enormous contribution to improving the quality of this work. Thank you.

The distribution maps presented in this book were drawn using data from several sources. We thank Barend Erasmus and Bryan Maritz for help with computing of maps, and James Harrison (SARCA) and Bill Branch for providing information on distributions. Bryan Maritz constructed the species richness map.

Many people have generously and graciously allowed us to publish their most stunning photographs. Specifically, in alphabetical order according to first name, we thank Adnan Moussalli, Andrew Turner, Atherton de Villiers, Bill Branch, Bryan Maritz, Colin Tilbury, Dave Honiball, David Maguire, Devi Stuart-Fox, Dick Bartlett, Duncan Mitchell, Jaco van Wyk, John Visser, Krystal Tolley, Marius Burger, Mark Marshall, Martin Whiting, Orty Bourquin, Randy Babb, Richard Boycott, Richard Boynton (of Critters and Creatures), Sarah Davies, Shirley Hanrahan, Steve Spawls, Tony Phelps, Vince Egan, Warren Schmidt and Wulf Haacke. The enthusiasm and willingness with which you acceded to our requests is an example of the camaraderie between southern African herpetologists.

Richard Boynton, Gavin Carpenter, Rob Deans, Liesl du Toit, Vince Egan, Mike Griffin, James Harvey, Mike Jaensch, Mike Perry, Gordon Setaro and Barry Stander kindly supplied specimens for us to photograph.

Spending time in the field is an opportunity to bond with like-minded people and benefit from their incredible herpetological knowledge. It is obviously not possible to list all of the people with whom we have done field work – the list would be too long – but we would like to thank the following, again in alphabetical order: Aaron Bauer, Bill Branch, Bryan Maritz, Chris Kruger, Donald Strydom, Gavin Masterson, Gordon Setaro, Jon Warner, Marius Burger, Mo Roedel, Paul Moler, Phillip Attenborough, Randy Babb, Sue McConnachie and Trevor Keith.

The herpetological community of southern Africa, through the guise of the Herpetological Association of Africa and the Southern African Reptile Conservation Assessment initiative, influenced and improved the content of this book in more ways than we can list. Additionally, our collective boss, the University of the Witwatersrand, provided us with the environment, latitude and luxury of freedom to allow us to take on this project. The staff of Fascination Books are also thanked for steering the ship in the right direction during Johan's extended absences.

As with the conception of a human, the creation of this field guide was exciting. However, bringing the 'child' into the world was also an unexpectedly painful, sapping exercise that seemed to fill all available gaps in our busy schedules. We thank Struik Publishers and the personnel at Struik, especially Pippa Parker, Colette Alves and Robin Cox for (reluctantly) subscribing to our concept of 'the mobile deadline'. Their continued support throughout the project can only be attributed to blind faith. We thank them also for being our safety net and asking the obvious questions.

But most of all, we thank our readers for buying this book. We ask you to use it in any way you can to promote the conservation of reptiles in southern Africa.

PREFACE

This book is aimed at wildlife enthusiasts who are interested in the reptiles of southern Africa. In some respects, it does not follow a conventional format for a field guide: rather than being dealt with individually, the majority of species are grouped according to their appearance, and occasionally a group includes species that are not even closely related to one another. One of the underlying philosophies used for clustering species into groups was: 'Could a layperson be expected to differentiate between two species without the aid of specialized equipment?' If not, the two species were placed in the same group. Many species of southern African reptiles can only be identified to species level with careful and detailed observation, with the aid of a binocular microscope. Even more frustrating for the non-expert, new molecular techniques are delineating species that cannot be differentiated from closely related species by morphology alone. This means that, in certain instances, positive identification to species level is simply beyond the capability of non-experts, and can even be a challenge for experts. Identification of reptile species is generally more difficult than it is for species of other vertebrate groups, such as birds or mammals. This is probably because their specific habitat requirements result in low dispersal abilities, increasing the potential for neighbouring populations to become genetically isolated and distinct, but with few physical differences. This is especially true for lizards that are dependent on specific types of rock or soil.

In certain instances, species have been grouped where two or more rare species are similar in habit, or where little is known of their biology. This allows space for more detailed notes on the biology of the better-studied species. Information on new discoveries resulting from ongoing research have therefore been included to give the reader a better 'feel' for the ecology, physiology and natural history of each group. An up-to-date list of species (at the time of going to press) in each group is provided. Information on the distribution and reproductive biology is also supplied, and conservation issues of threatened species are considered above and beyond the official 'Red Listings' of current conservation assessments.

Although this field guide is reasonably comprehensive in its coverage, 12 species have not been included in the species accounts. These species are either restricted to very small ranges in the northern extremes of southern Africa, or occur only in inaccessible localities. They are therefore not likely to be encountered by the vast majority of readers, and little is known about their biology. Specifically, omitted species are the Black and Yellow Burrowing Snake (*Chilorhinophis gerardi*), Olympic Snake (*Dromophis lineatus*), Semiornate Snake (*Meizodon semiornatus*), Cunene Racer (*Coluber zebrinus*), Lowland Swamp Viper (*Proatheris superciliarus*), Bouton's Skink (*Cryptoblepharus boutonii*), two species of Rock Lizard (*Australolacerta*), the Tree Lizard (*Holaspis guentheri*), two species of Leaf Chameleon (*Rhampholeon*) and the Tete Gecko (*Elasmodactylus tetensis*).

Graham Alexander   Johan Marais

Struik Publishers
(a division of New Holland Publishing
(South Africa) (Pty) Ltd)
Cornelis Struik House
80 McKenzie Street
Cape Town 8001

New Holland Publishing is a member
of Johnnic Communications Ltd.

Visit us at **www.struik.co.za**
Log on to our photographic website
www.imagesofafrica.co.za
for an African experience.

First published in 2007

ISBN 978 1 77007 386 9

Publishing manager: **Pippa Parker**
Managing editor: **Helen de Villiers**
Editor: **Colette Alves**
Design director: **Janice Evans**
Designer & illustrator: **Robin Cox**
Proofreader: **Glynne Newlands**

Reproduction by Hirt & Carter Cape (Pty) Ltd
Printed and bound by Sing Cheong Printing Company Limited

Front cover: Augrabies Flat Lizard; Back cover: Sungazer;
Page 1: Drakensberg Crag Lizard; Page 2: Cape Cobra;
Page 3: Giant Plated Lizard; Page 6: Green Water Snake (all Johan Marais)
Page 7: Cedarberg Dwarf Leaf-toed Gecko (Marius Burger)

CONTENTS

INTRODUCTION

Southern Africa is blessed with an extra-ordinarily diverse and rich reptile fauna that compares favourably with other parts of Africa of equivalent size. At the time of going to press, there was a total of 517 described species for the subregion (151 snakes, 338 lizards, 27 tortoises and one crocodile). Many more species, including new species of Tent Tortoise, Dwarf Chameleon, Sand Lizard, Flat Lizard, Flat Gecko and other geckos, are currently known or are being studied, but since they are still awaiting description in the scientific literature they cannot feature in this book. It is likely that many more novelties await discovery and that the real species number for southern Africa easily exceeds 600. This richness in reptiles is greater than that of the entire USA and is a largely unappreciated and undervalued part of southern Africa's natural heritage.

New scientific descriptions of southern African reptile species are proceeding at an unprecedented rate and this trend shows no sign of abating in the near future. In some respects it is surprising, since herpetology has a long and prestigious history on the subcontinent, beginning in the mid-seventeenth century. Herpetological interest grew strongly in the eighteenth and nineteenth centuries, driven by eminent herpetologists such as Sir Andrew Smith (1797–1850) and Wilhelm Peters (1815–1883), who collected and described many new species in the area. During the twentieth century, interest and expertise grew strongly and was championed by the likes of George Boulenger (1858–1937), John Hewitt (1880–1961), Arthur Loveridge (1891–1980) and Dr Vivian FitzSimons (1901–1975). There are several contemporary, influential herpetologists currently taking the study of reptiles forward. Donald Broadley, Bill Branch, Aaron Bauer and Wulf Haacke stand out as beacons, and are responsible for igniting a broad base of interest that is expanding at an exponential rate. Over the last decade, herpetology has become a focus at several universities in South Africa, and a surge in international collaborations in reptile research southern Africa illustrates that the region's herpetological richness is becoming more widely recognized. in

Sadly, reptiles have been neglected by most conservation plans and are generally ignored in conservation management in southern Africa. The most recent Red Data Book evaluating the conservation status of South Africa's reptiles was published more than 19 years ago; it is now largely obsolete, and does not comply with the latest internationally accepted IUCN (The World Conservation Union) criteria for the red listing of threatened species. The only other country in southern Africa whose reptiles have been 'comprehensively' evaluated is Swaziland. The IUCN standardized the categories, criteria and protocols for assigning levels of threat to species in the 1990s, but these standards have yet to be applied to most southern African reptile species. The few assessments that have been undertaken (see **www.IUCNredlist.org**) are based on scanty data and there is an obvious trend for the preferential assessment of large, charismatic species at the expense of small, cryptic ones. It is obvious that the current IUCN threat classifications for reptiles of southern Africa cannot always be taken at face value and are certainly not comprehensive. This state of affairs significantly undermines attempts at conservation efforts for reptiles in the subregion. For this reason, this field guide also highlights species that may be of conservation concern, but are not currently listed as threatened by the IUCN.

New and exciting developments are on the horizon: a collaborative research project, the Southern African Reptile Conservation Assessment (SARCA), was initiated in 2004, and is due to deliver a comprehensive conservation assessment of all reptile species occurring in South Africa, Lesotho and Swaziland in 2009. Readers are encouraged to download more information on this initiative from the internet (**www.reptiles.sanbi.org**), and to participate in the online submission of photographic data, which will be used in the most comprehensive conservation assessment of the subregion's reptiles to date. In this way, you will be able to contribute directly to the conservation of southern African reptiles.

Johan Marais

Johan Marais

HOW TO USE THIS BOOK

The reptiles featured in this book have been clustered into 116 species groups. These groups are arranged in a sequence that reflects the evolutionary relationships between the various species, in line with current understanding. The main groups appear as follows: snakes (pages 45–189), lizards (pages 190–349), crocodiles (pages 350–355) and finally, the Testudines (tortoises, terrapins and turtles; pages 356–395).

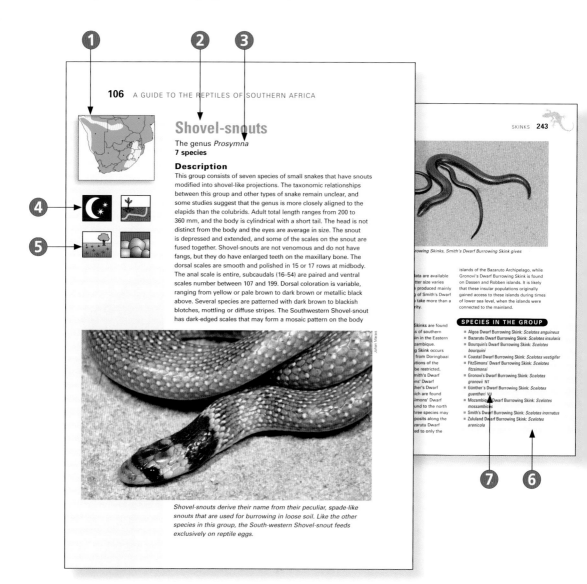

① **②** **③**

106   A GUIDE TO THE REPTILES OF SOUTHERN AFRICA

④

⑤

Shovel-snouts

The genus *Prosymna*
7 species

Description

This group consists of seven species of small snakes that have snouts modified into shovel-like projections. The taxonomic relationships between this group and other types of snake remain unclear, and some studies suggest that the genus is more closely aligned to the elapids than the colubrids. Adult total length ranges from 200 to 360 mm, and the body is cylindrical with a short tail. The head is not distinct from the body and the eyes are average in size. The snout is depressed and extended, and some of the scales on the snout are fused together. Shovel-snouts are not venomous and do not have fangs, but they do have enlarged teeth on the maxillary bone. The dorsal scales are smooth and polished in 15 or 17 rows at midbody. The anal scale is entire, subcaudals (16–54) are paired and ventral scales number between 107 and 199. Dorsal coloration is variable, ranging from yellow or pale brown to dark brown or metallic black above. Several species are patterned with dark brown to blackish blotches, mottling or diffuse stripes. The Southwestern Shovel-snout has dark-edged scales that may form a mosaic pattern on the body

Shovel-snouts derive their name from their peculiar, spade-like snouts that are used for burrowing in loose soil. Like the other species in this group, the South-western Shovel-snout feeds exclusively on reptile eggs.

SKINKS   **243**

rowing Skinks, Smith's Dwarf Burrowing Skink gives

ata are available
tter size varies
 produced mainly
g of Smith's Dwarf
 take more than a
rity.

islands of the Bazaruto Archipelago, while Gronovi's Dwarf Burrowing Skink is found on Dassen and Robben islands. It is likely that these insular populations originally gained access to these islands during times of lower sea level, when the islands were connected to the mainland.

Skinks are found
s of southern
in in the Eastern
ambique.
g Skink occurs
 from Doringbaai
tions of the
be restricted,
mith's Dwarf
ns' Dwarf
her's Dwarf
ich are found
imons' Dwarf
und to the north
hree species may
posits along the
zarutu Dwarf
ed to only the

SPECIES IN THE GROUP

- Algoa Dwarf Burrowing Skink: *Scelotes anguineus*
- Bazaruto Dwarf Burrowing Skink: *Scelotes insularis*
- Bourquin's Dwarf Burrowing Skink: *Scelotes bourquini*
- Coastal Dwarf Burrowing Skink: *Scelotes vestigifer*
- FitzSimons' Dwarf Burrowing Skink: *Scelotes fitzsimonsi*
- Gronovi's Dwarf Burrowing Skink: *Scelotes gronovii* NT
- Günther's Dwarf Burrowing Skink: *Scelotes guentheri* VU
- Mozambique Dwarf Burrowing Skink: *Scelotes mossambicus*
- Smith's Dwarf Burrowing Skink: *Scelotes inornatus*
- Zululand Dwarf Burrowing Skink: *Scelotes arenicola*

⑦ **⑥**

1 Distribution map: Each group is accompanied by a distribution map. The green areas on the map indicate the parts of southern Africa where at least one species of the group may be found. This 'area of occurrence' is only an estimate of the real distribution of the group since existing distribution data are not comprehensive and many parts of southern Africa have not been properly surveyed.

2 Group name: Each reptile group is given a common name. Where a group consists of a single species, the group name and species name are the same.

3 Group composition: This explicitly defines the group using scientific names at the most appropriate level.

4 Activity icons: These icons indicate whether the members of the group are active during the day or night.

 Diurnal – active primarily during the day.

 Nocturnal – active primarily during the night. Some 'nocturnal' species are more accurately described as 'crepuscular' as they are active for a period after sunset and then again before sunrise.

5 Habitat icons: These indicate the main habitat in which the members of the reptile group may be found. Some reptiles may be found in a variety of habitats.

ground

rock

tree

fresh water

shrub

sea

underground

sand dune

6 Species list: This lists the species (by common and scientific names) of each member in the reptile group.

7 Conservation status: Species that have been classified as threatened by the IUCN have the threat category recorded next to their names.

EX – Extinct
CR – Critically Endangered
EN – Endangered
VU – Vulnerable
NT – Near Threatened
DD – Data Deficient

Identification of reptiles

Many southern African reptiles, such as the Nile Crocodile and Southern African Python, have iconic status and are easily identified. Some species are less well known or are very similar in appearance to other, closely related species. In these cases, several more subtle characteristics may be of use in identification. Behaviour, geographic location and habitat are particularly useful for certain species. In others, the body shape or form, colour and patterning are diagnostic. Different species grow to various body sizes. In many reptile species, scale patterns and scale counts on the head and body are good keys to identification. Several of the basic scales counts and classifications are easy, but require correct identification of key scale types. The names and positions of scales are important for the identification of snakes, lizards and Testudines. Counts of the number of scale rows at midbody, and the number of ventral and subcaudal scales are also useful in identifying snakes. Generally, scale counts can only be made if the specimen is in the hand. In the case of venomous snakes, this is only feasible if the specimen is dead. Care should always be exercised when handling snakes, especially if they might be venomous.

Measurement of size

Body size is usually assessed by measuring the length of the reptile. Measures of the length of a snake or lizard can be made in two ways: the total length and the body length. As the name suggests, the total length is measured from the tip of the reptile's snout to the tip of its tail, and this is the usual way that snake size is reported in the popular literature. However, some snakes and many lizards can easily lose part or nearly all of their tail, and measures of total length of these individuals are arbitrary to a degree. Herpetologists overcome this problem by measuring the body length of snakes and lizards rather than total length.

The body length, also referred to as the 'Snout Vent Length', is taken from the tip of the animal's snout to its vent or cloaca.

Because the descriptions of species in this guide are aimed at aiding the naturalist (rather than the specialist herpetologist) in identification, the size of snakes is reported as total length. After all, it is not easy to gauge where a snake's body ends and the tail begins, unless the snake is in the hand. Lizard size is reported as body length since it is usually easy to judge where the tail begins, and lizards are often missing part of their tails.

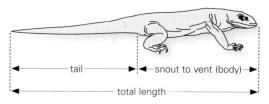

Measuring lizards and snakes

Size of tortoises, terrapins and turtles is made by measuring the length of the carapace. This is made as a straight measure in small species such as most of the tortoises and terrapins, but as a curved carapace length in the sea turtles as their large size makes measuring the straight carapace length impractical.

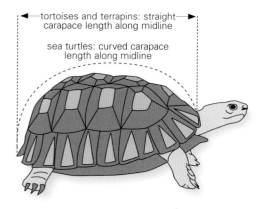

Measuring tortoises, terrapins and turtles

Scale counts

The simplest and most useful scale count for snakes is the number of rows at midbody. This is a measure of the number of longitudinal rows of dorsal scales (the ventral scale row is not counted) and is made midway between the head and cloaca, where the number of rows is at its maximum. This count can be made by progressing in a zig-zag fashion or by proceeding diagonally from one row to the next. Snakes usually have an odd number of scale rows at midbody since there is one row of scales that runs down the vertebral line of the back.

The 'ventral scale count' is a count of the total number of ventral scales along a snake's belly. The first ventral scale is defined as the first belly scale bordered on both sides by the first rows of dorsal scales, a rule that is known as the 'Dowling system'. The ventral scale count includes all ventral scales from the first one to the scale immediately in front of the anal scale.

The subcaudal scale count is the number of scales, or pairs of scales, under the tail. The count is made from the first scale or pair of scales that meet the lateral scales on either side of the tail, to the scale immediately in front of the terminal scale of the tail tip. In some instances, snakes may lose the original tail tip, and this will result in an incorrect count.

Body scale counts

 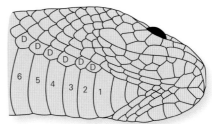

Midbody scale counts – the numbers show the two methods of counting rows at midbody. 'V' indicates ventral scales.

The Dowling system – the first ventral scale (numbered 1) is the most anterior belly scale in contact with the first dorsal row. 'D' indicates the first row of dorsal scales.

Scale counts on tails

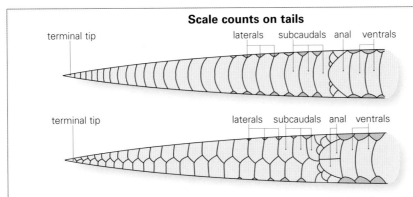

Scale counts on tails – subcaudal scales can be single (upper diagram) or paired (lower diagram), depending on the species. The anal scale may be entire (upper diagram) or divided (lower diagram).

Scale types and morphological traits

Scales on the heads and bodies of reptiles can be identified by their shape and relative position. The following diagrams can be used to identify key scales and morphological traits for reptiles in general. Scale names are similar for snakes and lizards, therefore only a snake example is provided. Chameleons have several unique traits that are diagnostic – these are illustrated opposite. Shields on the shells of tortoises, terrapins and turtles greatly facilitate identification. Naming conventions for these are provided on the page opposite.

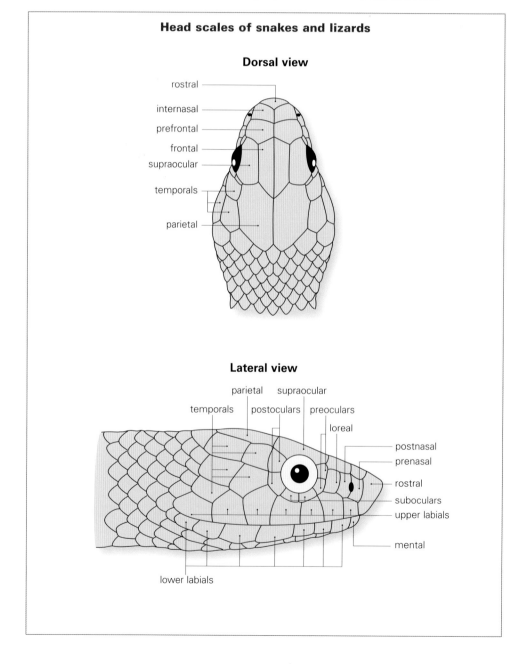

Head scales of snakes and lizards

Dorsal view

rostral
internasal
prefrontal
frontal
supraocular
temporals
parietal

Lateral view

parietal   supraocular
temporals   postoculars   preoculars
loreal
postnasal
prenasal
rostral
suboculars
upper labials
mental

lower labials

Chameleon morphological traits

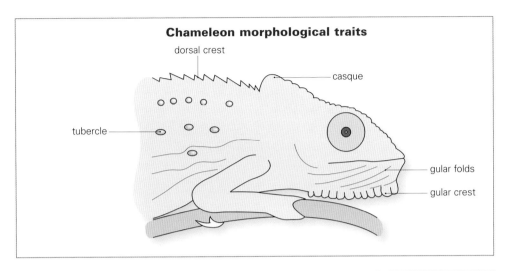

dorsal crest

casque

tubercle

gular folds

gular crest

Sea turtle shields

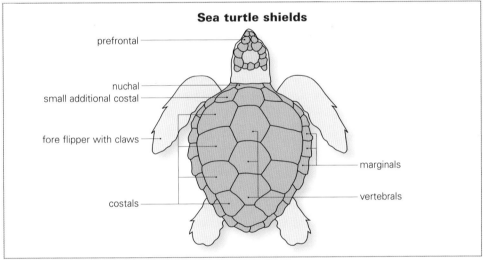

prefrontal

nuchal
small additional costal

fore flipper with claws

marginals

vertebrals

costals

Tortoise shields

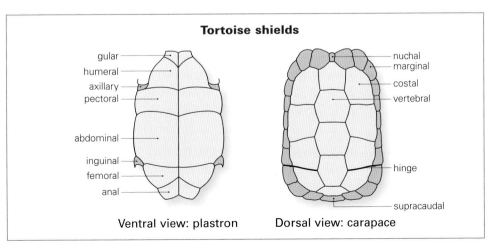

gular
humeral
axillary
pectoral

abdominal

inguinal
femoral
anal

nuchal
marginal

costal

vertebral

hinge

supracaudal

Ventral view: plastron   Dorsal view: carapace

Delalande's Beaked Blind Snake also goes by the scientific name Rhinotyphlops lalandei.

Naming systems

Two types of names have been used in this field guide: common and scientific. The choice of common names is largely a matter of personal preference, although a guiding principle of consistency is usually followed. In this guide, traditionally used common names have been applied where possible, but recent changes to the taxonomy of many southern African reptiles have necessitated the coining of several new names. Where we have had to create new names, we have chosen ones that are either descriptive or are directly derived from the scientific name.

The scientific naming system follows strict rules, and these names provide a great deal of information about how species are related. The naming system is hierarchical, and species are grouped into clusters according to their evolutionary relationships and the number of characteristics they share – the members of more inclusive groups (e.g. kingdoms and phyla) higher up the hierarchy have fewer shared traits than do members of less inclusive groups (e.g. genera and species).

An example of the scientific naming system: here, Delalande's Beaked Blind Snake is classified from the most inclusive level (Kingdom) to the most exclusive (species).

Kingdom:	**Animalia**
Phylum:	**Chordata**
Class:	**Reptilia**
Order:	**Squamata**
Family:	**Typhlopidae**
Genus:	***Rhinotyphlops***
Species:	***lalandei***

In the text of the field guide, any given species is usually referred to by its binomen – a pair of names that indicate the genus and species. For example, the scientific name of Delalande's Beaked Blind Snake is *Rhinotyphlops lalandei*, showing that it belongs to the genus *Rhinotyphlops* (and thus shares many characteristics with other member species of this genus), and has the specific epithet *'lalandei'*, the name that sets it apart from other members of the *Rhinotyphlops*. Conventionally, generic and specific names are always written in italics, but names at the other levels of the hierarchy are not.

DISTRIBUTION PATTERNS

This field guide covers the reptiles of Botswana (1), Lesotho (2), the southern half of Mozambique (3), Namibia (4), South Africa (5), Swaziland (6) and Zimbabwe (7). Thus, the geographic boundaries of the coverage are defined more by current political borders than by biogeographical principles. In the southern African subregion, species richness (the number of species in a given area) is generally highest in the northeastern extremes, declining to the south and west. However, there are also localized peaks in species richness: northern central Namibia is particularly rich in lizards, as is the southwestern Cape. Many species of reptile in KwaZulu-Natal and Mpumalanga are endemic to these areas and have small, patchy distributions, resulting in scattered local peaks in richness in these parts. Southern Mozambique appears to have a lower than expected richness. Future research will reveal if this observation is distorted by insufficient data.

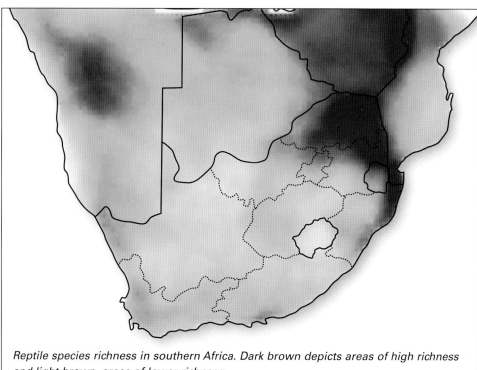

Reptile species richness in southern Africa. Dark brown depicts areas of high richness and light brown, areas of lower richness.

Centres of the distributions (where individuals of the species are most abundant) of the different species are clustered into two main areas over southern Africa: the southwestern Cape, and the lowlands of the northeastern parts of the region. These two assemblages of species are considered to have adapted to temperate and tropical environmental conditions respectively. A third assemblage of relatively few, arid-adapted species is found in the dry west. The distribution of the species in these three assemblages appears to be limited primarily by climatic factors. However, many species of lizard and several species of snake appear to be restricted to certain soil or rock types, and the ranges of these species may be small as a result. Not surprisingly, a high proportion of these 'substrate limited' species are either fossorial (burrowers) or rupicolous (rock-living).

Climatic and geological factors across southern Africa interplay to form several distinct ecoregions or habitat types (see map below). Each ecoregion has a unique assemblage of reptile species present, as a direct result of climate or geological conditions, or due to unique attributes of the ecoregion. For example, arboreal species may be restricted to ecoregions that have high densities of trees, or specialist feeders may be limited to those regions that have suitable prey types.

The ecoregions
Savanna
This is the most extensive ecoregion in the subregion, occurring over much of the northern parts of southern Africa. Savanna has a well-developed, grassy layer and a medium

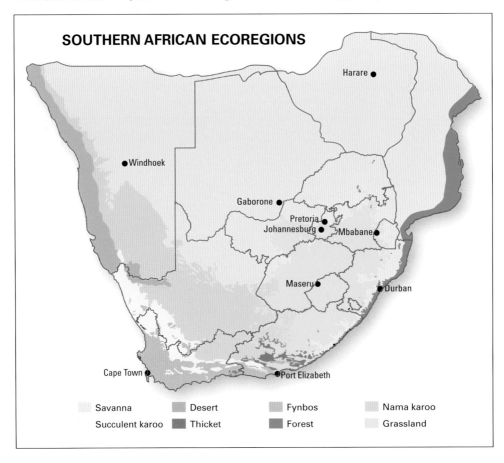

SOUTHERN AFRICAN ECOREGIONS

Savanna	Desert	Fynbos	Nama karoo
Succulent karoo	Thicket	Forest	Grassland

Johan Marais

The grassland ecoregion is one of the most threatened habitat types in southern Africa.

density of scattered trees. Rains occur during summer, and fire is an important regulator of the balance between density of grass and trees. Reptile species richness and endemism is extremely high, but this is partially a result of the large extent of the ecoregion. Few savanna reptiles are classified as threatened, and many have extensive ranges.

Forest

Forests are generally limited to the eastern and northeastern parts of southern Africa. Only relatively small patches of this ecoregion remain in South Africa, the most southerly of which occur in the Tsitsikamma and Knysna regions, and many of these have declined and are under further threat from human habitat transformation and exploitation. Forests vary greatly in plant species composition and richness, and may occur from sea level to high elevations. Reptile species richness is generally low in forests, but levels of endemism can be high in parts. Although there are currently few forest reptiles that are classified as threatened, the conservation status of many species is likely to worsen as forests become more fragmented and decrease in extent.

Grassland

The grassland ecoregion occurs over extensive parts of central eastern South Africa. It has undergone massive degradation on account of its situation across some of the most economically important parts of the country. At present, 80% has been irreversibly transformed and only 2% is formally conserved. Reptile richness is medium to low, and endemism is low. Because of the degraded state of this ecoregion, several species are of conservation concern, a situation that is likely to deteriorate further with continued urbanization in the area.

Thicket

The thicket ecoregion is highly fragmented and patchy, occurring mainly in the Eastern Cape and, to a very limited extent, in KwaZulu-Natal and the Western Cape. It is typified by dense, spiny, evergreen shrubs and trees. Species richness of shrubs and trees is very high. This ecoregion has been severely degraded over the last few decades and it is under-represented in conservation areas. Reptile species richness is generally low and there are very few endemic species, partially because of the limited extent and fragmented nature of the habitat. Although there are currently few threatened reptile species in the thicket ecoregion, the conservation status of many species is likely to worsen as this habitat becomes more fragmented and degraded.

Nama karoo

The nama karoo occurs extensively over the south-central parts of South Africa, extending through the central and western parts of Namibia. This heterogeneous ecoregion is typified by low rainfall and a vegetation mix of grasses, succulents, geophytes and annual forbs. Reptile species richness is generally low, and there are few endemic species. Few species that occur in this ecoregion are of conservation concern or classified as threatened.

Succulent karoo

The succulent karoo is relatively limited in extent and is restricted to the western parts of southern Africa, extending from the central Western Cape, northwards into coastal Northern Cape and coastal southern Namibia. The ecoregion is characterized by species of arid-adapted succulent-leaf scrubs. Rainfall is low and droughts are common. Reptile species richness is relatively high and a high proportion of the species are endemic. Many species are rupicolous (inhabiting rocky areas). Several species of reptiles found in succulent karoo are threatened, and this situation is likely to worsen drastically in response to climate change, since it is predicted that warming will reduce the extent of this ecoregion dramatically.

Desert

The Namib Desert is the only true desert in southern African and occurs in a narrow strip along the west coast of Namibia, extending only very marginally into South Africa. Rainfall is very low and sporadic, and the ecoregion is typified by shifting dune fields and ancient gravel plains. Vegetation occurs

The succulent karoo experiences low rainfall.

in very low densities and consists primarily of grasses (which are generally ephemeral) and specialized succulents. Trees may occur along drainage lines. Although reptile species richness tends to be low in this ecoregion, many species are desert specialists, and levels of endemism are thus relatively high. Because much of this ecoregion has experienced low levels of transformation, and substantial portions are designated conservation areas, few desert reptiles in southern Africa are of conservation concern. An exception to this may be species such as the Namaqua Dwarf Adder (*Bitis schneideri*) and Lomi's Blind Legless Skink (*Typhlosaurus lomiae*), which are affected by the impact of strip diamond mining.

Fynbos

Limited to the southern and western extremes of South Africa, the fynbos ecoregion is typified by a winter-rainfall pattern and extremely high plant species richness and endemism. A moderate number of reptiles occur in the region, but many of these tend to have relatively small ranges, and several are of conservation concern. It is likely that climate change will exacerbate the conservation status of many species in this habitat type, since it is predicted that warming will reduce the extent of the fynbos ecoregion considerably.

DIVERSITY OF REPTILES

The class Reptilia consists of four orders: Rhynchocephalia (tuataras); Squamata (snakes and lizards); Crocodylia (crocodiles) and Testudines (tortoises, terrapins and turtles). All but the Rhynchocephalia have representative species in southern Africa. There is only a single species of tuatara, which is endemic to offshore islands of New Zealand.

Reptiles were much more diverse in body size and form in the past and included the charismatic dinosaurs. However, there are still nearly 8 000 known living species. Reptiles occur throughout the warmer oceans of the world and are found on all continents apart from Antarctica. Although they are commonly – and incorrectly – thought of as being more primitive than birds and mammals, they show many derived characteristics and are adapted to a wide range of habitats. Their physiology is similarly complex and often differs radically from the more familiar mammals.

Marius Burger

Some lizards, such as this Rock Monitor, have unique and complex circulatory systems.

What is a reptile? There is no easy answer to this question. Usually, a taxonomic group is defined by a set of traits or characters that are shared by all members of the group, and are unique to that group alone. For example, birds can be identified by the presence of feathers since all birds, and only birds, have them. The problem is that reptiles don't really have any characters that set them apart unequivocally in this way. This difficulty has arisen because the class Reptilia consists of several ancient groups that are now distantly related and have diverged in many characteristics. In addition to the antiquity of the Reptilia, one of the reptilian orders, the Crocodylia, is more closely related to birds than it is to other reptiles. This means that the reptiles constitute a 'paraphyletic group' because not all of the descendants from the most recent common ancestor are included in the group (i.e. in this case, the birds are not). Although the 'paraphyletic problem' of the Reptilia has been known for a long time, traditional views have impeded the acceptance of a more correct phylogeny or schema. The simplest solution would be to elevate the currently recognized orders of the Reptilia to classes in their own right. The alternative would be to downgrade the class Aves (birds) to make it an order of reptiles, a change that would make for many unhappy ornithologists and exceedingly heavy field guides. It seems that the former solution is being adopted by some trail-blazing biologists.

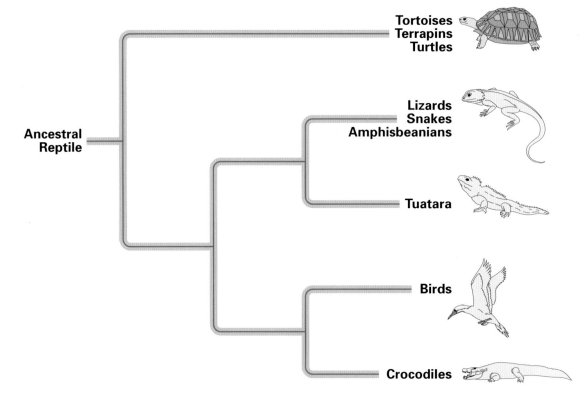

The evolutionary relationships between orders of living reptiles and birds. Reptiles are a 'paraphyletic group' because not all of the descendants from the most recent common ancestor are included in the group (birds are not). This cladogram also shows that crocodiles are more closely related to birds than they are to the other order of reptiles.

Reptiles have several characteristic features. These include traits such as: an impervious, scaly skin; air-breathing lungs; four limbs (although these have been secondarily lost in many species); a closed circulatory system, and a vomeronasal organ in the roof of the mouth called 'Jacobson's organ' (although this is absent in crocodiles). However, all of these traits are shared by at least some other classes of vertebrates (bony fish, amphibians, birds and mammals). Generally, reptiles have an incomplete ventricular septum between the two ventricles of the heart, allowing for the mixing of blood between the pulmonary and systemic parts of the circulatory system. This means that deoxygenated blood returning from the body can be pumped back to the body without first travelling to the lungs, an anatomical design that has traditionally been considered 'primitive'. However, crocodiles have completely separated ventricles and a circulatory system that has similarities to that of birds. In spite of having complete separation of pulmonary and systemic blood in the heart, crocodiles are able to shunt blood between the two circuits via a bridge in the arterial vessels called the 'foramen of Panizzae'. Although the mixing of arterial and pulmonary blood has been assumed to be a primitive and inefficient feature of the reptilian circulatory system, research indicates that shunting of blood is important to many aspects of reptilian physiology.

Johan Marais

Most reptiles, such as this Sungazer, have an incomplete ventricular septum.

SURPRISING RELATIONSHIPS

Crocodiles and birds are more closely related to each other than they are to other animals, and share a common ancestor. Both groups have descended from the archosaurs, a group that also gave rise to the dinosaurs. Crocodiles and birds share many common traits, including similarities of their circulatory systems and skeletons. The relationship between the two groups was originally shown by anatomical studies, but has recently been corroborated by research using new molecular techniques to compare the genes.

Recently developed molecular techniques are revolutionizing our understanding of the relationships between different species of reptiles and the sequence of evolutionary events that has led to present-day species. For example, it is now clear that both the snakes and amphisbaenians are merely unusual lizards and not equivalent groups to the lizards, as has been the view for the last 50 years. (Thus the correct term should be 'snakes and other lizards', rather than 'snakes and lizards'.) Even more surprising is the finding that lizards belonging to the families that are most closely related to snakes appear to be 'venomous'. Thus agamas, chameleons and monitors could technically be regarded as venomous, even though they do not have fangs (teeth that specifically deliver venom in a bite). They do, however, have salivary glands that produce proteins with a toxic action. Many of these proteins are very similar to those produced in the venom glands of snakes, suggesting that snakes were ancestrally venomous and that present-day non-venomous species must have secondarily lost the ability to produce venom. As these findings are very new and radically different from traditional views, they must still be tested and investigated further before their full implications can be properly evaluated.

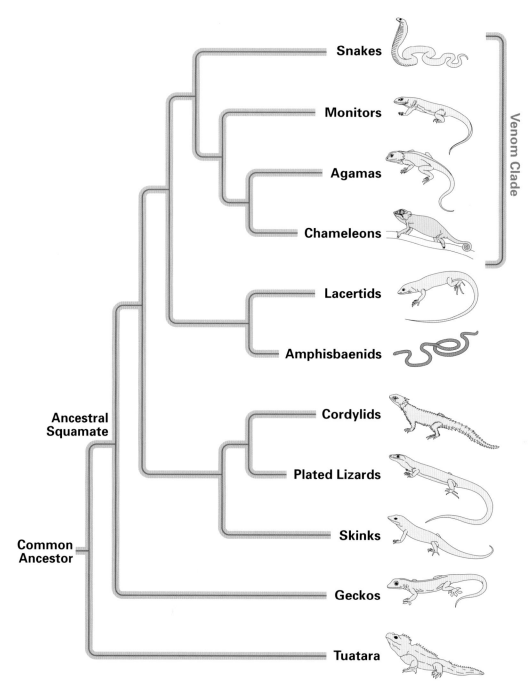

The evolutionary relationships of the Squamata, showing the relationship between lizards, snakes and amphisbaenians. Note that the snakes and several groups of lizards make up the 'Venom Clade' and that the lacertids are more closely related to Amphisbaenians than they are to other lizards (other schemes have also been proposed).

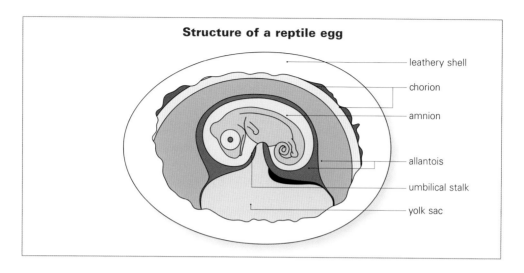

Structure of a reptile egg

- leathery shell
- chorion
- amnion
- allantois
- umbilical stalk
- yolk sac

Reptiles and birds lay eggs that differ significantly from those of amphibians and fish in that they have three fluid-filled sacs within a protective leathery or calcareous shell. The shell and fluid-filled sacs protect the embryo from physical damage, are permeable to gases needed for metabolism, and retard water loss so that the eggs can be incubated in relatively dry conditions. The first sac, the *allantois*, stores waste products of the embryo; the second is the *chorion*, which lies against the inner surface of the shell and has a rich network of blood vessels. Oxygen that diffuses across the shell is then transported in this network to the embryo. The third is the *amnion*, which contains the fluid-bathed embryo, physically protecting it and preventing its dehydration. There is also a yolk sac in which the yolk is stored as a food source for the developing embryo. A reptile egg is able to tolerate a much greater range of environmental conditions than an amphibian egg, allowing reptiles to be less dependent on water. It is therefore not surprising to see that reptiles are much more abundant in arid environments than are amphibians. In many species of snake and lizard the egg does not develop a shell, and development of the embryo occurs within the mother's body so that the young are born fully formed.

Marius Burger

Geckos are unique lizards as they lay hard-shelled, calcareous eggs.

BIOLOGY AND BEHAVIOUR

It is a curious fact that no species of terrestrial reptile migrates in the true sense of the word. The abilities of even the most mobile of land-living reptiles are completely overshadowed by the annual migrations of many species of bird and mammal that may move thousands of kilometres in response to the changing seasons. Why should there be such a clear difference between the ecologies and behaviours of terrestrial reptiles and that of birds and mammals? At the heart of the issue is a fundamental difference in the physiologies of the two groups: simply put, reptiles are adapted for 'going with the flow'. When conditions become testing, they sit tight and wait for better times. This strategy is most clearly demonstrated in a reptile's metabolic response to changing environmental temperatures. As the environment becomes colder, the reptile loses heat to the environment more quickly, resulting in a decreased body temperature. This causes the metabolic rate – the reptile's total energy expenditure – to decrease too, and the reptile becomes inactive until such time as the environmental temperatures increase again. In cold climates, this 'ectothermic' response may mean that a reptile becomes inactive for months at a time.

Marius Burger

Reptiles, such as this Karoo Tent Tortoise, are less mobile than most birds and mammals.

Marius Burger

Low metabolic rates allow reptiles to fast for long periods. Snakes can go for months without eating.

Birds and mammals have an entirely different strategy: when environmental temperatures decrease, they counteract the increased rates of body heat loss by elevating their metabolic rates. The extra heat produced by the body allows them to maintain a high and constant body temperature, even in cold environments and they can thus remain active when reptiles cannot. Shivering from the cold is one of several ways that we increase our metabolic rate. Thus, the 'endothermic' strategy of birds and mammals is to fight environmental effects on body temperature, but this comes at the cost of high energy expenditure. On average, birds and mammals have metabolic rates that are about 10 times that of reptiles of the same body mass, and birds and mammals have to adjust their food intake accordingly. Put another way, a meal lasts a reptile 10 times as long as it does a bird or mammal, and this is the reason why snakes are able to go for months without eating after a large meal. At low environmental temperatures, when the metabolic rates of reptiles are depressed and those of birds and

mammals elevated, the differences may be much greater – a bird or mammal may have a metabolic rate 100 times that of a reptile.

Reptiles' response to cold temperature impacts on almost every aspect of their biology. Low metabolic rates mean that activity levels are generally low, and fatigue sets in after brief bouts of intense exercise. Effectively, this precludes terrestrial reptiles from migrating in the way that birds and mammals can – they simply cannot sustain the levels of activity required to move such great distances. On the other hand, many species of bird and mammal that live in highly seasonal environments simply cannot gather enough energy to meet the demands of their endothermic lifestyles during lean times, and they must therefore either migrate to areas where there are more resources, or hibernate. Interestingly, the reptiles that come closest to migrating are the marine turtles: Leatherback Turtles (*Dermochelys coriacea*) have been recorded moving several thousand kilometres per year. The reason for this ability in an ectothermic reptile is the fact that swimming uses less energy than running or flying, and turtles tend to cover these great distances over extended periods, and not during intense bouts of activity, as is usually the case for migrating animals.

In spite of reptiles being ectothermic, many are able to regulate their body temperature within a narrow range through a combination of physiological and behavioural means, at least on occasions. In many respects, they are similar to birds and mammals in this regard; the only significant difference is that reptiles lack the ability to raise metabolism on demand as a heat generating mechanism. Thus, reptiles are able to vasodilate or vasoconstrict vessels in their circulatory systems to modify rates of heat exchange. They are able to modify heart rate to reduce or enhance the transport of heat by the circulatory system. Some species are able to pant as a means of evaporative heat loss. They are able to bask in sunlight to maximize heat gain (heliothermy), or flatten their bodies to achieve maximal contact with a warm surface (thignothermy). Even the choice of a refuge in which a reptile spends periods of inactivity has been shown to be motivated at least partially by the thermal characteristics of the refuge.

Every reptile has a preferred range of body temperatures; physiology and behaviour operate in concert so that the body temperature is close to the target when environmental conditions allow. Although there is variation from one species to the next, many snakes maintain their body temperatures at about 32 °C when possible. Many lizards select temperatures of about 36 °C, but some desert species choose body temperatures of up to 42 °C. Thus reptiles should not be seen as primitive or ineffective in comparison to mammals, but rather as successful organisms that have gone the route of economy when it comes to energy use. One of the advantages of an 'economy-class' lifestyle is a long life – individual Galapagos tortoises have been recorded

Orty Bourquin

Loggerhead Turtle hatchlings enter the sea shortly after hatching, and may travel thousands of kilometres in their first year.

living more than 150 years. Mammals are probably short-lived because they literally burn themselves out at a young age.

Reptiles are generally not thought of as social animals. However, there are several recently discovered examples, including some species of lizard, that are changing long-held views. Certain species of Australian skinks have been shown to live in small, stable family groups, and young living within family groups have better survival rates than those that do not. Data suggests that several species of southern African Girdled and Flat Lizard also have an array of complex social interactions.

HIBERNATION

Hibernation is a deep state of physiological inactivity experienced by certain mammals during winter. At this time, metabolism and all physiological processes are slowed to very low rates, and body temperature is regulated at these low levels by the metabolism of brown fat, a tissue type with the specific function of heat production. Reptiles that become inactive during winter are not hibernating in a strict physiological sense, since body temperature and metabolic rate are determined by the temperature of the hibernation site – they are not regulated by the reptile as they are in mammalian hibernators. Reptiles do not have brown fat and, during dormancy, metabolic rate is almost entirely dependent on body temperature.

Reproduction

All crocodilians, tuatara, most species of tortoise and terrapin, and some species of lizard have what is known as 'Temperature-dependent Sex Determination' (TSD), whereby the sex of the young is determined by the temperature of the egg prior to hatching. In addition to determining the sex, incubation temperature appears to affect several other attributes of the hatchlings, such as body size, growth rate and survival. As yet, TSD has not been found in any species of snake, and most species appear to have sex chromosomes, which fact appears to preclude TSD.

Although relatively few reptile species show any form of parental care of eggs or young once they have been laid, some species do remain with their eggs or young for a certain period. Female crocodiles vigorously protect their incubating eggs and newly hatched young. Several species of lizard and snake attend nests until hatching time, and some rattlesnakes are known to remain with young for weeks after birth. Female pythons actively attend their clutches until hatching time and the Southern African Python (*Python natalensis*) has recently been discovered to remain with the newly hatched young for more than two weeks. It is likely that more cases of maternal care of eggs and young will come to light with further research.

Although most reptiles lay eggs, many species of snake and lizard give birth to live young. Apparently, live birth (viviparity) has arisen many times through the retention of the eggs within the oviducts. (Viviparity has never evolved in tortoises, crocodiles or birds, possibly because the retention of eggs in the oviducts in these groups results in arrested development of the foetus.) Certain species of lizard, including three species of Typical Skink in southern Africa, are known to have some populations in which the females lay eggs and others where the females produce live young. Females of the Spotted Skaapsteker (*Psammophylax rhombeatus*) lay eggs with partially devel-

oped embryos. Instead of the normal three-month incubation for most snake eggs, Spotted Skaapsteker eggs take only about two weeks to hatch. It would appear that this species is on the evolutionary path to viviparity. In some species of viviparous snakes and lizards, the pregnant female develops what amounts to a placenta – a structure that facilitates the transfer of food and dissolved gases to the foetus.

Richard Boynton

A Southern File Snake laying a clutch of eggs.

Bill Branch

The shell of this Marsh Terrapin egg is soft and leathery, like that of most reptiles.

Lizards and snakes periodically shed their skin. Shedding frequency is governed primarily by growth rate.

Growth and shedding

To a large extent, growth rate in reptiles is determined by the ambient temperature, as well as the availability and quality of food. During lean times, growth may cease or even become negative. In many species, growth may continue indefinitely throughout life, a pattern that is referred to as 'indeterminate growth', although it does tend to slow with age.

Although some reptiles mature within a year, other species may take 10 or 20 years before becoming sexually active. Again, although certain species of lizard, such as Rough-scaled Lizards, may live for just over a year, many reptiles are exceedingly long-lived. Large pythons can live for more than 40 years, and crocodiles can exceed 100 years. Large tortoises have been known to have a lifespan of more than 150 years.

Reptiles shed their skin as they grow. The crocodiles, tortoises, terrapins and turtles do so on a more or less continuous basis, with small flakes or sheets of skin being lost in response to uninterrupted cell growth in the dermis. However, shedding in the tuataras and Squamata occurs in a cyclical pattern, with large patches or the complete outer covering being shed at once. The cycle consists of a long resting phase (from days to months), the length of which may be dependent on many factors such as temperature, season, age and food intake. This is followed by a period of cell proliferation and differentiation in the germinative layer of cells in the dermis (approximately 14 days). The old outer layer separates from the new inner layer and is sloughed off. In snakes and lizards with fused, transparent eyelids, the period of cell proliferation is revealed by a bluish or milky hue over the eye. During this time, they may have impaired vision and are irascible.

INDETERMINATE GROWTH

Most snakes never stop growing throughout their lives, and the rate is dependent mainly on temperature and food availability. However, growth slows markedly with age, and old snakes tend to increase more in girth than length. For example, Southern African Pythons (*Python natalensis*) increase in length very slowly once they attain a body length of approximately 4.5 m, but they become massively thick as they age. Therefore, reports of pythons exceed 6 m are unlikely, since their body mass would exceed 150 kg.

Senses

Reptiles rely on a variety of senses that provide them with information about their surroundings. The relative importance of the different senses depends on both the lifestyle and the ancestry of the species.

Vision

Reptiles generally have a well-developed and keen sense of vision. In most groups, the structure of the eye is similar to that of birds and mammals, with a lens, retina and cornea. Although Blind Snakes and Worm Snakes have only rods for light-sensitive cells on the retina, most other reptiles have rods and cones (of one type or another) and some can thus probably detect colour to some extent. In some species of lizard colour vision may be well developed. Pupils range from round in most diurnal species, to vertically elliptical in nocturnal ones. Many species of nocturnal gecko have a 'crennelated' or wavy edge to the pupil and, during the day, the iris may be closed to the extent that light can only enter the eye through four small notches.

Like birds, crocodiles have a nictitating membrane – a transparent additional eyelid that is used to sweep dirt off the surface of the eye. This membrane is closed over the eye when the crocodile is under water. All snakes and some species of lizard, including most species of gecko, have eyelids that are not movable, and therefore they cannot blink. Instead, they see through a transparent eyelid that is fused over the eye to form a protective spectacle. This spectacle is replaced with the rest of the skin during shedding.

Many burrowing species of snake and lizard have reduced eyes. The extent of reduction varies: the eyes may be reduced in size only, as is the case in several species of burrowing skink and Purple-glossed Snakes (*Amblyodipsas*) or reduced to light-sensitive eyespots that are situated entirely beneath the skin, as in the Blind Snakes (*Rhinotyphlops*, *Typhlops* and *Letheobia*)

and Worm Snakes (*Leptotyphlops*). Most species of Amphisbaenians lack external evidence of eyes – the eyes are situated deep beneath the skin and can probably only detect major differences in light levels.

Reptiles' eyes are generally located on the sides of the head. This gives them a wide field of view, but limits the field of binocular vision and thus their perception of depth. Depth perception is important in species that are arboreal and those that actively pursue their prey, and these species, therefore, generally tend to have wider fields or

The chameleon's eyes differ from those of other vertebrates in that each is controlled independently and is situated on a turret.

binocular vision. This is facilitated by more forward-facing eyes, a narrow snout and, in the most extreme cases, horizontally elliptical or keyhole-shaped pupils, as in the Boomslang and Vine Snakes. Although many species of snake appear to be better at detecting movement than they are at identifying stationary objects, the keen vision of these arboreal species allows them to detect stationary prey too.

Chameleons have very specialized eyes that allow for a wide field of view and excellent depth perception – something the chameleon needs when aiming its sticky tongue. The chameleon's eyes differ from those of other vertebrates in that each is controlled independently and is situated on a turret. This allows eye manoeuvrability and for both eyes to focus directly forwards on the same object.

Snakes focus their vision in an entirely different way to other vertebrates. Mammals, birds and most reptiles focus by contracting muscles around the lens, which pull on the lens, distorting it to adjust the focal distance. Snakes focus by moving the lens closer to or further from the retina. This difference suggests that ancestral snakes had reduced eyes, probably because they were fossorial.

Blind Snakes are colour-blind and have poor vision.

Smell

All reptiles have a sense of smell: odours are detected by sensory cells in the nasal cavity very much in the same way as in mammals. Many species depend on smell for detection of prey, predators and mates, although some lizards and crocodiles do rely primarily on sight for finding their food. The sense of smell is generally more acute and important to the lifestyle of those species that are nocturnal or live in subterranean darkness and cannot rely on vision. However, many diurnal species also depend largely on their sense of smell. Even tortoises appear to have the ability to locate a food source at a distance by detecting its scent.

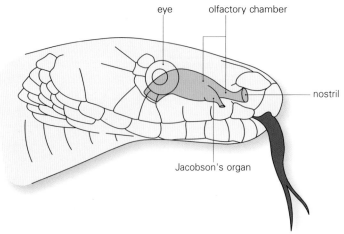

The vomeronasal organ, known as Jacobson's organ, is situated in the roof of the mouth and supplies the animal with sensory information on odours.

Most reptiles (excluding crocodiles) also have a vomeronasal organ known as 'Jacobson's organ'. This is a fluid-filled, bi-lobed sensory organ in the roof of the mouth that also supplies the animal with sensory information on odours. This sense is analogous to, but different from, the sense of smell and is better termed chemo-reception or vomerolfaction. It is especially well developed in snakes and some species of lizard, and is facilitated by the tongue of the animal. Although the tongue is not sens-itive to odours, it serves as the vehicle for the collection of odour particles as it waves up and down. It is then withdrawn into the mouth and the particles are transferred to the openings of the Jacobson's organ where the odours are detected.

The forked tongue of snakes and some species of lizard means that vomerolfaction can be directional and allows them to follow scent trails. Each of the two tongue tips supplies odour particles to the respective lobe of the Jacobson's organ, and the further apart the tongue tips are held while collecting odour particles, the better able the animal is to detect gradients in the strength of the scent. Thus, it is probably the advantage of being able to follow scent trails that has resulted in the evolution of the characteristic forked tongue of snakes and monitor lizards.

Hearing

Although all reptiles have middle and inner ears, only crocodiles and some lizards have a true outer ear. In addition, crocodiles and most geckos are able to close the ear cavity, and crocodiles do so when under water. The middle ear consists of a tympanum and two bones (the stapes and extracolumella), which are contained in an air cavity. All snakes lack external ears and a tympanum, but they are able to perceive some low-frequency airborne sounds. They hear mainly vibra-tions conducted through the ground, which are transmitted via the quadrate bones of the jaw.

Heat detection

Certain species of snake are able to detect warmth remotely with infrared heat recep-tors. Pythons and Boas have several of these receptors in shallow pits that are situated on labial scales of the upper and lower jaws.

The forked tongue of snakes can detect gradients in odour strength and allows them to follow scent trails.

Pit Vipers (none of which occur in southern Africa) have a pair of deep pits, one on each side of the upper jaw between the eye and nostril. The openings to these pits face forwards and their fields of detection overlap, giving these snakes stereoscopic infrared 'vision'. Heat receptors allow these snakes to detect warm-bodied prey in total darkness and may also be used for selecting appropriate basking sites. Experiments have shown that some species are able to detect temperature differences as small as 0.05 °C.

Activity patterns

Because reptiles are ectothermic, their activity patterns are governed by environmental conditions, making the patterns highly predictable. Although reptiles do become less active in winter, southern African species generally do not become completely dormant, even during the coldest months. For example, research has shown that Rinkhals (*Hemachatus haemachatus*) continue to emerge to bask each day during fine weather throughout winter. During this time they do not forage and remain in close proximity to their retreats to which they will quickly return if disturbed. The rarity of Rinkhals sightings during winter was previously assumed to indicate that they were in 'hibernation', when in fact it was due only to a change in activity patterns. It is likely that many other reptile species show similar shifts in activity in relation to season.

Each reptile species shows a particular daily activity pattern. Many species of lizard – especially the agamas, chameleons, monitors, lacertids, cordylids, plated lizards and skinks – are strictly diurnal, as are the tortoises. Most geckos are nocturnal. Although many species of snake are either diurnal or nocturnal, many are crepuscular, and are active for a period just after sunset and, possibly, again before sunrise. Some species, such as the Southern African Python (*Python natalensis*), forage during the night in summer, but are active only during the day in winter. Other species, such as the Nile Crocodile (*Crocodylus niloticus*) may be active during the day and night year-round.

Graham Alexander

The Rinkhals is able to raise its body temperature rapidly by basking with a spread hood.

Diurnal reptiles usually emerge from their retreats when temperatures are within the range that is suitable for activity. During the coldest months, this is usually near midday, when the sun's rays are warmest. However, temperatures are often too high at midday in summer, and reptiles that emerge earlier in the morning must return to their retreats to avoid overheating. They may then emerge again during the cooler afternoon. Therefore, many diurnal reptiles exhibit a unimodal (single peak) activity pattern during winter and a bimodal pattern during summer.

Lifestyles

Reptiles have adapted to a wide variety of habitats. Certain specialized species, such as Spotted Rock Snakes (*Lamprophis guttatus*) and Flat Lizards (*Platysaurus*), are found only in very particular habitats (in this case, exfoliating rock outcrops), while other species may occur in a range of habitat types. Certain lizards, such as Turner's Tubercled Gecko (*Chondrodactylus turneri*) spend periods of inactivity in one habitat (rock crevices) but may forage in another (on the ground surface). Habitat generalists tend to be more widely distributed than habitat specialists.

The majority of southern African reptiles, including all species of tortoise, the majority of snakes and many lizards, would be best categorized as terrestrial as they spend most of their time on the ground surface.

Many southern African lizard and snake species live underground. For these fossorial species, the substrate type is important and many avoid substrates that regularly become waterlogged or are too hard due to high clay content. Spade-snouted Worm Lizards are an exception in that they are able to burrow in hard substrates with their modified, spade-like heads. Often, suitable substrate types (such as aeolian sands) occur in isolated patches, resulting in fragmented distributions for species that depend on

them. In a similar way, strictly rupicolous species may be limited to specific rock outcrops and may occur only in restricted areas simply because they have been unable to disperse to other suitable sites.

Species that are strictly arboreal, such as Vine Snakes (*Thelotornis*) and most speciess of Green Snake (*Philothamnus*), are restricted mainly to the warmer northern and eastern parts of southern Africa. The southern parts of the subregion are not suitable for a strictly arboreal lifestyle, as temperatures can be low and the tops of trees are exposed to the elements. The Boomslang (*Dispholidus typus*), however, is an exception in that it occurs more widely and extends along the coastline to the southwestern Cape.

There are relatively few truly aquatic reptiles in southern Africa. Most notable and well known is the Nile Crocodile (*Crocodylus niloticus*), which is limited to permanent water in the northern and eastern parts of the subregion. Many species of freshwater terrapins are also dependent on permanent bodies of water. However, the Marsh Terrapin (*Pelomedusa subrufa*) is able to burrow into the mud of drying water bodies to aestivate until conditions become more favourable. Because of this adaptability

Marius Burger

As with many other species of lizard, Flat Lizards occur only on certain rock types.

to changing conditions, the Marsh Terrapin is much more widespread than the other species of freshwater terrapins in southern Africa. Several species of snake, including the Water Snakes (*Lycodonomorphus*), Marsh Snakes (*Natriciteres*) and the Bangweulu Swamp Snake (*Limnophis bangweolicus*), are also aquatic specialists that are restricted in occurrence to the close proximity of permanent water.

Only relatively few marine species of reptile are found in southern African waters. Five species of marine turtles visit our shores, but only two, the Leatherback Turtle (*Dermochelys coriacea*) and Loggerhead Turtle (*Caretta caretta*), regularly nest on southern African shores. A single species of sea snake, the Yellow-bellied Sea Snake (*Pelamis platura*), occasionally washes up on the coast. This is the most widespread species of sea snake and is truly pelagic, usually spending all its time in the open ocean. Generally, beached snakes are either sick or are washed ashore as a result of heavy seas.

Food and feeding

Reptiles feed on a great diversity of food types. Crocodiles are entirely carnivorous and prey almost exclusively on vertebrates, from fish to large antelope. Marine turtles feed on a variety of foods, ranging from marine invertebrates such as crabs, sponges and jellyfish to sea grass and algae. Freshwater terrapins are primarily carnivorous, and terrestrial tortoises are mainly vegetarian, but are known to supplement their diet occasionally with invertebrates and animal faeces. The majority of the Squamata are carnivorous, and this is true without exception for the snakes. Lizards feed primarily on invertebrates, although some of the larger species, such as the monitors, will take large vertebrate prey. A minority of lizards are at least partially vegetarian. This is most prevalent in species in the Iguanidae (a family of lizards that does not occur in southern Africa), but several southern African species, such as the Desert Plated Lizard, Giant Plated Lizard and Flat Lizards, do include vegetation in their diets.

Although many species of reptile are relatively unselective feeders, all are selective in the respect that they feed on a subset of the food that is available in the environment. There is a tendency for reptiles in food-scarce environments to eat a wider variety of prey.

Reptiles capture food either by lying in wait to ambush unsuspecting prey that is passing by, or by actively searching for it. Although many species use a combination of these two foraging modes, others use only one, and each mode has its advantages

Nile Crocodiles are ambush foragers and are able to cope with large prey items.

and disadvantages. For example, ambush foraging requires little energy, but generally results in low capture rates. These low capture rates usually result in ambush foragers being unselective when it comes to prey type or size. Alternatively, active foragers expend much more energy hunting for prey, but tend to have a much better success rate. In addition to this, they are able to include inactive and sessile food types on their menu since they are not reliant on their prey actively walking by. Ambush foragers are generally heavy-bodied with large heads, allowing them to cope with large prey items, and they generally have cryptic coloration, facilitating concealment when lying in ambush. They generally rely on their vision to detect passing prey. Active foragers tend to be slender and agile, using their speed to avoid danger or chase prey. Because of this, many are marked with prominent stripes that serve to confuse predators during escape. Although many species of active foragers also rely on good vision to find prey, many use olfaction to follow scent trails or detect retreat sites.

Once captured, small prey such as invertebrates may be swallowed alive. However, larger prey is more dangerous and is thus usually killed first. Generally, crocodiles use brute strength to hold prey under water until it drowns. Snakes are most specialized and use a variety of methods for dispatching prey, depending on the species. Constriction is an efficient way for nonvenomous species to kill: the body is coiled around the prey and pressure is applied to the thoracic cavity, overriding the pressure gradients in the heart. This results in rapid death due to cardiac failure. Highly venomous species are able to deliver a fatal dose of venom to their prey and wait while it takes effect.

In the majority of cases, reptiles simply swallow their food whole, with minimal processing in the mouth. This is certainly the case for the majority of snakes, since they have specialized heads, jaws and teeth that do not allow for chewing or for biting the

All snakes are carnivorous. Here, a Brown House Snake constricts a mouse.

victims into pieces. Although crocodile teeth are adapted for holding onto prey rather than for cutting, crocodiles are able to use their strength to tear chunks off their meals, either by rolling their bodies while biting or by violently shaking the meal. Lizards will generally use their jaws to crush the exoskeleton of their arthropod prey, thus facilitating the penetration of gastric juices in the stomach. Herbivorous reptiles tend to chew their food more thoroughly to improve digestion.

Snakes are the most specialized of the reptiles when it comes to swallowing large meals. Adaptations include a highly distensible gut and dermis, but the most obvious specializations are to the head and jaws. The bones of the skull are highly kinetic – there can be a great deal of movement between the various bones which, in other organisms, are tightly fused together. For example, the two sides of the lower jaw are not fused, as they are in other reptiles and mammals, and this allows the two sides to move independently and to be moved apart to accommodate large meals. In addition to this, the position and shape of the quadrate bone allows for a very wide gape. Thus, snakes are able to 'walk' their jaws over meals that may even exceed their own body mass.

FINDING AND OBSERVING REPTILES

The majority of reptiles are cryptic and secretive, since they are small and must avoid predators. Because of this, they are unobtrusive, even in environments where they may be the most abundant vertebrates. However, it is easier to detect reptiles in their natural environment if you have a good knowledge of their biology and natural history. For example, a basic understanding of activity patterns will clarify when various species are likely to be active, and knowledge of habitat selection will show where to concentrate the search. Most importantly, searching should be concentrated at the correct level – birders tend to look up and into the distance; reptile enthusiasts should focus near ground level.

Inactive reptiles can be located by searching for them in their retreats. Here, an understanding of a reptile's thermal needs is useful. A thin rock or piece of corrugated iron exposed to the sun's rays generally becomes too hot for reptiles to tolerate and will not be used as a retreat. Larger or partially shaded rocks and debris will remain within a tolerable thermal range for most reptiles and are worth investigating. Care should always be taken when lifting objects to find reptiles – lift the far side so that a surprised reptile does not feel trapped between you and the cover. Make sure that you carefully replace the object to its original position without crushing any animals beneath.

Road cruising, especially shortly after sundown during the warmer months, is an effective way of finding reptiles. Cruising should be slower than 40 km per hour so that you observe rather than crush reptiles that are crossing the road. After dark, use dimmed headlights, since this more effectively lights the road surface where reptiles are likely to be spotted.

When observing a reptile, attempt to remain motionless and at a safe distance. Their vision is generally tuned for motion detection, and rapid movement is therefore likely to startle the subject. Venomous snakes that feel threatened may bite in defence if the observer is within striking range. Carefully observe as many of the reptile's characteristics as possible. Practice hones the process and provides a reference for future observations. Most importantly, appreciate the world of reptiles that you have discovered.

Johan Marais

Reptiles are generally cryptic and unobtrusive. This Ovambo Tree Skink's colouring allows it to be camouflaged while basking.

SNAKEBITE

The incidence of death due to snakebite is very low in southern Africa, especially when compared to snakebite fatalities in parts of Southeast Asia and North Africa. For example, although actual numbers are not accurately known, there are probably fewer than 10 snakebite deaths per year in South Africa. In comparison, snakebite causes many thousands of deaths in India, Sri Lanka and the northern parts of Africa every year. This stark difference is probably due to the interplay of several factors: the species of snake found in the different areas, the densities of human populations and fundamental differences in human lifestyle. Probability of death after being bitten is also greatly influenced by standards of medical care and the speed with which a victim can get to appropriate medical facilities.

Marius Burger

The incidence of serious snakebite is relatively low in southern Africa.

Snake venom

Although more than half of the 151 species of snake in southern Africa have fangs and are technically venomous, only 16 species carry venom that is considered to be potent enough to be life-threatening. These include the Boomslang (*Dispholidus typus*), two species of Vine Snake (*Thelotornis mossambicanus* and *T. capensis*), the Coral Shield Cobra (*Aspidelaps lubricus*), the six species of Cobra (*Naja anchietae, N. annulifera, N. melanoleuca, N. nivea, N. nigricollis,* and *N. mossambica*), Rinkhals (*Hemachatus haemachatus*), the two species of Mamba (*Dendroaspis polylepis* and *D. angusticeps*), Puff Adder (*Bitis arietans*), Gaboon Adder (*Bitis gabonica*) and Berg Adder (*Bitis atropos*). Fatalities have been recorded from bites of a few other species, but these cases should be considered exceptional and may actually be the result of unusual sensitivity of the victim to the venom, or due to inappropriate treatment of the bite.

Generally, snake venom can be classified into four broad groups; neurotoxic (nerve destroying), cytotoxic (tissue destroying), haemotoxic (affecting blood chemistry) and myotoxic (paralyzing muscle), depending on the predominant symptoms shown in human victims. However, this schema is an extreme simplification of reality. Snake venom is essentially a specialized salivary excretion and the active component consists mainly of proteins and peptides. Any given species of venomous snake usually carries several different active proteins in its venom, and the principal effect of the venom may depend as much on the size and sensitivity of the victim as it does on the composition of the venom. Thus, the overriding symptom of Black Mamba envenomation in humans is neurotoxic in nature, but the same venom may also have a pronounced cytotoxic effect on a mamba's rodent prey.

Certain components of snake venom are common to several species and may be almost ubiquitous in venomous snake species. Other components may be found in only a single species, and many hundreds of different types of protein have now been identified in snake venoms – some even have medical application as potent anticoagulants. There are also known instances where snakes from different populations, but from the same species, have venoms of different potency or action (e.g. Berg Adder), while the composition of the venom in some species is known to change with the snake's age and diet.

Venom provides snakes with several advantages other than the obvious defensive benefits. For example, venom also serves an important function in the capture and despatch of prey, and dramatically speeds up the digestion of meals. In fact, the digestion-enhancing property of venom probably constitutes its single most important function for the snake: since snakes are not able to chew their meals, it is of great benefit that the venom injected into the prey can digest the meal from within. This is probably why there is a preponderance of venomous snakes in cold regions; digestion is otherwise impaired at low temperatures, since snakes are ectotherms.

Anti-snakebite serum

Two types of antivenom are available for treatment of snakebite in southern Africa. A general polyvalent anti-snakebite serum covers the bites of species that most commonly result in serious symptoms (Cobra, Rinkhals, Mamba, Puff Adder and Gaboon Adder), and is the serum that is provided in the conventional 'Snakebite First Aid Kit'. The second type is a monovalent anti-snakebite serum that is specifically for the treatment of Boomslang bites. This serum is not freely available and is only supplied to hospitals in known cases of Boomslang bites – which is a very rare occurrence. Fortunately, the slow action of Boomslang venom means that there is usually plenty of time for delivery. The venoms of Vine Snakes, Coral Shield Cobras, Berg Adders and all of the 'less venomous' species are not covered by any anti-snakebite serum, and antivenom should never be used in the treatment of bites by these snakes.

The antivenoms available for the treatment of southern African species are produced using horses. Briefly, the horses are injected with increasing doses of venom so that they build up a high level of immunity against the action of the venom. Horses treated in this way can, without any ill effect, tolerate doses of venom that would quickly kill horses that have not been immunized. Blood is then extracted from these 'immune' horses and is separated into two components: the red blood corpuscles and the blood serum (the 'serum' is simply the blood minus the red blood corpuscles, and includes water, immunoglobulins, other proteins, and various solutes). The red blood corpuscles are then returned to the circulatory system of the horse and the serum component is treated with pepsin, filtered and purified, before being packaged into 10 ml ampoules for use.

The anti-snakebite serum extracted from horse's blood contains the immunoglobulins produced by the horse against the action of the snake venoms with which it has been injected. These antibodies make the serum effective in the treatment of snakebite in humans. Unfortunately, the serum also contains several other constituents, including various proteins and antibodies produced by the horse against other pathogens to which it has been exposed during its lifetime. Given that there is, therefore, a veritable cocktail of constituents in the serum, it is not surprising that many people have allergic responses when treated with it. The intensity of the reaction can range from a mild bout of 'serum sickness' (which may be little more than the development of hives over the body) to a full-blown, heart-stopping anaphylactic reaction that can kill the patient in minutes – and much faster than any snake venom can. Because of this very significant and real danger, anti-snakebite serum should be administered only in serious cases where its use has clear and likely benefit, and where medical experts are on hand to deal with any resulting anaphylaxis.

Johan Marais

Puff Adders have large fangs, potent venom and are responsible for more serious bites than any other species in southern Africa.

For this reason also, the use of anti-snakebite serum as a first aid measure is strongly discouraged. In fact, many experts are of the opinion that during the 1900s more people in South Africa died from the treatment than from the snakebite (many deaths that are assumed to be due to envenomation may be due to the anaphylaxis resulting from the serum). Additionally, to be maximally effective, anti-snakebite serum should be administered intravenously (not by simple intramuscular injection), a procedure that should not be carried out by untrained people. Finally, first aid kits don't contain the volumes of serum required to make a significant and positive difference in serious bites – more than 150 ml may be needed, and the kits usually contain only 20 ml.

What to do in the case of snakebite

Given that anti-snakebite serum should not be administered routinely as a first aid measure, what should you do in the case of snakebite? It is extremely difficult to generalize, since many different variables can affect the situation: the most extreme bites can result in life-threatening symptoms within about an hour, while in other cases, bites from dangerous species result in no symptoms at all. In many circumstances, the 'pros and cons' of different procedures are simply unknown because they have never been measured scientifically. It is fundamentally important, however, that you don't panic (although our personal experience suggests that remaining calm may be difficult) and that you get the patient to an appropriate medical facility as a matter of urgency. In addition to this, knowledge of some basic facts (see box below) can be used to calm the patient) – even if the patient happens to be you.

How to minimize the chance of snakebite

- Wear boots when hiking – this will protect you from all but the most unlucky of bites.
- Do not allow the accumulation of rubble, building material, thick vegetation or other materials around your home – these could serve as refuges for snakes and their prey. Snakes are generally reluctant to venture into the open, where they are easy targets for predators.
- Do not tamper with snakes unless you have to, especially if you cannot identify the species. Intimidating a snake will cause the animal to become defensive and may lead to a bite.
- If you unexpectedly find yourself in close proximity to a snake, remain still or back away slowly. Snake vision is attuned to movement; remaining still or moving slowly will ensure that you become part of the background and will not be as threatening to the snake.

REASSURING FACTS ABOUT SNAKEBITE

- Only 16 southern African snake species are considered to be able to deliver a lethal bite. If you have been bitten, the snake may not necessarily be a dangerous one.
- Less than 1% of victims that get bitten by one of the 16 most dangerous species actually die from the bite.
- Generally, the symptoms take hours or days to become life-threatening – there is usually plenty of time to get to a hospital.
- Snakes are able to control the amount of venom injected during a bite. In many cases, the snake may choose not to inject any venom (a dry bite), or only a small amount when biting in defence.
- Bites can be treated symptomatically – it matters little if you don't know what type of snake has bitten you.
- Your chances of survival are much better than the victims of shark and crocodile attacks.

FIRST AID TREATMENT OF SNAKEBITE

What to do
- Note any distinguishing characteristics of the snake that may allow for a positive identification. Important characteristics include the body size, build, colour, body pattern, disposition and behaviour of the snake. Although not crucial to treatment, this information may help in the anticipation of symptoms.
- Try to keep the patient calm and offer reassurance, citing the points in 'Reassuring facts...'.
- Transport the patient to hospital as quickly as possible. Generally, it is more important to expedite this process than it is to apply other first aid measures.
- If the snake is long and slender, apply a pressure bandage to the bitten limb. The pressure bandage should be applied from the extremity towards the body trunk and should be applied with the pressure that is appropriate for a sprain (you are trying to slow the lymphatic system, not restrict blood flow). If in doubt, apply less pressure, or do not apply the bandage at all.
- Ensure that the patient is as inactive as possible: activity speeds up the transport of venom around the body.
- Elevate the bite site. This results in reduced blood flow to and from the bite site, slowing the spread of the venom.
- If the patient has difficulty breathing, or ceases breathing altogether, you may need to apply 'mouth to mouth' resuscitation during transport to hospital. Do not alarm the patient by attempting this prematurely.

Do not
- **Do not** try to kill the snake for identification purposes – bites are generally treated symptomatically. Attempting to capture or kill the snake often leads to a second bite.
- **Do not** use anti-snakebite serum as a first aid measure unless under exceptional circumstances (e.g. if you are a doctor, or if you are certain the snake was a Black Mamba or Cape Cobra and you are unable to reach a hospital within an hour).
- **Do not** cut the wound to bleed out the venom – this does not work.
- **Do not** apply a tourniquet unless under exceptional circumstances (e.g. if you are a doctor, or if you are certain the snake was a Black Mamba or Cape Cobra and you are unable to reach a hospital within an hour). Oxygen starvation of the limb can cause more damage than the envenomation, and is lifesaving only in very unusual circumstances.
- **Do not** allow the patient to consume alcohol. Alcohol will elevate metabolism and promote vasodilatation (widening of blood vessels), causing more rapid onset of symptoms.
- **Do not** attempt any form of electrical shock therapy – this has been shown not to work. Large doses of vitamins or heat treatment are also ineffective and are likely to cause more damage.

Treating venom in the eyes
- Wash the infected eye with copious amounts of water. There is little or no evidence that milk or diluted anti-snakebite serum is better than water, which is also more readily available.
- **Do not** rub the infected eye since this aggravates the condition.
- Once the eyes have been irrigated with sufficient water, transport the patient to hospital as quickly as possible.
- A positive identification of the snake will make little difference to the treatment. **Do not** try to catch or kill the snake – this will only place you in further danger.

ORDER: SQUAMATA

The order Squamata is easily the most species-rich order of living reptiles and includes nearly 8 000 species of lizards, snakes and amphisbaenians. A growing body of evidence has shown that two previously defined suborders within the Squamata, the Serpentes (snakes) and Amphisbaenia (amphisbaenians), are nothing more than unusual lizards. In fact, Monitor Lizards (Varanidae) are actually more closely related to snakes than they are to some other groups of lizards. Similarly, lacertid lizards (Lacertidae) are more closely related to amphisbaenians than they are to other families of lizards. Thus, these suborders are taxonomically invalid, and the Squamata should be regarded as 'the order of lizards', inclusive of unusual forms such as snakes and amphisbaenians. Squamates occur on all continents, apart from Antarctica, and on nearly all islands, except those in very cold climates. To some extent, squamates have also invaded the marine environment; sea snakes are an especially successful group, and Marine Iguanas (*Amblyrhynchus cristatus*) occur in coastal waters of the Galápagos Islands.

The Squamata is an ancient order that arose more than 200 million years ago. In total, the order Squamata contains at least 38 families and approximately 950 genera. The range of species, life histories and ecologies is extremely diverse, and the group is the most successful extant reptile lineage on Earth. Members of the order possess more than 50 shared derived characters, clearly demonstrating a common ancestry. One of the most interesting is the paired copulatory organs (hemipenes) of male squamates. Squamates also all have a scaly skin that is shed periodically, and the cloacal opening is transverse.

Johan Marais

The Squamata includes all species of snake, lizard and amphisbaenian, and is easily the most species-rich reptile order. The species pictured here is Wahlberg's Snake-eyed Skink.

SNAKES

Snakes are essentially a group of extremely specialized lizards and thus belong to the order Squamata. Snakes share many characteristics, suggesting that they have all descended from a common ancestor, which was probably a monitor-like, fossorial lizard. Currently, in excess of 3 000 species are known, divided into more than 450 genera and 18 families. There are 151 described species in southern Africa, one of which is an alien invasive, the Flowerpot Snake (*Ramphotyphlops braminus*). Southern African species are divided into 49 genera and seven families, and it is likely that further distinct genera and species will be identified in the subregion. Snakes occur on all continents apart from Antarctica. However, no snakes occur naturally in New Zealand, Ireland and many oceanic islands, and species diversity is generally low at high latitudes. Many species of snake are adapted for living in the marine environment, and one species, the Yellow-bellied Sea Snake (*Pelamis platura*), is truly pelagic, ranging over much of the Indopacific Ocean.

Snakes are elongate, limbless carnivores that have specialized in consuming large, infrequent meals. Many of the morphological characteristics that define snakes can be seen as adaptations to this extreme feeding strategy. Major modification of cranial anatomy has occurred, allowing for an exceedingly wide gape and a high degree of cranial kinesis (bones of the skull can move in relation to one another). The lower jaws are not fused together, but are connected by a very elastic ligament, allowing the two halves of the lower jaw to move independently of each other. The skin on the lower jaw is especially distensible. These adaptations allow snakes to consume meals that, in some instances, can exceed their own body mass. Because snakes' teeth are specialized for piercing, injecting venom and holding onto prey – rather than cutting it into pieces – snakes are unable to take bite-sized pieces of their victims or to chew chunks into smaller pieces, and prey must be swallowed whole.

The consumption of entire, large, unchewed meals is a digestive challenge for snakes. In addition to digestion being limited by the low body temperatures often experienced by reptiles, snakes' meals are difficult to digest because they present a small surface area for the action of the digestive juices. The ability to inject venom is thus probably primarily an adaptation for dealing with

Johan Marais

All snakes are carnivorous and generally eat large, infrequent meals. This Common Water Snake is engulfing a Sand Frog.

unchewed meals: venom is a type of saliva that has an impressive digestive function, and injection of venom into the meal means that digestion occurs from the inside too. It is therefore not surprising that a higher than average proportion of snakes in cold climates are venomous, even if only mildly so. Egg-eaters have a novel solution to the 'digestive problem': they consume only birds' eggs, which are cracked and squeezed in the Egg-eater's throat so that the liquid contents are emptied into the stomach, allowing for rapid and easy digestion. The eggshell is then spat out.

Snakes are able to endure long periods of fasting, living off fat reserves that are laid down after eating large meals. Because the digestive system is in a quiescent state much of the time, many species undergo a 'down-regulation' of the digestive system between meals. This atrophy results in the digestive system becoming reduced in size and non-functional and, as a consequence, leads to metabolic savings. It also allows for the partial atrophy of supporting organs, such as the heart, liver and kidneys, the down-regulation of which results in further metabolic savings. However, when a meal is ingested, the digestive system must be brought back into an active state quickly, a process that requires much energy. Overall, down-regulation benefits snakes that feed infrequently, since metabolic savings accrued during down-regulation exceed the start-up costs. But snakes that feed more frequently do not benefit from it, since the cumulative start-up costs exceed the energy saved by down-regulation.

Johan Marais

Slenderization allows snakes access to many microhabitats. This Viperine Bark Snake's slender body allows it access to narrow rock crevices.

Snakes are characterized by several other traits: a reduced number of bones in the skull; a total absence of a pectoral girdle and forelimbs; and the pelvic girdle and hind limbs are either rudimentary or entirely absent. In some groups, such as the pythons, the rudimentary hind limbs are present as small spurs, which are located on either side of the cloaca. Vertebrae have also generally increased in number, with nearly 500 in some species. Slenderization of the body has resulted in the elongation and reduction of internal organs. For example, the left lung is generally absent or extremely reduced in size. Snake eyes are covered with a transparent scale or spectacle, giving snakes a permanent, wide-eyed, unblinking stare. Ears are reduced and the tympana and eustachian tubes have

Many snakes that live in cold climates, such as this Berg Adder, are venomous.

been lost. The lack of an external ear means that snakes cannot easily hear air-borne sounds, but can detect low-frequency vibrations with the inner ear. The evolution of many of these attributes is strongly indicative of a fossorial ancestry.

The snake's forked tongue is often thought of as unique to the group. However, snakes' close lizard relatives, the monitors, have a tongue that is similar in anatomy and function. The tongue is elongate and forked, and is withdrawn into a sheath in the mouth when not in use. It serves as a directional chemical sampler – the wider the distance between the tips, the better the directionality. Volatile chemicals in the air (scent) and non-volatile chemicals from surfaces are collected by the tongue, then transported from the external environment to the bi-lobed Jacobson's organ in the roof of the mouth. The Jacobson's organ is especially sensitive to molecules of high molecular weight, and appears to operate as an important short-range sensory organ for identifying food and foe.

The majority of snakes lay eggs, but viviparity has evolved independently in different species. Although snakes are not typically thought of as showing any parental care, recent research has revealed that females of several species of rattlesnake remain in close association with their young for several weeks after birth. Pythons and several other snakes are also known to protect and/or incubate their eggs. Female Southern African Pythons not only incubate their eggs, but also remain with the young for more than two weeks after hatching.

BLIND SNAKES
Family: Typhlopidae

The family Typhlopidae is distributed throughout the tropics and some temperate parts of the world. Species occur variously throughout sub-Saharan Africa, subtropical South, Central and North America, and parts of the Caribbean, mainland Australia, the Indonesian archipelago and Southeast Asia, extending into parts of Eastern Europe. Currently, more than 233 species are known and are grouped into seven genera, although analysis using new molecular techniques may, in time, result in significant rearrangement of the family's taxonomy. Four genera comprising a total of nine species occur in southern Africa. One of these is an exotic species, the Flowerpot Snake (*Ramphotyphlops braminus*), the only exotic snake species confirmed to have populations established in southern Africa. Blind Snakes typically have a cylindrical body that is covered with tight-fitting, highly polished scales. The ventral scales are not enlarged. The head is blunt and is indistinct from the rest of the body, but some species have a well-defined, horizontal 'beak' on the snout, which facilitates burrowing. The skull is highly specialized and compact, and the few teeth are located on the maxillary bone on the upper jaw, and are minute and backward pointing. The eyes are reduced and are situated under a head shield. The tail is very short and ends in a sharp spine. Some species have internal vestiges of a pelvic girdle. These snakes are all highly adapted to a burrowing lifestyle.

Graham Alexander

Blind Snakes, such as Bibron's Blind Snake, typically have cylindrical bodies covered with tight-fitting, highly polished scales. This protects them from the bites of the ants and termites on which they feed.

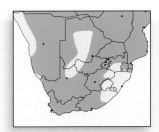

Beaked Blind Snakes

The genus *Rhinotyphlops*
5 species

Description

Beaked Blind Snakes have cylindrical bodies and small heads that are not distinct from the rest of the body. The eyes are reduced, often only visible as a dark spot under the skin. Beaked Blind Snakes have a hard-edged beaked snout that may be used for burrowing and that distinguishes them from other Blind Snakes. The tail is very short and ends in a spine. The coloration varies from beige to olive-brown, pink and pale bluish, sometimes with darker blotches. The scales are highly polished, smooth and close-fitting. Dorsal and ventral scale counts are high and range from 332–623. These snakes average 150–300 mm in length. Schlegel's Beaked Blind Snake and the Zambezi Beaked Blind Snake can grow to nearly 1 m.

Biology

Beaked Blind Snakes are burrowers and spend most of their lives underground. At the surface, they may be found in soil under rocks or logs or in moribund termite mounds. They may also come to the surface at night, especially after heavy rains. When handled, they often use their sharply pointed tail as a means of defence, digging it into their attacker. Diet consists of ants, termites and their larvae. Beaked Blind Snakes use a 'binge feeding' strategy, whereby the snake enters an ant or termite nest and binges on as many food items as possible in a short time. Several hundred ant larvae have been found in the stomachs of individuals that have recently fed. The cylindrical body with tight-fitting, smooth scales appears to be an

Delalande's Beaked Blind Snake spends most of its life underground, but may be found on the surface during the night.

adaptation, allowing Beaked Blind Snakes to resist bites from ants and termites, and possibly also as an adaptation to moving through soil. Large Beaked Blind Snakes often carry sizeable fat reserves, and the posterior half of the body may be distended by fat that is stored for over-wintering. Beaked Blind Snakes are not venomous and do not pose any danger to humans.

Schlegel's Beaked Blind Snake is restricted to the northern parts of southern Africa.

Schlegel's Beaked Blind Snake is one of the largest Blind Snakes and can reach almost 1 m in length.

Reproduction

Little is known about the reproductive biology of these snakes. Females produce between 2 and 14 eggs, although very large individuals have been known to produce up to 60. Eggs measure 20–43 x 9.5–12 mm.

Distribution

Beaked Blind Snakes are found throughout southern Africa in a variety of different habitats. Three species, Boyle's Beaked Blind Snake, Delalande's Beaked Blind Snake and Schinz's Beaked Blind Snake, are endemic to southern Africa.

Schinz's Beaked Blind Snake is usually pink in colour, often with brown blotches above.

SPECIES IN THE GROUP

- Boyle's Beaked Blind Snake: *Rhinotyphlops boylei*
- Delalande's Beaked Blind Snake: *Rhinotyphlops lalandei*
- Schinz's Beaked Blind Snake: *Rhinotyphlops schinzi*
- Schlegel's Beaked Blind Snake: *Rhinotyphlops schlegelii*
- Zambezi Beaked Blind Snake: *Rhinotyphlops mucruso*

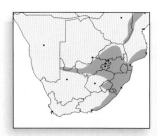

Typical Blind Snakes

The genera *Typhlops* and *Letheobia*
3 species

Description

Typical Blind Snakes have cylindrical bodies with highly polished, smooth, close-fitting scales and small heads that are not distinct from the rest of the body. The eyes are reduced to small dark spots just below the skin, and the nasal scales are undivided. Scales around the body are in 22 to 30 rows, and the dorsal scale count ranges from 236 to 300. These snakes vary in colour from shiny dark brown, dark grey, dark slate, or blackish brown to yellowish brown. The maximum length varies between 180 and 470 mm for adults, with a very short tail that ends in a spine.

Biology

Typical Blind Snakes, like their close relatives the Beaked Blind Snakes, are burrowers and spend most of their lives underground. They may be found in soil under rocks or logs, in moribund termite mounds and sometimes on the surface at night, especially after heavy rains. On warm, rainy summer nights, individuals are often seen crossing tarred roads. When handled, they use their sharply pointed tail for defence, digging it into the attacker. These snakes have no teeth in the lower jaw and feed on ants, termites and their larvae. Blind snakes use a 'binge feeding' strategy similar to that of Beaked Blind Snakes. Large Blind Snakes often carry substantial fat reserves, and the posterior half of the body may be distended by fat that is stored for over-wintering. Blind Snakes are not venomous and pose no danger to humans.

Johan Marais

Bibron's Blind Snake is usually a shiny dark brown, but may be slightly paler below.

Fornasini's Blind Snake is smaller than Bibron's Blind Snake and has a head that is the same diameter as its body.

Like other Blind Snakes, Fornasini's Blind Snake has vestigial eyes that are situated beneath the skin.

Bibron's Blind Snake lays eggs with well-developed embryos, which hatch after less than a week of incubation.

Reproduction

Females usually lay 2–14 thin-shelled eggs, measuring approximately 42 x 10 mm, but very large individuals may produce more. In Bibron's Blind Snake, embryos are well developed at the time of laying and eggs hatch after less than a week of incubation. Females of this species reportedly guard their eggs, and the young measure between 10 and 12.9 mm.

Distribution

Typical Blind Snakes are found mainly in the eastern half of southern Africa. Two of the three species that occur in southern Africa, Fornasini's Blind Snake and Bibron's Blind Snake, are endemic to southern Africa. The Southern Gracile Blind Snake just enters southern Africa in the northeast and has been recorded in northern Mozambique and eastern Zimbabwe.

SPECIES IN THE GROUP

- Bibron's Blind Snake: *Typhlops bibronii*
- Fornasini's Blind Snake: *Typhlops fornasinii*
- Southern Gracile Blind Snake: *Letheobia obtusus*

Flowerpot Snake

The species *Ramphotyphlops braminus*
1 species

Description

This group consists of one unique species that is currently the only
confirmed exotic invasive species of snake in southern Africa. It is
smaller than most of the other Blind Snakes, reaching a maximum
length of about 170 mm. The body is slim and cylindrical, and has
20 rows of polished, tight-fitting scales along the entire length.
Dorsal scales number 300–350 down the length of the body. The
head is rounded, with no evidence of a beak. The eyes are visible
but rudimentary, and the tongue is white. The tail is very short,
usually less than 3% of the body length, and has a conical spine at
the tip. Body colour is usually uniform brown, grey or blackish, but
the ventral parts may be paler than the dorsum, especially near the
head and tail.

Biology

Like all Blind Snakes, Flowerpot Snakes are fossorial, spending
most of their time underground, where they feed on termite and ant
larvae. Individuals are most easily located by searching under rocks,
as this appears to be a favourite sheltering site. As soon as the rock
is lifted, the exposed snake will quickly attempt to escape down
a hole. Flowerpot Snakes may be very abundant in certain areas,
and it is common to find up to five individuals under a single rock.

Johan Marais

*The Flowerpot
Snake is the only
foreign snake
species that is
confirmed to
have established
populations in
southern Africa.
This diminutive
species can be
locally abundant.*

All Flowerpot Snakes are female and are able to reproduce parthenogenetically.

Sandy, friable soils are favoured, possibly as it makes for easy burrowing, but the species also occurs in humic soils. These snakes are often trapped in pot plants, as they are easily incorporated with the potting medium. This has given the species its common name, and has also facilitated its human-assisted dispersal all over the world.

Reproduction

This is the only solely parthenogenetic snake known to science (rare cases of apparent parthenogenesis have been reported in other species). Only females have ever been found, and eggs do not require fertilization for embryonic development to proceed. The lack of males means that there is no possibility of sexual reproduction, and the young are clones of the mother. This attribute has aided the spread of this species around the world, since any single individual is capable of founding a new population. Clutches range from 2–7 small eggs (2 x 6 mm). Hatchlings are minute and are approximately 40 mm in length.

Distribution

This species is probably originally from Southeast Asia or Australia, but now has an almost cosmopolitan distribution. Currently, it is also known to occur in Florida, USA, and Mexico, many oceanic islands, and in several localities in East Africa, Madagascar and the East Indies. In southern Africa, the Flowerpot Snake occurs in coastal Mozambique as far south as Beira. Isolated populations are found in Durban and Cape Town in South Africa. The Cape Town population was probably established before the mid-1970s, but has remained limited in extent and shows little propensity for further expansion, probably as a result of the temperate climate in the area. The Durban population was only discovered in the mid-1980s, when it was apparently restricted to two small populations, but the range is now more extensive and appears to be expanding.

SPECIES IN THE GROUP

■ Flowerpot Snake: *Ramphotyphlops braminus*

WORM SNAKES
Family: Leptotyphlopidae

The family Leptotyphlopidae is composed of two genera and occurs throughout Africa (except in true desert), parts of Arabia, western India and South and Central America. Currently, 93 species are known, but this number is likely to grow as new techniques in molecular taxonomy are applied more extensively to the family. Twelve species, all belonging to the genus *Leptotyphlops*, occur in southern Africa, and eight of these are endemic to the subregion. Worm Snakes have small bodies that are cylindrical and slim with shiny, dark scales. Superficially, their appearance is more worm-like than snake-like. The head is indistinct and blunt, and the majority of species are virtually blind, with the vestigial eyes reduced to small black spots beneath the skin. The tail is short and the ventral scales are not enlarged. The upper jaw bears no teeth, and the lower jaw only a few. There are internal vestiges of a pelvic girdle. Worm Snakes have one oviduct and one lung. The small size and lack of distinguishing features makes species identification difficult without the aid of a dissecting microscope and much patience.

Johan Marais

Most Worm Snakes are superficially similar in appearance. Peters' Worm Snake is shown here.

Worm Snakes

The genus *Leptotyphlops*
12 species

Description

Worm Snakes are small and thin with cylindrical bodies and small heads that are indistinct from the rest of the body. These snakes are virtually blind; the eyes are greatly reduced and may be visible as small black spots. The forked tongue is usually small and white. Most Worm Snake species are superficially indistinguishable from one another and are either reddish brown to brown, or shiny black in colour, with smooth, tight-fitting scales. Scales are in 165–362 dorsal rows, 16–58 subcaudal rows, and either 10 or 12 rows around the tail. When dehydrated, these snakes may take on a silvery appearance due to overlapping scales losing contact with each other, causing more light to be reflected from scale surfaces. The length varies from 150–280 mm.

Biology

Worm Snakes are seldom encountered, and very little is known about their habits or biology. They may be found in soil under rocks or logs, or in moribund termite mounds. Large numbers of Worm Snakes may congregate in suitable cavities during winter. The diet consists primarily of small invertebrates, especially the larvae of termites and ants, and they have been observed following the scent trails of ants to the ant colony. It is thought that these snakes avoid attack by ants by mimicking their scent to avoid detection. Like Blind Snakes, Worm Snakes are binge feeders and appear to 'vacuum up' ant larvae using a fast oscillatory motion of the lower jaw. The jaw has been recorded opening and closing up to three times per second. Worm Snakes are not venomous and pose no danger to humans.

The Long-tailed Worm Snake has paler coloration than most other species of Worm Snake.

Randy Babb

Conservation

Although not currently listed as 'Threatened', the Southern Forest Worm Snake has a very restricted distribution, being limited to forested parts of the KwaZulu-Natal coast. It probably deserves a threatened listing, but more research is needed before its conservation status can be determined.

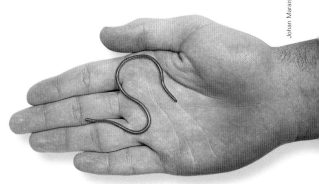

Johan Marais

Reproduction

Worm Snakes produce 2–7 small eggs, measuring about 10–22 x 3 mm. These eggs resemble rice grains and are sometimes attached like a string of sausages.

The Worm Snakes include the smallest species of snake in the world.

Distribution

Worm Snakes occur throughout most of southern Africa, although some species are restricted to small distributions.

Marius Burger

The Cape Worm Snake often has very dark body coloration.

Marius Burger

Incognito Worm Snakes spend most of their time underground or in termitaria, but may be forced to the surface after heavy rains.

Johan Marais

Worm Snakes are adapted for life underground: they have a blunt, indistinct head and vestigial eyes.

SPECIES IN THE GROUP

- Cape Worm Snake: *Leptotyphlops nigricans*
- Damara Worm Snake: *Leptotyphlops labialis*
- Distant's Worm Snake: *Leptotyphlops distanti*
- Incognito Worm Snake: *Leptotyphlops incognitus*
- Jacobsen's Worm Snake: *Leptotyphlops jacobseni*
- Long-tailed Worm Snake: *Leptotyphlops longicaudus*
- Namaqua Worm Snake: *Leptotyphlops occidentalis*
- Peters' Worm Snake: *Leptotyphlops scutifrons*
- Pungwe Worm Snake: *Leptotyphlops pungwensis*
- Slender Worm Snake: *Leptotyphlops gracilior*
- Southern Forest Worm Snake: *Leptotyphlops sylvicolus*
- Tello's Worm Snake: *Leptotyphlops telloi*

PYTHONS

Family: Pythonidae

The family Pythonidae consists of at least eight genera and 32 species, distributed throughout sub-Saharan Africa, South and Southeast Asia and Australia. Australia has the highest diversity, with four genera and 13 species. Only two species, both belonging to the genus *Python,* occur in southern Africa. Pythons are medium to very large, robust snakes and include some of the largest species of snake in the world. They are primitive and non-venomous, with pelvic spurs in the anal region (external evidence of a vestigial pelvic girdle). The ventral scales are relatively narrow and the number of dorsal scale rows is high. The lips have heat-sensitive pits that enable pythons to detect warm-blooded prey. All species are egg-laying, and several are known to be facultative endotherms due to the brooding female's ability to warm her body by muscle twitching.

Johan Marais

The Southern African Python is a large, robust snake that relies on constriction to kill its prey.

Anchieta's Dwarf Python

The species *Python anchietae*
1 species

Description

This is a small Python that is usually about 1.2 m, with a maximum length of 1.8 m. The scales have a beady appearance and are in 57–61 rows at midbody. The ventral scales are smooth but fairly narrow, and are only about a third of the body width. Coloration is reddish brown to dark brown with black-edged creamy white blotches on the dorsal parts, and the underside is paler. The head is very distinct from the neck, is covered with small scales and has reddish brown triangular markings bordered on each side by a creamy white, black-edged band. Three pairs of large heat-sensitive pits line the snout, and a row of smaller pits is positioned posteriorly on the lower jaw. The tail is generally short, with 46 to 57 paired subcaudal scales.

Biology

Anchieta's Dwarf Python is rare and is known from relatively few specimens. Little is known of its biology in the wild, but it is very popular in captive collections and many individuals have been exported illegally. In captivity it is active at night and rolls up in a defensive ball when threatened, much like its close relative, the Royal Python (*Python regius*) from West Africa. Prey includes rodents, such as gerbils and rats, and birds. In captivity it feeds readily on sparrows. Prey is seized and immediately constricted before being swallowed head first. This inoffensive species poses no danger to humans as it is nonvenomous and reluctant to bite.

Johan Marais

Anchieta's Dwarf Python is rare and is restricted to parts of central northern Namibia and parts of Angola.

Richard Boycott

Anchieta's Dwarf Python reaches a maximum length of about 1.8 m.

Conservation

In southern Africa, Anchieta's Dwarf Python is fully protected within its range by national conservation legislation. It is listed in Appendix II of CITES, but is not currently listed by the IUCN as 'Threatened'. Its rarity and high value in the pet trade may necessitate a future listing.

Reproduction

Small clutches of 4 or 5 eggs are produced in early summer. The eggs measure approximately 75 x 40 mm, and the young are about 500 mm in length. The hatchlings tend to be darker than the adults.

Distribution

Anchieta's Dwarf Python is restricted to the central northern parts of Namibia, extending further northwards into Angola.

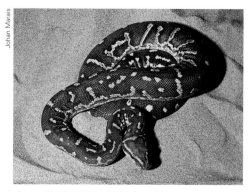

Johan Marais

Juvenile Anchieta's Dwarf Pythons are more strikingly marked than adults.

HEAT SENSORS

A variety of snakes, including Pit Vipers, pythons and Boas, have heat-sensitive pits situated either between the nostril and the eye or on the upper lip. In pythons these pits are situated between the scales on the lips and are capable of detecting infrared radiation. Even temperature fluctuations of less than 1 °C can be detected, enabling the snake to hunt warm-blooded prey in pitch darkness.

SPECIES IN THE GROUP

■ Anchieta's Dwarf Python: *Python anchietae*

Southern African Python

The species *Python natalensis*
1 species

Description

This is by far the largest snake species in southern Africa, reaching a maximum length of 5 m and mass of 60 kg. Many reports exaggerate the maximum length attained by the species, but it is doubtful that any specimens of more than 6 m have existed, even in historical times. The Southern African Python is a strong, muscular snake with a triangular head that is relatively distinct from the rest of the body. The eyes are moderate in size with vertical pupils. The snout has three pairs of large heat-sensitive pits, and several smaller pits are located posteriorly on the lower jaw. The head has a dark triangular marking on the crown and a dark line runs from the tip of the snout, through the eye to the back of the head. Body coloration is usually dark brown with grey-brown blotches and dark speckling above and widely spaced dark blotches on the sides. Older individuals and incubating females are often very dark in colour and may appear to be uniform black. Scales on the head are highly fragmented and small. Body scales are smooth, and are in 78–95 rows at midbody. Although the ventral scales are enlarged, they are narrower than is typical for snakes and are only about one third of the width of the body. The tail is relatively short and has 63–84 pairs of subcaudals. A pair of claws is located on the sides of the cloaca. These claws are much larger in males and are the external vestiges of limbs. Although they now play no part in locomotion, they appear to function in courtship, as the males uses them to tickle and stimulate the female.

Johan Marais

Southern African Pythons typically have a dark, triangular marking on the crown of the head and a dark line from the tip of the snout, through the eyes.

Graham Alexander

Southern African Pythons reach a maximum length of about 5 m and mass of 60 kg.

Biology

Although Southern African Pythons are active at night during warm seasons, they may be found abroad during the day at any time of the year and frequently bask at midday during winter. They will usually disappear surreptitiously into a retreat if approached while basking or, if near a body of water, will seek refuge in the water, where they can remain submerged for long periods. Pythons will freeze if surprised in the open, but will explode into activity at the slightest contact or molestation, striking out in self-defence.

Although Southern African Pythons employ a 'slow patrol' to search actively for food, they more often rely on ambush to catch prey. Favourite ambush positions include areas alongside animal paths and near water bodies, and they may submerge themselves in water to ambush prey that comes to drink. Prey is killed by constriction, and meals can exceed the python's own body mass. A wide variety of prey is taken, but warm-blooded species appear to be favoured, and the heat-sensitive pits appear to play an important role in prey location. Large adults of 4.5 m can ingest medium-sized antelope, but it is doubtful that even the largest Southern African Pythons can consume human adults, and most reported incidents of python attacks on humans are false or exaggerated. Recorded prey includes a variety of small birds and mammals, Grey Duiker, Impala, young Blesbok and Nyala, Vervet Monkey, African Wild Dog, and Cheetah. Cold-blooded prey includes fish, Monitor Lizards and Crocodiles. The Southern African Python has been recorded feeding on duck eggs and even carrion on occasions.

Conservation

The Southern African Python is listed as 'Vulnerable' in the most recent South African and Swaziland Red Data Books. These ratings are based on the fact that Southern African Pythons are specifically exploited for human consumption. It is unlikely that this species will retain this threat classification when reassessed using the latest IUCN criteria, since it appears to be quite common in certain areas and is widespread. Populations do, however, appear to be declining in some areas, and local populations in Durban and the Eastern Cape have reportedly been extirpated. Causes of mortality are varied: many are inadvertently killed on roads, for their skins or for fat for the muti trade. A more recent cause of mortality is electrocution on electric game fences. The rapid expansion of the game farming industry in southern Africa could result in electric fences becoming a threat to populations in the future.

Reproduction

Southern African Pythons mate between June and September. During this time, receptive females become more active and are often seen crossing roads when they are moving from one retreat site to another. Males actively follow the scent trails left by females, and up to 13 may be found in attendance of a single female, but aggression or rivalry between the males during mating is unknown. Depending on the size and condition of the female, 30–60 eggs (as many as 100 in exceptional cases) are laid between October and December. The eggs measure about 100 mm in diameter, weigh 130–160 g, and are usually laid underground in termite mounds or in Aardvark burrows. Clutches have been laid on the surface in very exposed situations, but it is likely that such clutches would have reduced hatching success. The female coils around the eggs to protect and warm them. Python eggs appear to be more sensitive to low temperatures than other snake eggs, and hatching success drops markedly if the clutch is not maintained at temperatures above 28 °C. Unlike some other python

Dave Honiball

Pythons are renowned for their ability to ingest large meals. This Southern African Python is swallowing an adult Common Duiker.

Graham Alexander

Unlike some other brooding pythons that raise their body temperature by shivering, female Southern African Pythons do so by basking on the surface when it is sunny. The brooding females take on a darker coloration, making basking more efficient.

species, brooding Southern African Pythons are unable to raise their body temperature by shivering, but do so by basking on the surface when it is sunny. After raising her body temperature, the incubating female returns to her eggs and warms them by coiling tightly around the clutch. Brooding of the clutch facilitates and accelerates incubation. During this time the female allows her body temperature to reach near-fatal body temperatures of around 40 °C during bouts of basking. Her large size helps maintain the temperature of the eggs at or above 28 °C through the night. Body temperatures selected by brooding females are significantly higher than those selected by non-brooding pythons, which are usually just below 32 °C. Research indicates that it is the inability of brooding females to maintain high clutch temperatures in cooler climates that limits the species to warm areas.

Brooding females fast for the duration of incubation and may lose more than half their body mass over this period. The young measure between 500 and 700 mm in length and weigh about 100 g. The female and the young remain at the nest site for two weeks after the clutch hatches, and can be found basking near the nest entrance during the day. During this period the female coils around the empty eggshells at night and the young climb into her coils. It is likely that the young stay warmer at night due to this behaviour, and it may speed up the

Graham Alexander

Southern African Pythons rely on several senses – including sight, smell, vomerolfaction and heat detection – to detect potential prey and predators.

digestion of remaining egg yolk in their stomachs. However, the mother does not actively protect the young, is unusually timid and retiring at this time and is generally the first to flee at a sign of danger. The young shed their skin about 12 days after hatching and disperse a day or two later. Females can take some time to regain body mass lost during brooding and only lay eggs every second or third year. Southern African Pythons may take more than 10 years to reach sexual maturity in the wild, but can develop much quicker in captivity.

Distribution

The Southern African Python is widespread in bushveld, savanna and forest, and is found throughout most of southern Africa excluding the southern, central and Western Cape, southern Namibia and central Botswana. The southernmost population is in the Eastern Cape and is isolated from other populations by a distance of approximately 350 km. It was purported to have become extinct in 1927, when the supposed last specimen was captured in the Bathurst district. However, occasional reports still originate from this area and 34 pythons were 'reintroduced' into the Great Fish River Nature Reserve near Grahamstown in the Eastern Cape between 1980 and 1986 in an attempt to re-establish the species in this area. Unfortunately, little follow-up monitoring of the translocation has been made. Some evidence suggests that the species has recently extended its range southwards in Gauteng and in the Northern Cape, possibly as a result of climatic warming.

Danger to humans

Although not venomous, large pythons are capable of inflicting bites that may occasionally require medical attention. Incidents of attacks on humans are grossly exaggerated and there is very little hard evidence of pythons attacking people. Several cases of supposed python attacks have turned out, on more thorough investigation, to be human attacks on pythons.

Johan Marais

The Southern African Python can be found in a wide variety of microhabitats, including trees, rocky areas and water.

CONSTRICTING PREY

Several snakes, mainly those that lack fangs and venom, kill their prey by constriction. The prey is generally seized with strong, sharp teeth and quickly wrapped in the snake's coils. The snake senses the prey's bodily movement, including heartbeat, with its coils and will apply more pressure in those areas. Such pressure quickly kills mammalian prey by cardiac and circulatory arrest, and not merely through suffocation as is usually assumed. Snakes do not need to anchor their tails in order to constrict prey.

SPECIES IN THE GROUP

■ Southern African Python: *Python natalensis*

AFRICAN BURROWING SNAKES
Family: Atractaspididae

The Atractaspididae is a small, essentially African family of snakes. It occurs throughout most of sub-Saharan Africa, with only one species being found out of Africa – on the Arabian Peninsula, and in parts of Israel and Jordan. The family has two well-defined subfamilies, but relationships between genera within the Atractaspididae, and its taxonomic relationship to other snake families, are still under investigation. As currently delineated, the family includes 14 genera and at least 66 species. Nineteen species, constituted into seven genera, occur in southern Africa. One genus is endemic to the region. African Burrowing Snakes are small to medium cylindrical snakes with small heads that are not very distinct from the rest of the body. They have no loreal scale – a scale between the preocular and nasal scales; only African Burrowing Snakes and elapids lack this scale. Most species are primarily fossorial and have small eyes, smooth shiny scales and a short tail. Some species show additional adaptation to burrowing in the form of compact skulls or elongated snouts. A wide variety of fang types occurs in the family, ranging from a completely fangless species to grooved rear fangs, front fixed fangs and front movable fangs. The venom of some species is of medical significance, and the bites of some species have resulted in the death of humans. Many of the species in this family are nondescript, leading to confusion with harmless species.

African Burrowing Snakes, such as this Transvaal Quill-snouted Snake, generally have cylindrical bodies, heads that are not very distinct from the body and small, beady eyes.

Stiletto Snakes

The genus *Atractaspis*
3 species

Description

This group is made up of three nondescript species of snake
that all have a similar body form, coloration and behaviour. They
have previously been known by many names including Mole
Viper, Burrowing Adder and Burrowing Asp, but these names are
inappropriate and their usage should be discouraged. Adult total
length is usually about 400 mm, but specimens of 700 mm are
known. The body is slim and cylindrical and the tail is short, usually
ending in a sharp point. The head is indistinct from the neck, the
eyes are small and beady, and the snout is usually pointed. There
is no loreal scale. The Beaked Stiletto Snake has an obvious sharp
edge along the jawline. Stiletto Snakes are so-named because they
have very large, hollow mobile fangs situated in the front of the
mouth. The lower jaw is relatively small and a bite usually involves
only one fang, which is exposed out of the side of the mouth and is
used in a stabbing fashion without the mouth really being opened.
Midbody scales are in 19–27 rows, the anal shield is entire (very
occasionally divided) and the 18–27 subcaudals are unpaired,
although the subcaudals of the posterior half of the tail of the
Eastern Congo Stiletto Snake are usually paired. Ventral scale counts
number 193–260. The body is usually purple-brown, grey-brown or
black above, with a creamy white or dark brown to black belly.

Johan Marais

*Because it is often
confused with
nonvenomous
species, the non-
descript Southern
Stiletto Snake is
responsible for
many serious bites
among novice
herpetologists.*

Biology

Stiletto Snakes are primarily fossorial and are often found under logs or stones or in moribund termite mounds. They come to the surface at night to forage, especially after summer rains. These snakes are surprisingly active hunters and move about rapidly on the surface in a characteristically jerky fashion. Molested specimens will usually arch their necks with the head pointing down at an angle as though trying to burrow into the ground. This posture is misleading since a Stiletto Snake in this position is primed to bite, and will do so without hesitation if handled. These snakes tend to respond to threats with erratic body movements, head-hiding and cloacal discharge.

The diet consists mainly of a variety of burrowing reptiles, small rodents, frogs and other snakes. When catching its prey in a burrow, a Stiletto Snake will usually make use of one fang and will rake backwards to allow the fang to penetrate the prey. However, when on the surface and not restricted by a burrow, Stiletto Snakes will seize prey firmly in their jaws with both fangs penetrating.

Reproduction

Little is known about reproduction in Stiletto Snakes. Apparently all species lay small clutches of between 3 and 8 eggs. Incubation time and hatchling size have not yet been recorded.

Distribution

The Southern Stiletto Snake is widespread in southern Africa, occurring throughout the northern and eastern parts. This species inhabits a wide variety of habitats including moist savanna, lowland forest, grassland, arid savanna and karoo scrub. The Beaked Stiletto Snake has a more restricted, endemic distribution, occurring in central northern Namibia, southeastern Botswana, and parts of the Northwest, Gauteng and

Stiletto Snakes have large fangs. Here, the fang of a Southern Stiletto Snake is exposed.

Body coloration of Southern Stiletto Snakes is variable. This individual has a white belly; others are uniformly brown.

Marius Burger

The more placid Beaked Stiletto Snake is easily distinguished from the Southern Stiletto Snake by the prominent edge along its jawline.

Limpopo provinces in South Africa. As it is a secretive species, it is likely that it is more widespread than current records suggest. The Eastern Congo Stiletto Snake is widespread in West and Central Africa, only entering southern Africa in the Caprivi Strip.

Danger to humans

Several attributes make Stiletto Snakes much more dangerous than their nondescript appearance would suggest. They are easily mistaken for a variety of harmless or docile species, including Wolf Snakes (*Lycophidion*) and Purple-glossed Snakes (*Amblyodipsas*), and are thus misguidedly handled by inexperienced herpetologists. They are irascible and will not hesitate to bite, and because the bite does not usually involve a conventional strike, it comes without warning. Stiletto Snakes have very large, backward-pointing fangs, which can be manoeuvred into a finger even if the snake is restrained behind the head. When picked up by their tails they are also able to twist and quickly climb up their own bodies, to deliver a surprising bite to the uninitiated. These characteristics result in many novice snake catchers being bitten, and these snakes are responsible for more snakebites than any other species in areas where they are common. Although the three species that occur in southern Africa are not regarded as deadly, their bites can be painful and may lead to tissue loss as a result of necrosis. The venom has a primarily cytotoxic effect in humans, leading to local pain, swelling and necrosis. Polyvalent antivenom is not effective in treatment and must not be administered.

SAFE HANDLING OF SNAKES

Although experienced herpetologists may be able to catch certain venomous snakes safely by the tail or others by gripping them behind the head, Stiletto Snakes cannot be handled safely. Many herpetologists have attempted to restrain Stiletto Snakes behind the head, only to be bitten in the process. As these snakes have large backward-facing fangs under the upper lip, they are able to bite even when restrained.

SPECIES IN THE GROUP

- Beaked Stiletto Snake: *Atractaspis duerdeni*
- Eastern Congo Stiletto Snake: *Atractaspis congica*
- Southern Stiletto Snake: *Atractaspis bibronii*

Centipede-eaters

The genus *Aparallactus*
4 species

Description

Four southern African species belong to this group. Centipede-eaters are all similar in body form and size. They are small snakes with cylindrical bodies that vary in total length from 200–450 mm. The head is almost indistinct from the body and is torpedo shaped. The eyes are small and have round pupils. A minute fixed fang is situated on the posterior of the maxillary bone, just below the eye. There is no loreal scale. The scales on the body are smooth and shiny and are in 15 rows at midbody. The anal shield is undivided, the subcaudals (29–65) are not paired and ventral scales number between 126 and 186.

Coloration and patterning varies between species, but all have a collar on the neck. The Black-headed Centipede-eater is yellow, reddish brown or grey-brown in colour with a black head and black collar that narrows on the sides of the neck. Mozambique Centipede-eaters are similar to Black-headed Centipede-eaters in coloration, but the collar on the neck is twice as broad. The Reticulated Centipede-eater is brown to olive-grey above, often with dark-edged scales that give a reticulated effect. Juveniles of this species have a black collar followed by 12 dark blotches down the body, which fade with age. The Black Centipede-eater usually has two yellow collars on the neck and a whitish underside.

Centipede-eaters feed almost exclusively on centipedes. Here, a Black-headed Centipede-eater bites into its meal.

Johan Marais

The Reticulated Centipede-eater sometimes includes scorpions in its diet.

Zimbabwe and southern Mozambique. The *Black-headed Centipede-eaters have a black head and a broad, black bar on the neck.*

Biology

Centipede-eaters are burrowers and are usually found in loose soil under stones, rotting logs or debris, or in moribund termite mounds. Several individuals may congregate in a single termite mound. These snakes are nocturnal and very active after summer rains. Centipede-eaters are quick to bite when first handled, but they soon become docile. Their fangs are relatively short and seldom pierce the skin. Their venom poses no threat to humans. They feed almost exclusively on centipedes, seizing the prey in their jaws and chewing along the length of the centipede while the venom takes effect. If bitten by the centipede, the snake will release and start the chewing process again.

Reproduction

All the species in this group are oviparous, laying small clutches of 2–4 elongate eggs (32 x 5 mm) during summer. The young are between 90 and 120 mm in total length.

Distribution

Centipede-eaters are restricted to the eastern half of southern Africa. The Black-headed Centipede-eater is most widespread, occurring extensively in lowland forest, montane forest, moist savanna and grassland, from north of the subregion, south into the Eastern Cape. The Reticulated Centipede-eater occurs in

remaining two species are more restricted. The Mozambique Centipede-eater, the only endemic species in the group, is restricted to the Inhambane region of southern Mozambique, where it is very rare and has not been recorded for more than 100 years; the Black Centipede-eater is restricted to eastern Zimbabwe, but does occur more widely to the north of southern Africa.

Body coloration is variable in Black-headed Centipede-eaters. This individual is reddish brown. Others may be yellow, grey-brown or beige.

SPECIES IN THE GROUP

- Black Centipede-eater: *Aparallactus guntheri*
- Black-headed Centipede-eater: *Aparallactus capensis*
- Mozambique Centipede-eater: *Aparallactus nigriceps*
- Reticulated Centipede-eater: *Aparallactus lunulatus*

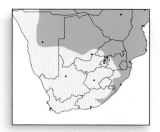

Natal Black Snakes and Purple-glossed Snakes

The genera *Macrelaps* and *Amblyodipsas*
5 species

Description

The five species in this group are burrowers that have stocky, cylindrical bodies, relatively small heads that are not distinct from the body and small eyes with round pupils. The total length in adults ranges from a maximum of 320 mm in the Eastern Purple-glossed Snake to just over 1 m in the Common Purple-glossed Snake. The head is blunt and the tail is short. Grooved rear fangs are situated just below the eyes. All species have smooth, highly polished scales. There is no loreal scale. Rows of midbody scales number 25 or 27 in the Natal Black Snake, 19 or 21 in the Common Purple-glossed Snake, 17 in the Natal Purple-glossed Snake, and 15 in the Eastern Purple-glossed Snake and Kalahari Purple-glossed Snake. The Purple-glossed Snake species have 15–39 pairs of subcaudals, and the Natal Black Snake has 35–50 unpaired subcaudals. Likewise, the anal shield is divided in all Purple-glossed Snakes, but undivided in the Natal Black Snake. There are between 120 and 215 ventral scales.

Johan Marais

The Natal Black Snake can be distinguished from Purple-glossed Snakes by the presence of single subcaudals.

Johan Marais

There are conflicting reports about the Natal Purple-glossed Snake. It has been reported laying eggs and producing live young.

The majority of species in this group are inky or jet black above and below, and the Purple-glossed Snakes have an iridescent purplish sheen. The two species that differ in coloration are the Eastern Purple-glossed Snake, which has white or yellow on the upper lip, throat and two scales on the lower flank, and the Kalahari Purple-glossed Snake, which is yellow with a broad purplish band down the centre of the back. It may also have purple-black blotches on the belly. The species in this group become dull silver-grey prior to shedding.

Biology

All members of this group are fossorial and may be found under rotting logs and large stones, and in animal burrows. They may also be exposed during excavations. These snakes forage through leaf litter in search of food and are active on warm overcast days and warm damp nights. They favour deep sandy or humic soils in well-wooded forest areas and along streams. Suitable habitat ranges from coastal lowland forest to Kalahari sand. These shy, elusive snakes are rarely encountered and are docile and reluctant to bite. Some may hide their head under body coils. Prey includes frogs, snakes, small rodents, legless lizards and amphisbaenians. Although these snakes are all venomous, they also use constriction to subdue large prey. The Natal Black Snake has also been recorded including carrion in its diet.

Reproduction

All species in the group have been recorded as laying eggs. Surprisingly, the Natal Purple-glossed Snake has also been reported to have produced live young. Natal

Bill Branch

The eastern form of the Eastern Purple-glossed Snake often has yellow on the belly.

The Common Purple-glossed Snake is the largest Purple-glossed Snake and can reach a length of just over 1 m.

Black Snakes lay clutches of between 3 and 10 large eggs (approximately 45 x 28 mm) in summer. The young are between 200 and 290 mm in length. Purple-glossed Snakes lay clutches of 3–11 eggs (approximately 29 x 17 mm).

Conservation

A subspecies of the Eastern Purple-glossed Snake (*Amblyodipsas microphthalma nigra*) is listed as 'Restricted' in the most recent South African Red Data Book, but is not listed by the IUCN as 'Threatened'. This subspecies has a very restricted distribution and little is known about its biology.

Distribution

Most of the species in this group are restricted to the eastern parts of southern Africa, Botswana and northern Namibia. The Natal Black Snake occurs in eastern KwaZulu-Natal, extending into the Eastern Cape. The Natal Purple-glossed Snake occurs from southern KwaZulu-Natal northwards into Mpumalanga and Limpopo provinces in South Africa. The Common Purple-glossed Snake has a wide distribution from southern KwaZulu-Natal northwards into Mpumalanga, Gauteng, Limpopo province, Mozambique, eastern and northern Botswana, most of Zimbabwe, extending north of southern Africa. The Eastern Purple-

glossed Snake is found in Mozambique and northern Limpopo province. The Kalahari Purple-glossed Snake occurs in the northwestern Namib, most of Botswana and western Zimbabwe. All species, except for the Common Purple-glossed Snake and the Kalahari Purple-glossed Snake, are endemic to southern Africa.

Danger to humans

Although these snakes have not been responsible for many serious cases of snakebite, the venom of the Natal Black Snake can result in loss of consciousness in humans and is potentially dangerous. Purple-glossed Snakes are reluctant to bite. Their venom has not been studied, but it is unlikely to be dangerous. Polyvalent antivenom is not effective in treatment and must not be administered.

SPECIES IN THE GROUP

- Common Purple-glossed Snake: *Amblyodipsas polylepis*
- Eastern Purple-glossed Snake: *Amblyodipsas microphthalma*
- Kalahari Purple-glossed Snake: *Amblyodipsas ventrimaculata*
- Natal Purple-glossed Snake: *Amblyodipsas concolor*
- Natal Black Snake: *Macrelaps microlepidotus*

Quill-snouted Snakes

The genus *Xenocalamus*
4 species

Description

The four species in this group have a peculiar elongate, quill-shaped head and very pointed snout. The body form is slim and cylindrical. The head is not distinct from the body and the lower jaw is under-slung and reduced. The eyes are small with round pupils and there is no loreal scale. Immovable rear fangs are situated on the maxillary bone below the eyes. The tail is relatively short and has a blunt end. Adults usually reach a length of between 300 and 500 mm, but specimens of up to 850 mm have been recorded. Midbody scales are in either 15 or 17 rows, the subcaudals (22–37) are paired and the anal scale is divided. Ventral scales number between 183 and 248. Quill-snouted Snakes are usually black above, yellow on the flanks and white or pale yellow below, but several other colour phases exist. Some specimens of the Transvaal Quill-snouted Snake are more uniformly black above with pale-centred or yellow-edged scales that give a fine, chequered pattern. Individuals that are plain black above and below are also known. The Elongate Quill-snouted Snake is usually lemon-yellow to light purple-brown with a double row of brownish blotches. Some specimens have a whitish sheen on the head and neck.

Biology

Quill-snouted Snakes are fossorial and occur in sandy soils. They are seldom seen on the surface, but may be found in termite mounds

Quill-snouted Snakes, such as this Transvaal Quill-snouted Snake, are easily recognizable: they have a quill-shaped head, a pointed snout and a slim, cylindrical body.

Johan Marais

Bill Branch

The Bicoloured Quill-snouted Snake is typically dark above and pale below, but colours vary from one individual to the next.

or under rotting logs. At times they may be driven to the surface by water-logging after excessive rain, or uncovered during excavations. These snakes are generally slow-moving, docile and very reluctant to bite. When handled, they use their sharp snouts as a defence, but this poses no threat to humans. They feed largely on amphisbaenians, but will also eat burrowing skinks. It is likely that their peculiar snouts are adapted to grasp amphisbaenians in the confines of a narrow burrow. Likewise, some amphisbaenian species have blunt tails that appear to function as burrow-sized plugs to prevent Quill-snouted Snakes from biting their tails.

Conservation

The Transvaal Quill-snouted Snake is listed as 'Rare' in the latest South African Red Data Book and 'Data Deficient' by the IUCN. All of the Quill-snouted Snakes are secretive and seldom encountered. Research is needed to determine the conservation status of all species in the group.

Reproduction

Very little is known about Quill-snouted Snake reproduction. All species are oviparous and lay small clutches of between 2 and 4 eggs (28–47 x 6–15 mm). The young of one clutch measured 200 mm in length.

Distribution

Quill-snouted Snakes are restricted to sandy substrates in the northern half of southern Africa and have patchy distributions. The Transvaal Quill-snouted Snake, which has limited distribution, and the Save Quill-snouted Snake are endemic to southern Africa.

SPECIES IN THE GROUP

- Bicoloured Quill-snouted Snake: *Xenocalamus bicolor*
- Elongate Quill-snouted Snake: *Xenocalamus mechowii*
- Save Quill-snouted Snake: *Xenocalamus sabiensis*
- Transvaal Quill-snouted Snake: *Xenocalamus transvaalensis* **DD**

Harlequin Snakes

The genus *Homoroselaps*
2 species

Description

This group consists of two species that are small with cylindrical bodies, smooth, polished scales and a blunt head, which is not distinct from the neck. The eyes are small with round pupils and there is no loreal scale. Small, immovable fangs are situated in the front of the mouth and resemble those found in the elapids. Adult length ranges between 200 and 320 mm in the Striped Harlequin Snake, and between 300 and 650 mm in the Spotted Harlequin Snake. Striped Harlequin Snakes are also much slimmer than Spotted Harlequin Snakes. Harlequin Snakes have 15 rows of scales at midbody, the anal shield is divided and subcaudals (22–43) are paired. Ventral scales number between 160 and 239. The Striped Harlequin Snake is black above with a conspicuous yellow stripe down the centre of the back from the nose to the tip of the tail. The lips, belly and outer scales on the flanks are creamy white to yellowish white. The Spotted Harlequin Snake has two distinct, geographically based, colour patterns. Specimens from the southern and western parts of the distribution are yellowish white with regular black bars or blotches and a wide bright orange or red vertebral stripe. The belly is light yellowish with large dark blotches. In the northern parts of the distribution, specimens are blackish above with a yellow dot on each scale and a bright orange to yellow stripe down the centre of the back, from the crown of the head to the tip of the tail. An area of intergradation exists between Port Elizabeth and East London where the two colour phases are mixed. The taxonomic relationship between the colour phases needs investigation.

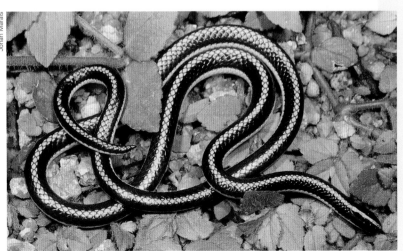

Johan Marais

Harlequin Snakes are small and innocuous. Striped Harlequin Snakes are rare and are listed by the IUCN as 'Near Threatened'.

The head of Harlequin Snakes is not distinct from the body, but the eyes are more prominent than those of other African Burrowing Snakes.

Biology

Harlequin Snakes are docile and rarely attempt to bite, even when captured. They spend most of their lives underground, sometimes burrowing in loose soil, foraging for legless skinks and Worm Snakes. The Spotted Harlequin Snake may be locally common in some areas and is usually found in deserted termite mounds or under rocks.

The Striped Harlequin Snake is very poorly known as it is so seldom encountered. Although the venom may cause some discomfort, it is not considered dangerous to humans.

Reproduction

Spotted Harlequin Snakes lay 6–16 eggs (approximately 20 x 10 mm) that take about

In the south of its range, the Spotted Harlequin Snake is usually yellowish white with regular black bars or blotches and a wide, bright orange or red vertebral stripe.

In the northern parts of its distribution, the Spotted Harlequin Snake is blackish above with a yellow dot on each scale and a bright orange to yellow stripe down the centre of the back.

two months to hatch. The hatchlings have a total length of approximately 140 mm. The Striped Harlequin Snake lays small clutches of 2–4 minute elongated eggs.

Conservation

The Striped Harlequin Snake is listed by the IUCN as 'Near Threatened'. It is also listed in the South African Red Data Book as 'Rare' and in the Swaziland Red Data Book as 'Data Deficient'. This species is a grassland specialist; most recorded specimens have been found in moribund termite mounds. Land transformation due to wide-scale commercial agriculture is thought to pose a significant threat to the species, since ploughing destroys suitable termite mounds.

Distribution

The Spotted Harlequin Snake has a temperate distribution and is found in fynbos, coastal forest, moist savanna and grassland in the Western and Eastern Cape, extending northwards into KwaZulu-Natal, Free State, Gauteng, Limpopo and Mpumalanga in South Africa, and Lesotho. An isolated population occurs in coastal Namaqualand. The Striped Harlequin Snake is much more restricted and has a patchy distribution in the highveld grasslands of Gauteng and Free State, extending to moist savanna in KwaZulu-Natal, Mpumalanga and Limpopo provinces. It is endemic to South Africa.

African Burrowing Snakes lack a loreal scale.

SPECIES IN THE GROUP

- Spotted Harlequin Snake: *Homoroselaps lacteus*
- Striped Harlequin Snake: *Homoroselaps dorsalis* **NT**

COLUBRIDS
Family: Colubridae

Colubridae is the world's largest, most morphologically heterogeneous family of snakes. The family has an extensive distribution in tropical and temperate climes and is found on all continents except Antarctica. It is excluded from the western and southern parts of Australia, where it is replaced with the Elapidae as the most species-rich family of snakes. Colubrids are often referred to as 'typical snakes' and the family includes at least 12 subfamilies, many of which are likely to be shown to be families in their own right, based on new molecular research techniques. Colubridae includes more than 70% of all snake genera, more than 302 in total, and comprises more than 1 827 species. Twenty-seven genera and 78 species occur in southern Africa. Most species have nine enlarged scales on top of the head. The head tends to be distinct from the neck and the eyes are well-developed, although there are exceptions. Most species do not have fangs, but some have rear fangs that are grooved and attached to the posterior part of the maxillary bone, just below the eye. The vast majority of colubrids are either harmless or nearly so, but a few species carry potent venoms that are of medical significance. Ventral scales are wide and span the width of the belly. Most of these snakes are terrestrial, arboreal, rock-living or aquatic, although few species show a tendency towards a fossorial existence.

Johan Marais

Colubrids, such as this Angola Green Snake, are often referred to as 'typical snakes'.

Water Snakes

The genus *Lycodonomorphus*
4 species

Description

The four species of Water Snake in this group are similar in body form, size, coloration and behaviour. They are small to medium-sized snakes with rectangular heads that are distinct from the body. Usually, adult total length is between 450 and 850 mm, but the Dusky-bellied Water Snake can reach a length of 1.2 m. The eyes are medium-sized and the pupils can be either round or elliptic. Water Snakes have no fangs and are not venomous. The scales on the body are smooth and highly polished. Midbody scales are either in 19 or 21 rows, the anal shield is undivided and the subcaudals (37–89) are paired. Ventral scales number 154–179. The tail is medium in length. Dorsal coloration is generally plain olive-brown to dark brown. The belly can be mother-of-pearl, pink or yellowish. The Floodplain Water Snake has a pale stripe on the upper lip and the belly might have dark markings. The Dusky-bellied Water Snake has dark spots on the upper lip and dark markings on the belly that form a jagged, dark band.

Biology

Water Snakes are semi-aquatic, inhabiting margins of streams, vleis and damp areas in grassland. The Dusky-bellied Water Snake is especially aquatic, swims well and can spend extended periods in water. The Common Water Snake and the Floodplain Water Snake are nocturnal, but the Mulanje Water Snake and the Dusky-bellied Water Snake are active during the day, hunting along shaded streams in search of food.

As with other Water Snakes, this Common Water Snake has a distinctive yellow-pink belly.

Common Water Snakes are nocturnal and forage for frogs along the banks of streams and other wetland areas.

Water Snakes are harmless and reluctant to bite, even when captured. Some Dusky-bellied Water Snakes are an exception to this, but the bites are harmless to humans. The Common Water Snake and the Dusky-bellied Water Snake can be very common in suitable habitat. Water Snakes generally feed on frogs, tadpoles and fish, but are also known to take nestling birds and rodents. Prey is often seized underwater and immediately constricted. Dusky-bellied Water Snakes can swallow large meals without coming to the surface for air, but the other Water Snakes will generally carry large prey to the water's edge before it is ingested.

Reproduction

All members of this group are oviparous and lay clutches of between 4 and 23 eggs (20–42 x 12–22 mm) in midsummer. Eggs take just over two months to hatch and the young are between 150 and 220 mm in length.

Distribution

Water Snakes are restricted mainly to the wetter, eastern parts of southern Africa. The Common Water Snake, the most widespread member of the group, has a temperate distribution, ranging from the southwestern Cape, through the eastern parts of South Africa. An isolated population occurs in central eastern Zimbabwe. The Dusky-bellied

Water Snake is restricted to parts of the Eastern Cape, KwaZulu-Natal, Gauteng and Mpumalanga provinces of South Africa. The Floodplain Water Snake occurs on the coastal plain of Mozambique, extending into the northeastern extremes of South Africa. In southern Africa, the Mulanje Water Snake is limited to eastern Zimbabwe, but occurs more extensively to the north. The Common Water Snake and Dusky-bellied Water Snake are endemic to southern Africa.

The Dusky-bellied Water Snake has black speckling or barring on the belly.

SPECIES IN THE GROUP

- Common Water Snake: *Lycodonomorphus rufulus*
- Dusky-bellied Water Snake: *Lycodonomorphus laevissimus*
- Floodplain Water Snake: *Lycodonomorphus obscuriventris*
- Mulanje Water Snake: *Lycodonomorphus leleupi*

Brown House Snake

The species *Lamprophis capensis*
1 species

Description

This group currently includes one well-known species. However, a previously described subspecies from Namaqualand (*Lamprophis capensis mentalis*) may turn out to be a full species. Brown House Snakes are medium-sized, robust snakes with an average adult length of between 600 and 900 mm. Specimens from KwaZulu-Natal are larger, sometimes reaching as much as 1.4 m. The rectangular head is distinct from the body. The eyes are medium-sized and have elliptical pupils. Specimens from Namaqualand have large, bulging eyes. Brown House Snakes have no fangs and are not venomous. Midbody scale rows range from 25 to 35, the anal shield is entire and the subcaudals (45–71) are paired. Ventral scale counts range from 186 to 226. Body coloration is usually reddish brown to chocolate brown. Each side of the head usually bears pale stripes, one running from the tip of the nose through the eye to the back of the head, and the other from the eye to the angle of the jaw. These light markings might extend onto the neck and fade towards the posterior parts. The belly is shiny and pearly white.

Biology

As the name indicates, Brown House Snakes frequent human habitation in search of rodents, which form an important part of their diet. They are nocturnal and are extremely effective rodent control agents that can devour an entire nest of young in a single meal. In addition to rodents, Brown House Snakes will consume lizards, shrews, bats, birds, small eggs and, occasionally, even

Marius Burger

The Brown House Snake is one of the most common and widespread snakes in southern Africa. It is a useful rodent control agent that is often found around houses.

Brown House Snakes vary geographically. Top left: KwaZulu-Natal. Top right: Mozambique. Bottom left: Limpopo province. Bottom right: Namaqualand.

certain species of frog. A large specimen from KwaZulu-Natal killed and consumed a hatchling Nile Crocodile (*Crocodylus niloticus*) in captivity. Brown House Snakes are often discovered during domestic cleaning operations, especially when old building material is removed. Since they pose no danger to humans, are beneficial for pest control and are easy to identify, they should be left in peace. Brown House Snakes settle well in captivity and make the ideal 'first snake' pet for young, budding herpetologists.

Reproduction

Between 5 and 18 white eggs (approximately 40 x 20 mm) are laid in summer, and females are known to produce several clutches per year. Eggs generally take about three months to hatch, but clutches that are laid late in the season on the Highveld can overwinter and take more than six months to incubate. Hatchlings measure between 190 and 260 mm in length.

Distribution

The Brown House Snake is found throughout most of southern Africa and is excluded only from desert dune fields and the Lesotho highlands.

Brown House Snakes from the arid western parts of southern Africa typically have large eyes with a pale iris.

SPECIES IN THE GROUP

■ Brown House Snake: *Lamprophis capensis*

Olive House Snake

The species *Lamprophis inornatus*
1 species

Description

Olive House Snakes are medium-sized, robust constrictors that have an average adult length of between 700 and 900 mm but can occasionally exceed 1 m. The relatively long head is distinct from the body, and is more rounded than that of Brown House Snakes. The eyes are small to medium in size and have vertical pupils. Olive House Snakes have no fangs and are not venomous. Midbody scale rows range from 21 to 25, the anal shield is entire and the subcaudals (45–70) are paired. Ventral counts range from 170 to 196 and both dorsal and ventral scales are highly polished. Body coloration is uniform, and ranges from olive-green, olive-grey to black above and slightly paler below, especially in the chin and throat regions. The upper lip is sometimes pale grey. Because Olive House Snakes are plain, they are easily confused with other species, including the Black Mamba (*Dendroaspis polylepis*).

Biology

Olive House Snakes are nocturnal and terrestrial, and appear to favour moist habitats near wetlands. They are unusual in the respect that they are normally active in misty, cold conditions or during light drizzle. The diet includes rodents, shrews and lizards, and they are partial to eating other snakes. Olive House Snakes are not venomous and pose no threat to humans.

Johan Marais

Olive House Snakes often forage during misty nights when it is drizzling. They have smooth, dark, glossy scales, which help to camouflage them in these conditions.

With the exception of a pale lower jaw, Olive House Snakes are generally uniformly dark in coloration and are easily mistaken for Black Mambas by amateurs.

In some parts of their range, Olive House Snakes are almost black in colour.

Reproduction

Females lay clutches of between 5 and 15 eggs (approximately 42 x 22 mm) in summer. Eggs take approximately three months to hatch and the young are between 190 and 240 mm in length.

Distribution

Olive House Snakes are limited to the more temperate parts of the subregion and occur in moist savanna, lowland forest, grassland and fynbos. They occur in the southwestern Cape and the eastern parts of South Africa. The distribution is fragmented and patchy, but the species can be locally abundant.

SPECIES IN THE GROUP

■ Olive House Snake: *Lamprophis inornatus*

Spotted Rock Snake

The species *Lamprophis guttatus*
1 species

Description

This group includes a single species that has unique patterning on the body and is a strict habitat specialist. Spotted Rock Snakes are small and slender, averaging 400 to 600 mm in length, with a maximum of 650 mm. The head is very flat and broad, and is probably an adaptation for accessing narrow crevices. The body can also be flattened to some extent. The eyes are medium-sized, copper-brown and have vertical pupils. There are no fangs and the species is not venomous. Midbody scale rows range from 21 to 25, the anal shield is entire and the subcaudals (46–72) are paired. There are between 186 and 230 ventral scales, and the dorsal and ventral scales are smooth and highly polished. Spotted Rock Snakes are usually very attractively marked, but coloration and patterning does vary among populations. Generally, the dorsum is yellowish brown to pinkish grey, with reddish brown to dark brown blotches or spots arranged in adjacent or alternate pairs that may form a zigzag pattern down the back. Specimens in the Northern Cape are usually light to medium brown or mustard-brown with very dark spots that decrease in size towards the tail. The underside is white to yellowish white.

Biology

Spotted Rock Snakes are habitat specialists, occurring in rocky habitats that provide suitable shelter under exfoliating rock flakes and in narrow rock crevices. They are nocturnal and hunt for crevice-living lizards. In captivity, they will also take small rodents. However, Spotted Rock Snakes do not always settle well in captivity.

Johan Marais

The Spotted Rock Snake uses cracks under exfoliating rocks as retreats during the day and hunts for rupicolous lizards at night.

Populations of Spotted Rock Snakes are isolated as they are only found in certain rocky environments. This isolation has resulted in big differences in patterning and coloration between populations.

Conservation

The Spotted Rock Snake is not listed by the IUCN as 'Threatened' and is not listed in any of the Red Data books. However, it is rare, especially in the eastern half of its distribution, and is very popular in the pet trade. Populations are localized and are exploited once discovered because they are easily found under rock flakes. The collection of these snakes causes a certain degree of habitat damage, as rock flakes are broken off the bedrock.

Reproduction

Small clutches of between 3 and 6 eggs (38 x 20 mm) are laid in summer.

Distribution

The Spotted Rock Snake is widespread in the southern and eastern parts of South Africa. The distribution also extends up the West Coast into southern Namibia. The species occurs in fynbos, karoo scrub, grassland, moist savanna and lowland forest. Populations are highly fragmented and scattered, and abundances vary greatly.

The flattened head of the Spotted Rock Snake allows it to access narrow cracks in pursuit of its lizard prey.

SPECIES IN THE GROUP

■ Spotted Rock Snake: *Lamprophis guttatus*

Aurora House Snake

The species *Lamprophis aurora*
1 species

Description

Aurora House Snakes are small to medium-sized snakes that have a 'typical' snake body shape, a head that is distinct from the body and smooth, polished dorsal scales. Adult total length varies from 450 to 600 mm, and large specimens occasionally reach 900 mm. The eyes are relatively small and the pupils are vertically elliptical. There are no fangs and the species is not venomous. There are 21 or 23 midbody scale rows, the anal shield is entire and the subcaudals (35–58) are paired. There are between 165 and 185 ventral scales. Coloration is striking: adults are shiny olive-green with a bright orange to yellow vertebral stripe from the top of the head to the tip of the tail, and a yellowish to greenish white underside. Juveniles are usually darker in colour, and each dorsal scale is olive-green with a pale green bar running through it, giving a somewhat speckled appearance. The head may also have pale green mottling, but the orange vertebral stripe is as prominent as it is in adults. Individuals from the Western Cape tend to be more colourful than those from Gauteng. Juveniles may be confused with the striped phase of the Spotted Harlequin Snake (*Homoroselaps lacteus*).

Biology

Aurora House Snakes are secretive and nocturnal. They favour damp localities, but are found in a wide variety of habitat types, including fynbos, moist savanna and grassland. They often make use of moribund termite mounds as retreat sites in grasslands. They are inoffensive and seldom attempt to bite, even when captured. Aurora House Snakes hunt for lizards, frogs and nestling rodents at night and kill prey by constriction.

Tony Phelps

The Aurora House Snake can easily be recognized by the bright orange to yellow vertebral stripe that runs from the top of the head to the tip of the tail.

Aurora House Snakes are secretive, but are often unearthed in moribund termitaria.

The Aurora House Snake's pupil is vertically elliptical, but may appear almost round in response to low light.

Conservation

Although this species is not officially classified as 'Threatened', it is uncommon and populations appear to be decreasing in certain areas. In Gauteng, a large proportion of previously suitable habitat has been destroyed due to farming activities and urban sprawl. Aurora House Snakes are also highly prized in the pet trade.

Reproduction

Clutches of 8–12 eggs (approximately 35 x 20 mm) are laid in summer. The hatchlings are 200–225 mm in length.

Distribution

The Aurora House Snake is restricted to the southern and eastern parts of South Africa. It is endemic to South Africa.

Juvenile Aurora House Snakes have a more speckled appearance, making them look superficially similar to one of the colour phases of the Spotted Harlequin Snake.

SPECIES IN THE GROUP

- Aurora House Snake: *Lamprophis aurora*

Lesser House and Rock Snakes

The species *Lamprophis fiskii*, *L. fuscus* and *L. swazicus*
3 species

Description

This group includes three related snake species. They generally
have slender bodies with smooth, polished scales. The Swazi Rock
Snake has prominent eyes, but the eyes are relatively small in Fisk's
House Snake and the Yellow-bellied House Snake. Adult length
ranges from 400 to 500 mm in length in the Yellow-bellied House
Snake and Swazi Rock Snake. Fisk's House Snake is smaller, usually
250–350 mm, but a maximum length of almost 400 mm is known.
These snakes do not have fangs and are not venomous. Fisk's House
Snake has either 21 or 23 midbody scale rows, the Yellow-bellied
House Snake has 19, and the Swazi Rock Snake has 17 rows. The
anal shield is entire and the subcaudals are paired. Ventral counts
range from 165 to 208. Fisk's House Snake is lemon-yellow above
with dark brown spots in a double alternating or single series down
the back. The lips and underside are creamy white in colour. The
Yellow-bellied House Snake is plain olive-brown to light brown or
yellow-brown above with yellow lips, sides and belly. The Swazi
Rock Snake is dark reddish to beige or light brown above with a
cream to white belly.

Biology

All three species are poorly known. Fisk's House Snake is known
from only a few specimens that have been found on roads at night.
When molested, it will coil and uncoil the front part of the body while
hissing in self-defence. This snake appears to be restricted largely to
karoo scrub. Captive individuals have fed on geckos, and a Burchell's

Johan Marais

*The Yellow-bellied
House Snake is a
rare species that
occurs in isolated
populations in
fynbos scrub,
grassland and
arid savanna.*

Sand Lizard (*Pedioplanis burchelli*) was found in the stomach of an individual caught in the wild. These snakes constrict their prey. The Yellow-bellied House Snake is also secretive and nocturnal, and has been found in moribund termite mounds and under rocks in fynbos scrub, grassland and arid savanna. They are docile and make no attempt to bite when handled. The diet consists mainly of lizards and rodents. The Swazi Rock Snake shelters in narrow rock crevices and under exfoliating rock flakes on rocky outcrops. It feeds on lizards and may take small birds.

Reproduction

A female Fisk's House Snake produced 8 eggs in summer, and a Swazi Rock Snake that was collected in October was carrying 7 elongate eggs (29–36 x 10–13 mm).

Conservation

All three species are secretive, appear to be extremely rare and have very restricted distributions. They are all listed as 'Rare' in the South African Red Data Book, and the two species that occur in Swaziland (the Yellow-bellied House Snake and the Swazi Rock Snake) are both listed as 'Data Deficient' in the Swaziland Red Data Book. Fisk's House Snake is listed as 'Vulnerable' and the Yellow-bellied House Snake and Swazi Rock Snake as 'Near Threatened' by the IUCN. More information on the biology of these species is needed to assess their conservation status adequately.

The Swazi Rock Snake is restricted to rocky habitats in parts of Swaziland and northeastern South Africa.

Distribution

Fisk's House Snake occurs primarily in nama karoo in the western half of South Africa, both in the Northern Cape and Western Cape. The Swazi Rock Snake and the Yellow-bellied House Snake occur in the eastern parts of South Africa, the latter extending south into the Western Cape. All three species appear to have highly fragmented and isolated populations.

Fisk's House Snake is very rare and little is known about its ecology. Fewer than 30 individuals have been recorded and the species has been classified as 'Vulnerable'.

SPECIES IN THE GROUP

- Fisk's House Snake: *Lamprophis fiskii* **VU**
- Swazi Rock Snake: *Lamprophis swazicus* **NT**
- Yellow-bellied House Snake: *Lamprophis fuscus* **NT**

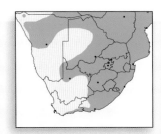

Wolf Snakes

The genus *Lycophidion*
8 species

Description

Eight closely related species make up this group. All are small with flat heads, and although the body is typically cylindrical, it can also flatten to allow entry into narrow crevices. None of the species has fangs or venom, but they are aptly named Wolf Snakes because they have long teeth that are adapted for grasping smooth-scaled prey. Adult length varies from 250 mm to a maximum of about 560 mm, depending on the species. They have small eyes and the head is only slightly distinct from the neck. Midbody scales are in 17 rows, the anal shield is entire and the subcaudals (19–52) are paired in all species. There are between 140 and 214 ventral scales. Most species are light to dark brown, reddish brown, purple-brown or black, sometimes with white stipples or flecks that can be quite pronounced. The Spotted Wolf Snake usually has a paired series of dark blotches down the back that may form crossbars. Both the Pygmy Wolf Snake and the Dwarf Wolf Snake have stippled white bands around the snout.

Biology

Wolf Snakes are secretive, nocturnal and mainly terrestrial or rock-living. More widespread species, such as the Common Wolf Snake, inhabit a wide variety of habitats such as lowland forest, fynbos, moist savanna, grassland and karoo scrub. The more restricted species are generally found in specific habitat types, such as arid

Johan Marais

Wolf Snakes, such as this Common Wolf Snake, have smooth, polished scales and a head that is not very distinct from the body. They are easily mistaken for Stiletto Snakes by amateurs.

rocky areas or woodland. They may shelter under stones, logs or dead aloes and in moribund termite mounds. These snakes are slow-moving and actively hunt for prey, including lizards and snakes. Their flat

Common Wolf Snakes lay between three and 10 eggs in early summer.

The snout and sides of the head are pale in the Pygmy Wolf Snake.

SPECIALIST FEEDERS

Several snake species feed on a specific prey type, often an animal that is not easily subdued by most other predators. Skinks, for instance, are extremely abundant worldwide but, because of their powerful bodies with small limbs (or no limbs) and overlapping scales, many predators find it difficult to catch and hang on to them. Wolf Snakes have evolved strong, long, recurved teeth that enable them to catch skinks, which form an important part of their diet.

heads and long recurved teeth are thought to be used to extract sleeping lizards from their retreats. When molested, Wolf Snakes typically flatten the entire body and jerk around as if striking, but do not usually even open their mouths. They are inoffensive, reluctant to bite and are not venomous.

Reproduction

All members of this group are oviparous. Females lay small clutches of between 3 and 10 eggs (22–31 x 6–15 mm) in early summer. Hatchlings are 120–196 mm in length.

Distribution

The Common Wolf Snake is widespread, occurring throughout the eastern half of southern Africa, extending into northern Namibia, but it appears to be absent from all but the eastern extremes of Botswana. The other species in the group are much more restricted in distribution. The Namibian Wolf Snake and Hellmich's Wolf Snake are found in the northwestern parts of Namibia. The Spotted Wolf Snake only just enters southern Africa in the Caprivi Strip, and the Eastern Wolf Snake is found only in the Inhambane region and Bazaruto Archipelago in Mozambique. The Pygmy Wolf Snake is endemic to northern KwaZulu-Natal, and the Dwarf Wolf Snake is restricted to the central Mozambique plain. The Variegated Wolf Snake has scattered populations in the northeastern parts of South Africa and Zimbabwe.

SPECIES IN THE GROUP

- Common Wolf Snake: *Lycophidion capense*
- Dwarf Wolf Snake: *Lycophidion nanum*
- Eastern Wolf Snake: *Lycophidion semiannule*
- Hellmich's Wolf Snake: *Lycophidion hellmichi*
- Namibian Wolf Snake: *Lycophidion namibianum*
- Pygmy Wolf Snake: *Lycophidion pygmaeum*
- Spotted Wolf Snake: *Lycophidion multimaculatum*
- Variegated Wolf Snake: *Lycophidion variegatum*

File Snakes

The genus *Mehelya*
3 species

Description

This group consists of three unusual, small to large species, all with a body shape that is characteristically triangular in cross section. The dorsal body scales are raised, strongly keeled and can be widely separated from each other, making the derivation of the common name obvious. Adult length for the Southern File Snake and the Angola File Snake is about 1 m, but specimens of nearly 1.7 m are known. The Black File Snake is much smaller, averaging 350–500 mm. File Snakes have a flat, rectangular head that is distinct from the body. The small to medium eyes have broadly elliptical pupils and a peculiar, beady appearance. They have no fangs and are not venomous. Midbody scales are in 15–19 rows, the anal shield is entire and the subcaudals (44–79) are paired. Ventral scales number between 165 and 268. Coloration is similar in all species and is generally a uniform grey to blackish colour above, with an ivory to dark grey belly. The Southern File Snake has an obvious white vertebral stripe.

Biology

File Snakes are nocturnal and secretive, and appear to be relatively rare, although recent surveys have shown the Black File Snake to be fairly abundant in places. These snakes often hunt after heavy rains. The diet of the Southern File Snake and the Angola File Snake consists primarily of other snakes, including venomous species such as the Black Mamba (*Dendroaspis polylepis*) and Puff Adder (*Bitis arietans*). They appear to have some degree of immunity to snake venom. File Snakes also eat toads and small rodents. The Black File Snake seems to be more of a lizard specialist. File Snakes generally do not attempt to bite, even when captured.

Johan Marais

File Snakes derive their names from their triangular bodies and very keeled scales. This Southern File Snake also has a prominent white vertebral line.

The Black File Snake does not grow as large as other File Snakes and is more secretive.

Reproduction

All species in this group are oviparous. Female Southern File Snakes lay clutches of 5–13 eggs (approximately 50 x 25 mm) and are known to lay more than one clutch per season. The hatchlings are between 290 and 450 mm in length. Black File Snake clutches are small, averaging 3–6 eggs. The hatchlings are about 200 mm long.

Distribution

The Southern File Snake occurs in lowland forest and moist savanna in the eastern half of southern Africa, extending into Zimbabwe, eastern and northern Botswana and northern Namibia. The Angola File Snake is restricted to rocky mountainous regions in the Namib Desert, extending northwards into Angola. The Black File Snake is found in lowland forest and moist savanna in eastern KwaZulu-Natal, Mpumalanga and Limpopo provinces of South Africa, Swaziland, most of Zimbabwe and eastern Botswana, with isolated records from the central Namib.

SPECIES IN THE GROUP

- Angola File Snake: *Mehelya vernayi*
- Black File Snake: *Mehelya nyassae*
- Southern File Snake: *Mehelya capensis*

File Snakes have a flat, rectangular head that is distinct from the body.

Slug-eaters

The genus *Duberria*
2 species

Description

These short, stocky snakes have small heads that are not distinct from the body. Adult length ranges from 250 to 440 mm. The eyes are relatively small and the pupils are round. Slug-eaters have no fangs and are not venomous. Midbody scales are in 15 rows, the anal shield is entire and the subcaudals (20–51) are paired. There are between 91 and 142 ventral scales. The Common Slug-eater has a distinct broad, reddish brown band down the centre of the back flanked with a greyish band on either side. The belly is cream to yellowish white, edged with a black or grey dotted line on either side. The Variegated Slug-eater is dark brown above with three rows of dark spots or blotches down the back that may form crossbars. These markings fade with age. The belly is dirty white with darker markings, especially towards the rear.

Biology

Slug-eaters are shy, slow-moving, inoffensive snakes that seldom attempt to bite, even when captured. The Common Slug-eater is known to roll up in a tight spiral with its head concealed in the coils in self-defence, leading to its Afrikaans name *tabakrolletjie*, or tobacco roll. They are able to produce a pungent scent from their glands, which may be employed in self-defence. Slug-eaters generally prefer damp localities, but may occur in grassland, moist savanna, lowland forest and fynbos. As the common name indicates, Slug-eaters feed exclusively on slugs and land snails, and forage among leaf litter and decaying vegetation in search of food, often following slime trails of their prey. They are primarily diurnal but are sometimes active at night.

Slug-eaters, such as this Common Slug-eater, have stocky bodies and the head is not distinct from the neck.

Tony Phelps

Common Slug-eaters have a distinct broad, reddish brown band down the centre of the back flanked with a greyish band on either side of the body.

Johan Marais

Variegated Slug-eaters have several rows of dark spots or blotches down the back that may form crossbars.

Reproduction

Females are viviparous, producing between 6 and 22 young in late summer measuring 80–110 mm in length.

Distribution

The Common Slug-eater is much more widespread than the Variegated Slug-eater. It has a typical temperate distribution, occurring from the Western Cape, east and northwards along the axis of the eastern escarpment into Limpopo province in South Africa. An isolated population that has subspecific status occurs in eastern Zimbabwe. The Variegated Slug-eater is endemic to northern KwaZulu-Natal and southern coastal Mozambique.

SPECIES IN THE GROUP

- Common Slug-eater: *Duberria lutrix*
- Variegated Slug-eater: *Duberria variegata*

Mole Snake

The species *Pseudaspis cana*
1 species

Description

Mole Snakes are medium to large, powerful constrictors with small heads that are not distinct from the neck. The snout is pointed and is adapted for burrowing. Adult length averages about 1.4 m, but individuals measuring over 2 m are known, especially from the Western Cape. The eyes are relatively large and prominent, and the pupils are round. The scales on the dorsal parts have a peculiar 'beady' or 'bobbly' appearance but are generally not keeled (some specimens from the Western Cape exhibit slight keeling) and are fairly polished. Midbody scales are in 25–31 rows, the anal shield is divided and the subcaudals are paired. Colour and patterning vary considerably. Juveniles usually have dark, zigzag markings on a reddish brown to greyish brown dorsal colour. Adults are usually light grey to light brown, dark brown, brick red, or even black above and yellowish below, sometimes with darker infusions.

Biology

Mole Snakes are diurnal, but spend a large portion of their time underground. Their strong bodies and robust snouts allow them to push their way through soft sand, but they also make extensive use of rodent and mole burrows. When approached, adults will generally flee, but juveniles freeze in their tracks and rely on camouflage to avoid detection. Although Mole Snakes are often portrayed as the

Mole Snakes are large, robust snakes that are widely distributed throughout southern Africa. They are especially common in fynbos and grasslands.

Mole Snakes from the Cape are often dark in coloration.

archetypal harmless snakes that make wonderful pets, they are often belligerent and are willing to bite, especially when first handled. Apart from loud hissing, vicious striking and the secretion of a strong, musky odour from their cloaca, they are also able to inflict bite wounds that are more serious than those from most other non-venomous snakes. This is because some of the teeth of the Mole Snakes' lower jaw have a cutting edge along their inner curve. Once a Mole Snake bites onto a finger, it is able to pull the lower jaw backwards using the upper jaw as a lever, slicing the teeth of the lower jaw

through the flesh to make two parallel cuts. If not immediately removed, it will rotate its head right around the finger, causing lacerations that can encircle a finger. This unique method of biting probably aids Mole Snakes in dispatching dangerous mole-rats underground, where the physical limitations of the burrow prevent the snake from constricting its prey in the conventional way. The diet is varied and includes rats, mole-rats, golden moles, gerbils and birds and their eggs. Mole Snakes on Robben Island feed on sea bird eggs, which are swallowed whole. Juveniles feed primarily on lizards.

Mole Snakes are diurnal and have large eyes with round pupils.

Juvenile Mole Snakes have vivid markings on the body. These markings fade with age.

COLOUR VARIATION

Colour and markings often vary tremendously within a single species of snake. In many species, such as the Garter Snakes of the genus *Elapsoidea*, the juveniles may have vivid colours that fade with age. In other snakes, such as the Mole Snake (*Pseudaspis cana*) and Boomslang (*Dispholidus typus*), juveniles differ in colour from the adults. Adult colour variation is also common, and species such as the Mole Snake or Cape Cobra (*Naja nivea*) vary from black to brown or orange and beige, sometimes with bright speckling. This variation makes snake identification extremely difficult for the novice. In some instances the colour variation among adults may be an adaptation for camouflage in their habitat. Horned Adders (*Bitis caudalis*) from the bright red Kalahari sands are often more brightly coloured than those from the Namib Desert.

Graham Alexander

Large Mole Snakes bite readily and the resulting wounds may require stitches.

Reproduction

Mating occurs in November. Mole Snakes are very unusual in that males fight rivals by biting them viciously. Most adult male Moles Snakes bear scars from previous fights that tend to be concentrated either on their necks or tails. Cuts may encircle the tail completely, and bites on the body often expose ribs. Males appear, remarkably, to recover from these injuries, which often appear to be very serious. Females are viviparous, giving birth to 25–50 young in late summer. As many as 95 young have been produced by a single female. The newborn snakes measure between 200 and 310 mm in length.

Distribution

Mole Snakes are found throughout most of southern Africa, but are most common in areas with sandy substrates, and where mole-rats are common.

Danger to humans

Although Mole Snakes are not venomous, a bite from one of these snakes can result in significant cuts (due to the cutting edge on their teeth) that may require stitches.

SPECIES IN THE GROUP

■ Mole Snake: *Pseudaspis cana*

Marsh and Swamp Snakes

The genera *Natriciteres* and *Limnophis*
3 species

Description

Two species of Marsh Snakes and the Bangweulu Swamp Snake make up this group. All are small, relatively nondescript, typical snakes, with cylindrical bodies and small heads. The two species of Marsh Snakes are smaller, reaching an adult length of about 350 mm. The Bangweulu Swamp Snake is slightly larger, reaching a maximum length of 500 mm. The head is barely distinguishable from the rest of the body, and the eyes have round pupils. Marsh and Swamp snakes are not venomous and have no fangs. Midbody scales are in 17 or 19 rows, and both the anal shield and the subcaudals (45–87) are divided. There are between 125 and 153 ventral scales. Marsh Snakes are pale brown to dark brown above with a darker stripe down the centre of the back, often edged with minute light spots or flecks. The underside is yellow to yellow-orange with dark edges. The Bangweulu Swamp Snake is olive-brown above with a pale stripe on either side that runs along the length of the body. The belly is creamy white, yellow or brick red.

Biology

Marsh and Swamp snakes are active at night and during the mornings. They are always found close to vleis, pans or marshy areas, where they hunt for small fish, frogs, tadpoles, fish-eating spiders and flying termites. These snakes seek refuge under stones, logs and in crevices in the clay banks of streams. Like some of the Sand Snakes (*Psammophis*), they will spin their bodies if grasped by the tail, often snapping off the tail tip in an attempt to escape. They have a gentle disposition and generally do not bite.

The secretive Southern Forest Marsh Snake is usually found in close proximity to water.

Johan Marais

The Bangweulu Swamp Snake is restricted to the central northern parts of southern Africa.

The Olive Marsh Snake occurs in the northern and eastern extremes of southern Africa, extending northwards.

Reproduction

All three species are egg-laying. The females lay small clutches of 3–11 eggs (22 x 15 mm) in summer.

Distribution

The Bangweulu Swamp Snake is restricted to the Okavango and Zambezi drainage basins. The Olive Marsh Snake occurs in Mozambique, Zimbabwe, the Caprivi Strip and the Okavango in Botswana, extending northwards. The Southern Forest Marsh Snake is more restricted and is limited to northern coastal KwaZulu-Natal and the southern extremes of Mozambique. Another population occurs on the eastern highlands of Zimbabwe, extending into central Mozambique.

SPECIES IN THE GROUP

- Bangweulu Swamp Snake: *Limnophis bangweolicus*
- Olive Marsh Snake: *Natriciteres olivacea*
- Southern Forest Marsh Snake: *Natriciteres sylvatica*

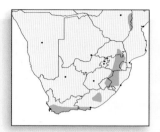

Many-spotted and Mountain Snakes

The genera *Amplorhinus* and *Montaspis*
2 species

Description

The two species that comprise this group have cylindrical bodies with heads that are only slightly distinct from the body. Adult length is approximately 500 mm. The eyes are moderately sized with round pupils. These snakes are venomous and have grooved fangs situated on the maxillary bone approximately below the eye. The dorsal scales are smooth and polished. Many-spotted Snakes have 17 rows of scales at midbody and Cream-spotted Mountain Snakes have 21. The anal shield is entire and subcaudals (53–91) are paired. Ventral scales number between 133 and 154. Many-spotted Snakes are either uniform green or olive to olive-brown with dark brown spots. They may also have a pale stripe along either side of the body. White or yellowish edging to scales may give the snake a flecked appearance. The belly is dull green to olive- or bluish green. Cream-spotted Mountain Snakes are chocolate brown to shiny blackish brown above with cream spots on the head and upper lip. The chin and throat are cream, and the belly is dark brown with pale-edged scales and creamy spots that fade towards the tail.

The Many-spotted Snake is common in swampy areas.

Marius Burger

Biology

Snakes of both species are secretive. The Many-spotted Snake is common, especially in the Cape, but the Cream-spotted Mountain Snake is extremely rare and only a few specimens have been found since its description in 1991. They are diurnal and will forage for food in wet, swampy areas and riverside vegetation. The Many-spotted Snake feeds on frogs, lizards and small rodents and the Cream-spotted Mountain Snake is known to feed on frogs, but is likely to include lizards and small rodents in its diet too. Many-spotted Snakes bite when handled and may coil in a tight spring like a Slug-eater (*Duberria lutrix*). Cream-spotted Mountain Snakes never attempt to bite, but flatten their body and move with jerky movements, often emitting a foul-smelling substance from the cloaca. The mild venom carried by these snakes poses no threat to humans.

Conservation

Although not currently listed by the IUCN as 'Threatened', the Cream-spotted Mountain Snake has a very restricted distribution and appears to be rare.

Reproduction

Cream-spotted Mountain Snakes are oviparous and lay small clutches of about 6 eggs. Many-spotted Snakes are viviparous, giving birth to litters of 8–13 young in late summer. The young are between 120 and 200 mm in length.

Distribution

The Many-spotted Snake has a temperate distribution, occurring in the Western Cape, Cape Fold Mountains, western KwaZulu-Natal and Mpumalanga Drakensberg, and in eastern Zimbabwe. The Cream-spotted Mountain Snake is known only from mountain streams and vleis at high altitude in the KwaZulu-Natal Drakensberg and adjacent northeastern Lesotho. Both species are endemic to southern Africa.

Marius Burger

The green phase of the Many-spotted Snake is less common than the brown phase.

Johan Marais

The Cream-spotted Mountain Snake is rare and is restricted to high altitudes in the KwaZulu-Natal Drakensberg and adjacent Lesotho.

SPECIES IN THE GROUP

- Cream-spotted Mountain Snake: *Montaspis gilvomaculata*
- Many-spotted Snake: *Amplorhinus mutimaculatus*

Shovel-snouts

The genus *Prosymna*
7 species

Description

This group consists of seven species of small snakes that have snouts modified into shovel-like projections. The taxonomic relationships between this group and other types of snake remain unclear, and some studies suggest that the genus is more closely aligned to the elapids than the colubrids. Adult total length ranges from 200 to 360 mm, and the body is cylindrical with a short tail. The head is not distinct from the body and the eyes are average in size. The snout is depressed and extended, and some of the scales on the snout are fused together. Shovel-snouts are not venomous and do not have fangs, but they do have enlarged teeth on the maxillary bone. The dorsal scales are smooth and polished in 15 or 17 rows at midbody. The anal scale is entire, subcaudals (16–54) are paired and ventral scales number between 107 and 199. Dorsal coloration is variable, ranging from yellow or pale brown to dark brown or metallic black above. Several species are patterned with dark brown to blackish blotches, mottling or diffuse stripes. The Southwestern Shovel-snout has dark-edged scales that may form a mosaic pattern on the body

Shovel-snouts derive their name from their peculiar, spade-like snouts that are used for burrowing in loose soil. Like the other species in this group, the South-western Shovel-snout feeds almost exclusively on reptile eggs.

Johan Marais

Jan's Shovel-snout has striking markings. This species is restricted to northern KwaZulu-Natal and southern Mozambique.

and a dark collar followed by smaller bands and blotches that fade toward the tail. Most species have creamy white or yellow bellies, but the East African Shovel-snouts may have a brownish white or even dark brown belly.

Biology

Shovel-snouts are secretive and seldom encountered. The majority burrow in loose sand close to the surface and may be found under rocks or logs or in termite mounds. Visser's Shovel-snout is the exception, as it inhabits deep rock crevices. These snakes feed virtually exclusively on reptile eggs, especially soft-shelled eggs, but at least some of the species include hard-shelled gecko eggs in their diet. Both the eggshells and their contents are swallowed. The large teeth on the maxillary bone are thought to be used for cutting into soft-shelled reptile eggs. Shovel-snouts have also been reported to feed on small geckos and skinks.

Shovel-snouts are inoffensive small snakes that do not bite, even when first

Marius Burger

The Two-striped Shovel-snout is found under stones and logs in sandy areas.

handled. Rather, they are inclined to coil up like a watch-spring when threatened, coiling and uncoiling rapidly. Jan's Shovel-snout and the East African Shovel-snout have also been observed waving the anterior part of the body to and fro as a defensive behaviour.

Sundevall's Shovel-snout is often found in moribund termitaria. It is inoffensive and does not bite in defence.

The East African Shovel-snout occurs widely over the northeastern parts of southern Africa.

Reproduction

All Shovel-snouts are egg-layers and lay small clutches of between 2 and 5 eggs (19–39 x 7–12 mm). The young are between 100 and 145 mm long.

Distribution

Shovel-snouts are distributed widely over much of southern Africa, with one or two species occurring in most parts of the subregion. They are absent only from some of the dune fields along the west coast of Namibia, parts of the Northern Cape and Eastern Cape in South Africa, and the eastern parts of Lesotho. Jan's Shovel-snout has a very restricted distribution, occurring only in northern coastal KwaZulu-Natal and southern Mozambique. Visser's Shovel-snout only just enters the northwestern parts of Namibia, but is more widespread in Angola.

SPECIES IN THE GROUP

- Angola Shovel-snout: *Prosymna angolensis*
- East African Shovel-snout: *Prosymna stuhlmannii*
- Jan's Shovel-snout: *Prosymna janii*
- Southwestern Shovel-snout: *Prosymna frontalis*
- Sundevall's Shovel-snout: *Prosymna sundevalli*
- Two-striped Shovel-snout: *Prosymna bivittata*
- Visser's Shovel-snout: *Prosymna visseri*

Western Keeled Snake

The species *Pythonodipsas carinata*
1 species

Description

This group consists of a single, unique species that bears a superficial resemblance to a small adder. Adult Western Keeled Snakes average 500 mm, with a maximum length of 800 mm. They have flat, triangular heads that are distinct from the body, and large eyes with vertical pupils. The scales on the head are small and irregular, very much like those of adders and pythons. Midbody scales are in 21 rows, the anal shield is entire and the subcaudals (41–55) are paired. The body is cylindrical, and coloration may be similar to that of some small adders. The dorsal parts are light orange-yellow to greyish with a double series of dark grey-brown blotches that form crossbars or a zigzag pattern down the back and onto the tail. There are smaller, less prominent spots or bars on the sides, and the belly is white, sometimes with dark spots.

Biology

This is a terrestrial nocturnal snake that prefers rocky desert areas. Because of its nocturnal habits, excellent camouflage and preference for rocky habitat, it is seldom encountered but appears to be far more common than previously thought. Western Keeled Snakes have large back fangs but are reluctant to bite. The venom is of no consequence to man. They feed largely on lizards, especially geckos and skinks, and constrict their prey. Rodents are also taken. It is said that Western Keeled Snakes mimic the Horned Adder (*Bitis caudalis*).

Johan Marais

The Western Keeled Snake bears a superficial resemblance to a small adder as it has a large triangular head.

Reproduction

Although no reproductive data are known for this species, it is likely that the Western Keeled Snake lays eggs.

Distribution

The Western Keeled Snake occurs from southwestern Namibia northwards into Angola. It is restricted to rocky desert areas.

Western Keeled Snakes are nocturnal and have vertical pupils.

The body markings and coloration of Western Keeled Snakes ensure that they are well camouflaged in their natural environment.

SPECIES IN THE GROUP

■ Western Keeled Snake: *Pythonodipsas carinata*

Beaked Snakes

The genera *Rhamphiophis* and *Dipsina*
2 species

Description

The Beaked Snakes are small to medium-sized snakes that have peculiar and distinctive hooked snouts. Adult length is approximately 350 mm in the Dwarf Beaked Snake, but the Rufous Beaked Snake is much larger and more robust, reaching a maximum length of about 1.2 m. The head is distinct from the body, and the eyes are large with round pupils. Beaked Snakes are mildly venomous and have immovable fangs situated near the back of the maxillary bone, below the eye. The body is cylindrical with smooth scales, and midbody scales are in 17 or 19 rows. There are between 144 and 194 ventral scales and the anal shield is divided. The Rufous Beaked Snake has 87–118 pairs of subcaudals, but the Dwarf Beaked Snake has only 28–45. The Rufous Beaked Snake is yellowish brown to pale red-brown above with dark-edged scales. The head has a diagnostic dark streak on either side, extending from the nostril through each eye, and the underside is usually creamy white. The Dwarf Beaked Snake varies from pale buff to light greyish brown with darker blotches or spots, which may fuse to form crossbars. The neck has a darker V-marking, and a dark stripe runs on either side of the head from the nose through the eye to the back of the head. The underside is creamy white with dark spots.

Johan Marais

The Dwarf Beaked Snake is restricted to the western parts of southern Africa and may be locally abundant.

The Rufous Beaked Snake is restricted to the northeastern parts of southern Africa. The eyes are large with a dark streak running through them.

Biology

These diurnal snakes use both ambush and active searching to locate their prey. Rufous Beaked Snakes feed on rodents, lizards, small snakes, frogs and small birds. The juveniles reportedly also feed on insects. Dwarf Beaked Snakes feed primarily on lizards. Rufous Beaked Snakes inhabit termite mounds and animal burrows; Dwarf Beaked Snakes may hide under stones or in loose sand at the base of bushes. They are docile snakes that may hiss but seldom attempt to bite. The Rufous Beaked Snake has the peculiar habit of holding its head in an elevated position while jerking it from side to side. The Dwarf Beaked Snake may assume a coiled position, mimicking the Horned Adder (*Bitis caudalis*) when threatened. The venom is mild and inconsequential to humans.

Reproduction

Both snakes are oviparous. Rufous Beaked Snakes lay clutches of 7–18 eggs (approximately 38 x 24 mm). The young are approximately 300 mm in length. Dwarf Beaked Snakes lay small clutches of 2–4 eggs (approximately 25 x 8 mm). The young are between 110 and 130 mm in length.

Distribution

The Rufous Beaked Snake occurs in the northeastern extremes of South Africa, into southern and central Mozambique, eastern and northwestern Zimbabwe and northern Botswana. The Dwarf Beaked Snake is restricted to the western parts of southern Africa, from the Western Cape northwards into the Northern Cape, southwestern Botswana and southern and western Namibia. The Dwarf Beaked Snake is endemic to southern Africa.

The Dwarf Beaked Snake has a strongly pointed snout and round pupils.

SPECIES IN THE GROUP

- Dwarf Beaked Snake: *Dipsina multimaculata*
- Rufous Beaked Snake: *Rhamphiophis rostratus*

Bark Snakes

The genus *Hemirhagerrhis*
2 species

Description

Bark Snakes are small and slender with a small head that is barely distinct from the body. Adults reach a length of just over 300 mm. The eyes are moderate in size and have round pupils. Bark Snakes are mildly venomous and have small immovable fangs near the back of the maxillary bone, just below the eyes. The smooth midbody scales are in 17 rows, and the ventral scales number 154–183. The subcaudals (52–98) are paired and the anal shield is divided. These snakes are grey to grey-brown with a darker vertebral stripe flanked by blackish spots that often fuse to form crossbars or a zigzag pattern. The darker markings may also form triangles and become paler towards the tail, which is often yellow or orange in colour. The belly is dirty white to brownish, with darker mottled patches.

Biology

Eastern Bark Snakes are found under the bark of trees and in rotting logs, and are sometimes found emerging from logs that are placed on fires. Viperine Bark Snakes are more rupicolous, living in deep rock cracks where they hunt for lizards, especially diurnal geckos.

Bark Snakes are small and slender, reaching a total length of just over 300 mm.

Unlike the Eastern Bark Snake, the Viperine Bark Snake inhabits rock crevices.

The Eastern Bark Snake lives under the bark of trees and is most abundant in mopane veld.

Skinks and frogs are also included in the diet. Like Vine Snakes (*Thelotornis*), Bark Snakes swallow their prey while hanging in a head-down position. They are very docile, even when handled for the first time, seldom attempting to bite, and the mild venom has little effect on humans.

Reproduction

Bark Snakes lay small clutches of 2–8 eggs (24 x 6 mm).

Distribution

The Eastern Bark Snake is found in savanna and lowland forest in the northeastern half of southern Africa. The Viperine Bark Snake occurs in arid savanna in north-central Namibia.

SPECIES IN THE GROUP

- Eastern Bark Snake: *Hemirhagerrhis nototaenia*
- Viperine Bark Snake: *Hemirhagerrhis viperinus*

Skaapstekers

The genus *Psammophylax*
3 species

Description

This group consists of three species of slender, medium-sized snakes. Adult length ranges from 650 mm to about 1.2 m. The head is distinct from the neck and the eyes are large with round pupils. All three species are mildly venomous and have immovable fangs near the back of the maxillary bone, below the eyes. The body is cylindrical with smooth, polished scales. Midbody scales are in 17 rows, the anal shield is divided and the subcaudals (49–84) are paired. Ventral scales number between 139 and 177. Spotted Skaapstekers vary from yellowish brown to pale olive with three or four rows of dark-edged blotches. These markings may form zigzag or longitudinal lines along the body. Specimens from Eastern Cape and KwaZulu-Natal may be more striped. The underside is white to yellowish with spots and blotches. The Striped Skaapsteker is grey to olive-grey or brown with three well-defined, black-edged dark brown stripes that extend along the length of the body. The narrowest of the three stripes is down the centre of the back and may have a fine yellow stripe down its centre. The two dark lateral stripes pass through the eyes. The upper lip and belly are creamy or yellowish white. The Grey-bellied Grass Snake is plain grey to olive-brown with three thin dark lines that may be flecked with white. The upper lip and belly are dirty white to grey.

Graham Alexander

Skaapstekers, such as this Spotted Skaapsteker, are active, diurnal snakes that rely on speed to escape from predators.

Biology

Skaapstekers are terrestrial, active foragers, hunting for food in the day and early evening. Adults feed on rodents and nestling birds; the young take frogs, other snakes and lizards, especially skinks. Small fish are also taken by the Grey-bellied Grass Snake. Skaapstekers are alert and fast, and are quick to disappear into grass when disturbed, and then freeze in their tracks and use camouflage to avoid detection. They will struggle violently when captured. The venom is mild and is inconsequential to humans.

Reproduction

Both the Striped Skaapsteker and the Spotted Skaapsteker are oviparous, laying clutches of 5–30 eggs (20–35 x 10–18 mm) in summer. The young are 130–240 mm in length. Female Spotted Skaapstekers coil around eggs during incubation. The eggs have partially developed embryos at the time of laying and hatch after about two weeks. The Grey-bellied Grass Snake is viviparous, producing up to four young that are 150–155 mm in length.

SHEEP KILLER

The common name Skaapsteker, Afrikaans for 'sheep killer' (or more literally, 'sheep stinger'), is rather misleading as this snake possesses a mild venom that is not capable of killing even a new-born lamb. Skaapstekers are common where Cape Cobras (*Naja nivea*) occur and were probably wrongly blamed for sheep deaths, the Cape Cobra being the real culprit. The venom of the Skaapsteker has no effect on humans.

Distribution

The Spotted Skaapsteker occurs from the Western Cape, northwards through the Eastern Cape, KwaZulu-Natal, the Free State, Mpumalanga, Gauteng and Limpopo provinces of South Africa, extending into eastern Zimbabwe. Scattered records are known from Namaqualand and Namibia. The Striped Skaapsteker occurs from the Free State into Gauteng, the Northwest and Limpopo provinces of South Africa, into eastern and northern Botswana, Zimbabwe,

Graham Alexander

The Spotted Skaapsteker's body patterning varies over its range. This individual from the KwaZulu-Natal midlands is less spotted than those from the Cape.

Graham Alexander

The body patterning of Striped Skaapstekers provides good camouflage in grassland habitat.

northern Namibia and north of southern Africa. The Grey-bellied Grass Snake is widespread north of southern Africa, but only just enters the subregion in the Chobe floodplain.

Johan Marais

Skaapstekers have round pupils and very good vision.

Johan Marais

The Grey-bellied Grass Snake only just enters southern Africa in the Caprivi.

SPECIES IN THE GROUP

- Grey-bellied Grass Snake: *Psammophylax variabilis*
- Spotted Skaapsteker: *Psammophylax rhombeatus*
- Striped Skaapsteker: *Psammophylax tritaeniatus*

Olive Grass Snake

The species *Psammophis mossambicus*
1 species

Description

This group contains a single species – a large, robust snake. The Olive Grass Snake has an average adult length of about 1 m, but specimens of 1.8 m have been recorded. The head is distinct from the body, and the eyes are large with round pupils. These snakes are venomous and have relatively large immovable fangs situated near the back of the maxillary bone, more or less below the eyes. The dorsal scales are smooth but not highly polished, and the body is cylindrical with a long tail. Midbody scales are in 17 rows, the anal shield is divided and the subcaudals (82–121) are paired. There are between 150 and 180 ventral scales. Body coloration is uniform olive-brown above, sometimes with black-edged scales on the back. Young specimens may have distinct striping on the body, with a broad dark band down the back, beige on the flanks and a fine yellow vertebral line. Individuals with vivid markings are difficult to distinguish from some of the other species in the genus. However, stripes fade with age and Olive Grass Snakes grow much larger and are more robust than any of the Sand or Whip snakes (other *Psammophis* spp). Olive Grass Snakes have scattered, black-edged scales on the neck and chin. The lips are pale with darker spots or blotches, and the belly is white to yellowish, sometimes with darker spots. The size, build, coloration and behaviour of Olive Grass

Bryan Maritz

The Olive Grass Snake is the largest of the Sand and Whip snakes, reaching a length of almost 2 m.

Snakes often result in large individuals being misidentified as Black Mambas.

Biology

Olive Grass Snakes are extremely fast, alert, diurnal snakes that use speed to escape from danger. Usually, they will disappear quickly into a clump of thick vegetation and remain motionless until flushed, resulting in a sprint to the next clump. Like Black Mambas, Olive Grass Snakes often lift the anterior third of their bodies off the ground for a better view of their surroundings, giving the impression that they are very aware of their environment. Diet is varied and consists mainly of lizards, small mammals, birds, frogs and snakes. Olive Grass Snakes are even known to eat Black Mambas and Puff Adders. Generally, they will bite and hold their prey until the venom takes effect, and large individuals are capable of carrying the struggling prey in the mouth with the head held high. Olive Grass Snakes are nervous and will not hesitate to bite when first handled. They usually tame quickly.

Reproduction

Females lay clutches of 10–30 eggs (28–40 x 10–20 mm) in summer. The hatchlings measure 270–300 mm in length.

Distribution

The Olive Grass Snake occurs in moist savanna and lowland forest from the KwaZulu-Natal coast, northwards into Mpumalanga and Limpopo provinces of South Africa, Swaziland, Mozambique, Zimbabwe, northern Botswana and northern Namibia.

Danger to humans

Olive Grass Snakes have not been considered much of a threat to humans. However, their large size and wide gape means that they could potentially deliver significant volumes of venom in a bite.

Although the venom is not well-studied and has conventionally been considered to be relatively mild, recent research indicates that it has the potential to be dangerous. Recorded bites have resulted only in local pain and swelling, but Olive Grass Snakes should be handled with caution and bites should be avoided.

Juvenile Olive Grass Snakes are easily confused with Short-snouted Sand Snakes.

FEEDING STRATEGIES

Snakes can either hunt actively or lie in ambush, waiting for prey to come to them. Many of the slender snakes (such as the Sand Snakes and Whip Snakes) that are active during the day will travel great distances in search of food, expending much energy while chasing fast-moving lizards. Many of these chases are in vain. Some of the larger, more stocky snakes, like Puff Adders (*Bitis arietans*), tend to ambush their prey, a strategy that results in conservation of energy but also fewer meals. Many species use a combination of the two strategies, and switch from ambush to active hunting as their hunger increases.

SPECIES IN THE GROUP

■ Olive Grass Snake: *Psammophis mossambicus*

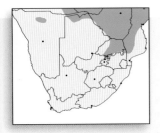

Dwarf Whip Snake

The species *Psammophis angolensis*
1 species

Description

This group consists of a single, diminutive species that has an adult length of 300–400 mm. It is much smaller and more slightly built than other Sand Snakes (*Psammophis* spp). Dwarf Whip Snakes have a head that is fairly distinct from the body and moderate-sized eyes with round pupils. The dorsal scales are smooth and slightly shiny. They are mildly venomous and have small, immovable fangs situated near the back of the maxillary bone. Midbody scales are in 11 rows, the anal shield is divided and the subcaudals (58–80) are paired. There are between 133 and 157 ventral scales. Dwarf Whip Snakes are strikingly patterned and are beige above with a broad dark brown stripe down the centre of the back. The sides bear thin, dark dorsolateral stripes on either side. The head is dark brown with three narrow pale crossbars and the neck has one or two dark collars. The lips, throat and belly are white or yellow.

Biology

Dwarf Whip Snakes are very secretive, using their speed and vigilance to avoid detection. Little is known about their biology apart from the fact that they are diurnal and largely terrestrial. They feed on small lizards and frogs and are reluctant to bite, even when first handled. Their small mouths, minute fangs and inoffensive disposition mean that they pose no threat to humans.

The small Dwarf Whip Snake is easily identified by its characteristic patterning and small size.

Johan Marais

Johan Marais

Dwarf Whip Snakes are alert and active. They have large eyes and good vision which allows them to avoid detection.

Johan Marais

The Dwarf Whip Snake reaches a maximum length of 500 mm.

Reproduction

Three to five small eggs (approximately 20 x 6 mm) are laid in summer.

Distribution

The Dwarf Whip Snake occurs in the northeastern parts of southern Africa, including Mozambique, Zimbabwe, northern Botswana, northern Namibia (including Caprivi), and Mpumalanga, Limpopo, Gauteng and Northwest provinces in South Africa.

SPECIES IN THE GROUP

- Dwarf Whip Snake: *Psammophis angolensis*

Sand and Whip Snakes

The genus *Psammophis*, excluding *P. mossambicus* and *P. angolensis*
11 species

Description

This group includes 11 species of sleek, highly active snakes that go by the names of Sand Snakes or Whip Snakes. Nearly all have stripes, and the head is fairly distinct from the body. Adult length ranges from about 800 mm to 1.2 m. They have moderate to large eyes with round pupils. All species are mildly venomous and have medium-sized immovable fangs situated far back on the maxillary bone, just below the eyes. The bodies are cylindrical with long tails, and the dorsal scales are smooth and moderately polished. The majority of the species have 17 midbody scale rows, but Jalla's Sand Snakes and Crossed Whip Snakes usually have 15. The anal shield is divided and the subcaudals (61–156) are paired. There are between 134 and 201 ventral scales. Coloration includes browns, reds, olives, greys and yellows. Most species are striped, but an unmarked phase in Crossed Whip Snakes is relatively common, and plain Leopard Whip Snakes have also been recorded. The majority of Sand Snakes also have a white or yellow dashed vertebral line that runs the length of the body. Stripes are often black-edged. Some species have bright yellow bellies; others have white or cream bellies.

Johan Marais

Most species of Sand Snake, such as this Crossed Whip Snake, rely on their speed and camouflage in grassland to escape predators.

The Short-snouted Sand Snake is found mainly in grassland and moist savanna.

The Cape Whip Snake is restricted to a small range in the southwestern Cape.

The strikingly marked Leopard Whip Snake.

Biology

Sand Snakes are fast, alert, diurnal snakes that actively forage for their prey. They feed largely on lizards, especially lacertids and skinks, but also take rodents, birds and other snakes. They are largely terrestrial but some, such as the Western Stripe-bellied Sand Snake, often climb into low shrubs to bask. These snakes are very quick and dash to the closest clump of vegetation, shrub or rock crevice when disturbed. They will remain motionless there until the danger has passed or they are flushed. If grasped by the tail, they typically thrash about, and may snap

The Namib Sand Snake's distribution is restricted to arid areas.

A Kalahari Sand Snake surveys its surroundings.

Western Stripe-bellied Sand Snakes will often bask in low vegetation.

The Karoo Whip Snake is restricted to the arid western parts of southern Africa.

off their tails. Most species will also bite readily. The venom may cause some minor discomfort but poses no threat to humans.

Reproduction

Sand Snakes lay small clutches of 3–8 eggs (approximately 26 x 8 mm) in summer. The young are 220–240 mm in length.

Conservation

The Cape Whip Snake is listed in the South African Red Data Book as 'Vulnerable'. It has a restricted range and is threatened by habitat destruction. This species is not currently classified by the IUCN as 'Threatened'.

Distribution

Sand Snakes are distributed widely over most of southern Africa, with up to five species occurring in some parts. They are common in a variety of habitats, including grassland, savanna, bushveld and succulent and nama karoo, and can be abundant in suitable habitat. All species are relatively widespread, apart from the Cape Whip Snake, which is restricted to the southwestern Cape.

SPECIES IN THE GROUP

- Cape Whip Snake: *Psammophis leightoni*
- Crossed Whip Snake: *Psammophis crucifer*
- Eastern Stripe-bellied Sand Snake: *Psammophis orientalis*
- Jalla's Sand Snake: *Psammophis jallae*
- Kalahari Sand Snake: *Psammophis trinasalis*
- Karoo Whip Snake: *Psammophis notostictus*
- Leopard Whip Snake: *Psammophis leopardinus*
- Namib Sand Snake: *Psammophis namibensis*
- Short-snouted Sand Snake: *Psammophis brevirostris*
- Western Stripe-bellied Sand Snake: *Psammophis subtaeniatus*
- Western Whip Snake: *Psammophis trigrammus*

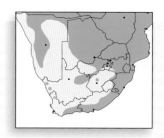

Green Snakes

The genus *Philothamnus*
5 species

Description

This group contains five species of medium-sized, slender Green
Snakes that have large eyes with dark round pupils. One species,
the Natal Green Snake, currently has two subspecies that will likely
prove to be full species with further research. Adult length varies
from a maximum of 1 m in the Angola Green Snake to 600 mm
in the more diminutive Green Water Snake. The head is distinct
from the body and has a relatively flat top. Although Green Snakes
do not have fangs and are not considered to be venomous in the
conventional sense, research on their saliva has shown it to be
toxic, but not dangerously so to humans. Midbody scales are in
15 rows, and the dorsal scales are smooth with a slight polish.
There are between 140 and 204 ventral scales. The tail is long,
the subcaudals (73–166) are paired and the anal shield is divided.
Coloration is striking and is usually a bright emerald green above,
often with black spots or crossbars on the anterior half of the body.
The underside is greenish white to yellowish, and ventral and
subcaudal scales are distinctly keeled in some species. Ornate
Green Snakes have a yellow-edged, reddish brown vertebral stripe
that extends from the head to the tip of the tail. The belly is white
to creamy bronze. The skin between the dorsal scales may be black,
and overlaps on the scales conceal white or turquoise flecks in some
species. In the western parts of its range, the Spotted Bush Snake is
a distinct copper colour on the posterior half of the body.

Bryan Maritz

*Green Snakes, such
as this Spotted
Bush Snake, are
excellent climbers
and spend much of
their time in trees.*

The Spotted Bush Snake has three upper labials touching the eye.

The Angola Green Snake has a single anterior temporal and black spots on the neck.

The Green Water Snake has a single anterior temporal and a plain neck.

The eastern form of the Natal Green Snake.

The western form of the Natal Green Snake.

Biology

These snakes are active, diurnal hunters. The group includes arboreal (Spotted Bush Snake, Natal Green Snake) and semi-aquatic (Green Water Snake, Ornate Green Snake, Angola Green Snake) species. Green Snakes have keen vision, and when foraging for food they often undulate their necks from side to side in a serpentine fashion while keeping the body perfectly still, giving an appearance of foliage blowing in the wind. Prey includes frogs, chameleons, geckos, nestling birds, fish and insects. Individuals sleep in crevices in logs and trees or on the outer edges of branches high up in trees. They will drop to the ground if approached by predators. When cornered, they will inflate their throats to expose the brightly coloured interstitial skin and do not hesitate to bite. Green Snakes do not pose a threat to humans, but are often needlessly killed in the mistaken belief that they are Boomslangs (*Dispholidus typus*) or Green Mambas (*Dendroaspis angusticeps*).

ADAPTED FOR CLIMBING

Some snakes, such as the Spotted Bush Snake, are especially adapted for an arboreal existence. These snakes have strongly keeled ventral scales that enable them to climb up the rough bark of trees. They are notorious for climbing up bricked walls and seeking shelter among the asbestos or tin roofs of outbuildings, where they search for geckos. A particular advantage of living in trees is that the snake can sleep on utstretched, thin, leafy branches. Should a predator approach, the snake can drop quickly to the ground in order to escape.

Reproduction

All species of Green Snake are egg-layers and produce clutches of between 3 and 16 eggs (20–43 x 8–18 mm). The hatchlings range in length from 150 to 300 mm, depending on the species.

The Green Water Snake has a long slender body. It is usually found in fairly close proximity to water.

Johan Marais

Green Snakes, such as this Natal Green Snake, can be distinguished from Green Mambas and Boomslangs by its dark eyes and the coppery edge to the iris.

Some Green Water Snakes have brown spots on the anterior parts of the body.

Distribution

Green Snakes inhabit a variety of habitat types, mainly in the eastern and northern parts of southern Africa. The Natal Green Snake and the Green Water Snake occur furthest south, extending into the southern Cape. The Spotted Bush Snake has the widest distribution and occurs from the Eastern Cape, northwards through the northeastern parts of South Africa, into Mozambique, Zimbabwe, Botswana and extensively in the northern half of Namibia. The Ornate Green Snake is restricted to the Okavango Swamps and eastern Zimbabwe, extending further north. The Angolan Green Snake is found in northern KwaZulu-Natal, Mozambique, eastern and central Zimbabwe, northern Botswana, the Caprivi Strip and central Namibia.

SPECIES IN THE GROUP

- Angola Green Snake: *Philothamnus angolensis*
- Green Water Snake: *Philothamnus hoplogaster*
- Natal Green Snake: *Philothamnus natalensis*
- Ornate Green Snake: *Philothamnus ornatus*
- Spotted Bush Snake: *Philothamnus semivariegatu*

Egg-eaters

The genus *Dasypeltis*
3 species

Description

The three species in this group are small to medium-sized snakes with small, bullet-shaped heads and rough, strongly keeled dorsal scales. Adults average 600 mm and have a maximum length of just over 1 m. The eyes are moderate in size and have vertical pupils. The mouth is virtually toothless and lacks fangs or venom. Midbody scales are in 21–27 rows, the anal shield is entire and the subcaudals (38–109) are paired. There are between 180 and 259 ventral scales. Rhombic Egg-eaters are light to grey-brown above with a series of dark rhombic or round blotches down the back, and narrow dark bars down either side of the body. An irregular dark 'V'-marking occurs on the neck and the head. Occasional pale individuals are also known. Southern Brown Egg-eaters are uniform yellowish brown, olive or dark brown dorsally, with paler flanks and belly. The East African Egg-eater is pinkish brown, with up to five dark 'V'-markings on the head and neck. A brown vertebral stripe runs down the centre of the back, interrupted by regular pale patches. The sides of the body have narrow dark vertical bars, and the belly is creamy white to pink with grey to brown stippling.

Egg-eaters have rough, keeled scales and a blunt head that is not very distinct from the neck. This Rhombic Egg-eater is gaping as part of its defensive posture.

Johan Marais

The Southern Brown Egg-eater has no markings on the body. This species is restricted to the eastern parts of South Africa and Swaziland.

Biology

Egg-eaters are nocturnal and arboreal or terrestrial. In grasslands, they regularly shelter in moribund termite mounds or beneath rocks. They feed exclusively on bird eggs and have an extraordinary ability to locate them. These snakes have several adaptations for eating eggs, including a very flexible lower jaw and distensible skin in the neck region. The mouth is stretched over the bird egg, which passes through the throat and into the neck region, where the shell is cracked length-wise by a series of bony protrusions that project ventrally from the neck vertebrae. The egg is then squeezed so that it collapses, and the contents are swallowed. The shell is regurgitated as a neat boat-shaped package.

When confronted with danger, Egg-eaters coil and uncoil their bodies in a 'U' shape, rubbing their strongly keeled dorsolateral scales against each other. This action produces a hissing or rasping sound that is similar to the hissing of more dangerous snakes. They also strike out viciously with their mouth agape. The Rhombic Egg-eater has a dark inner lining to the mouth that adds dramatic effect to this act. Egg-eaters are completely harmless to humans but are often needlessly killed in the mistaken belief that they are Night Adders (*Causus*).

Reproduction

Clutches of between 6 and 28 eggs (21–46 x 8–21 mm) are laid and females may produce more than one clutch per season. The Southern Brown Egg-eater's eggs have numerous small pimple-like protrusions on the surface. Hatchlings are between 200 and 280 mm in length.

The Rhombic Egg-eater has vivid markings and is often confused with venomous species, which it appears to mimic. This individual comes from Namaqualand and has similar markings to the Horned Adders in the area.

SPECIES IN THE GROUP

- East African Egg-eater: *Dasypeltis medici*
- Rhombic Egg-eater: *Dasypeltis scabra*
- Southern Brown Egg-eater: *Dasypeltis inornata*

COPING WITH BIG MEALS

Snakes are renowned for their ability to eat large food items, and the Egg-eaters are champions in this regard. They cope easily with eggs that are more than four times the diameter of their heads. This is possible because the throat region has highly elastic skin, and because the lower jaws are connected anteriorly by a highly elastic ligament and are not fused together as they are in most other animals. Snakes do not dislocate their jaws when feeding – this would render them incapable of feeding. They effectively 'walk' their jaws over their prey, using the teeth on both the upper and lower jaws to assist in the process. Egg-eaters, however, have to push their jaws over the smooth egg, and it is suspected that lubrication may be provided from glands situated behind the eyes.

Distribution

The Rhombic Egg-eater is widespread throughout most of southern Africa and also occurs extensively to the north. It appears to be excluded only from true desert, closed-canopy forest and high mountain ranges. The Southern Brown Egg-eater occurs from the Eastern Cape northwards into KwaZulu-Natal, Mpumalanga and Limpopo provinces. It is endemic to southern Africa. The East African Egg-eater is restricted to the northeastern parts of southern Africa and is found from northern KwaZulu-Natal into Mozambique and eastern Zimbabwe.

The East African Egg-eater is found mainly in lowland forest in the northeastern parts of southern Africa.

Egg-eaters are renowned for their ability to engulf birds' eggs that are much larger than their heads.

Tropical Water Snakes

The genus *Crotaphopeltis*
2 species

Description

This group contains two species, one widespread and the other restricted. Both are small to medium-sized snakes with distinct flat heads, large eyes and vertical pupils. Adult length is between 450 and 750 mm in the Herald Snake, and between 400 and 700 mm in the Barotse Water Snake. Both species are mildly venomous and have relatively large immovable fangs near the back of the maxillary bone, just below the eyes. The dorsal scales are smooth and highly polished. Herald Snakes have either 19 or 21 rows of scales at midbody; the Barotse Water Snake has 17. The anal shield is entire and the subcaudals (24–47) are paired. There are between 139 and 174 ventral scales. Herald Snakes are olive-green to grey above with white speckles that form indistinct transverse bars, especially in juveniles. The head is darker than the body and is often iridescent black, especially after shedding. The upper lip is red to orange-red, yellow or white, and the underside white or cream. The Barotse Water Snake is iridescent grey-brown to grey with dark-edged scales and a white to pale brown belly.

Biology

Both species are terrestrial, but are often associated with wetlands, where their prey is concentrated. They are nocturnal, and actively hunt for frogs and toads. Once the snake has bitten its prey, it hangs on while the venom takes effect. The Barotse Water Snake inhabits papyrus swamps and is not well known. When threatened, the Herald Snake raises its head and flattens it horizontally, displaying the upper lips while hissing and striking, often with the mouth agape. Herald Snakes bite readily, but the Barotse Water Snake is docile, even when captured. Both species have small venom glands, and the mild venom is of little consequence to humans.

Herald Snakes are also sometimes known as Red-lipped Heralds or Red Lips. However, not all individuals of the species have this striking characteristic.

Johan Marais

Bryan Maritz

Herald Snakes flatten their heads and strike viciously at their attacker.

Reproduction

Clutches of between 6 and 19 eggs (25–32 x 10–13 mm) are laid in summer. The hatchlings are between 130 and 180 mm in length.

Distribution

The Herald Snake is common throughout the wetter eastern half of southern Africa, from the Western Cape to Zimbabwe, extending north of the subcontinent. The Barotse Water Snake is restricted largely to the Okavango Swamps, extending its range along the Chobe River and into the upper Zambezi.

Marius Burger

Body colour of Herald Snakes varies from olive-green to brown or grey above. The species can be identified by the presence of white speckles on the body.

NAMED BY A NEWSPAPER

The existence of the Herald Snake was first announced in a newspaper called *The Eastern Cape Herald*, hence the common name of this snake.

SPECIES IN THE GROUP

- Barotse Water Snake: *Crotaphopeltis barotseensis*
- Herald Snake: *Crotaphopeltis hotamboeia*

Tiger Snakes

The genus *Telescopus*
2 species

Description

The two species in this group are instantly recognizable by their golden yellow to buff dorsal coloration with prominent black bars. A third species awaits formal description in scientific literature and is not covered here. Tiger Snakes are small to medium sized with a generally slender body form. Adult length ranges from 600 m to nearly 1 m. The head is very distinct from the body, and the eyes are large and bulbous with vertical pupils. These snakes are mildly venomous and have immovable fangs far back on the maxillary, just below the eyes. Midbody scales are in 17–21 rows, the anal shield is divided but is occasionally entire and subcaudals (51–83) are paired. There are between 190 and 247 ventral scales. The Common Tiger Snake has 22–70 black crossbars or blotches on the body and tail, while Beetz's Tiger Snake has 30–39 dark black blotches on the back and 12–20 on the tail. It also usually has a dark blotch on the crown of the head. The underside is uniform pink, buff or yellowish.

Biology

Tiger Snakes are nocturnal, seeking shelter in narrow rock crevices or under the bark of trees during the day. Though largely terrestrial, they climb well, and Common Tiger Snakes are often found in trees while they search for food. These snakes are very active after summer rains, and many are killed by cars while crossing roads. They feed on lizards, fledgling birds, bats and small rodents. If

Tiger Snakes, such as this Beetz's Tiger Snake, are highly distinctive and easily recognized.

Johan Marais

Graham Alexander

The Common Tiger Snake has between 22 and 70 black crossbars or blotches on the body and tail.

confronted, they put up an impressive display, lifting the head off the ground, drawing it back and striking quite viciously. Beetz's Tiger Snake is usually found in rocky areas and probably shelters in rock crevices. The mild venom poses no threat to humans.

Reproduction

Females lay between 3 and 20 eggs (24–55 x 10–17 mm). Hatchlings are between 170 and 230 mm in length.

Distribution

Tiger Snakes are found in a variety of habitats, from desert to nama karoo, savanna and forest. The Common Tiger Snake is widespread in the northern and northeastern parts of southern Africa, occurring in KwaZulu-Natal, Mpumalanga, Limpopo, Gauteng and Northwest provinces in South Africa, through Swaziland, Mozambique, Zimbabwe, Botswana and the northeastern and highveld regions of Namibia, extending southwards into the

Richtersveld. Beetz's Tiger Snake is found from the Cedarberg to the southwestern Free State, northwards through the Northern Cape into Namibia. It is absent from the Namib Desert.

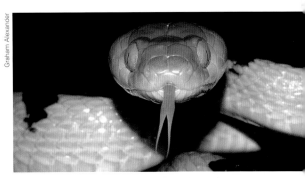

Graham Alexander

Tiger Snakes are nocturnal. They have large, prominent eyes with vertically elliptic pupils.

SPECIES IN THE GROUP

- Beetz's Tiger Snake: *Telescopus beetzii*
- Common Tiger Snake: *Telescopus semiannulatus*

Cat-eyed Tree Snakes

The genus *Dipsadoboa*
2 species

Description

The two species in this group are slender snakes with distinct heads and large eyes with vertical pupils. Adult length ranges from 450 mm to about 850 mm. Cat-eyed Tree Snakes are mildly venomous and have immovable fangs situated near the back of the maxillary bone, just below the eye. The dorsal scales are smooth and polished and there are 17 rows of midbody scales. Ventral scale counts range from 170 to 197, and the anal shield is entire. There are 75 to 106 subcaudals, which are paired. Body coloration is usually a red-brown to light brown above, with faint whitish crossbars. The head is faintly spotted or marbled with white, and the belly is creamy white, sometimes with darker speckling. Cross-barred Tree Snakes have a distinct brown stripe on either side of the head that extends from the nose through the eye to the angle of the jaw.

Biology

Cat-eyed Tree Snakes are attractive nocturnal snakes that shelter under loose bark, in hollow tree trunks, in thatched roofs and in shaded plant debris during the day. They emerge at dusk to hunt for food, which includes lizards, frogs, toads and, occasionally, small rodents. Because of their preference for geckos and frogs they are often encountered near human dwellings. When threatened, they coil loosely into a striking position with a flattened head that is raised off the ground. The strike is relatively slow and deliberate, and the mouth is held open. The mild venom is of no consequence to humans.

Cat-eyed Tree Snakes, such as this Marbled Tree Snake, have large, prominent eyes. They use their keen vision to detect prey.

Johan Marais

Johan Marais

The long, agile body of the Marbled Tree Snake alludes to its climbing abilities.

Reproduction

Females lay clutches of between 7 and 9 small eggs (approximately 25 x 12 mm) in summer. Hatchlings are approximately 180 mm in length.

Distribution

The Marbled Tree Snake is restricted to lowland forest and moist savanna in the eastern parts of southern Africa, extending from northern KwaZulu-Natal into Mpumalanga, Mozambique and eastern Zimbabwe. The Cross-barred Tree Snake is restricted to southern Mozambique in southern Africa, but does occur further north.

Bill Branch

In southern Africa, Cross-barred Tree Snakes are known only from the coastal parts of Mozambique.

Bill Branch

Marbled Tree Snakes feed on frogs, as well as on chameleons and geckos.

SPECIES IN THE GROUP

- Cross-barred Tree Snake: *Dipsadoboa flavida*
- Marbled Tree Snake: *Dipsadoboa aulica*

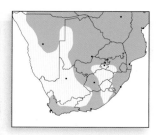

Boomslang

The species *Dispholidus typus*
1 species

Description

Although the single species in this group is very distinctive, it is often confused with the Green Mamba (*Dendroaspis angusticeps*) and harmless Green Snakes (*Philothamnus*). Boomslangs are medium to large snakes that have a very large, blunt head and enormous eyes. The pupils are round, but are slightly lobed in the front, allowing binocular vision. Boomslangs are highly venomous and usually have three large immovable fangs near the back of the maxillary bone, below the eyes. Adult length ranges from 1.2 to 2 m and the dorsal scales are strongly keeled, giving a rough appearance. Midbody scales are in 17–21 rows, the anal shield is divided and the subcaudals (104–142) are paired. There are between 164 and 201 ventral scales. Coloration is very varied. Females are usually olive-brown with a dirty white belly. Males are usually bright green, sometimes with black between the scales, giving a cross-barred appearance. In some areas, males are dark brown to black with a bright yellow or dark grey belly. Hatchlings are dull grey to brown in colour, usually with a little blue and orange in the throat region, which is usually only visible when the neck is inflated. Hatchlings' eyes are a vivid emerald green colour that darkens with age.

Biology

Boomslangs are arboreal and only rarely descend to the ground to hunt, bask or move from one tree to another. They are mainly diurnal and rely on their cryptic coloration to avoid detection. The diet is varied and includes chameleons and other tree-living lizards, birds, their nestlings and eggs. They will also eat frogs and small mammals such as rats and mice. Prey is usually consumed in a tree while in a head-down position so that the prey hangs from the mouth. The prey is not released after the initial bite and is chewed while the venom takes effect. Boomslangs are often

Boomslangs vary greatly in colour, but can be identified by their distinctive head shape and keeled dorsal scales. This adolescent still bears its juvenile coloration and patterning.

Marius Burger

Boomslangs have well-developed binocular vision: each pupil is lobed in the front and the snout is shaped to allow the snake to see directly forward.

mobbed by small birds and sometimes use the opportunity to catch a meal. While hunting, the neck may be undulated from side to side, with the head and body held perfectly still. The function of this behaviour is not clear, but it could serve to improve camouflage. There are reports of several individuals congregating in the same tree.

Boomslangs are docile and are typically very reluctant to bite. When cornered, they will put on an impressive display that includes inflating the neck region to expose colours that are usually hidden by the overlap of scales. The neck and anterior third of the body is held straight and stiff, so that the head is slightly raised. The tongue is menacingly flickered in a slow, deliberate fashion. Given the opportunity, Boomslangs will quickly flee into thick vegetation where they use their camouflage to avoid any further confrontation, but if directly grasped they may bite.

Reproduction

Females lay between 8 and 27 eggs (27–53 x 18–37 mm) in hollow tree trunks or in rotting logs late in spring. The young are between 290 and 380 mm in length.

Juvenile Boomslangs usually have distinctive green irises.

Distribution

The Boomslang is widely distributed throughout much of southern Africa excluding most of Lesotho, the central Highveld and the drier western half of South Africa and southern Namibia. It is found in a variety of habitats including arid and moist savanna, lowland forest, grasslands and fynbos.

Marius Burger

Boomslangs spend most of their time in trees and will usually only descend to the ground to move to another tree, retrieve prey or lay eggs.

Danger to humans

Boomslang venom is potently haemotoxic and can cause severe symptoms that require medical treatment. Although the initial symptoms after a bite may appear to be relatively minor, involving only the oozing of blood-stained serum from the bite wounds, they can later become life-threatening. Severe headaches, nausea, vomiting and abdominal pain usually commence several hours after the bite, followed later by swelling, haemorrhaging and a suite of associated blood-related maladies. Specific Boomslang antivenom is effective in treatment, which may require extensive blood transfusion. Fortunately, very few bites have been recorded. It is a misconception that because Boomslangs are 'back-fanged', they can only deliver an effective bite on a finger or hand. Boomslangs are able to open their mouths wide enough, and the fangs are positioned forward enough in the mouth to allow them to deliver an effective bite almost anywhere on a human body.

Tony Phelps

Boomslangs rely on their vision to detect predators and prey.

SPECIES IN THE GROUP

■ Boomslang: *Dispholidus typus*

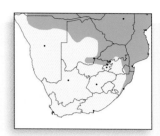

Vine Snakes

The genus *Thelotornis*
2 species

Description

There are two southern African species in this group. Vine Snakes, also sometimes call Twig Snakes, are medium sized, have slender bodies and a unique mottled patterning that makes them perfectly camouflaged in the branches of trees. Adult length ranges from 800 mm to 1.2 m. The head is elongated and the large eyes have keyhole-shaped pupils. The dorsal body scales are slightly keeled and are not polished. The tail is long. Midbody scales are in 17 or 19 rows, and between 144–177 ventral scales. The subcaudal scales (127–173) are paired. The Southern Vine Snake is ash grey to grey-brown above with darker and lighter flecks of black, orange and pink, and one or two dark blotches on the side of the neck. The head is pale blue-green above and is speckled with dark brown or black, as is the chin and throat. There is sometimes a black 'Y'-shaped marking on the crown of the head. The upper lip has a wide pale band that runs from the snout to the back of the head and there is a dark oblique band from the eye to the upper jaw. The belly is pinkish white to grey with brown speckles. The tongue is bright red with a black tip. The Eastern Vine Snake differs from the Southern Vine Snake in that it has a plain green head with a dark speckled 'Y'-marking on the crown. Both the chin and throat are white.

Biology

Vine Snakes are arboreal and generally move slowly, relying on their excellent camouflage to escape detection. Although at home in trees, they tend to favour low bushes and shrubs from where they inspect the ground below for passing prey. Vine Snakes tend to perch motionlessly until food is spotted. The prey is then approached in short bursts of movement and is finally seized with

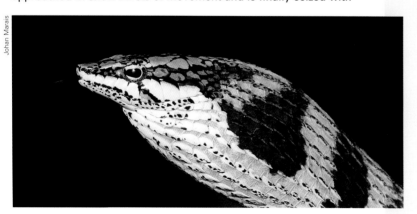

Johan Marais

Vine Snakes will react to molestation by inflating their necks and stiffening the anterior part of the body.

a lunge. It is held firmly in the jaws while the venom takes effect and the fangs may be firmly embedded in the prey to encourage envenomation. Vine Snakes prey on chameleons and other lizards, frogs, snakes, small mammals and occasionally birds. Surprisingly, burrowing Rain Frogs (*Breviceps*) are frequently eaten.

Vine Snakes may remain in the same position for several days, but can move

Vine Snakes, such as this Southern Vine Snake, rely on their camouflage to avoid confrontations.

This Eastern Vine Snake has highly modified pupils that allow for good binocular vision. The pupils are lobed to the extent that they are horizontally elliptic and become keyhole-shaped when contracted.

swiftly when disturbed. These snakes are generally timid and reluctant to bite, but if provoked will inflate the neck, exposing the bright skin between the scales. They may resort to lunging strikes, interspersed with slow tongue flicking.

Reproduction

Male combat occurs during the mating season. Females lay clutches of between 4 and 18 eggs (25–41 x 12–17 mm). The hatchlings are between 220 and 370 mm in length.

Distribution

Vine Snakes inhabit lowland forest and savanna. The Southern Vine Snake occurs from KwaZulu-Natal, Limpopo, Mpumalanga and North West provinces of South Africa, extending into Mozambique, Swaziland, Zimbabwe and the northern and eastern parts of Botswana and northern Namibia. In southern Africa, the Eastern Vine Snake occurs in Mozambique, but extends to the north of the subregion.

Danger to humans

Very few Vine Snake bites have been recorded. However, these snakes carry dangerous haemotoxic venom that can cause life-threatening symptoms. Initially, symptoms may appear to be minor, with local swelling and slight bleeding. However, this may be followed by more substantial haemorrhaging from the bite wound, internally, and from any other wounds or scratches on the body. There is no effective antivenom available for this species and treatment may require transfusions in serious cases. Human fatalities are known but are rare.

SPECIES IN THE GROUP

- Eastern Vine Snake: *Thelotornis mossambicanus*
- Southern Vine Snake: *Thelotornis capensis*

ELAPIDS
Family: Elapidae

The Elapidae is divided into two subfamilies, the Elapinae (terrestrial species) and the Hydrophiinae (sea snakes). The family probably has the widest distribution of any snake family, since the terrestrial species occur throughout most of Africa, Arabia, India, Southeast Asia, the Indonesian archipelago, Australia, South America and southern North America, while marine species occur extensively in the Indian and Pacific oceans. Although the division of the family into terrestrial and marine species has been long-standing (some authorities even consider them to be separate families), it is likely to be proved artificial since recent research suggests that at least two marine lineages have arisen from the Australian terrestrial elapids independently. The family has 60 genera and more than 315 species. In southern Africa there are six genera, and a total of 16 species. All species in the family are venomous and have relatively short, immovable hollow fangs situated on the anterior part of the maxillary bone, near the front of the mouth. Many carry potent neurotoxic venoms that can result in serious bites. There is no loreal scale and the head is usually distinct from the body, at least in southern African species. Ventral scales are the width of the belly (but may not be in sea snakes) and dorsal scales are usually smooth, but the Rinkhals is a well-known exception that has keeled dorsal scales. The body form of African elapid species is usually slender, and the snakes are active and agile. Marine species have several adaptations to their environment, and the tail is usually flattened into an oar that propels the snake effectively in water. Generally, elapids have well-developed eyes and appear to rely on vision more than do other snakes. Most African elapids are egg-laying, but the majority of the marine species and several Australian species give birth to live young.

Most species of African elapids, such as this Western Barred Spitting Cobra, are large, alert snakes. Many carry potent venom.

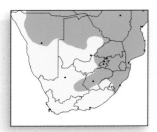

African Garter Snakes

The genus *Elapsoidea*
4 species

Description

There are four species in this group, all small to medium sized with smooth scales. Adult length ranges from 400–770 mm. The head is small and is barely distinct from the rest of the body, the eyes are medium sized and dark, and the snout is rounded. All African Garter Snakes are venomous and have short immobile fangs near the front of the mouth. The dorsal scales are polished and there are either 13 or 15 rows of scales at midbody. The anal shield is entire, the subcaudals (13–60) are paired and the tail is very short. Ventral scale counts range from 131 to 181. Although there is a fair amount of variation in coloration and pattern between and within species, there are some general commonalities: juveniles are brightly banded, but these bands usually fade with age; adults tend to be uniform grey to black, sometimes with faint banding. Colours tend to be paler below, ranging from white to a pale shade of the dorsal colour. Juvenile Günther's Garter Snakes are black with 16–20 light crossbars on the back and 2–4 on the tail. Juvenile Angolan Garter Snakes have a white head and black back with 12–19 white bands on the body and two or three on the tail. Juvenile Zambezi Garter Snakes have a white head and are black above with 12–17 white to pale yellow bands on the body and tail. The light bands are a half to one-third the width of the darker bands. Juvenile Sundevall's Garter Snakes have between 16 and 34 pale, pink or reddish bands on the body and 2–4 on the tail.

Sundevall's Garter Snake has prominent banding over the body, typical of Garter Snakes. These bands tend to fade as the snakes age.

Johan Marais

The Zambezi Garter Snake is sometimes plain in coloration.

In southern Africa, Günther's Garter Snake is restricted to the central and northern parts of Zimbabwe.

Biology

Little is known about the life history of these shy, secretive snakes because they are so seldom encountered. They are nocturnal and spend their days hiding under rocks, in termite mounds or underground, and appear to be partially fossorial. Garter Snakes are relatively slow-moving, inoffensive and very reluctant to bite, even when captured, but can be induced to coil and hiss if molested. The diet consists primarily of reptiles and, to a lesser degree, amphibians.

Reproduction

Clutches of between 4 and 10 eggs (20–40 x 8–16 mm) are laid in summer.

Distribution

Günther's Garter Snake occurs on the central plateau of Zimbabwe, extending into areas north of southern Africa. The Angolan Garter Snake is found in northern Namibia, the Caprivi Strip, northwestern Botswana and further north. The Zambezi Garter Snake ranges from northern KwaZulu-Natal through Swaziland, Mozambique, and Mpumalanga, Limpopo, Northwest and Northern Cape provinces of South Africa, into eastern Botswana, Zimbabwe and areas north of southern Africa. Sundevall's Garter Snake occurs mainly in the eastern parts of southern Africa, from southern Mozambique south to just into the Eastern Cape province of South Africa, extending inland to Free State and Gauteng provinces and Swaziland. It also occurs in the west from northern Namibia to eastern Botswana.

Danger to humans

Very little is known about the venoms of Garter Snakes other than that it may cause nausea, immediate pain and stiffness, blurred vision and even loss of consciousness. They should be regarded as dangerous. Polyvalent antivenom is not effective in treatment and should not be administered.

Like most African elapids, Sundevall's Garter Snake lays eggs.

SPECIES IN THE GROUP

- Angolan Garter Snake: *Elapsoidea semiannulata*
- Günther's Garter Snake: *Elapsoidea guentheri*
- Sundevall's Garter Snake: *Elapsoidea sundevalli*
- Zambezi Garter Snake: *Elapsoidea boulengeri*

Coral Shield Cobra

The species *Aspidelaps lubricus*
1 species

Description

The single species in this group is one of the most attractive snakes in southern Africa. Coral Shield Cobras are small cobra-like snakes with an average adult length of approximately 500 mm and a maximum of 750 mm. It has a chunky flat head with an enlarged rostral scale on the snout. The head is distinct from the body and the medium-sized eyes are black. Coral Shield Cobras are venomous and have small immovable fangs near the front of the mouth. Dorsal body scales are smooth and highly polished and there are 19, occasionally 21, rows at midbody. The anal shield is entire and the subcaudals (17–36) are paired. There are between 139 and 179 ventral scales. Coloration and patterning varies geographically. In the southern parts of the range the body is orange-yellow to coral red above with 20 to 47 narrow, evenly spaced black crossbars that may encircle the body and tail. The underside is yellowish white with black crossbars, but the darker crossbars may fade with age. This species also has a short, black, vertical stripe from the top of the head through the eye to the upper jaw, and another dark stripe that runs from the top of the head to the back of the jaw. In the northern parts of its range it has a dark or sometimes pale head, dull grey to yellowish body, and 24–66 indistinct crossbars on the back.

Biology

Coral Shield Cobras spend most of their lives underground, sheltering under rocks or in burrows. They are particularly active at night after summer rains, when they may be seen crossing roads. Their diet includes lizards (especially legless skinks), small snakes

In the southern parts of its range, the Coral Shield Cobra is brightly coloured and has black crossbars on its body.

Marius Burger

The enlarged rostral scale on the nose of Coral Shield Cobras is an adaptation for burrowing.

and rodents, and it has been suggested that they catch diurnal lizards while they are sleeping since they feed in the early evenings or at night. If confronted, the Coral Shield Cobra will immediately raise the front third of the body off the ground, spread a very narrow but distinct hood, hiss with purpose and strike repeatedly, usually with the mouth closed. These snakes bite readily and possess fairly potent neurotoxic venom.

Reproduction

Males engage in combat during the mating season. Females lay between 3 and 11 eggs (approximately 50 x 18 mm) in the summer, and sometimes more than one clutch in a season. The hatchlings range in length from 150–200 mm.

Distribution

The Coral Shield Cobra inhabits rocky outcrops, stony and dry sandy regions, arid savanna, succulent and nama karoo and fynbos in the western parts of southern Africa. It occurs from southern Angola, through central and southern Namibia into the Karoo, the southern Free State and Western Cape, extending into the Eastern Cape in South Africa.

Coral Shield Cobras show their close relationship to the true cobras in their defensive behaviour. However, they are able to spread only a narrow hood.

Danger to humans

Coral Shield Cobras carry neurotoxic venom that has resulted in human fatalities. However, bites from individuals from the southern parts of the range have been less significant and have not resulted in life-threatening symptoms. Polyvalent antivenom is not effective in treatment and should not be administered.

SPECIES IN THE GROUP

■ Coral Shield Cobra: *Aspidelaps lubricus*

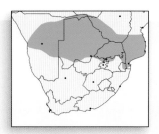

Shield Cobra

The species *Aspidelaps scutatus*
1 species

Description

Shield Cobras are short, stocky snakes with blunt, broad heads that are just distinct from the rest of the body. The most obvious feature of this species is a very large rostral scale covering the tip of the snout. This protective scale is an adaptation that allows Shield Cobras to bulldoze through loose sand. Adult length is between 400 and 450 mm, but occasionally very large specimens of up to 750 mm are found in the eastern parts of the distribution. The eyes are black, medium sized and prominent. The nostrils are large and open laterally. There are usually 21 or 23, occasionally 25, scale rows at midbody, and the anal shield is entire. Subcaudals (19–39) are paired and there are between 108 and 125 ventral scales. Colour is quite variable, but usually salmon pink to orange-brown or reddish brown above with a series of brown blotches over the back and tail. The head and most of the lower throat region are black, and this colouring may encircle the neck but the upper neck region is usually white. The underside is white to yellowish. Specimens from the eastern part of the distribution often have distinct large black blotches on the back and sides of the body.

Biology

Shield Cobras are nocturnal and are usually found under rocks or in rodent burrows during the day. They emerge to forage during

Shield Cobras are very stocky and have a pronounced rostral scale, which is used for bulldozing through soft sand.

Colin Tilbury

Shield Cobras from the eastern parts of the range have a pale head and body.

Shield Cobras from the western and central parts have a dark head and body.

the early evening and night, when they are commonly encountered on tarred roads. The diet is varied and consists of amphibians, lizards, other snakes and small mammals. Even winged termites are eaten. Since most of the prey species are also nocturnal, it suggests that Shield Cobras hunt active prey. When molested, Shield Cobras may play dead, but are renowned for their usual cantankerous performance of raising the anterior quarter of the body off the ground, hissing and striking repeatedly. The strikes can be sufficiently vigorous to move the entire body of the snake a short distance. These snakes cannot spread a hood.

Reproduction

Females lay clutches of between 4 and 14 eggs (30 x 18 mm) and may remain coiled around the eggs during incubation. Hatchlings are between 159 and 180 mm in length.

Distribution

Shield Cobras occur in sandy and stony regions of central, northeastern and central Namibia, from the coastal areas across most of Botswana into southwestern Zimbabwe, the Northwest, Limpopo, northern Gauteng and Mpumalanga provinces of South Africa, into southern Mozambique and the Gonarezhou National Park in southeast Zimbabwe. The species is endemic to southern Africa.

Danger to humans

Little is known about the venom, but bites have resulted in mild neurological symptoms accompanied by pain. One human fatality has been reported. Polyvalent antivenom is not effective in treatment and should not be administered.

Female Shield Cobras are known to guard their eggs.

SPECIES IN THE GROUP

- Shield Cobra: *Aspidelaps scutatus*

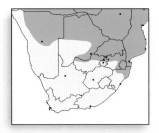

Bushveld Cobras

The species *Naja annulifera* and *N. anchietae*
2 species

Description

Two large robust cobra species belong to this group. Adult Bushveld Cobras range from 1.5–2.5 m in length. The head is large and is reasonably distinct from the body. The eyes are medium sized with round pupils. Bushveld Cobras are venomous and have relatively small, immobile fangs near the front of the mouth. The dorsal body scales are smooth but are not highly polished. There are either 17 or 19 rows of scales at midbody, the anal shield is entire and the subcaudals (51–65) are paired. Ventral scale counts range from 175 to 203. Both Bushveld Cobra species have banded and plain phases. The banded phase has 7–11 bluish black cross bands interspaced by broad yellow to yellow-brown cross bands. The lighter bands are about half the width of the darker bands. The plain phase is yellowish to greyish brown or bluish black above, with a yellow belly with darker mottling. Both species have a dark throat band that is more conspicuous in juveniles.

Biology

Bushveld Cobras often take up residence in a retreat for years if not disturbed. They can be active during the night or day, and will often forage for food at dusk. The diet is varied and consists of rodents, toads, birds, eggs, lizards and other snakes. They bask during the morning, usually close to their retreats, into which they will

Bushveld Cobras, such as this Snouted Cobra, are large-bodied and can reach a length of more than 2.5 m. A small proportion of individuals of both species in the group is banded.

Johan Marais

disappear if disturbed. Although they are not aggressive, they will stand their ground if cornered, raise the anterior third of the body and spread a broad hood in an impressive display. Individuals will occasionally play dead if molested.

Reproduction
Females lay clutches of 8–33 eggs (47–60 x 25–35 mm) in early summer. Hatchlings range from 220 to 340 mm in length.

Distribution
The Snouted Cobra is found primarily in savanna and occurs from KwaZulu-Natal northwards into the lowveld of Mpumalanga and Limpopo provinces, Mozambique, Zimbabwe, Botswana and areas north of southern Africa. Anchieta's Cobra favours wooded areas along rivers and wetlands in arid savanna, and is found in northern Namibia, northern Botswana and western Zimbabwe.

Danger to humans
Bushveld Cobras bite readily and possess potent neurotoxic venom that can lead to respiratory failure and death. Some bites have also resulted in limited cytotoxic symptoms. Polyvalent antivenom is effective in treatment. Victims require urgent hospitalization and treatment.

Snouted Cobras may be mottled or have indistinct, broken banding on the body.

Anchieta's Cobra spreads a broad hood in a typical defensive posture.

Cobras, such as this Snouted Cobra, may use their hood to increase heating while basking.

SPECIES IN THE GROUP

- Anchieta's Cobra: *Naja anchietae*
- Snouted Cobra: *Naja annulifera*

Forest Cobra

The species *Naja melanoleuca*
1 species

Description

Forest Cobras are large, reaching a maximum length of around 2 m. They have large, angular heads that are not distinct from the body, and slender to robust bodies with highly polished smooth dorsal scales. The eyes are moderate in size with round pupils. Forest Cobras carry potent venom and have relatively short immobile fangs near the front of the mouth. There are usually 19 rows of scales at midbody, but specimens with 17 or 21 are occasionally found. The anal shield is entire, the subcaudals (63–72) are paired and there are between 201 and 214 ventral scales. The head, neck and forepart of the body are usually yellowish brown flecked with black, becoming darker towards the back. The underside is creamy white to yellow and may have darker blotches.

Biology

This species is usually associated with closed-canopy coastal forest in KwaZulu-Natal, lowland forest and moist savanna. It is an active, alert snake that climbs well, often foraging in low bushes, but is equally at home on the ground and in water. It is active at dawn and dusk, but also hunts for food during overcast weather. Otherwise, it is fond of basking. The Forest Cobra is a shy, elusive snake that is quick to disappear into the closest thicket if disturbed. If cornered, it will spread a narrow hood and will bite readily.

Forest Cobras have smooth, polished scales. Body coloration becomes darker posteriorly. There is often a pale band across the neck.

Bryan Maritz

The Forest Cobra has a long, narrow hood and is able to raise its head high off the ground. The ventral side of the hood is a mustard yellow; the dorsal side is usually dark brown with flecks.

Reproduction

Males are known to engage in combat during the mating season, twisting their bodies around one another as if in a wrestling match. Females lay clutches of 11–26 eggs (46–61 x 24–32 mm) in summer. The young are between 270 and 400 mm in length.

Distribution

Forest Cobras occur in KwaZulu-Natal from just north of Durban, northwards into southern and central Mozambique, and eastern Zimbabwe. The species is widespread in East and West Africa.

Danger to humans

This is an extremely dangerous species that has potent neurotoxic venom. Fortunately, few people are bitten due to the Forest Cobra's restricted distribution and shy, retiring nature. Victims of serious bites require urgent hospitalization and antivenom treatment. Polyvalent antivenom is effective.

SPECIES IN THE GROUP

■ Forest Cobra: *Naja melanoleuca*

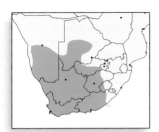

Cape Cobra

The species *Naja nivea*
1 species

Description

The Cape Cobra is a medium-sized snake with a slender body and a head that is distinct from the body. Adults usually attain a length of between 1.2 and 1.4 m, but occasionally specimens of up to 2.3 m are recorded. The eyes are medium sized with round pupils. Cape Cobras carry potent venom and have relatively short immobile fangs near the front of the mouth. The dorsal scales are smooth and are highly polished, with either 19 or 21 rows at midbody. The anal shield is entire, the subcaudals (50–68) are paired and there are 195–227 ventral scales. Coloration is very variable, ranging from light, sandy brown, to yellow or reddish brown or black. The most common patterning includes the following phases: shiny dark brown to blackish above; bright yellow, sometimes with darker speckling; and bright shiny orange-brown to brown with darker or lighter mottling. The yellow phase is widespread, but the other phases occur only in restricted areas. Juveniles have a broad band in the throat region that is visible when they spread a hood.

Biology

Cape Cobras are active mainly during the day, but may also forage for food in the evenings. Although they are largely terrestrial, they are renowned for raiding Sociable Weaver nests and prey readily on eggs and fledglings of any suitably sized birds. The diet also includes rodents, lizards, toads and other snakes. Rodent burrows, moribund termitaria and rock crevices are used as retreats. Cape Cobras adapt well to life in low-density suburbia and squatter

Juvenile Cape Cobras usually have a prominent dark band across the neck.

Marius Burger

Cape Cobra body coloration often matches the environment.

Cape Cobras come in a variety of colours; this one is a striking lemon-yellow.

settlements, and frequent human dwellings on farms. They have a generally nervous disposition and will put on an impressive display of hood-spreading and striking if cornered or molested. They bite readily and are responsible for the majority of snakebite deaths among humans in South Africa. However, as with other snakes, if given the chance, they prefer to flee rather than engage in confrontation. Cape Cobras are probably responsible for most of the stock losses that are blamed on the relatively harmless Spotted Skaapsteker (*Psammophylax rhombeatus*).

Reproduction

Clutches of between 8 and 20 eggs (60–69 x 24–30 mm) are laid in midsummer. The hatchlings measure between 340 and 400 mm.

Distribution

The Cape Cobra is found in fynbos, succulent and nama karoo, arid savanna and the Namib Desert. It is restricted to the Western Cape, Eastern Cape, Northern Cape and Free State provinces in South Africa, extending into Botswana and Namibia. It is endemic to southern Africa.

Danger to humans

The Cape Cobra is one of the deadliest snake species in southern Africa. It has powerful neurotoxic venom, the most potent of any African cobra. Victims require urgent hospitalization and treatment. Symptoms include drooping eyelids, difficulty in swallowing, respiratory failure and flaccid paralysis. Polyvalent antivenom is effective, but must be administered promptly (within hours). Artificial respiration may be necessary to combat the effects of flaccid paralysis.

SPECIES IN THE GROUP

- Cape Cobra: *Naja nivea*

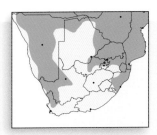

Spitting Cobras

The species *Naja nigricollis* and *N. mossambica*
2 species

Description

At present there are two species in this group, the Black-necked Spitting Cobra and Mozambique Spitting Cobra. Ongoing research using molecular techniques suggests that two subspecies of the Black-necked Spitting Cobra – the Western Barred Spitting Cobra (*Naja nigricollis nigricincta*) and the Black Spitting Cobra (*Naja nigricollis woodi*) – together form a species that is distinct from the Black-necked Spitting Cobra. Spitting Cobras are medium to large, robust cobras with broad heads and blunt snouts. The Black-necked Spitting Cobra is the largest, with adults averaging 1.4 m and occasionally growing to 2 m. The Mozambique Spitting Cobra is smaller, and reaches a length of about 1.2 m. The head is fairly rectangular and the eyes are medium sized with round pupils. All Spitting Cobras carry potent venom, which can be delivered by biting or spitting using small immovable fangs near the front of the mouth. The dorsal body scales are smooth and polished, and are in 17–25 midbody rows. The anal shield is entire and the subcaudals (51–69) are paired. Ventral scales number between 176 and 228. These cobras are able to spread relatively wide hoods, and Black-necked Spitting Cobras and Mozambique Spitting Cobras have dark distinctive transverse bars across the hood. These cobras are a uniform dark olive-brown to grey-brown above with a salmon pink to red belly. However, the Western Barred Spitting Cobra is brown to pinkish with between 50 and 85 vivid, evenly spaced black crossbars on the body and up to 32 on the tail. These crossbars usually encircle the body completely, and the hood and throat are completely black. The Black Spitting Cobra is black above with a dark grey belly, while juveniles are grey above with a black head and neck.

Like other Spitting Cobras, the Western Barred Spitting Cobra has a broad hood that does not extend far down the neck. These cobras do not stand very tall in their defensive posture.

Johan Marais

Graham Alexander

The Mozambique Spitting Cobra is the most common cobra in the northeastern parts of southern Africa. The underside of the hood is typically salmon pink with black bars.

Biology

Spitting Cobras may be active during the day or night, and bask during the morning. They are largely terrestrial but climb into trees and shrubs while actively searching for food. Their diet is varied and includes toads, small mammals, birds, lizards, fish, eggs, snakes and even insects. They may use retreats such as termite mounds, rodent burrows, hollow tree trunks and rock crevices for extended periods, and the Mozambique Spitting Cobra has been recorded sharing retreats with other species such as Black Mambas (*Dendroaspis polylepis*).

When confronted in the open, Spitting Cobras will usually spread a hood, and if approached they will spit venom at the face of the attacker. If molested while in a crevice, Spitting Cobras are able to spit without raising a hood. They are generally nervous snakes and are willing to bite if given the opportunity.

Reproduction

Females lay clutches of between 10 and 22 eggs (29–37 x 17–24 mm), and the hatchlings are between 230 and 370 mm in length.

Johan Marais

Spitting Cobras have round pupils and are diurnal.

Conservation

A subspecies of the Black-necked Spitting Cobra, the Black Spitting Cobra (*Naja nigricollis woodi*), is listed as 'Rare' in the South African Red Data Book. Better data collection since the publication of the Red Data Book has shown that this species is not as rare as originally thought. It is not listed by the IUCN as 'Threatened'.

Distribution

The Black-necked Spitting Cobra only just enters our range at the Caprivi Strip, whereas the Western Barred Spitting Cobra occurs from central Namibia northwards

Marius Burger

The Black Spitting Cobra is a subspecies of the Black-necked Spitting Cobra and occurs in the arid western parts of southern Africa.

and the Black Spitting Cobra from central Namibia southwards into Namaqualand, as far south as Citrusdal in the Western Cape. The Mozambique Spitting Cobra occurs from southern KwaZulu-Natal northwards into Mozambique and Mpumalanga, Gauteng, Limpopo and North West provinces, Zimbabwe, eastern and northern Botswana, and northeastern Namibia, northwards.

Johan Marais

The Black-necked Spitting Cobra is the largest of the Spitting Cobras and can reach a length of 2 m.

Danger to humans

Spitting Cobras, especially the Mozambique Spitting Cobra, are common and are responsible for many snakebite cases in southern Africa. The venom is potent and has both cytotoxic and neurotoxic components, and victims need to be hospitalized urgently. Symptoms include local swelling, serious local tissue damage and 'skip' lesions. Bites can be life threatening. Polyvalent antivenom is effective, but must be administered promptly (within hours). Bites can also result in organ failure. These snakes also spit their venom, which can cause intense pain. Venom molecules bind to the corneal protein and cause swelling around the eye. Venom should be washed from the eye immediately using water.

SPECIES IN THE GROUP

- Black-necked Spitting Cobra: *Naja nigricollis*
- Mozambique Spitting Cobra: *Naja mossambica*

Rinkhals

The species *Hemachatus haemachatus*
1 species

Description

This stocky, cobra-like snake averages 1 m, but may reach a maximum length of 1.5 m. It is unique among southern African elapids in that it has keeled dorsal scales that are not polished. The head is distinct from the neck and the snout has a relatively sharp point. The eyes are prominent and the pupils are round. There are either 17 or 19 midbody scale rows, the anal shield is entire and the subcaudals (30–47) are paired. Coloration and patterning vary according to geographic locality, but on the Highveld the body is usually olive to dark brown or charcoal grey above. The ventral scales are more polished, and may range from pale grey to black, with 1–4 white crossbars on the throat. Some specimens lack the white bars altogether, but when the white bars are present they are very prominent when the hood is displayed. Populations in KwaZulu-Natal, the Eastern Cape and Zimbabwe typically have a dorsum that is prominently banded with narrow crossbars of creamy white, bright yellow or orange.

Biology

Although often assumed to be nocturnal, the Rinkhals is primarily diurnal and basks in the morning before setting out on active foraging bouts within a few hundred metres of its retreat. Foraging may also

The Rinkhals has a defensive posture that is similar to that of cobras, and is able to spread a typical cobra-like hood.

take place at night in the summer months. During the winter months, emergence is delayed until around 09h00–10h00, but individuals will remain active throughout the year and will bask on most fair-weather days. The selected body temperature is about 32 °C, and they will move from the basking site into shade once the body reaches this level. The species is very effective at regulating its body temperature in a temperate climate, and can maintain a body temperature of more than 30 °C during the day, even on cold days.

If approached, Rinkhals will usually retreat quickly if given the opportunity, but if cornered they will lift about half of their body off the ground and present a broad hood to intimidate the attacker. Once hooded, they will readily spit venom at their attackers, drawing the head back and throwing the raised part of the body forward to help project the venom. Venom can be sprayed up to about 2 m and is directed in the general direction of danger. If further threatened by their attackers, Rinkhals will play dead by twisting the anterior portion of the body sideways or upside down and will let the mouth gape open. The tongue may even be left hanging out of the mouth. If handled while shamming, Rinkhals usually hang limp, but can also 'come back to life' and bite quickly with little warning.

A wide variety of prey is taken, but Rinkhals are most partial to toads and some individuals will eat nothing else. Most snakes will also feed on lizards, rodents, birds, their eggs and other snakes. Eggs the size of domestic fowl eggs are taken and swallowed whole.

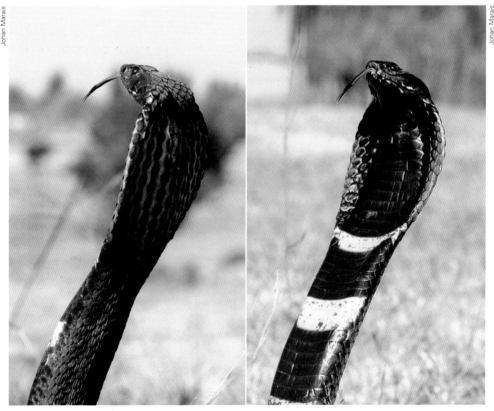

Among other characteristics, the Rinkhals differs from cobras in that it has keeled dorsal scales that are not polished. The ventral scales, although not highly polished, are smooth.

If threatened, the Rinkhals will often play dead by twisting the anterior portion of the body sideways or upside down. Rinkhals from KwaZulu-Natal are often banded.

Reproduction

Unlike the cobras, this species is a live-bearer, producing 20–30, but as many as 63, young in late summer. The young average 160–220 mm and rear up and spread small hoods from birth.

Distribution

The Rinkhals is a southern African endemic with a classic temperate distribution. It occurs from sea level in the Western Cape, through the Cape Fold Mountains, northwards along the eastern escarpment from the Western and Eastern Cape, through KwaZulu-Natal grasslands into Gauteng and adjacent areas. The species is limited to higher altitudes in the northern parts of its distribution and there is a relict population in the Inyanga area of Zimbabwe. Rinkhals prefer grasslands, moist savanna and fynbos, and may be locally common in parts of its range, especially in pristine highveld grasslands.

Danger to humans

Although Rinkhals venom is potentially deadly, it is not as potent as that of the cobras, and fatalities are rare. The venom has neurotoxic and cytotoxic components, causing pain and swelling within minutes of the bite. Within hours, symptoms may include nausea, vomiting, drowsiness, double vision and there may be some local necrosis. Respiratory failure is unlikely. Polyvalent antivenom is effective in treatment. These snakes also spit their venom, which can cause intense pain. Venom molecules bind to the corneal protein and cause swelling around the eye. Venom should be washed from the eye immediately with water.

SPECIES IN THE GROUP

■ Rinkhals: *Hemachatus haemachatus*

Black Mamba

The species *Dendroaspis polylepis*
1 species

Description

Black Mambas are very large, slender, agile snakes with distinct, relatively large heads. Adult length is usually between 2.4 and 3 m, but very large specimens that approach or even exceed 4 m have been recorded. They are the largest venomous snakes in Africa. The head is infamously coffin-shaped and lacks a loreal scale. The eyes are medium sized and have round pupils. Black Mambas are highly venomous and have short, immobile fangs near the front of the mouth. The dorsal body scales are smooth and have a slightly matt, almost satiny sheen. There are 23 or 25 rows or scales at midbody, the anal shield is divided and the subcaudals (109–132) are paired. There are between 248 and 281 ventral scales. The tail is long. General body colour is usually dark olive to greyish brown or gunmetal grey, with colours becoming darker with mottling posteriorly that may form indistinct oblique bars on the body. Juveniles are pale grey to olive. The belly is silver to pale grey. The inside of the mouth is inky black.

Biology

Black Mambas are primarily terrestrial, but do venture into shrubs and bushes, especially to bask after eating. They are active foragers and will feed on any suitably sized mammals including rodents, squirrels and rock hyrax – there is even a record of a Black Mamba eating a young Blue Duiker. Birds are frequently taken. Black Mambas occur in a wide variety of habitat types, including forest, bushveld and savanna, and select rocky areas that offer suitable retreat sites. They will make use of a single retreat for extended periods and are known to share residence with other Black Mambas or even individuals of other species such as the Mozambique Spitting Cobra (*Naja mossambica*). Black Mambas are fast-growing, can reach a length of nearly 2 m at one year of age and can have a lifespan of more than 20 years.

Black Mambas are generally not black – the common name is said to be derived from the black interior of its mouth.

Marius Burger

The abilities and disposition of Black Mambas are legendary, but public perception of the species is based largely on misinformation. Black Mambas are not aggressive and will choose retreat over attack. However, they have a nervous disposition and are inclined to bite if cornered or harassed. Apparently, some bites have resulted from the victim inadvertently coming between the mamba and its place of refuge. Generally, Black Mambas avoid humans and seldom permit close approach, but individuals become quickly habituated to human presence and can live in close proximity to humans for years, often entirely undetected. The threat display of an anxious Black Mamba is impressive and entails the snake raising as much as the anterior third of its body off the ground, spreading a long, narrow hood, and gaping to expose the dark interior of the mouth. If the aggressor is within striking range, the mamba will not hesitate to bite repeatedly if provoked.

Reproduction

Mating occurs in spring and males engage in combat, twisting their bodies and necks around each other in an attempt to push the competitor to the ground. Females lay clutches of between 6 and 17 eggs (approximately 70 x 32 mm) in summer. The young measure 400–600 mm.

Distribution

The Black Mamba occurs from the northern extremes of the Eastern Cape northwards through KwaZulu-Natal and Limpopo provinces of South Africa, Swaziland, Mozambique, Mpumalanga, Zimbabwe, Botswana and northern Namibia, but is absent from true desert.

Danger to humans

The Black Mamba is one of the most dangerous snakes in the world and is arguably the most dangerous snake in Africa. Its large body size, nervous temperament.

and potent neurotoxic venom are a lethal combination that has resulted in many fatal bites. Symptoms progress rapidly, beginning with excessive sweating and proceeding to paralysis and respiratory failure, sometimes within an hour. Serious bites can also directly affect heart function. Urgent hospitalization is essential. Polyvalent antivenom is effective, but must be administered before symptoms have become acute, and a large dosage may be needed.

Marius Burger

The profile of a Black Mamba showing the characteristic 'smile of death'.

Johan Marais

Black Mambas are able to spread a narrow hood. They may also gape, showing the black interior of the mouth.

SPECIES IN THE GROUP

■ Black Mamba: *Dendroaspis polylepis*

Green Mamba

The species *Dendroaspis angusticeps*
1 species

Description

Green Mambas are large, slender, agile snakes with distinct, relatively large heads. Adult length is usually between 1.8 and 2.5 m. The head is coffin-shaped and there is no loreal scale. The eyes are medium sized, yellow-brown and have small, round dark pupils. Green Mambas are highly venomous and have short, immobile fangs near the front of the mouth. The dorsal body scales are smooth and slightly polished. There are 19 (rarely 17 or 21) midbody scales and the subcaudals (99–126) are paired. The anal shield is divided. There are between 201 and 232 ventral scales. Body coloration is a brilliant green above and below, sometimes with occasional yellow scales scattered on the dorsum.

Biology

Green Mambas are strictly arboreal and spend most of their time in the upper canopy in coastal forest. They rarely descend to the ground and sleep high in trees, usually in an exposed position coiled up on a branch. Their camouflage is extremely effective and they can easily avoid detection in trees. If confronted, they will quickly and gracefully disappear into thick vegetation. Green Mambas are not nearly as nervous as Black Mambas, will generally not gape in threat and are more reluctant to bite. They are often confused with the non-venomous Green Snakes (*Philothamnus*), which are usually much

Green Mambas are large, slender snakes with brilliant green coloration, sometimes with occasional yellow scales.

Johan Marais

The Green Mamba's pupils are round and dark, and the irises are golden in colour.

slimmer and have dark eyes with an orange inner rim to the iris.

Green Mambas rely on their cryptic coloration to ambush prey and also actively hunt for birds, their eggs and fledglings, and small tree-living mammals such as bats. Chameleons are also taken by juveniles, but mammals and birds are preferred.

Reproduction

Males engage in combat, intertwining their necks and bodies in an attempt to push each other down. Mating takes place in trees with the tails hanging down. Between 6 and 17 eggs (approximately 50 x 26 mm) are laid in summer, usually in a hollow tree trunk or in leaf litter. The young are between 300 and 450 mm in length.

Distribution

This species is restricted to evergreen lowland forest and moist savanna. In South Africa, it is restricted to the strip of dense coastal vegetation close to the sea, occurring from southern KwaZulu-Natal and Eastern Cape, northwards. It also occurs in the forest of eastern Zimbabwe.

Danger to humans

Green Mambas are shy, reclusive snakes that are rarely encountered. Consequently, bites are rare. Their neurotoxic venom is much less toxic than that of the Black Mamba, but victims still require urgent hospitalization. Symptoms are similar to those from Black Mamba bites, but are not as extreme. Polyvalent antivenom is effective in treatment.

Green Mambas are strictly arboreal and rarely descend to the ground.

SPECIES IN THE GROUP

- Green Mamba: *Dendroaspis angusticeps*

Yellow-bellied Sea Snake

The species *Pelamis platura*
1 species

Description

This group consists of a single species. Yellow-bellied Sea Snakes are very distinctive and are specialized for a marine existence. They have extremely reduced ventral scales, a laterally compressed body and a paddle-like tail. Adult total length usually ranges from 600 mm to 1 m. The head is depressed, bullet-shaped and only just distinct from the body. There are large scales on top of the head, but no loreal scale. The mouth opening slants upwards near the angle of the jaw. The nostrils can be closed by valves, open directly upwards and are set far back on the head. Yellow-bellied Sea Snakes superficially resemble eels but are air-breathing and, like all snakes, have a forked tongue that they flicker underwater. They are venomous and have very small, immovable fangs situated about halfway between the tip of the snout and the eye. The dorsal scales do not overlap and are approximately hexagonal in shape. There are 49–67 rows of scales at midbody and 264–406 ventral scales that are fragmented and almost indistinguishable from the dorsal scales. There are several slightly enlarged scales just anterior to the cloaca, but there is no true anal shield. Subcaudals cannot be distinguished from the dorsal scales on the tail. Coloration is distinctive: the upperparts of the body are black and the underparts bright yellow. The tail is yellow with black blotches.

Dick Bartlett

Yellow-bellied Sea Snakes are pelagic, and most spend their entire lives at sea. Sick inividuals may become stranded.

Bill Branch

The Yellow-bellied Sea Snake is adapted to the marine environment. The nostrils are situated high on the snout and can be closed by valves.

Biology

Yellow-bellied Sea Snakes are truly pelagic and are found great distances from land in the open ocean. They rest in the vicinity of sea slicks, areas of calm water where surface currents converge, where they may aggregate in huge numbers. When at rest, these snakes float motionlessly at the surface, often hidden in *Sargassum* seaweed or among flotsam. They ambush small fish from these positions, striking downwards with their buoyant bodies braced against the water surface. Their venom quickly paralyses fish, which are eaten underwater. Yellow-bellied Sea Snakes have very few predators, and most predatory fish and sea birds avoid them, possibly because of their venomous bite. Naïve fish from the Atlantic Ocean (where Yellow-bellied Sea Snakes do not occur) will eat them, but immediately regurgitate them, suggesting they are distasteful.

These snakes are accomplished divers, diving deeper than 50 m and staying underwater for more than three hours on a single breath. The oxygen needed for a dive is stored in an enlarged lung, which has a posterior air sac that serves to increase the lung volume. Since Sea Snakes cannot resist the effects of hydrostatic pressure on the air in the body, the lung compresses as the snakes dive deeper. Normally positively buoyant at the surface, they become neutrally buoyant at approximately 4 m, and negatively buoyant below this, making deep dives less energy demanding. Yellow-bellied Sea Snakes are also able to absorb oxygen through their skin and can meet more than a third of their needs this way. Nearly all the carbon dioxide produced by metabolism is lost through the skin. Gas exchange across the skin is most efficient immediately after shedding. The skin is shed frequently, and is achieved at sea by the snake forming a knot with its body, and then moving the knot towards its tail. This action scrapes off the old skin.

The body temperature of Yellow-bellied Sea Snakes resting at the surface can be as much as 2.4 °C higher than the water

Yellow-bellied Sea Snakes are occasionally washed ashore during storms.

temperature. Although this temperature difference is not large, it is nonetheless impressive, given that Sea Snakes are small and therefore have a relatively large surface area over which heat is lost to the water. Water temperature appears to be a primary limiting factor for the species, and these snakes are excluded from waters below 18 °C, but can survive for short periods at water temperatures down to 11 °C. Strandings from the west coast of southern Africa are probably vagrants that could not survive for long in the cold Benguela Current.

Yellow-bellied Sea Snakes are awkward and almost helpless on land. Individuals washed up on the coast are often sickly and do not usually survive long. Strandings are probably quite common on the east coast, but have only been recorded on two occasions on the West Coast. The species generally has a docile temperament and is not inclined to bite, even when handled.

Reproduction

Small litters of between 2 and 8 young, measuring about 250 mm in length, are born at sea.

Distribution

The Yellow-bellied Sea Snake has a massive range, occurring throughout the warm Indian and Pacific oceans from the east coast of Africa to the west coast of the Americas. The species does not occur in the Atlantic, probably because the waters off the southern tip of Africa and South America are too cold to allow dispersal of snakes into the Atlantic.

Danger to humans

Little is known about the venom of the Yellow-bellied Sea Snake, but it appears to be potent. It is primarily neurotoxic in its action and very small quantities are produced. In addition to this, the small fangs reduce chances of effective envenomation. Few bites have been recorded, and even young human victims have recovered without complications. Polyvalent antivenom is probably ineffective as a treatment.

SPECIES IN THE GROUP

■ Yellow-bellied Sea Snake: *Pelamis platura*

VIPERS
Family: Viperidae

The Viperidae family includes all Vipers, Adders, Night Adders, Rattlesnakes and other Pit Vipers. The family is divided into four subfamilies, which collectively contain 36 genera and at least 259 species. It is distributed throughout most of the world with the exception of Antarctica, Australia and most oceanic islands, but extends into higher latitudes than other snakes. Three genera and 15 species occur in southern Africa, eight of which are endemic. All species in the Viperidae are venomous and have large fangs situated on a highly modified maxillary bone in the front of the mouth. The maxillary bone can rotate due to a unique articulation with the palatine bone, allowing the fangs to fold back against the roof of the mouth when not in use, and to erect when the mouth is opened. The fangs have an enclosed duct on the anterior face, making for a highly efficient venom delivery system. Many species carry potent venoms that have mainly cytotoxic components and appear to facilitate the digestion of food in the stomach, allowing some species to digest food in cold climates. The majority of species have broad, triangular heads and relatively short, stocky bodies. Scalation on the head is usually highly fragmented, although Night Adders (*Causus*) and Fea's Viper (*Azemiops feae*) have large head scales. The body usually has many rows of keeled dorsal scales and broad ventral scales. The left lung is usually absent or greatly reduced, and a tracheal lung is present in most instances. Species may be terrestrial, arboreal or partially aquatic, and the majority of species are ambush foragers.

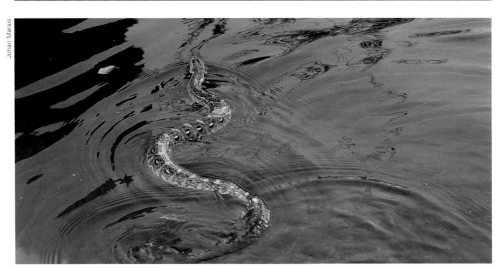

Vipers generally have broad, triangular heads and relatively short, stocky bodies. Even thick-set snakes, such as this Puff Adder, are capable swimmers.

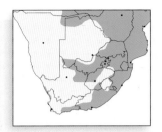

Night Adders

The genus *Causus*
2 species

Description

Night Adders have a more slender body than do most other adders, and, atypically for adders, they have large scales on the head. Two species with similar markings occur in southern Africa. Adult length ranges between 500 mm and 1 m in the Rhombic Night Adder, and between 300 and 430 mm in the Snouted Night Adder. The head is hardly distinct from the body and the eyes are moderately sized with round pupils. The movable fangs are situated near the front of the mouth but are relatively small by adder standards. The venom glands are extremely large and extend from below the eye, down the neck. The dorsal scales on the body appear to have a satin texture and are indistinctly keeled to smooth. There are either 17 or 19 midbody scale rows, the anal shield is entire and the subcaudals (10–33) are mainly paired, although Rhombic Night Adders may have several unpaired subcaudals scattered along the tail. There are between 108 and 155 ventral scales. The Snouted Night Adder has an upturned snout that is probably used for pushing through loose sand. Night Adders have a very distinctive broad, dark symmetrical

Graham Alexander

Night Adders, such as this Rhombic Night Adder, are easily identified by the presence of the prominent 'V' on the top of the head. They differ from other Vipers in having large scales on their heads.

'V'-marking on the crown of the head, which extends from between the eyes to the back of the jaws. Body coloration is light grey to light brown above with large dark, sometimes white-edged, rhombic or triangular markings on the dorsal parts of the body and tail. The belly is pearl white to light grey and blackish in juveniles.

Biology

The common name is inappropriate, as Night Adders are more accurately described as crepuscular or diurnal. They shelter in moribund termite mounds and under logs or stones, and will often bask in the morning. They are most active at sunset. Most individuals have a docile disposition and will generally flee when molested. If cornered, they will inflate their bodies, hiss and strike, often with the mouth remaining closed. These snakes are terrestrial but are often found near wetlands, probably as they prey on amphibians. Unlike most other species of adder, Night Adders actively search for their prey. Toads are favoured, and Night Adders are immune to the toxins produced in the toad's skin.

Reproduction

Mating occurs in early spring, and males engage in combat, wrestling and pushing each other onto the ground. Rhombic Night Adder females lay clutches of between 7 and 26 eggs (approximately 30 x 17 mm). More than one clutch may be laid in a season, but this is probably rare for southern African specimens. Incubation takes about three months, and the body length of the young ranges from 130 to 160 mm. Snouted Night Adders lay small clutches of between 3 and 9 eggs (approximately 25 x 12 mm) in summer, and the young measure just over 100 mm.

Distribution

Night Adders occur in moist savanna, lowland forest and fynbos. The Rhombic Night Adder ranges from the Western Cape

Johan Marais

The Snouted Night Adder can be distinguished from the Rhombic Night Adder by its upturned snout.

through the Eastern Cape, KwaZulu-Natal, Mpumalanga and Limpopo provinces of South Africa, extending into Swaziland, Mozambique, Zimbabwe, northern Botswana and the Caprivi Strip in Namibia. The Snouted Night Adder occurs in parts of KwaZulu-Natal, Mpumalanga and Limpopo provinces, Swaziland, Mozambique and Zimbabwe. Both species occur more extensively north of southern Africa.

Danger to humans

The venom is mildly cytotoxic, causing pain, local swelling and, in some cases, acute discomfort. Night Adders are generally not considered dangerous and antivenom is ineffective in treatment.

SPECIES IN THE GROUP

- Rhombic Night Adder: *Causus rhombeatus*
- Snouted Night Adder: *Causus defilippii*

Puff Adder

The species *Bitis arietans*
1 species

Description

The Puff Adder is one of Africa's most renowned snakes and is instantly recognizable. It is a large, heavily built species with a large, relatively flat head that is distinct from the body. Adult length is generally around 900 mm, but individuals are known to exceed 1.5 m, especially in the northern parts of the distribution. The head is covered with small scales, the eyes are relatively small and the pupils are vertical. The nostrils are large and are directed upwards. Puff Adders are highly venomous and have very large, movable fangs near the front of the mouth. The dorsal scales on the body are strongly keeled and are in 29–41 rows at midbody. The anal shield is entire and the subcaudals (14–38) are paired. Ventral scales number 123–147. Coloration and body patterning vary geographically and within populations. There are usually regular, darker, chevron-like markings on the back, and dark bars on the tail. The crown of the head usually bears a large blotch that is separated from a blotch on the snout by a light line between or just behind the eyes. Two dark oblique bands line the sides of the head, one below and one behind the eye. Puff Adders from many localities may be quite drab and are patterned in shades of brown, beige and yellow, but specimens from the Eastern Cape, Western Cape and KwaZulu-Natal are often brightly marked with black and bright yellow.

Although patterning and coloration vary, the crown of the head of all Puff Adders has a light line between or just behind the eyes. The head is covered with small scales.

Johan Marais

The Puff Adder is a heavily built species with a large, relatively flat head that is distinct from the body. The dorsal scales are strongly keeled and there are usually regular, darker, chevron-like markings on the back.

Biology

The Puff Adder is one of the most common and widespread species in southern African. It is usually fairly slow-moving and relies on camouflage to avoid detection. This is very effective, and Puff Adders are seldom encountered despite being common in certain areas. True abundance is sometimes revealed only when males actively search for mates. Because Puff Adders will generally freeze in their tracks if approached, they have been labelled as 'lazy', but this is an effective way of avoiding predators. They are mainly terrestrial in habit, and will take up ambush positions in thick grass or under bushes. They are known to climb into low bushes to bask and have been recorded several metres up in the branches of trees. Some individuals are belligerent and will hiss and strike. The neck is drawn back into an 'S'-shape before the snake lunges forward to strike. Puff Adders are capable of fast strikes of more than 5 m per second but, contrary to common belief, they do not strike backwards. They move slowly in a straight line using reticular, caterpillar-like locomotion when unthreatened. If molested, however, they will move quickly in the normal serpentine manner, usually with the head and anterior third of the body held slightly off the ground in a striking posture, facing the attacker.

Their diet consists primarily of rodents, but any suitably sized mammals, birds, lizards, toads, snakes and juvenile tortoises are taken. Puff Adders generally avoid being injured by their prey by releasing large victims immediately after the initial bite. The victim soon dies and the snake follows the scent trail with its flickering tongue. Smaller prey items may be bitten and held.

Reproduction

Mating takes place in bouts of intense activity in autumn, winter or spring when males actively search for females. Males also engage in combat, with the anterior third of the body held off the ground and entwined with that of the competitor. Each male endeavours to get his head on top his rival's and to force his body to the ground. Litters of between 20 and 40 young are born in late summer. Exceptional litters of up to 80 young are known, and a captive Kenyan

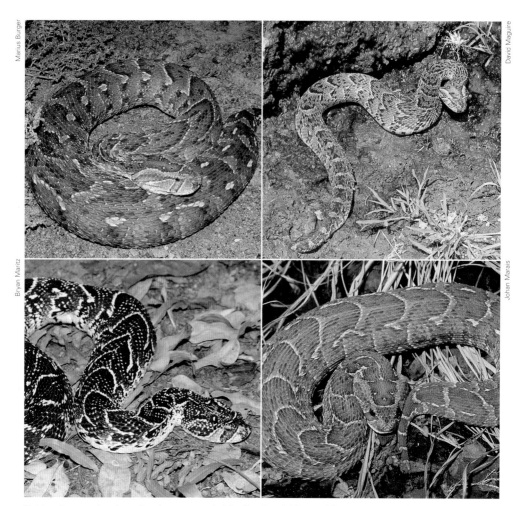

Patterning and coloration is very variable, both within and between populations.

specimen was reported to have produced 156 young. The young have a body length of between 150 and 200 mm.

Distribution

The Puff Adder is widespread throughout most of southern Africa except for dense forests, true desert and mountain tops.

Danger to humans

The Puff Adder is responsible for more cases of serious venomous snakebite in southern Africa than any other species. The venom is potently cytotoxic and causes extreme pain, swelling, blistering and necrosis, and can be life-threatening. Immediate hospitalization is essential. Polyvalent antivenom is effective but must be administered promptly (within hours), and a large dosage may be needed. Bites may result in compartment syndrome (where intense swelling compromises blood flow) and multiple organ failure. Secondary infection associated with the bite site may increase necrosis considerably.

SPECIES IN THE GROUP

■ Puff Adder: *Bitis arietans*

Gaboon Adder

The species *Bitis gabonica*
1 species

Description

The Gaboon Adder is Africa's largest adder and is an extreme animal in many respects. It is bulky and uniquely patterned, making it instantly recognizable. Adult length of southern African specimens ranges from 900 mm to 1.2 m, but much larger specimens of nearly 2 m and 10 kg are known from Central and East Africa. Gaboon Adders have large, flat, triangular heads that are very distinct from the body, and small, horn-like scales above each nostril. The head is covered with small scales. The eyes are relatively small with vertical pupils, and the tongue is black with a red tip. These snakes have long, movable fangs near the front of the mouth and are contenders for having the largest snake fangs. The fangs of large specimens can exceed 40 mm in length. The Gaboon Adder has 33–46 midbody scale rows, 124–140 ventral scales and 17–33 pairs of subcaudals. The anal shield is entire. This snake is sometimes referred to as the Butterfly Adder on account of its beautiful colours and markings. The body has shades of light and dark brown, buff, purple and pink, with a broad broken, buff vertebral stripe interspersed with evenly spaced dark hourglass markings. The sides of the body are covered with complex buff, purple and brown markings, and black-edged purple triangles jut from the belly. The head is buff to chestnut or white, with a narrow dark brown median line and a dark blotch above the angle of the jaw. A dark triangle lies on either side of the head, the apex entering the eye and extending to the angle of the jaw. A second dark triangle or blotch extends downwards from the eye to the jaw. These two triangles are merged in some specimens. The underside of the body is yellowish to buff with dark blotches.

Johan Marais

Gaboon Adders are instantly recognizable. Their markings blend into the colours of the forest floor.

During winter, Gaboon Adders in southern African move to the forest edge so that they can bask more effectively.

Biology

Gaboon Adders lead an extremely low-energy lifestyle and are probably the most sedentary snakes in the world. Individuals have been observed remaining in one position for months at a time, and their coloration and body markings make them extremely cryptic and difficult to detect in the leaf litter of the forest floor. They usually remain completely motionless, their attention to proceedings revealed only by the alert, attentive movement of their eyes. Occasional bouts of activity occur primarily during the night, when individuals may be found crossing roads. In South Africa, Gaboon Adders will often choose patches of sunlight on the forest floor during summer, but in winter they appear to favour the forest margin, probably as they are able to bask more effectively in the more exposed situation. It has also been suggested that they are attracted to forest margins because prey is more plentiful there. In eastern Zimbabwe, Gaboon Adders may be locally abundant and still occur on tea plantations, especially where patches of natural forest remain.

Compared with other adders, Gaboon Adders are surprisingly placid. When molested, they will emit a series of long, drawn-out hisses while lifting the forepart of the body off the ground in a striking position, but even then they are reluctant to strike. Usually, their camouflage ensures that they escape detection.

Their diet consists mainly of rodents, but also includes hares, ground birds, toads, small monkeys and duiker. Gaboon Adders have even been recorded eating domestic cats. An ambush strategy is typically used and, unlike most other adders and vipers, Gaboon Adders often hang on to their prey after biting. The venom is potent and usually kills the prey very quickly.

Reproduction

In southern Africa, mating occurs in bouts during the winter and spring, and males become much more active and mobile during this time as they search for females. Males are also known to engage in combat at this time, wrestling and even striking at each other with closed mouths. Litters of between

16 and 30 young are born in late summer. The body length of the young varies between 250 and 320 mm. Two cases of hybridization between Gaboon Adder and Puff Adder have been reported. These oddities were intermediate between the two species in both colour pattern and morphology.

Conservation

The Gaboon Adder is listed as 'Vulnerable' in the South African Red Data Book, but is not listed by the IUCN as 'Threatened'. In the wider context, the species is plentiful in parts of its distribution, but southern African populations, especially those in South Africa, are at risk and have declined significantly over recent decades. Declines are mainly the result of habitat destruction and transformation, but illegal collecting for the pet trade has probably also had a detrimental effect. Dukuduku Forest near St Lucia in South Africa was a former stronghold, but the population has recently been decimated in this area. Although extremely difficult to census, South African Gaboon Adders appear to be genuinely rare, and research into management of this population and its taxonomic relationship to other populations is currently underway, and is desperately needed.

Distribution

Distribution is restricted, apparently in two isolated areas in southern Africa. A population occurs in the montane forests of the eastern escarpment of Zimbabwe, extending into the forests of central Mozambique. The most southern population is found mainly in South Africa, along the northern KwaZulu-Natal coastal plain. Natural populations appear to occur from Richards Bay in the south, northwards into southern Mozambique. A translocation project moved nearly 200 specimens from Dukuduku Forest to Mtunzini on the KwaZulu-Natal coast. Although Mtunzini is south of the historical distribution of

the species, continued occasional sighting reports suggest that a population may have established in the area.

Danger to humans

Gaboon Adders carry large quantities of potently cytotoxic venom. A full bite is life-threatening and requires immediate hospitalization and treatment. Polyvalent antivenom is effective, but must be administered promptly (within hours), and a large dosage may be needed. Bites are very painful, and symptoms include significant swelling, blistering and bleeding, with a risk of compartment syndrome (where intense swelling compromises blood flow) and multiple organ failure. Secondary infection may increase necrosis considerably. Very few bites have been recorded in southern Africa.

Johan Marais

Gaboon Adders are ambush foragers and will eat any birds or mammals that are small enough to swallow. They have been recorded eating meals that exceed their own body mass.

SPECIES IN THE GROUP

■ Gaboon Adder: *Bitis gabonica*

Berg Adder

The species *Bitis atropos*
1 species

Description

Although all Berg Adders currently belong to a single species, geographically isolated populations that show unique differences may prove to be distinct species. Berg Adders are small snakes, with an adult length ranging from 300 to 400 mm. Very large specimens with a body length of up 600 mm have occasionally been recorded. The head is triangular and is distinct from the body, and there are no horns or ridges above the eyes. Berg Adders are venomous and have large movable fangs near the front of the mouth. The dorsal body scales are strongly keeled and are in 27–33 rows at midbody. The anal shield is entire and the subcaudals (15–31) are paired. Ventral scales number between 118 and 144. Colour and patterning vary geographically. The crown of the head usually bears a dark arrow mark flanked by light stripes. The dorsal coloration ranges from olive-grey to dark brown or black with a silvery white dorsolateral stripe that extends from behind the eye to the tip of the tail. This line may be very faint in some individuals. Above each dorsolateral line is a series of dark triangular or semicircular pale-edged markings with similar, but smaller, markings below the line, forming a geometric pattern. Khaki or reddish brown individuals with faint markings occur near Belfast in Mpumalanga province in South Africa. The belly is usually off-white to dark grey.

Berg Adders are typical Vipers with a thick-set body and triangular head.

Marius Burger

Biology

Berg Adders can be abundant in suitable habitat and are usually encountered when they are basking in grass tussocks, on rocky ledges or in footpaths. The species is known for its bad temperament, and individuals will hiss loudly and strike repeatedly if molested. The diet consists mainly of lizards and small rodents, but amphibians, including Rain Frogs (*Breviceps*), are also eaten, as are birds and other snakes. Juveniles feed primarily on frogs and toads.

Reproduction

Mating starts in autumn and females give birth to litters of 4–16 young in late summer. The young measure between 90 and 150 mm. Females can produce more than one litter from a single mating. Captive males engage in combat, biting one another in the head region.

Distribution

Berg Adders occur from sea level in the southern and Western Cape, along the Cape Fold Mountains from the Cedarberg to Port Elizabeth, and northwards with populations in the KwaZulu-Natal Drakensberg, the Mpumalanga Drakensberg, and the Chimanimani and Inyanga mountains in Zimbabwe. Suitable habitat includes montane grassland, sourveld and mountain fynbos. Berg Adders generally appear to be limited to cool areas, and populations at lower latitudes are restricted to high altitudes, resulting in these populations being marooned on mountain tops. These isolated populations are also genetically isolated from their neighbours and could be considered to be 'species in the making'.

Danger to humans

Berg Adders are locally abundant and are often encountered while they are basking during the morning. Mountain climbers and hikers are at risk, as they may place their hands on unsighted hand holds while

Johan Marais

Berg Adders are limited to cool areas, and populations in the northern parts of the distribution are restricted to high altitudes.

climbing. Despite the generally belligerent attitude of Berg Adders, surprisingly few people are bitten. The venom is potent and can result in some alarming neurological symptoms, including drooping eyelids, blurred vision and loss of the senses of taste and smell. Respiratory failure can also occur between 6 and 36 hours after the bite. Some symptoms, such as those that affect sight, can persist for years or even prove permanent. Bites also result in cytotoxic effects, but these are not as serious as in Puff Adder (*Bitis arietans*) bites. Polyvalent antivenom is not effective, and should not be administered. Several human fatalities have been recorded, especially from bites in the southern and Western Cape.

SPECIES IN THE GROUP

■ Berg Adder: *Bitis atropos*

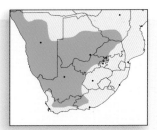

Horned Adder

The species *Bitis caudalis*
1 species

Description

Horned Adders are small, robust snakes that are usually between 250 and 400 mm in length, reaching a maximum of 600 mm. They usually have a distinct single horn above each eye. The head is triangular and distinct from the rest of the body. These snakes have relatively large movable fangs, situated in the front of the mouth. The body scales are keeled and in 21–31 rows at midbody. The anal shield is entire and the subcaudals (16–40) are paired. Colours and patterning vary geographically. Individuals from the Kalahari are usually buff to red above; those from the central Cape are greyer to dark olive-brown. Specimens from the Namib Desert are light reddish brown to light sandy grey. There are three series of spots or blotches dorsally: a median row of dark elongate quadrangular blotches flanked by two dorsolateral rows of smaller dark blotches that are usually pale-centred and sometimes pale-edged. A dark bar usually extends from the eye down to the jaw. The underside of the snake is white to yellowish white with dark spots on the chin and throat. The tongue is mostly black. Males have much longer tails than females, and some individuals have a dark tail tip.

Biology

Horned Adders are terrestrial snakes that are able to bury themselves in loose sand, leaving only the eyes and top of the

Horned Adders have a single prominent horn above each eye.

Johan Marais

head exposed. They also lie in ambush in the shade of shrubs, where they are well camouflaged. These snakes are capable of sidewinding on loose sand. If molested they will coil, inflate their body, hiss loudly and strike repeatedly. Horned Adders are most active at dusk and often leave a distinct track that is easy to follow. They feed largely on lizards, but will also take frogs, small rodents and birds. The dark tail tip is wiggled as a lure to attract prey to within striking distance.

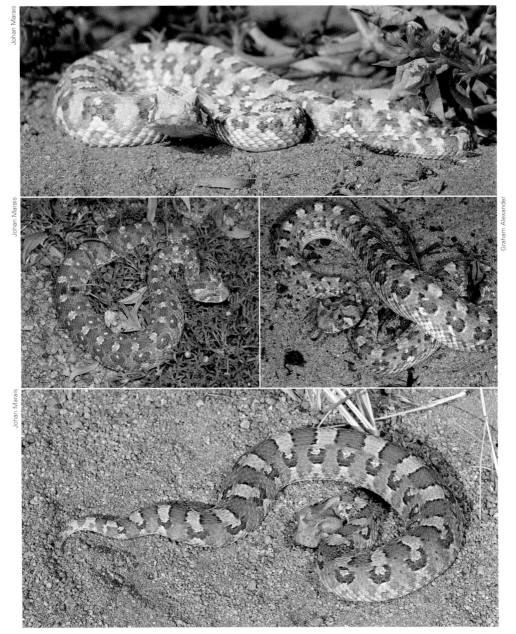

The body patterning and coloration of Horned Adders vary geographically.

Horned Adders are widespread and occur in most of the more arid parts of southern Africa.

Reproduction

Males are known to engage in combat during the mating season, wrestling each other into the ground but not biting in the process. Usually, 3–8 (but as many as 27) young are born in summer, roughly at the same time many lizard eggs hatch. The young measure between 100 and 150 mm in length.

Distribution

The Horned Adder inhabits dry sandy regions in the Namib Desert, succulent and nama karoo and dry savanna. It is widespread throughout the arid western half of the region, extending eastwards into southern Botswana, southern Zimbabwe, and North West, Limpopo and Gauteng provinces of South Africa.

Danger to humans

The venom is mildly cytotoxic, causing pain and swelling and perhaps some necrosis, but is not life-threatening. Polyvalent antivenom is not effective and must not be administered.

A Horned Adder in a defensive posture, ready to strike.

SPECIES IN THE GROUP

■ Horned Adder: *Bitis caudalis*

Dwarf Dune Adders

The species *Bitis schneideri* and *B. peringueyi*
2 species

Description

This group includes two species of small adders. One species, the Namaqua Dwarf Adder, is the smallest adder in the world, averaging 200 mm with a maximum length of around 300 mm. Péringuey's Adder is slightly larger, ranging from 200 to 250 mm with a maximum length of 330 mm. In Péringuey's Adder, the eyes are on top of the flat head, facing almost directly upwards. The Namaqua Dwarf Adder has small eyes situated more laterally on the head, with small ridges above each eye. These snakes have relatively large movable fangs situated in the front of the mouth. Midbody scales are in 23–31 rows and the dorsal scales are strongly keeled. The anal shield is entire and the subcaudals (15–30) are paired, although the first few may be single in the Namaqua Dwarf Adder. The Namaqua Dwarf Adder is grey to brownish grey above with three series of dark brown to black pale-centred blotches down the back. The belly is greyish to dirty yellow, and both the back and belly have dark speckles. Where this snake occurs on red sand, the body colour may be orange-red. Péringuey's Adder is orange-brown to pale sandy grey with three rows of faint to dark, sandy brown or greyish black spots down the body. The spots on the side are pale-centred. The belly is white but may have dark reddish brown spots along the sides. About 25% of Péringuey's Adders and some Namaqua Dwarf Adders have a black tail tip.

Johan Marais

Dwarf Dune Adders, such as this Péringuey's Adder, show several adaptations to their desert habitat.

Johan Marais

Péringuey's Adders are proficient at sidewinding on unstable dunes.

Graham Alexander

The body coloration of Namaqua Dwarf Adders tends to match the colour of the sand in their habitat.

Biology

The two species of Dwarf Dune Adders are sand dune specialists found exclusively on the wind-blown desert sands along the West Coast. Both species are adept at sidewinding, which is the most effective way for snakes to negotiate soft, hot, unstable dune sand. During the day they may use a peculiar shuffling movement of the body to bury themselves into loose sand so that just the top of their heads, or in the case of Péringuey's Adders, only the eyes, are exposed. They occasionally move from one shrub to the next, shuffling into the sand for a while and then moving on, leaving distinct tracks in the sand that can be followed for 100 m or more. These snakes bask early in the mornings, especially on overcast days. Péringuey's Adders use their tail tips to lure their prey within striking distance, and Namaqua Dwarf Adders may do the same. They drink water that collects on their bodies from the condensation of fog that blows in from the cold Atlantic Ocean. Prey consists of skinks, lizards, small mammals and amphibians.

Reproduction

Péringuey's Adders give birth to litters of 3–10 young in late summer. The young are between 80 and 135 mm in length. Namaqua Dwarf Adders produce litters of between 3 and 7 young, which are 110–130 mm in length.

Conservation

The Namaqua Dwarf Adder is listed by the IUCN and the South African Red Data Book

Johan Marais

Namaqua Dwarf Adders are generally found on semi-stable, partially vegetated dunes on the West Coast.

as 'Vulnerable'. It is threatened by habitat destruction resulting from alluvial diamond mining. Illegal collecting for the pet trade is a threat for both species of Dwarf Dune Adders.

Distribution

The Namaqua Dwarf Adder inhabits semi-stable vegetated coastal sand dunes, from Little Namaqualand to Lüderitz Bay in Namibia. Péringuey's Adder is found in the soft, wind-blown dunes of the Namib Desert, from Rotkop in southern Namibia northwards into Angola.

Danger to humans

These small adders have only small quantities of venom that usually results in relatively mild symptoms. However, some bites have resulted in neurotoxic symptoms, and bites should be taken seriously. Polyvalent antivenom is not effective and must not be administered.

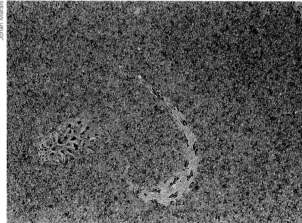

Johan Marais

Péringuey's Adders often bury themselves in the loose sand, leaving little more than their eyes exposed.

SPECIES IN THE GROUP

- Namaqua Dwarf Adder: *Bitis schneideri* **VU**
- Péringuey's Adder: *Bitis peringueyi*

Dwarf Adders

Selected species from the genus *Bitis*
6 species

Description

The six species of Dwarf Adders in this group are small, with stout bodies and eyes that are situated laterally on the head. The head is distinct from the body, and adult length varies from 225–560 mm. Midbody scale rows number 25–31. The dorsal scales are keeled, the anal shield is entire and the subcaudals (21–37) are paired. These snakes have relatively large movable fangs situated in the front of the mouth. Some species of Dwarf Adder have scale tufts forming up to four distinct horns above each eye, whereas others have a single small horn or lack horns altogether. The Many-horned Adder has 2–4 distinct horns above each eye and is grey to greyish brown or reddish brown above, with three or four rows of 22–31 dark angular blotches that may be pale-edged. The markings on the upper rows are usually larger than those on the lower rows and may fuse to form large rectangular markings. The crown of the head has a large, dark, arrow-shaped marking. The side of the head has a dark oblique streak that runs from the eye to the jaw. The underside is white to dirty brownish grey and may have darker stippling. The Desert Mountain Adder is not quite as stout as the Many-horned Adder and lacks horns. It is ash to dark grey or brown above with 16–34 dark crossbars and a plain head. The belly is light grey to dusky with darker infusions. The Plain Mountain Adder also lacks horns, is dull yellowish brown and usually has 19–24 faint, darker

Dwarf Adders, such as this Many-horned Adder, are generally stocky in build and irascible in disposition.

Johan Marais

The Southern Adder is restricted to coastal fynbos in the southwestern Cape.

blotches or spots on each side. The belly is cream to light brown and may have dark speckling. The Red Adder may have tufts of small scales above each eye or no horns whatsoever. It is very pale red above with virtually no pattern, or dull brown to reddish brown with 18–30 paired darker blotches. This species may have a dark triangle on the head as well as dark stripes that radiate from the eye to the jaw. The belly is dirty cream to grey and has dark infusions. The Albany Adder has small tufts of scales above the eyes and is boldly patterned in grey, white and black, with 15–22 dark dorsolateral blotches that may fuse towards the tail. The belly is cream-grey and may have darker infusions. The Southern Adder may or may not have small tufts of horns above each eye. It is grey with dark stipples and 22–28 dark brown to black-and-white blotches. It has a dark arrow-shaped marking on the crown of the head and dark markings that radiate from the eye to the jaw. The underside is pale grey-white with dark markings on the sides.

The Albany Adder is found only around Algoa Bay in the Eastern Cape.

Biology

Dwarf Adders become active in the early evening when they hunt for food, but they are also active in the early morning. These snakes seek refuge in rock cracks, under rocks and rock slabs, in grass tussocks and in rodent burrows. When confronted, they may hiss loudly and strike. Dwarf Adders from colder regions that experience snow may go into hibernation. Although not much is known about their diet, Dwarf Adders are known to feed on ground-living lizards, small rodents, birds and amphibians. They have been observed climbing quite high into shrubs to bask.

Reproduction

Very little is known about the reproduction of most of the Dwarf Adders. Between 4 and 14 young are produced in late summer, measuring 120–160 mm. A captive Desert Mountain Adder produced five young, averaging 150 mm.

Conservation

Several of the Dwarf Adders have very restricted distributions and are rare. Urban development and collecting for the illegal pet trade also pose threats. The Plain Mountain Adder is listed by the IUCN as 'Vulnerable' and 'Restricted' in the South African Red Data Book. This species occurs in montane grasslands, which are also at threat due to overgrazing.

Distribution

The Many-horned Adder is found in mountainous regions, rocky outcrops, gravel plains and mountain fynbos from the Western Cape through Namaqualand and into southern Namibia. The Desert Mountain

The Plain Mountain Adder is rare and has been classified by the IUCN as 'Vulnerable'.

The Many-horned Adder can be distinguished from other Dwarf Adders by the tufts of horns over each eye.

Johan Marais

The Desert Mountain Adder occurs on rocky hillsides along the lower Orange River, from Augrabies to the Richtersveld, and in southern Namibia.

Adder lives on mountain slopes and sparsely vegetated rocky hillsides along the lower Orange River, from Augrabies to the Richtersveld and into southern Namibia. The Plain Mountain Adder is found on mountain slopes in the Sneeuberg, from Graaff-Reinet to Cradock. The Red Adder is restricted to rocky mountain fynbos and succulent karoo, from the Cedarberg further inland to parts of the nama karoo. The Albany Adder has an extremely limited range in succulent thickets in the Algoa Bay area of the Eastern Cape. The Southern Adder is restricted to low-lying coastal fynbos not higher than 200 m above sea level in the southwestern Cape. Much of this snake's former habitat has been destroyed.

Andrew Turner/Sarah Davies

The Red Adder is found in the Cedarberg and Little Karoo.

Danger to humans

Little is known about Dwarf Adder venom since few bites have been recorded. The venom of some species may be quite potent, but the yields are minute, so that although the bites may be very painful, they pose no real threat. Polyvalent antivenom is not effective and must not be administered.

SPECIES IN THE GROUP

- Albany Adder: *Bitis albanica*
- Desert Mountain Adder: *Bitis xeropaga*
- Many-horned Adder: *Bitis cornuta*
- Plain Mountain Adder: *Bitis inornata* **VU**
- Red Adder: *Bitis rubida*
- Southern Adder: *Bitis armata*

LIZARDS

The lizards are an 'artificial' grouping of species that make up part of the order Squamata. Snakes form a natural group within the lizards and should be seen merely as a group of specialized lizards that belong to the same order; they are treated separately here only because of traditional perceptions. More than 4 500 described species of lizards are known in the world. These are classified into more than 504 genera and 20 families. A total of 338 species in 48 genera and nine families are known to occur in southern Africa. However, new discoveries and taxonomic reassessments are likely to increase the species number to at least 400 for southern Africa. Lizards occur on all continents of the world except Antarctica. They are generally very good at dispersing to new localities and are found on many oceanic islands, including most tropical islands, no matter how remote. Their highest diversity is in the semi-arid parts of Australia and southern Africa, where both the species number and density of individuals can be astonishing. Many lizards appear to be limited to their particular ranges by substrate type rather than by climatic factors, as is more usual in other vertebrates. A lizard species may therefore be found either only on a particular rock type or only on/in a particular soil type. Patterns and changes in the distribution of a lizard species may thus be affected by geological processes as much

Johan Marais

Many lizard species, such as this Drakensberg Crag Lizard, occur only on particular types of rocky outcrop and their distributions are limited because of it.

as by climate. This, in turn, has had an important impact on patterns of speciation of lizards in southern Africa.

Lizards differ from snakes in that the two halves of a lizard's lower jaw are fused at a suture, and the bones of the upper jaw are firmly joined to the rest of the skull. Many, but certainly not all, species of lizards have well-developed limbs. In some species, the legs are greatly reduced or have been lost altogether, probably as an adaptation to either burrowing or grass-swimming. Similarly, although most lizards have movable eyelids, Snake-eyed Skinks (*Panaspis*) and nearly all geckos have fused eyelids (the universal condition in snakes), and these lizards see through the transparent eyelids that form spectacles over their eyes. Fused eyelids offer physical protection for the eyes, reducing rates of dehydration. Many types of lizards are able to shed their tails easily as an antipredatory strategy. The shed tail wiggles, acting as a lure to draw the predator's attention away from the escaping lizard. The tail is rapidly regenerated if the lizard has

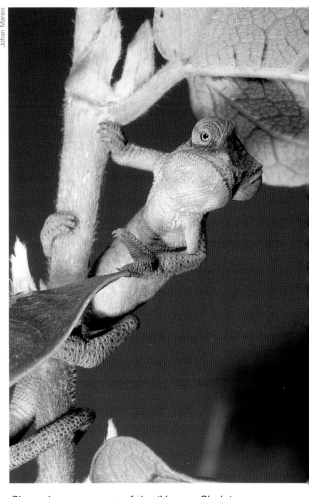

Chameleons are part of the 'Venom Clade'.

access to an adequate food supply. Some lizards, such as the agamas, chameleons and monitors, are unable to shed their tails in this way and cannot regenerate them if they are lost through injury.

Although no southern African lizards are considered to be venomous in the conventional sense, recent research has revealed that the group of lizards most closely related to snakes do produce toxins in their saliva. This group, including all snakes, has been named the 'Venom Clade', and southern African members include the agamas, chameleons and monitors. All studied examples have been shown to have salivary glands that produce toxins that have venomous action.

Most southern African lizards are insectivorous and will feed on any palatable invertebrates of an appropriate size. Some of the larger species, such as the monitors, are generalist carnivores and will consume anything they can subdue,

Marius Burger

The bright body coloration of male Flat Lizards is important for attracting mates.

including other lizards, snakes, birds and their eggs, small mammals, invertebrates and even tortoises. Although no purely herbivorous species of lizards are found in southern Africa, some species – such as the Giant Plated Lizard, Crag Lizards, Girdled Lizards and Flat Lizards – include a significant amount of vegetation in their diets. In such instances, easily digestible soft flowers and fruit appear to be favoured. The most herbivorous species in southern Africa is the Desert Plated Lizard, which feeds primarily on the semi-succulent thorns of the Nara (*Acanthosicyos horrida*), a desert plant, and on grass seeds and detritus.

Reproductive biology is highly diverse in lizards. The majority of species lay relatively large clutches of soft-shelled eggs, but the geckos typically lay two hard-shelled eggs in each clutch. Many species of lizard give birth to live young and, within some species, individuals from certain populations lay eggs, while individuals from other populations give birth to live young. Some live-bearing species have highly developed inter-uterine structures that function in a similar way to the mammalian placenta to nourish the developing foetus. Many species also show remarkably complex social structures. Some species of Girdled Lizard maintain social groups, while some species of Australian skink live in small family units where the presence of the parents improves the survival rates of the young.

AGAMAS
Family: Agamidae

Agamid Lizards are restricted to the Old World and are found in Africa (excluding Madagascar), southeastern Europe, tropical and temperate Asia, New Guinea, Australia and the Solomon Islands. Totals of 52 genera and more than 381 species occur worldwide. Twelve species belonging to two genera occur in southern Africa. Agamas are medium to large lizards that generally have a squat body form and a large, distinct head. The teeth are usually differentiated into incisors and canines; the eyes are small with round pupils and movable eyelids. The scales on the head are small and slightly rough. The body is also covered with small, rough, spiny or keeled scales and tubercles, and there may be a crest of enlarged, raised scales along the vertebral line. Limbs are well developed and digits have strong, recurved claws. The tail is normally longer than the body and is not shed. The majority of agamas are rock-living or terrestrial, although some are arboreal. Most species are insectivorous – some of the southern African species appear to feed primarily on ants; some species that occur in north Africa are herbivorous. Nearly all species lay eggs.

Johan Marais

Agamas, such as this Southern Rock Agama, have squat bodies covered in small, rough, spiny or keeled scales.

Agamas

The genus *Agama* and *Acanthocercus atricollis*
12 species

Description

Eleven species of agama are found in southern Africa, all of which have a very similar and characteristic appearance, with small rough, spiny scales over the dorsal parts of the plump body. They are medium to large lizards with body lengths ranging from 60 to 170 mm in adults. The head is large and round, and always very distinct from the body. Although prominent, the eyes are relatively small and the eyelids are movable. The ear openings are large and easily visible in most species, but small in the Southern Spiny Agama, Etosha Agama and Makgadikgadi Spiny Agama. The body tends to be squat and the scales on the dorsal parts of the body are always strongly keeled, with some drawn into spines. In some species, spiny scales form rows that run the length of the body, but in others these scales are scattered randomly over the dorsal parts. Several species have a dorsal crest of raised scales, although this may be feebly developed in some individuals. Although the ventral scales tend to be feebly keeled in most species of southern African agamas, they are smooth in the Ground Agama and Southern Tree Agama. Agamas' legs are well developed, with a long claw on each of the well-developed toes for climbing. The tail is usually longer than the body, but is shorter in Anchieta's Agama. In species such as the Etosha Agama and Southern Spiny Agama, the tail is longer

Male Southern Rock Agamas develop a white vertebral stripe during the breeding season.

Johan Marais

It is easy to see why Tree Agamas are also known as Blue-headed Lizards.

Knobel's Agama is similar to the Southern Rock Agama, but grows larger.

than the body in males, but shorter in females. Tails are thin in comparison to the robust body.

Body coloration generally matches the substrate, and the lizards rely on camouflage as a means of protection from predation. Terrestrial species, such as the Ground Agama, are generally reddish brown with blotches and irregular bars on the body; rock-living and arboreal species tend to be greyer, but have similar blotching. Reproductively active individuals, especially males, become brightly coloured. In several species, such as the Southern Tree Agama, Ground Agama, Southern Rock Agama, Knobel's Agama and Peter's Ground Agama, the male's head can become intensely blue. Breeding Southern Tree Agama males usually also have a broad yellow dorsal stripe that connects to the yellow on the tail. Male Southern Rock Agamas usually have a white vertebral stripe. Male Namibian Rock Agamas and Kirk's Rock Agamas have

a bright yellow head, blue-grey body and yellow tail during the breeding season. Female Namibian Rock Agamas also develop yellow blotches and stripes on the head and bright orange flashes behind the armpits, which become brighter in the breeding season. Males of terrestrial species, such as the Etosha Agama and Southern Spiny Agama, may develop a colourful and patterned gular area. Patterning includes barring or a network of dark lines.

Ground Agamas will often select a basking site that is a good vantage point.

Biology

Different species of agama have adapted to various microhabitats and have different lifestyles: some are strictly arboreal, whereas others are rock-living or terrestrial. Ground Agamas are primarily terrestrial but will use low bushes as basking sites. All agamas are strictly diurnal and spend the night asleep in their retreats. Terrestrial species dig burrows, rock-living species use rock crevices and arboreal species use either a hole in a tree trunk or a gap under loose bark. During the active part of the day, agamas are alert and use speed to escape danger. Southern Tree Agamas evade danger by moving around the trunk and fleeing into the upper branches. Many agama species are fairly social. Rock Agamas can form dense colonies on rock outcrops, and the Southern Tree Agama appears to form family groups, centred around clusters of suitable trees. Some evidence suggests that Ground Agamas form monogamous pairs during the breeding season. Agamas are able to change their body coloration quickly, much like a chameleon, although the range of change is not as great. Brightly coloured males will assume the camouflage colour of the females when under threat, and even dead individuals undergo a colour change if placed in sunlight for some time.

Agamas are unusual in that some species appear to feed almost exclusively on ants and termites. Ants are not usual fare for other lizards since they are too acidic to be palatable. A certain amount of vegetation may also be included in the diet, especially that of the Namibian Rock Agama.

The Mozambique Agama is restricted to eastern Zimbabwe and central Mozambique.

Ground Agamas have distinctive throat patterns that vary between populations.

Male Southern Spiny Agamas become yellow-green during the breeding season.

A gravid female Southern Spiny Agama searching for a suitable location to lay her clutch.

Reproduction

Males tend to grow larger than females and develop brighter breeding coloration. They display to rivals and females, with head bobbing and body posturing. Although well established hierarchies keep fighting to a minimum, rival male Southern Tree Agamas can engage in savage battles. Agamas are egg-layers, the female laying the clutch in a hole she has dug. The clutch size is generally large, ranging from 5–18, and averaging about 10 eggs. Eggs are laid in midsummer and take about two months to hatch.

Namibian Rock Agamas occur in the northwestern parts of Namibia.

Distribution

Most species have large distributions, and several species may be encountered at particular localities. The Makgadikgadi Spiny Agama is restricted to the Makgadikgadi pan, and the Etosha Agama is limited to the Etosha pans and surrounding areas. The distribution of Knobel's Agama is centred over the mouth of the Orange River, and is restricted to the southwestern extremes of Namibia and the northwestern extremes of the Northern Cape. Collectively, agamas occur over most of southern Africa and are excluded only from parts of the Namib Desert.

SPECIES IN THE GROUP

- Anchieta's Agama: *Agama anchietae*
- Etosha Agama: *Agama etoshae*
- Ground Agama: *Agama aculeata*
- Kirk's Rock Agama: *Agama kirkii*
- Knobel's Agama: *Agama knobeli*
- Makgadikgadi Spiny Agama: *Agama makarikarica*
- Mozambique Agama: *Agama mossambica*
- Namibian Rock Agama: *Agama planiceps*
- Peter's Ground Agama: *Agama armata*
- Southern Rock Agama: *Agama atra*
- Southern Spiny Agama: *Agama hispida*
- Southern Tree Agama: *Acanthocercus atricollis*

CHAMELEONS
Family: Chamaeleonidae

Chameleons are found throughout much of Africa, Madagascar, the southern Arabian peninsula, southern Spain, southern India and Sri Lanka. Fossils indicate that they were once more widespread. Eight genera and more than 162 species are known. Three genera comprising 19 species occur in southern Africa. The skull is characteristic and usually forms a bony casque with prominent crests and tubercles. The eyes are large and turret-like, with a thick granular lip and small central opening for the pupil, and movable eyelids. The eyes are very mobile and can move independently of each other. The tongue is club-shaped, very extensible and is used to capture prey. External ears are lacking. The body is laterally compressed and covered with granular scales, which may be interspersed with enlarged tubercles. Limbs are long and well developed, and the digits are opposed, to facilitate grasping. The tail cannot be shed and is usually strongly prehensile. Nearly all species are arboreal and diurnal. Chameleons are renowned for their ability to change colour rapidly and for their slow, deliberate movement. Both egg-laying and viviparous species exist.

Johan Marais

The laterally compressed body and turret-like eyes set this Flap-neck Chameleon apart from lizards in other families.

Dwarf Chameleons

The genus *Bradypodion*
15 species

Description

This group currently includes 15 described species, but the number is likely to grow significantly as the genus is better researched. The taxonomy is still in an uncertain state, mainly due to many small, isolated populations, but genetic research is being used to redefine the species. As the name suggests, Dwarf Chameleons are small; adults are 45–100 mm in body length, excluding the tail. They have a typical unmistakable chameleon appearance, and the skin covering the body usually has large tubercles scattered on the flanks and legs. The eyes are turret-like and can be directed independently of each other, or both can be directed forwards for binocular vision, which is used for judging distance. The tail is as long as, or longer than, the body. All the species in this group have a moderate to well-developed casque, a raised structure on the back of the head that gives their heads a triangular profile. The casque is fairly pointed in some species and extends the head posteriorly in others. Many species have a gular crest, which consists of a series of scaly flaps along the midline of the lower jaw. Gular folds may also be present in the distensible skin of the lower jaw. These folds run the length of the lower jaw, but are only noticeable if the chameleon exposes them in display. Most species also have a dorsal crest, which consists of a row of enlarged compressed scales that extend along the midline of the back. Dorsal crests may be poorly developed in some species, but are well developed in others, such as the Little Karoo Dwarf Chameleon – the crest extends along the entire length of the body and halfway along the tail, giving it the appearance of

Devi Stuart-Fox/Adnan Moussalli

A male Wolkberg Dwarf Chameleon displays to another male.

Two male Knysna Dwarf Chameleons: the dominant individual is brightly coloured while the subordinate one becomes drab.

a minute dinosaur. Both dorsal and gular crests may be especially well developed in adult males. The legs are well developed and the feet have five toes, each with a prominent claw. The toes are arranged so that three oppose the other two, allowing for effective grasping.

Body coloration is usually a mottled brown, sometimes with an irregular pale lateral stripe. Some adult males develop bright breeding colours, which vary greatly among species. For example, adult male Knysna Dwarf Chameleons are a brilliant emerald green above, with large blue-green or reddish brown patches on the flanks, and yellow below. The head is usually blue-grey to grey on the sides of the casque, and the skin in the gular folds is yellow. Cape Dwarf Chameleon males are a lighter green,

The gular grooves of the Western Dwarf Chameleon can be a variety of bright colours, including orange, yellow or black.

with broad yellow lateral stripes containing maroon patches on the body and in the temporal area, whereas male Natal Midlands Dwarf Chameleons are an olive-green with yellow and cream patches in the gular region, on the flanks, and the edges of the casque and dorsal crest. However, in some other species, such as the KwaZulu Dwarf Chameleon, male coloration differs little from the mottled browns of the female. As with other types of chameleon, Dwarf Chameleons are able to change colour very rapidly and become almost black when stressed. They generally turn pale beige when sleeping, making them easy to find by torchlight.

Biology

Dwarf Chameleons can occur at high densities in favourable habitat, but populations seem to fluctuate unpredictably through time. Some species become very difficult to find during winter – it is possible that they hibernate underground – but others can be found throughout the year on exposed perches. Further research is required to reveal the reasons for the extraordinary changes in the detectability of certain species. All Dwarf Chameleons are arboreal, and the majority of species are found in forests or fynbos. Forest species, such as Setaro's Dwarf Chameleons or the Wolkberg Dwarf Chameleon, often climb into the high canopy, making them difficult

Krystal Tolley

The Cape Dwarf Chameleon is restricted to the southwestern Cape.

to locate. KwaZulu Dwarf Chameleons may be especially common in reedbeds, and several species are also found in grasslands, though it would appear that this is marginal habitat into which young individuals are forced. The ecotone between forest and grassland appears to be a favoured habitat for some species because of the superior basking opportunities. Dwarf Chameleons are heliothermic (using the sun's rays to raise body temperature) and they climb into exposed positions in the morning to bask. They rely on their cryptic coloration and ability to change colour as camouflage. However, when approached closely they may move out of view to the other side of a branch or drop to the ground if directly threatened. They have been transported to new habitats by human agency, intentionally as pets or as unintentional stowaways on plants. This has resulted in feral populations being established in Johannesburg, Alexander Bay, Walvis Bay and other localities.

Dwarf Chameleons generally catch their food by waiting in ambush for passing insects or by patrolling through vegetation in search of prey. Meals are caught with the rapid extension of the long, sticky tongue, which equals the length of the chameleon's body. Diet consists mainly of small grasshoppers and other small flying insects, although small beetles and spiders have also been recorded.

Johan Marais

The Western Dwarf Chameleon occurs on semi-stable dunes and strandveld along the West Coast of South Africa.

Conservation

The highly restricted distributions and the high level of threat to some of the favoured habitats have resulted in several species being classified by the IUCN as 'Threatened'. Elandsberg's Dwarf Chameleon is listed as 'Critically Endangered', and Setaro's Dwarf Chameleon is listed as 'Endangered'. Both the Natal Midlands Dwarf Chameleon and the Qudeni Dwarf Chameleon are listed as 'Near Threatened'. Although several species of Dwarf Chameleon certainly deserve threatened classifications, it is doubtful that the current listings accurately reflect the true situation. For example, the Kentani Dwarf Chameleon, which is not currently listed, is probably in far more need of conservation management than Setaro's Dwarf Chameleon. Research on the taxonomy of Dwarf Chameleons is crucial in order to resolve these issues.

Reproduction

During the breeding season, adult males become very brightly coloured and engage in

Adult Natal Midlands Dwarf Chameleons have well developed casques and prominent facial tubercles.

ritualized displays that includes head bobbing, expansion of the gular region to display the colours of the gular folds and posturing with one of the forelimbs extended. Displays frequently escalate into vicious fights that result in one of the contestants being bitten or dislodged from his perch. Mating occurs in spring, and females give birth to 5–20 live young. Many species are very productive and females may produce 2–3 litters per season. Newborns are attached to the surrounding vegetation by the sticky foetal membranes from which they emerge. They are able to grasp and climb immediately. The young feed voraciously on small insects such as fruit flies. Growth is rapid, with maturity being reached in one or two years. Lifespan is about three or four years.

Distribution

Dwarf Chameleons typically occur in isolated populations that are limited to very small patches of suitable habitat. The historical changes in the distributions of the various species appear to have been closely linked to changes in the extent and fragmentation of natural forests. It therefore

The Elandsberg Dwarf Chameleon is listed by the IUCN as 'Critically Endangered'.

A KwaZulu Dwarf Chameleon catches a meal by rapidly extending its long, sticky tongue.

seems likely that, on many occasions, populations were split, diverged and then joined and interbred again. This reticulate evolutionary pattern has resulted in complex relationships among populations. The distributions of the various species can be divided into two groups: a coastal group, whose distributions are limited to small areas close to the coastline, and an inland group situated along the eastern escarpment. Generally, only one species occurs in any particular area.

Setaro's Dwarf Chameleon has been listed by the IUCN as 'Endangered'.

SPECIES IN THE GROUP

- Cape Dwarf Chameleon: *Bradypodion pumilum*
- Drakensberg Dwarf Chameleon: *Bradypodion dracomontanum*
- Eastern Cape Dwarf Chameleon: *Bradypodion ventrale*
- Elandsberg Dwarf Chameleon: *Bradypodion taeniabronchum* **CR**
- Kentani Dwarf Chameleon: *Bradypodion kentanicum*
- Knysna Dwarf Chameleon: *Bradypodion damaranum*
- KwaZulu Dwarf Chameleon: *Bradypodion melanocephalum*

- Little Karoo Dwarf Chameleon: *Bradypodion gutturale*
- Natal Midlands Dwarf Chameleon: *Bradypodion thamnobates* **NT**
- Pondo Dwarf Chameleon: *Bradypodion caffer*
- Qudeni Dwarf Chameleon: *Bradypodion nemorale* **NT**
- Setaro's Dwarf Chameleon: *Bradypodion setaroi* **EN**
- Swartberg Dwarf Chameleon: *Bradypodion atromontanum*
- Western Dwarf Chameleon: *Bradypodion occidentale*
- Wolkberg Dwarf Chameleon: *Bradypodion transvaalense*

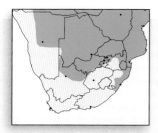

Flap-neck Chameleon

The species *Chamaeleo dilepis*
1 species

Description

This group consists of a single species of large chameleon with a maximum body length of 150 mm. It has a strongly prehensile tail equal to the length of its body. The body is laterally compressed, with a ridge running along the length of the back and another above each eye. The common name of this chameleon is derived from the large occipital flap that extends from the posterior edge of the head, covering part of the neck. However, the size of this flap varies over the range of the species and is almost lacking in some populations, especially those found in southeastern parts of the range. The variation in flap size was previously used by taxonomists to divide Flap-neck Chameleons into several varieties. Careful analysis, however, suggests there are no clear boundaries between large-flapped and small-flapped populations, and that flap size is also dependent on sex and age, with adult males having the largest flaps. The typical chameleon eyes are turret-like and can be directed independently of each other, or both can be directed forwards for binocular vision, which is used during prey capture. The back angle of the jaw curves downwards. The legs are well developed and the feet each have five toes with a prominent claw on each, arranged so that three oppose the other two. Males have an additional small projection on the posterior of each back foot, the function of which is not known.

The Flap-neck Chameleon is widespread and common.

Johan Marais

Johan Marais

The Flap-neck Chameleon has a low casque and relatively smooth skin.

While awake, resting and unstressed, the body coloration is usually an emerald green with white lateral longitudinal bars. However, this species is renowned for its ability to change colour, varying from almost black when stressed, through all shades of green, yellow and brown. Handling usually induces black spots over the entire body, and light and dark green blotches often cover most of the body when the chameleon is on the move. The body becomes a washed out whitish green or yellow when the animal is asleep, making sleeping Flap-neck Chameleons easy to find at night with a spotlight. The skin between the scales on the throat of the adult male is usually orange, and this interstitial skin is used in display between rivals.

Biology

Adults are usually found in trees or shrubs, but hatchlings appear to favour perching on grass stems. Flap-neck Chameleons can be common in suitable habitat and may occur in high densities, although their cryptic coloration helps them avoid detection.

However, individuals can be spotted as they attempt to cross roads. When moving over open ground, these chameleons appear to be unsure of themselves and progress with a peculiar back and forth see-sawing motion. During such times, while exposed and out of their element, many chameleons are killed by vehicles and predators. Flap-neck Chameleons feed on insects such as grasshoppers, beetles, flies and butterflies, snaring them with their long, sticky tongue, which can equal the total body length when fully extended. These chameleons forage by means of ambush or by slowly patrolling through vegetation. They respond to danger by inflating their bodies, hissing, gaping and changing body coloration to dark mottled shades. When highly agitated, the occipital flaps are raised forward, making the animal appear larger still. The shade of coloration can also depend on body temperature: when body temperature is low and the chameleon is basking in the mornings, the body darkens to absorb more solar radiation. This can be fine-tuned so that the side of the body facing the sun is perceptibly darker than the side in shadow. Flap-neck Chameleons are more difficult to find during the winter months, and individuals have reportedly been unearthed during cold conditions. This suggests that these chameleons 'hibernate', but this requires confirmation. This behaviour may also protect them from winter veld fires in grassland areas. Although populations of Flap-neck Chameleons persist in some suburban areas, intensive landscaping and highly manicured gardens ultimately result in local declines and extinctions.

Reproduction

It is easy to determine the gender of adult Flap-neck Chameleons, as males have a pronounced swelling at the base of the tail and a small spur projecting backwards on each hind foot. Mating takes place in early to mid-summer, when males display and sometimes fight each other. In late summer, females dig a hole in which they lay 25–60 small eggs. Egg laying can take much time as everything is done in the slow and deliberate manner typical of chameleons. Eggs are deposited in layers, each of which is covered by a layer of soil. When the entire clutch has been laid, the hole is filled and the surface is patted down carefully. Eggs can incubate for almost a year, and only hatch the following spring or summer. Hatchlings dig themselves out of the nest and often perch in groups of 3–4 in close proximity to the nest for several days after hatching.

Distribution

The Flap-neck Chameleon is the most widespread and common chameleon in southern Africa. It occurs throughout Zimbabwe, Botswana, Mozambique, northeastern Namibia, excluding the western extremes, and the central and northern parts of South Africa. It is found in a wide variety of habitats, but is most common in savanna, bushveld and coastal forests. It may also be abundant around wetlands where the vegetation is protected from fire.

Johan Marais

A Flap-neck Chameleon shedding its skin.

> ### EYE MOVEMENT IN CHAMELEONS
>
> Most lizards are capable of focusing each of their eyes on a different object simultaneously, but chameleons have mastered this. Each eye can scan almost 180°, and the only blind spots are close up, immediately above and below the body. The brain deals with the two vastly different images by switching between them rapidly, concentrating on the image from each eye for about a second before moving to the other. Chameleons have much more acute vision than do humans.

SPECIES IN THE GROUP

■ Flap-neck Chameleon: *Chamaeleo dilepis*

Namaqua Chameleon

The species *Chamaeleo namaquensis*
1 species

Description

This group includes a single species of large chameleon that is quite unmistakable in its appearance. It has a maximum body length of 160 mm. The tail is short – about two thirds the length of the body – and much less prehensile than that of most other chameleon species. It is often carried fully extended, especially when the animal is on the ground. These chameleons have a very robust body and head, giving them an almost bulbous appearance. The most striking characteristic is the row of large, knob-like tubercles on the ridge that runs the length of the back. Viewed from the side, these tubercles give the back a zigzag outline and give the chameleon the appearance of a small dragon or dinosaur from a children's story book. The eyes, well-developed legs and grasping feet are all typically chameleon-like. Coloration is generally beige or olive-brown to reddish, often with black spots scattered over the entire body. When stressed, Namaqua Chameleons can turn almost completely black and will open the mouth to expose the yellow lining.

Biology

Despite the fact that its grasping feet and legs appear perfectly suited for a life in trees, the Namaqua Chameleon spends much of its time on the ground, moving between shrubs in its sparsely vegetated habitat. Namaqua Chameleons are also surprisingly

Johan Marais

The Namaqua Chameleon spends much of its time on the ground or in low bushes.

accomplished at running and can be difficult to catch. However, they typically move more slowly on the ground as they patrol for food. They are also known to ambush prey from perches in small shrubs. Out of necessity, they eat a wide variety of prey and will attempt to turn anything small enough into a meal. The most common prey items are beetles, especially tenebrionid beetles which are plentiful in the chameleon's habitat, although they also prey on locusts, lizards and small snakes. During times of plenty, Namaqua Chameleons gorge themselves, laying down fat reserves to see them through periods when food is scarce. They are thought to be territorial and will usually fight vigorously when they meet other members of the species. The Namaqua Chameleon is found in warm environments and shows adaptations that prevent overheating. The most obvious of these is the use of orientation: the chameleon will face the sun during the hottest part of the day, presenting the minimum surface area to the warming rays, or it will climb into a low shrub to avoid the hot ground.

Namaqua Chameleons occur in the arid, western parts of southern Africa in habitat that is not conventionally considered suitable for chameleons.

The Namaqua Chameleon can be identified by the presence of a series of knob-like tubercles on the ridge that runs the length of the back.

Reproduction

Males are usually smaller than females and are, therefore, forced to cling to the female's side during mating. About 20 eggs (measuring 20 x 13 mm) are laid in each clutch, with up to three clutches being laid per year. Incubation time depends on temperature, resulting in winter eggs taking longer to hatch (about 115 days) than summer eggs (about 90 days). In a similar fashion to Flap-neck Chameleons, the eggs are laid in a hole dug by the female at the base of a shrub. Eggs are deposited in layers, the female covering each layer with soil before depositing the next batch. When the entire clutch has been laid, the hole is filled and the surface patted down carefully. The hatchlings dig themselves out during the night, thereby avoiding high daytime temperatures.

Distribution

The Namaqua Chameleon is restricted to the western parts of southern Africa and occurs in arid scrub vegetation and coastal dunes. Its range extends from Little Namaqualand and nama karoo in the south, northwards into Namibia, where it is widely distributed in the western and southern parts, and northwards into southern Angola.

SPECIES IN THE GROUP

■ Namaqua Chameleon: *Chamaeleo namaquensis*

MONITORS
Family: Varanidae

These lizards are confined to the Old World and are found throughout Australia, where species richness is highest, and in Southeast Asia and Africa (excluding Madagascar). The single genus, *Varanus*, includes about 59 known species. The two species that occur in southern Africa are easily the largest lizards in the subregion. The neck is long and the tongue is deeply forked and snake-like. The eyes are well developed with round pupils, and the eyelids are movable. Ear openings are distinct. Monitor lizards are robust, with well-developed legs and a strong, recurved claw on each digit. Scales on the head are small and do not overlap. The scales on the dorsal part of the body are rounded and may be raised, and those on the ventral surface are more rectangular and are arranged in transverse rows. The laterally compressed tail is generally much longer than the body. It cannot be shed or regenerated, but is used as a whip in self-defence. Monitor lizards inhabit a wide variety of habitats, including aquatic, terrestrial and arboreal. All monitors lay eggs.

Johan Marais

Monitors are large, alert, active lizards that have snake-like forked tongues.

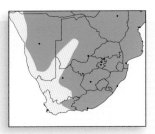

Rock Monitor

The species *Varanus albigularis*
1 species

Description

This is the second-largest species of lizard in southern Africa, reaching a body length of about 800 mm. The tail is a little longer than the body and is laterally compressed, but is more cylindrical than that of the Water Monitor (*Varanus niloticus*). The head is distinct from the neck, and the neck is about as long as the head. The snout is bulbous and convex, giving the head an angular, box-like appearance. In this respect, it differs markedly from the slender snout of the Water Monitor. The tongue is pink or bluish, and forked like that of a snake. Eyes are well developed, with scaly movable eyelids, and the nostrils are slit-like and backward facing, situated between the tip of the snout and the eyes, but nearer the eyes. The oval-shaped tympanum is situated far back on the head and is about the same size as the eyes. The Rock Monitor's body is covered with bead-like, granular scales, and those on the tail may be slightly keeled. Legs are strong and muscular and each of the toes has a strong prominent, curved claw that is used for digging and defence.

Colour is generally a dirty brown, but can range from beige to greyish brown. Light beige spots form about five crossbars over the back. The beige spots are larger on the flanks of the body and coalesce to form large blotches. The ventral surface is more or less uniform beige. About nine beige bars cross the tail. The sides of the head and neck are beige with brown spots. The patterning in large Rock Monitors tends to become more drab with age, and some individuals appear almost uniform brown.

Biology

These lizards are primarily terrestrial but will often climb trees and may spend a large proportion of their time on rocky outcrops. They

The Rock Monitor can be distinguished from the Water Monitor by its bulbous, convex snout.

Graham Alexander

are diurnal, active foragers and can cover considerable distances on long, rambling patrols in search of food. They feed primarily on invertebrates, especially beetles and millipedes, but they will also eat snakes, lizards, small tortoises, rodents, birds, eggs and carrion. They usually have a retreat in a rock fissure, a hole in a tree, or in a termitarium. Rock Monitors defend themselves by biting, scratching and lashing out with the tail. Although tail lashing looks impressive, it produces little more than a stinging sensation and is incapable of breaking skin or bone. However, their bite is powerful and they tend to hold on for a considerable time. Although the teeth are relatively small, they are easily capable of breaking through skin. The claws are also very effective in defence. When all else fails, Rock Monitors will sham death.

Although wild-caught adult Rock Monitors rarely tame in captivity, hatchlings raised in captivity become exceptionally tame and make good pets. Some tamed individuals will feed from the hand. They are long-lived and relatively slow-growing.

Rock Monitors regularly climb trees and may bask several metres above the ground.

Conservation

The skin and fat of Rock Monitors are used in the muti trade, and the skin used to be highly prized in the leather industry. Because of these threats, it was listed in the first Reptile Red Data Book in South Africa. However, it is widely distributed and abundant and has been taken off the Red List. It remains on CITES Appendix II.

Reproduction

Clutches usually number 10–40 eggs, although clutches of over 50 have been recorded. The soft-shelled eggs are about 60 x 35 mm and are laid in a hole dug by the female in a carefully selected site. She then covers them with soil, filling the hole. Incubation can take more than 10 months.

Distribution

The Rock Monitor is widely distributed in the savannas and arid parts of southern Africa, occurring over much of Namibia, Botswana, Zimbabwe and southern Mozambique. It is found widely in South Africa, and is excluded only from the Western Cape and Namaqualand. There is some evidence of recent range extension in the Northern Cape.

Juvenile Rock Monitors are more vividly marked than adults.

SPECIES IN THE GROUP

■ Rock Monitor: *Varanus albigularis*

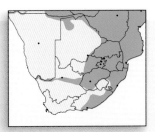

Water Monitor

The species *Varanus niloticus*
1 species

Description

This is the largest species of lizard in southern Africa, reaching a body length just short of a metre, excluding the tail. The laterally compressed tail is about 1.5 times the length of the body. The head is reasonably distinct from the neck, which is about twice as long as the head. The snout is elongated, tends to be concave dorsally, and is more pointed and slender than that of the Rock Monitor (*Varanus albigularis*). The tongue is forked and dark, and looks very much like that of a snake. The eyes are well developed, with scaly, movable eyelids. Nostrils are round and obvious, and are situated between the tip of the snout and the eyes, slightly closer to the tip of the snout. The tympanum is large, almost round in shape, and is situated far back on the head. Bead-like, granular scales cover the body. Those on the posterior half of the tail are weakly keeled, whereas all other scales are smooth. Legs are strong and muscular, and each toe has a strong, prominent, curved claw.

Water Monitors are generally dark, ranging from almost black to grey or dirty brown. Yellow spots form about eight crossbars over the dorsal parts of the body and coalesce to form yellow blotches ventrally. About a dozen yellow bars cross the tail, and the head is also intricately patterned with yellow. Large Water Monitors tend to become more drab with age, with the contrasting black and yellow fading to shades of brown and beige. However, some individuals retain the striking patterning into adulthood.

Although the body coloration of adult Water Monitors may become duller with age, their markings are usually more vivid than those of Rock Monitors.

Johan Marais

Johan Marais

Juvenile Monitors are vividly marked.

Johan Marais

Water Monitors are capable diggers and will raid nests, such as this terrapin nest, for the eggs..

Biology

Water Monitors are terrestrial, semi-aquatic lizards that are usually found close to water. They are active foragers and may venture some distance away from water in their search for food, but they are most often seen basking along riverbanks. These monitors are accomplished climbers and will often bask on branches overhanging water; if disturbed they will launch themselves into the water, sometimes from a considerable height. Water Monitors are consummate swimmers, propelling themselves with lateral undulations of the tail in a style very similar to that of a crocodile. When swimming, the legs are adpressed to the sides of the body and play no part in propulsion. In the face of danger, they can swim underwater for considerable distances and time. They are not selective feeders and will eat almost anything that they can overpower,

including frogs, crabs, invertebrates, lizards, snakes, birds and small mammals. They are notorious for raiding poultry houses and stealing eggs and young chickens. These lizards also raid crocodile nests and can be responsible for high rates of egg loss for tortoises and turtles. In the face of danger, Water Monitors defend themselves vigorously by biting and scratching. Like Rock Monitors, Water Monitors lash their tails in defence. Tail lashing is relatively inoffensive in comparison to the bite, which is powerful and can be maintained as a vice-like hold for a considerable time while the claws are used to rake the attacker. The teeth are not particularly sharp, especially in adults, but are easily capable of breaking skin and causing bruising. When all else fails, they resort to shamming death, but are more reluctant to resort to this behaviour than are Rock Monitors.

Conservation

Like the Rock Monitor, the Water Monitor's skin and fat are used in the muti trade, and the skin is used in the leather industry. The species was listed in South Africa's first Reptile Red Data Book, but it is widely distributed and abundant, and has subsequently been removed from the Red List. It remains on CITES Appendix II.

Reproduction

The female excavates a hole in an active termitarium, and lays 40–60 soft-shelled eggs, each about 50 x 35 mm in size. In their efforts to repair the damage, the termites seal the eggs in, inadvertently providing a humid, warm environment and protecting the eggs from predation. Incubation is slow, even by reptile standards, usually taking 9–10 months. The hatchlings dig themselves out of the nest.

Distribution

Largely limited to the eastern half of southern Africa, but extending west along the Orange River and into the Okavango system. It occurs over most of Zimbabwe and Mozambique, but is limited to the eastern extremes of Botswana. In South Africa, Water Monitors occur throughout Limpopo, Mpumalanga and KwaZulu-Natal provinces, and into the Eastern Cape and Free State. Water Monitors have recently established a feral population in Florida, USA, as a result of the escape or release of pet monitors.

Water Monitors frequently bask on branches, often above open water.

Water Monitors are generalist carnivores and will eat a wide variety of prey.

SPECIES IN THE GROUP

- Water Monitor: *Varanus niloticus*

LACERTIDS
Family Lacertidae

Lacertids are restricted to Asia, Europe and Africa, with the highest species richness in Africa and Europe. Three species have been introduced into North America. The two subfamilies include a total of 31 genera and more than 279 species. Thirty-seven species occur in southern Africa, but current research suggests the existence of several cryptic species, and the count is likely to increase in the future. Most species of lacertids have small, granular dorsal scales and large, rectangular ventral scales arranged in regular transverse and longitudinal rows. The head scales are large and symmetrical. The limbs are always well developed and the tail is usually much longer than the body. The tail can be shed and regenerates rapidly. Most species are terrestrial, although some are rock-living or arboreal. All southern African species lay eggs.

Johar Marais

Most species of lacertids, such as this Spotted Desert Lizard, have small, granular dorsal scales on the body and large, symmetrical head scales.

Sand Lizards and related species

The genera *Heliobolus, Meroles, Nucras* and *Pedioplanis*
27 species

Description

Members of this group all have a similar build and lifestyle. They
include the Bushveld Lizard, seven species of Desert Lizard, eight
species of Sandveld Lizard, and 11 species of Sand Lizard. All have
well-developed legs, especially the hind legs, with long toes, and
most species are built for speed. Some of the Sandveld Lizards,
however, have a more serpentine build, slightly smaller legs and are
not quite as speedy as other members of the group. The adult body
length (excluding tail) averages 55 mm but varies among species,
ranging from 35 to 110 mm. The head is distinct from the body and
a well-defined collar crosses the throat. This collar is a fold of skin
that gives the appearance of a cut across the neck. The eyes are well
developed, with movable eyelids, and the tail is longer than the
body. As with many other lizards in this family, the back has a matt
skin with small granular scales that do not overlap. This gives the
skin a dry, slightly wrinkly appearance. The belly scales are larger,
fairly shiny and arranged in longitudinal rows.

Coloration and pattern vary among species, but most have
a certain degree of camouflage and blend in with the terrain
where they occur. In fact, coloration appears to vary from one
population to the next within the same species, probably because
each population evolves colours that match the substrate where
it is found. Most of the species have some degree of longitudinal
striping and spotting, which further aids in camouflaging them. The

*The Shovel-snouted
Lizard lives on sand
dunes and uses its
snout for burrowing
in the loose sand.*

Johan Marais

Johan Marais

Spotted Desert Lizards wait in concealed positions for passing insect prey.

belly scales are usually white or cream. The sexes exhibit only minor differences in coloration. Most species have a fairly sharp or pointed snout, particularly so in the Shovel-snouted Lizard, which is a desert sand dune specialist endemic to the Namib Desert. However, some of the Sandveld Lizards have well-rounded, blunt snouts. The blunt snouted species also tend to be more brightly coloured and some, such as the Spotted Sandveld Lizard and the Western Sandveld Lizard, have striking black-and-white patterning on their anterior half, and a plain red posterior.

Biology

These lizards are terrestrial, diurnal reptiles. Many are active foragers, patrolling in search of prey. Other species are ambush foragers, darting out from concealed positions under bushes or rocks to catch passing prey. Most species dig holes at the base of bushes or under rocks and remain in well-defined home ranges, with which they become very familiar. Their speed and familiarity with their home range makes them very difficult to catch, but individuals translocated into a neighbour's territory are much less able to

Johan Marais

Smith's Desert Lizard is found only on semi-stable dunes of coastal southern Namibia and Namaqualand.

avoid capture in unfamiliar surroundings. Species that live in mobile sand dunes do not excavate burrows but will dive into and swim through the loose sand to avoid predators, escape the heat or sleep. Most Sand Lizards occur in hot, dry environments and some are known to allow their body temperatures to reach almost 40 °C. They are able to tolerate temperatures of 44 °C, which would easily kill many other reptiles.

The Shovel-snouted Lizard is renowned for characteristically lifting opposite feet alternately in what appears to be a comical dance but serves to avoid prolonged contact of each foot with the hot surface. Similar behaviours are shown by the Desert Plated Lizard and by some Typical Skinks, but the 'dance' is not nearly as ritualized in these other species. Daily activity patterns also show adaptation to hot environments: during the summer months, lizards are most active during the early morning and

Sandveld Lizards, such as Delalande's Sandveld Lizard, are longer and more serpentine in body form than other lacertids.

The Ornate Sandveld Lizard occurs in the northeastern parts of southern Africa.

The Western Sandveld Lizard has striking black-and-white patterning on its anterior half, with a plain red posterior.

late afternoon (bimodal activity pattern); in winter they are active during midday. Although the diet of these lizards typically includes most invertebrates that are small enough to overpower (adult and larval beetles, termites, grasshoppers, scorpions, spiders, cockroaches), species that are desert specialists are known to eat vegetable matter such as grass seeds. The larger species are also known to eat other small lizards. Although these lizards can shed their tail, this only happens when it is actually grasped by a predator. The tails do regenerate. Hatchling Bushveld Lizards have very different colours from the adults, a black body with white spots and a brown tail that blends with the substrate, whereas adults are typically brown with stripes. The coloration and very unusual stiff-legged walk of juveniles suggests that they mimic Oogpister Beetles (*Anthia*), which are able to deliver a nasty bite and squirt formic acid up to 350 mm when threatened. The young Bushveld Lizards' mimicry is thought to provide them with some measure of protection from predators.

Reproduction

Lizards in this group lay 1–9 soft-shelled eggs, usually during the summer months. Reproduction may be unseasonal in some species, especially desert species, such as the Wedge-snouted Desert Lizard, which appears to respond proximally to rainfall.

The Spotted Sand Lizard is the most abundant and widely distributed Sand Lizard in southern Africa.

Like other Sand Lizards, the Namaqua Sand Lizard is diurnal and retreats to its burrow during the night.

The Plain Sand Lizard is restricted to the extreme northwestern parts of South Africa and southern Namibia.

Juvenile Bushveld Lizards protect themselves from predators by mimicking Oogpister Beetles.

Eggs are laid in burrows excavated under rocks, at the base of dunes or under bushes. Several clutches may be produced in one season. Growth is rapid in some species, with juveniles reaching adult size in a matter of months, but can be much slower in others, with juveniles taking up to three years to reach maturity. Active-foraging species usually have faster growth rates than ambush foragers.

Distribution

These lizards typically inhabit arid, sandy areas and many species are limited to the western part of southern Africa. Up to five species can be found at some localities, where they may be the dominant diurnal lizards. Species inhabit savanna, desert dunes, desert flats, gravel plains and fynbos. Delalande's Sandveld Lizard, Burchell's Sand Lizard and the Cape Sand Lizard occur in grasslands in the southeastern parts of southern Africa.

SPECIES IN THE GROUP

- Bushveld Lizard: *Heliobolus lugubris*
- Knox's Desert Lizard: *Meroles knoxii*
- Reticulated Desert Lizard: *Meroles reticulatus*
- Shovel-snouted Lizard: *Meroles anchietae*
- Small-scaled Desert Lizard: *Meroles micropholidotus*
- Smith's Desert Lizard: *Meroles ctenodactylus*
- Spotted Desert Lizard: *Meroles suborbitalis*
- Wedge-snouted Desert Lizard: *Meroles cuneirostris*
- Blue-tailed Sandveld Lizard: *Nucras caesicaudata*
- Delalande's Sandveld Lizard: *Nucras lalandii*
- Holub's Sandveld Lizard: *Nucras holubi*
- Karoo Sandveld Lizard: *Nucras livida*

- Ornate Sandveld Lizard: *Nucras ornata*
- Spotted Sandveld Lizard: *Nucras intertexta*
- Striped Sandveld Lizard: *Nucras taeniolata*
- Western Sandveld Lizard: *Nucras tessellata*
- Angolan Sand Lizard: *Pedioplanis benguellensis*
- Burchell's Sand Lizard: *Pedioplanis burchelli*
- Cape Sand Lizard: *Pedioplanis laticeps*
- Husab Sand Lizard: *Pedioplanis husabensis*
- Kaokoveld Sand Lizard: *Pedioplanis gaerdesi*
- Namaqua Sand Lizard: *Pedioplanis namaquensis*
- Plain Sand Lizard: *Pedioplanis inornata*
- Short-headed Sand Lizard: *Pedioplanis breviceps*
- Spotted Sand Lizard: *Pedioplanis lineoocellata*
- Waterberg Sand Lizard: *Pedioplanis rubens*
- Western Sand Lizard: *Pedioplanis undata*

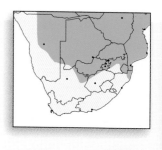

Rough-scaled Lizards

The genus *Ichnotropis*
3 species

Description

This is a small group of lizards, with only three species occurring in southern Africa. Although Rough-scaled Lizards have a similar build and size to Sand Lizards, they differ in three easily discernible characteristics: they lack a collar across the neck, the head scales are rough and they have fairly large, spiny, overlapping scales on the back. As with Sand Lizards, the eyelids are movable and scaly. Body length is 50–70 mm in adults. The tail is long and usually exceeds the body length.

Coloration differs markedly among the species: the Cape Rough-scaled Lizard has striking markings and colours, with a coppery back and black stripes down the flanks, extending onto the tail. The dark stripes are white-edged and there may be some reddish brown blotches just above the black stripes. The belly is usually white in all species, but the chin and throat of breeding Cape Rough-scaled Lizard males can become a bright yellow. The Cape Rough-scaled Lizard does not generally exceed 60 mm in body length. Although the Caprivi Rough-scaled Lizard has similar patterning to the Cape Rough-scaled Lizard, it lacks the white edging to the black stripes and is larger, reaching a body length (excluding tail) of 70 mm. The coloration and patterning of the Common Rough-scaled Lizard are similar to those of the Sand Lizards, with three indistinct longitudinal light stripes from snout to tail. Dark brown spots on a sandy-brown background occur next to the light stripes and form a patchwork pattern on the dorsum.

Graham Alexander

Rough-scaled Lizards, such as this Common Rough-scaled Lizard, have rough head scales and spiny dorsal scales on the body.

Biology

Rough-scaled Lizards are terrestrial, highly active and fast-moving. They tend to live in well-drained, sandy areas where grass is sparse. They dig holes at the base of grass tussocks or trees and retreat into these burrows at night or when temperatures are not suitable for activity. During the winter, activity levels peak at midday. In summer these lizards retreat into their burrows during the midday heat and are active mainly during the morning and, to a lesser extent, in the cooler afternoons. They will also retreat to their burrows when they perceive danger. When active, Rough-scaled Lizards search for prey by patrolling their home ranges and actively hunting. Prey includes most invertebrates that are small enough to overpower, especially termites. The Cape Rough-scaled Lizard and Common Rough-scaled Lizard are fast-growing and have

short lifespans, with most individuals living for less than a year. Where these species occur together, staggered life cycles (see *Reproduction*, below) ensure that adults of the two species never occur in the same area at the same time. It has been argued that this staggering of life cycles is an adaptation to reduce competition for food, but this has not been unequivocally demonstrated. In any event, these lizards often occur together with other species of Sand Lizards that have longer lifespans and prey on the same food items. The Caprivi Rough-scaled Lizard does not appear to be an annual species, though not much is known about its life history due to its rarity and restricted distribution.

Reproduction

All species produce 3–12 soft-shelled eggs in a clutch. More than one clutch may be laid in any one season. The female excavates a

Marius Burger

The Common Rough-scaled Lizard is found in sandy areas, and is active and fast-moving.

Marius Burger

Cape Rough-scaled Lizards mate in spring and lay eggs in summer.

burrow about 100 mm deep into which the eggs are laid and then covered with sand. The Cape Rough-scaled Lizard lays eggs from November to December and the hatchlings emerge from January to February. The Common Rough-scaled Lizard lays eggs from April to May and the hatchlings emerge from October to November.

Distribution

Rough-scaled Lizards are restricted mainly to savanna and are, therefore, limited to the northern parts of southern Africa, including the northeastern parts of Namibia, Botswana, Zimbabwe and Mozambique. In South Africa, Rough-scaled Lizards occur in North West, northeastern Northern Cape, Limpopo, Gauteng and Mpumalanga provinces. The Cape Rough-scaled Lizard occurs down the South African east coast, reaching its southern limits on the north coast of Durban in KwaZulu-Natal. The Caprivi Rough-scaled Lizard is restricted to the western Caprivi Strip, northeastern Ovamboland and the northwestern extremes of Botswana.

Bill Branch

The Cape Rough-scaled Lizard has a coppery back and black stripes down the flanks, extending onto the tail.

SPECIES IN THE GROUP

- Cape Rough-scaled Lizard: *Ichnotropis capensis*
- Caprivi Rough-scaled Lizard: *Ichnotropis grandiceps*
- Common Rough-scaled Lizard: *Ichnotropis squamulosa*

Mountain Lizards

The genus *Tropidosaura*
4 species

Description

Four species of Mountain Lizard are currently recognized, all of which are endemic to southern Africa, but the taxonomy is under review. Mountain Lizards are similar in build to Rough-scaled Lizards, but tend to have slightly smaller legs and a more cylindrical body form. Adult body length varies from about 52 mm to 66 mm, and the long, cylindrical tail exceeds the body length. The head is noticeably short, and the neck usually has an indistinct gular fold. However, the gular fold may be completely absent or indiscernible in certain individuals. The enlarged scales on the head are relatively smooth. The tympanum is obvious and exposed, with the lower edge of the oval in line with the jawline. The eyelids are movable and scaly. The body is covered with rough, spiny, overlapping scales that give the lizards a particularly rough appearance. The Common Mountain Lizard has keeled scales on the sides of the neck, but these are granular in the other Mountain Lizards.

Coloration tends to be quite dull above, with about five pale stripes running from the head onto the tail. Stripes may be spotty and diffuse in the Cape Mountain Lizard and relatively indistinct in Cottrell's Mountain Lizard. Various bright colours such as red, yellow, orange and blue may be infused in the stripes, especially in the lateral and ventral parts of breeding males. Although the head tends to be the same olive-greenish background colour of the body, it may include some bluish green and brown spots. The belly is bluish with dark edges to the scales in most species, but in the Common Mountain Lizard it is greenish white with dark spots. The tail is green-blue.

Mountain Lizards, such as this Common Mountain Lizard, have rough scales on the body and enlarged, relatively smooth scales on the head.

Johan Marais

Essex's Mountain Lizard occurs in montane grasslands of northern and southern Lesotho, extending marginally into South Africa.

Biology

Very little is known about the habits and biology of Mountain Lizards. They appear to be mainly terrestrial, living among rocks and heather in mountainous areas and sometimes on mountain summits. Fynbos and mountain grassland appear to be the favoured vegetation types, and the lizards will use the vegetation as cover and basking sites. Some species dig shallow holes under rocks, which are used as retreats during the night and when the lizards are under threat. Most of the species are shy and retiring, but they are fond of basking and do so even when air temperatures are low.

Cape Mountain Lizards are primarily terrestrial, living among rocks and heather in mountainous areas.

The Cape Mountain Lizard is restricted to the Cape Fold mountains, extending as far east as Port Elizabeth.

Yellow spots on the flanks of male Common Mountain Lizards become bright orange during the breeding season.

Reproduction

It is likely that all Mountain Lizards lay eggs. The few existing records indicate that 2–8 eggs are laid early in summer in holes dug in the ground or under rocks.

Distribution

Mountain Lizards are endemic to South Africa. As their name suggests, they are restricted to mountainous areas and are limited to the Cape Fold Mountains in the south, the Amatola Mountains in the Eastern Cape, and the Drakensberg escarpment and foothills in KwaZulu-Natal, Eastern Cape and the Free State of South Africa. Because Mountain Lizards are limited to mountaintops, populations tend to be isolated from each other.

Cottrell's Mountain Lizard is restricted to the eastern parts of Lesotho and adjacent South Africa.

The Cape Mountain Lizard is restricted to the Cape Fold Mountains, extending as far east as Port Elizabeth.

SPECIES IN THE GROUP

- Cape Mountain Lizard: *Tropidosaura gularis*
- Common Mountain Lizard: *Tropidosaura montana*
- Cottrell's Mountain Lizard: *Tropidosaura cottrelli*
- Essex's Mountain Lizard: *Tropidosaura essexi*

AMPHISBAENIANS
Family: Amphisbaenidae

These unusual worm-like lizards have a soft skin that forms numerous rings or annuli around the legless body. They are distributed throughout much of Africa, Turkey, the Arabian and Iberian peninsulas, South and Central America, Florida and the Caribbean. Historically, amphisbaenians were classed as lizards, but were subsequently placed in a separate suborder within the Squamata named the Amphisbaenia. However, recent molecular evidence has revealed a close relationship between amphisbeanians and lacertid lizards, and they are, therefore, now considered to be highly specialized, burrowing lizards. Internally, members of the Amphisbaenidae show many derived characteristics that include a reduced right lung, a unique middle ear, vestigial eyes and backward-pointing nostrils. All African amphisbeanians are elongate, cylindrical and legless. The annuli that cover the body are made up of smooth, square scales (two annuli for each vertebra of the body). The skin is loosely attached to the body and can move independently of the trunk, an adaptation that facilitates burrowing. Most species are medium to small, and they generally feed on invertebrates. Some species lay eggs, but others appear to give birth to live young. Four of the 18 genera and 17 of the 154 species occur in southern Africa.

Marius Burger

Amphisbaenians are elongate, cylindrical and legless and superficially resemble earthworms.

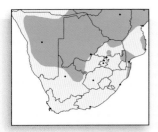

Round-headed Worm Lizards

The genera *Chirindia* and *Zygaspis*
7 species

Description

This group consists of seven species of small Worm Lizards that have slender bodies with distinct annuli and round snouts. Body length varies from 140 to 280 mm. The tail is short in comparison to the body and is bluntly rounded at the end. Although the tail can be shed, it does not regenerate. Lang's Round-headed Worm Lizard and Swynnerton's Round-headed Worm Lizard have highly fused head scales. Eyes may appear as dark spots under the skin or may not be evident.

Coloration is usually fairly uniform and may vary from pink to dark brown, purple-brown, or purple above and pale below. Colours may become darker towards the tail. The Black Round-headed Worm Lizard has variegated scales that are primarily black on the dorsal parts and white below.

Biology

Round-headed Worm Lizards are rarely found and are consequently very poorly known. They tend to be found under stones, logs or other debris in sandy or humic soils. The Ferocious Round-headed Worm Lizard is reputed to bite when handled. Their diet includes ants, termites and other small insects.

Reproduction

Few data exist on reproduction, but clutches appear to be small, numbering from 1–4 very elongate eggs.

Round-headed Worm Lizards, such as this Kalahari Round-headed Worm Lizard, have blunt heads and vestigial eyes that appear as spots beneath the skin.

Marius Burger

Van Dam's Round-headed Worm Lizards may be found under stones in sandy areas.

Distribution

Round-headed Worm Lizards are limited mainly to the northern half of southern Africa. Most species are restricted to small distributions in the northern and northeastern extremes of South Africa, the eastern extremes of Zimbabwe, and Mozambique. The Kalahari Round-headed Worm Lizard occurs more widely and is found throughout the central eastern parts of Namibia, Botswana, the northern parts of central South Africa, Zimbabwe and parts of Mozambique.

Round-headed Worm Lizards, such as this Black Round-headed Worm Lizard, are often mistaken for earthworms.

Like other members in this group, the Kalahari Round-headed Worm Lizard has an obvious jaw and nostrils, and an internal skeleton.

SPECIES IN THE GROUP

- Lang's Round-headed Worm Lizard: *Chirindia langi*
- Swynnerton's Round-headed Worm Lizard: *Chirindia swynnertoni*
- Black Round-headed Worm Lizard: *Zygaspis nigra*
- Ferocious Round-headed Worm Lizard: *Zygaspis ferox*
- Kalahari Round-headed Worm Lizard: *Zygaspis quadrifrons*
- Van Dam's Round-headed Worm Lizard: *Zygaspis vandami*
- Violet Round-headed Worm Lizard: *Zygaspis violacea*

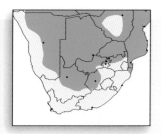

Spade-snouted Worm Lizards

The genera *Monopeltis* and *Dalophia*
10 species

Description

The 10 species in this group have hard, horizontal, nail-like snouts that are covered with one or two horny scales. Spade-snouted Worm Lizards are relatively large, ranging from 285 to 560 mm in body length. The body is cylindrical with distinct annuli and four to six enlarged, rectangular pectoral scales on the throat. The tail is very short in comparison to the body, has a rounded tip and cannot be shed. Tails of the Blunt-tailed Worm Lizard and Long-tailed Worm Lizard have a terminal pad. Body coloration varies from pink to whitish pink or reddish brown, sometimes with grey or brown speckles or blotches on the back. The ventral parts are usually pink.

Biology

Spade-snouted Worm Lizards are capable of burrowing in hard soils and may be abundant in certain habitats. These reptiles feed on termites and beetles.

Reproduction

The Cape Spade-snouted Worm Lizard gives birth to 1–3 young. Clutches of 4 eggs have been recorded in the Blunt-tailed Worm Lizard.

Distribution

Spade-snouted Worm Lizards are found mainly in the northern half of southern Africa. The Cape Spade-snouted Worm Lizard extends south into the western parts of the Free State province of South Africa, while the Dusky Spade-snouted Worm Lizard extends south on the Kalahari sand deposits in the Northern Cape province.

Spade-snouted Worm Lizards, such as this Cape Spade-snouted Worm Lizard, are easily identified by the hard, horny scales that cover the snout.

Johan Marais

The Slender Spade-snouted Worm Lizard occurs in deep alluvial sands over much of Botswana, northeastern Namibia and coastal Mozambique.

The Cape Spade-snouted Worm Lizard is found in the central northern parts of South Africa, extending marginally into eastern Botswana.

SPECIES IN THE GROUP

- Anchieta's Spade-snouted Worm Lizard: *Monopeltis anchietae*
- Cape Spade-snouted Worm Lizard: *Monopeltis capensis*
- De Coster's Spade-snouted Worm Lizard: *Monopeltis decosteri*
- Dusky Spade-snouted Worm Lizard: *Monopeltis infuscata*
- Kalahari Spade-snouted Worm Lizard: *Monopeltis leonhardi*
- Slender Spade-snouted Worm Lizard: *Monopeltis sphenorhynchus*
- Zambezi Spade-snouted Worm Lizard: *Monopeltis zambezensis*
- Zimbabwe Spade-snouted Worm Lizard: *Monopeltis rhodesiana*
- Blunt-tailed Worm Lizard: *Dalophia pistillum*
- Long-tailed Worm Lizard: *Dalophia longicauda*

SKINKS
Family: Scincidae

Most species of skink are terrestrial, rock-living or fossorial in habit, and are gener-ally diurnal and extremely active. Many of the fossorial or semi-fossorial species have undergone limb reduction to the extent that several have lost external evidence of limbs altogether. The skinks are essentially cosmopolitan, but the highest species richness occurs in Australia, southern Asia and Africa. They also occur on many islands in the Indian Ocean. A total of 127 genera and more than 1 305 species occur worldwide. They are second only to the geckos in species richness in southern Africa, with 10 genera and 74 species currently described. Skinks have tight-fitting, overlap-ping, shiny scales. The head is not usually distinct from the neck and is covered with large, symmetrical head scales. These features and the cylindrical body result in a robust body form that has proved to be ecologically successful, and skinks can be extremely abundant and speciose in some environments. Tails are easily shed and regenerated. Although some species lay eggs, many are live-bearing and some have even developed the skink equivalent of a placenta for nourishing the developing young. Most skinks feed on invertebrates, which are actively hunted.

Marius Burger

Skinks, such as this Montane Speckled Skink, generally have tight-fitting, overlapping shiny scales and a cylindrical body.

Legless Burrowing Skinks

The subfamily Acontinae (*Acontias*) and the genus *Typhlacontias* (Burrowing Skinks)
22 species

Description

This is a diverse group comprising 22 species of Legless Burrowing Skinks. Although the group includes some fairly distantly related species and does not form an inclusive taxonomic unit, all the members have a similar body form and lead a similar subterranean lifestyle. All have a large and obvious rostral scale on the snout. The rostral often differs slightly in colour from the rest of the head scales, and a groove in the rostral runs from the nostril to the posterior edge of the rostral scale. All of the species in this group lack any trace of external limbs, apart from FitzSimons' Burrowing Skink and the Speckled Burrowing Skink, which have tiny, rudimentary hind limbs. Most Legless Burrowing Skinks are fairly stout, but there are exceptions, such as Brain's Blind Legless Skink, which has a slim build. The tail is short and stubby and is only a fraction of the body length. Scales on the body are shiny, overlapping and tight fitting, and the head scales tend to be enlarged and often unpaired. There are no external ear openings. The body length of most species is 60–300 mm. However, the group also includes the largest Legless Skink, the Giant Legless Skink, which reaches a maximum length of 500 mm and has a particularly stocky build. Although most of the species have a blunt snout, Meyer's Blind Legless Skink has a sharp horizontal edge on the snout. Legless Skinks have conspicuous eyes with movable eyelids, but the eyes appear sunken and differ markedly from those of snakes. The eyes of the Woodbush Legless Skink and Blind Legless

Johan Marais

Many species of skink, such as this Coastal Legless Skink, lack any external trace of limbs.

Skinks are small and do not have movable eyelids; those of Burrowing Skinks are only rudimentary and appear as dark spots beneath the head scales.

Coloration varies among species: the body can be olive-brown, grey-brown, uniform black, yellow, yellow-white, creamy white or even pink. Body scales may be spotted or longitudinally striped.

Biology

They are sually found in fairly friable soil, under rocks and logs, or around the base of shrubs or grass tufts. Some species

Cape Legless Skink

Giant Legless Skink

Thin-tailed Legless Skink

Variable Legless Skink

Striped Blind Legless Skink

Boulenger's Blind Legless Skink

of Legless Skink are found in leaf litter and humus and can live in more moist conditions. Members of this group are found in a wide variety of vegetation types including montane grassland, highveld grassland, savanna, forest and semi-stable dunes. Not much is known about the diet of many of the species, but some will eat a wide variety of invertebrates including earthworms, termites, spiders, beetle larvae and centipedes. The Giant Legless Skink is even known to eat small burrowing reptiles and frogs. The Striped Blind Legless Skink has been observed feeding on surface-living insects, catching them by ambush from below. Species that live in dunes often leave symmetrical wavy tracks in the sand when moving just below the surface. Dune-living species and species that live in very sandy soils usually escape by burying themselves rapidly when unearthed. Species that live in more compact soils are usually slower moving. These species are also often forced to the surface after heavy rains because compact soils easily become waterlogged. The Giant Legless Skink is known to bask on the surface in the mornings and is often observed sunning itself on road sides. They are often misidentified as snakes, and killed.

Cuvier's Blind Legless Skink

Cregoi's Blind Legless Skink

Conservation

Woodbush Legless Skink and Lomi's Blind Legless Skink are both listed by the IUCN as 'Vulnerable' on account of their very restricted distributions, apparent rarity and, in the case of Lomi's Blind Legless Skink, possible impacts resulting from alluvial diamond mining in its habitat.

Reproduction

All species in the group are viviparous and most appear to give birth to 1–3 young in summer. The Giant Legless Skink has been recorded giving birth to as many as 14 young in a single litter. However, no information is available on reproduction for some of the rare species.

Brain's Blind Legless Skink

Golden Blind Legless Skink

Johan Marais

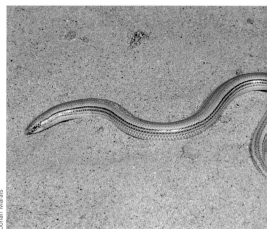

Johan Marais

The Striped Legless Skink closely resembles the Striped Blind Legless Skink.

The Speckled Burrowing Skink is found in sparsely vegetated desert in the northwestern extremes of Namibia.

Distribution

Overall, Legless Burrowing Skinks occur in most parts of southern Africa, but are not found over much of western Namibia, central Zimbabwe and Lesotho. In South Africa, they are excluded from the eastern Free State province, southern and western KwaZulu-Natal, and central North West province. For many species in the group, distribution appears to be limited primarily by soil type, resulting in many of the species' distributions being quite different from those of other species of reptiles, and many species of Legless Burrowing Skink have relatively small, patchy ranges. Because of the preference for sandy substrates, species of Blind Legless Skinks and Burrowing Skinks tend to be more prevalent along the west coast of southern Africa. Many of the Legless Skinks occur more widely in the interior; some appear to be associated with Kalahari sand deposits, but others are limited to high-lying areas.

SPECIES IN THE GROUP

- Cape Legless Skink: *Acontias meleagris*
- Giant Legless Skink: *Acontias plumbeus*
- Percival's Legless Skink: *Acontias percivali*
- Short-headed Legless Skink: *Acontias breviceps*
- Thin-tailed Legless Skink: *Acontias gracilicauda*
- Variable Legless Skink: *Acontias poecilus*
- Woodbush Legless Skink: *Acontophiops lineatus* VU
- Coastal Legless Skink: *Microacontias litoralis*
- Striped Legless Skink: *Microacontias lineatus*
- Boulenger's Blind Legless Skink: *Typhlosaurus vermis*
- Brain's Blind Legless Skink: *Typhlosaurus braini*
- Cregoi's Blind Legless Skink: *Typhlosaurus cregoi*
- Cuvier's Blind Legless Skink: *Typhlosaurus caecus*
- Gariep Blind Legless Skink: *Typhlosaurus gariepensis*
- Golden Blind Legless Skink: *Typhlosaurus aurantiacus*
- Lomi's Blind Legless Skink: *Typhlosaurus lomiae* VU
- Meyer's Blind Legless Skink: *Typhlosaurus meyer*
- Striped Blind Legless Skink: *Typhlosaurus lineatus*
- FitzSimons' Burrowing Skink: *Typhlacontias brevipes*
- Kalahari Burrowing Skink: *Typhlacontias rohani*
- Speckled Burrowing Skink: *Typhlacontias punctatissimus*
- Western Burrowing Skink: *Typhlacontias johnsonii*

Snake-eyed Skinks

The genus *Panaspis*
2 species

Description

Snake-eyed Skinks have small, cylindrical bodies with smooth, shiny scales. The body is usually about 50 mm long but only about 6 mm wide, and the tail may be slightly longer than the body. The legs are small and although each limb usually has five toes, some toes may be missing on some limbs. Lack of toes in some specimens may be genetically based, because it is very common in certain populations. The eyelids are permanently fused and the lower eyelid, which covers the eye, is transparent. Snake-eyed Skinks are therefore unable to blink, a characteristic they have in common with snakes and from which they derive their common name. Coloration and patterning vary geographically, according to species and sex, and also in response to the breeding season. Usually, the body is a coppery or golden brown. A broad, dark brown, white-edged stripe runs down each side of the body, from the tip of the snout to the tip of the tail. Often six fine, dark longitudinal lines run down the back, although the dorsum of some individuals is plain. Some individuals may also have dark spots on the sides of the neck, extending to the anterior part of the chest. Mating occurs between August and December, and during this time males develop a bright reddish orange colour on the neck and belly. The two species found in southern Africa are very similar in appearance and habit, and were in fact considered a single species until they were divided into two species in 2000, following a detailed taxonomic investigation. The two species are differentiated primarily by the shape of the scales under the feet. Wahlberg's Snake-eyed Skink usually has a white

Johan Marais

Snake-eyed Skinks, such as this Wahlberg's Snake-eyed Skink, have transparent eyelids that are permanently fused over the eye.

belly when not in breeding coloration. The Spotted-neck Snake-eyed Skink usually lacks the white edging of the lateral stripes, is usually smaller than Wahlberg's Snake-eyed Skink and has small white spots on each side of the neck.

Biology

Snake-eyed Skinks are generally found in leaf litter on the forest floor or in grass, especially in sandy areas. In certain regions, such as Durban, Snake-eyed Skinks are common in suburban gardens and utilize mown lawn and the mulch in flowerbeds.

Their body form is well adapted to these microhabitats, and the lizards can effectively 'swim' through the grass or leaf litter without much use of their limbs. Individuals with missing toes do not appear to be at any disadvantage in this regard and are as mobile as fully toed individuals. They are usually found under rocks, rotting logs or debris, and respond to being exposed by quickly darting into the undergrowth. Snake-eyed Skinks are active foragers and their diet includes most small invertebrates that are found in leaf litter, such as ants, termites, small woodlice and crickets.

Wahlberg's Snake-eyed Skinks are active foragers and feed on small invertebrates.

The Spotted-neck Snake-eyed Skink can be found in grass or leaf litter.

Wahlberg's Snake-eyed Skink has a broad, dark brown, white-edged stripe down each side of the body.

The Spotted-neck Snake-eyed Skink has white spots on the sides of the neck, which are diagnostic for the species.

Reproduction

Eggs, measuring about 4 x 8 mm, are laid in summer. These are soft-shelled and can number from 2 to 6 per clutch. Clutches are laid under logs or in leaf litter, and communal clutches that number more than 30 eggs are known. Incubation takes about one month, and hatchlings literally 'burst' out of their eggs and begin foraging almost immediately. Growth is rapid, and individuals mature within a year. They are also fairly short-lived, with a lifespan of about two years.

Distribution

They are restricted mainly to the northern and eastern parts of southern Africa. Usually only one of the two species occurs in any one area, but there are areas where they overlap, in Limpopo province and in the eastern parts of Zimbabwe. Wahlberg's Snake-eyed Skink is limited mainly to the northeastern parts of southern African, and the Spotted-neck Snake-eyed Skink is found mainly in the central north.

FUSED EYELIDS

Many species of lizard, including most of the geckos and all snakes, have fused eyelids. This means that the eyes are permanently closed and the eye 'sees' through a transparent lid. The evolution of fused eyelids may be for protection of the eyes, especially in species that live underground, or to reduce water loss from the body. In some lizard species that have movable eyelids, water loss across the eye accounts for more than 60% of the body's water loss.

SPECIES IN THE GROUP

- Spotted-neck Snake-eyed Skink: *Panaspis maculicollis*
- Wahlberg's Snake-eyed Skink: *Panaspis walbergii*

Legless Dwarf Burrowing Skinks

Legless and near-legless species of the genus *Scelotes*
10 species

Description

The 10 members of this group are all slender, legless (or have only minute hind leg buds) and small, ranging from 65 to 110 mm in body length. The tail is usually slightly shorter than the body, but may be slightly longer in the Mozambique Dwarf Burrowing Skink and FitzSimons' Dwarf Burrowing Skink. The body is cylindrical and is covered with polished, tight-fitting scales. The head is blunt, is not distinct from the neck and has a relatively square snout. The eyes are well developed with movable eyelids. Ear openings are usually absent and although FitzSimons' Dwarf Burrowing Skink, Mozambique Dwarf Burrowing Skink and Gronovi's Dwarf Burrowing Skink do have minute openings, these can only be seen under magnification. Tails are easily lost and regenerate quickly.

Body coloration is generally dominated by coppery or dark browns, and longitudinal stripes usually run the length of the body onto the anterior parts of the tail. Pale stripes are especially prominent in FitzSimons' Dwarf Burrowing Skink and the Mozambique Dwarf Burrowing Skink, running from the snout and fading slightly as they progress dorsolaterally along the body. Often, scales on the flanks or dorsal parts are individually flecked with black or dark brown spots, which can also give the impression of longitudinal striping. Gronovi's Dwarf Burrowing Skink is paler in coloration, with several rows of dark spots along the body and a dark stripe on either side of the head, through the eyes. There is blue on the tail of the Mozambique Dwarf Burrowing Skink and FitzSimons' Dwarf Burrowing Skink. The belly is usually pale.

Legless Dwarf Burrowing Skinks, such as this Smith's Dwarf Burrowing Skink, are slender and have polished, overlapping scales.

Johan Marais

The Zululand Dwarf Burrowing Skink occurs in coastal dunes, from southern Mozambique as far south as Lake Sibaya.

Biology

Legless Dwarf Burrowing Skinks require loose, friable sands in which to burrow. Locomotion is achieved by 'sand swimming' and these skinks appear to occur from the surface layers to a depth of about 200 mm. They are most often found at the sand surface under rocks, logs or debris, and make their escape by rapidly burrowing to deeper levels when exposed. Dependence on specific substrate types means that populations are easily isolated on islands of sand amid unsuitable, compact soils, and this natural fragmentation of substrates is the primary reason for the restricted ranges of many species. Although some species are extremely difficult to find, especially during the winter, population densities can be relatively high in localized habitat patches. The substrate at the forest edge appears to be ideal habitat, at least for some species such as Smith's Dwarf Burrowing Skink. This microhabitat offers sufficient shade as well as patches of sunshine, allowing skinks to regulate their body temperature in the leaf litter at the surface during the day. Generally, individuals appear to remain in relatively small home ranges, even over extended periods. Diet consists of small invertebrates such as woodlice, small crickets and termites, which may be hunted on the surface. It is likely that lifespan is relatively long and may exceed five years.

Conservation

Gronovi's Dwarf Burrowing Skink is listed by the IUCN as 'Near Threatened' on account of its restricted distribution. Günther's Dwarf Burrowing Skink is currently listed by the IUCN as 'Vulnerable', but deserves a higher threat rating since it is known only from one specimen that was collected in

The Mozambique Dwarf Burrowing Skink can be locally common in the sands and loamy soils of the KwaZulu-Natal north coast.

Bourquin's Dwarf Burrowing Skink is restricted to grasslands in the KwaZulu-Natal midlands.

'Port Natal' in 1886; it may even be extinct. The currently unlisted Smith's Dwarf Burrowing Skink should also be classified as threatened, because it is restricted to a small distribution along the coast around Durban and is undergoing range reduction due to urban development. Currently, only 3.6 km² of occupied habitat remain, and the species probably deserves a rating of 'Critically Endangered'. Its dependence on friable sand means that it cannot survive in areas with lawns where the grass roots impede locomotion, but small populations do appear to persist in flowerbeds. Urban development has also severely fragmented the range of Smith's Dwarf Burrowing Skink; even roadside curbing can act as an insurmountable barrier. The threat status of FitzSimons' Dwarf Burrowing Skink, Bourquin's Dwarf Burrowing Skink, the Coastal Dwarf Burrowing Skink and the Zululand Dwarf Burrowing Skink is also in need of evaluation.

FitzSimons' Dwarf Burrowing Skink is similar to the Mozambique Dwarf Burrowing Skink but lacks all traces of hind limbs.

Gronovi's Dwarf Burrowing Skink occurs in the southwestern Cape.

As is typical of Dwarf Burrowing Skinks, Smith's Dwarf Burrowing Skink gives birth to live young.

Reproduction

All the species for which data are available give birth to live young. Litter size varies from 2 to 5, and young are produced mainly in late summer. The young of Smith's Dwarf Burrowing Skink appear to take more than a year to reach sexual maturity.

Distribution

Legless Dwarf Burrowing Skinks are found in the eastern coastal areas of southern Africa, from the Algoa Basin in the Eastern Cape, northwards into Mozambique. Gronovi's Dwarf Burrowing Skink occurs in the southwestern Cape, from Doringbaai to Graafwater. The distributions of the individual species tend to be restricted, especially in the case of Smith's Dwarf Burrowing Skink, FitzSimons' Dwarf Burrowing Skink and Günther's Dwarf Burrowing Skink, all of which are found in or around Durban. FitzSimons' Dwarf Burrowing Skink is also found to the north as far as Kosi Bay. Up to three species may occur together on sand deposits along the Maputoland coast. The Bazarutu Dwarf Burrowing Skink is restricted to only the

islands of the Bazaruto Archipelago, while Gronovi's Dwarf Burrowing Skink is found on Dassen and Robben islands. It is likely that these insular populations originally gained access to these islands during times of lower sea level, when the islands were connected to the mainland.

SPECIES IN THE GROUP

- Algoa Dwarf Burrowing Skink: *Scelotes anguineus*
- Bazarutu Dwarf Burrowing Skink: *Scelotes insularis*
- Bourquin's Dwarf Burrowing Skink: *Scelotes bourquini*
- Coastal Dwarf Burrowing Skink: *Scelotes vestigifer*
- FitzSimons' Dwarf Burrowing Skink: *Scelotes fitzsimonsi*
- Gronovi's Dwarf Burrowing Skink: *Scelotes gronovii* NT
- Günther's Dwarf Burrowing Skink: *Scelotes guentheri* VU
- Mozambique Dwarf Burrowing Skink: *Scelotes mossambicus*
- Smith's Dwarf Burrowing Skink: *Scelotes inornatus*
- Zululand Dwarf Burrowing Skink: *Scelotes arenicola*

Johan Marais

Short-legged Dwarf Burrowing Skinks

Legged species of the genus *Scelotes, Proscelotes* and *Sepsina*
13 species

Description

The 13 species in this group are all small, slender skinks that have reduced limbs. They are placed in this group on the basis of their superficial resemblance to one another, but some of the members may not be that closely related. The maximum body length for the various species ranges from 55 to 130 mm, and tail length is usually about equal to body length, but is much longer in Arnold's Skink. The body is cylindrical and is covered with polished, tight-fitting scales. The head is not distinct from the neck, and the snout varies from blunt to fairly pointed. Eyes are well developed with movable eyelids. Ear openings are generally minute, and are completely hidden in the Cape Dwarf Burrowing Skink. Limbs are generally very small. The degree of limb reduction varies and several of the species lack forelimbs altogether. All species have small hind limbs and the number of digits on the limbs varies from one species to the next. Digits are usually minute. The tail is cylindrical and is easily shed. Dorsal coloration varies from a dark or coppery brown in the Montane Dwarf Burrowing Skink and Cape Dwarf Burrowing Skink to pale beige and silvery white in the Bloubergstrand Dwarf Burrowing Skink and Silvery Dwarf Burrowing Skink. Individual scales often bear dark spots and several species, such as the Striped Dwarf Burrowing Skink, Lowveld Dwarf Burrowing Skink and Limpopo Dwarf Burrowing

The Montane Dwarf Burrowing Skink has small but well-developed legs.

Johan Marais

The Bloubergstrand Dwarf Burrowing Skink was first discovered in 2001.

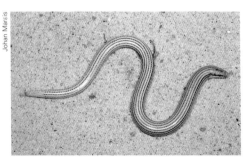

The Striped Dwarf Burrowing Skink has well-developed hind limbs but no forelimbs.

Skink, are prominently striped with light or dark longitudinal stripes that run the length of the body. A dark stripe often runs from the snout through the eyes, and the tails of several species may be infused with blue. Belly coloration is generally paler than that of the dorsal parts.

Biology

Short-legged Dwarf Burrowing Skinks are usually found in leaf litter or in friable sand. Generally, the species with more developed limbs are leaf litter specialists, whereas the sand swimmers show a greater degree of limb reduction. One species with well-developed but small limbs, the Montane Dwarf Burrowing Skink, occurs in montane, grassy areas. This is a poorly known group, and new species continue to be discovered:

the Bloubergstrand Dwarf Burrowing Skink, which was only discovered in 2001, is known from only three specimens.

Conservation

Kasner's Dwarf Burrowing Skink is listed by the IUCN as 'Vulnerable' on account of its restricted distribution and habitat degradation within its distribution. A subspecies of the Limpopo Dwarf Burrowing Skink (*Scelotes limpopoensis albiventris*) is listed in the latest Red Data Book on South African reptiles, also on account of its restricted distribution. Although not currently listed as 'Threatened', the recently discovered Bloubergstrand Dwarf Burrowing Skink probably deserves a 'Threatened' status on account of it being known from only a few specimens and its highly restricted distribution.

The Limpopo Dwarf Burrowing Skink gives birth to live young. Full-term foetuses can be seen through the belly of this gravid female.

Reproduction

Currently, nothing is known about reproduction in Albert's Burrowing Skink and the Angola Burrowing Skink. Most of the Dwarf Burrowing Skinks (*Scelotes*) appear to give birth to live young, with litter size varying from 1 to 4. Females give birth in late summer. Arnold's Skink has been reported both to lay eggs and to give birth to live young. This may show true variation within the species or is indicative of the presence of more than one cryptic species within the group.

Distribution

The distributions of the various species of Short-legged Dwarf Burrowing Skinks are clustered in three distinct areas: Albert's Burrowing Skink and the Angola Burrowing Skink occur in the northern parts of Namibia, extending northwards into Angola. Arnold's Skink, Limpopo Dwarf Burrowing Skink, Lowveld Dwarf Burrowing Skink and Montane Dwarf Burrowing Skink occur variously along the eastern escarpment of Zimbabwe, Mpumalanga escarpment, Lowveld and Limpopo River Valley. The third cluster includes the remaining species and is centred in the southwestern Cape, extending along the Cape south coast and succulent karoo, and up the West Coast into southern central Namibia.

Kasner's Dwarf Burrowing Skink is listed by the IUCN as 'Vulnerable' due to its limited distribution.

The Limpopo Dwarf Burrowing Skink has small limbs and prominent dorsolateral pale stripes on the body.

The Cape Dwarf Burrowing Skink is restricted to southern Namibia and Namaqualand.

SPECIES IN THE GROUP

- Albert's Burrowing Skink: *Sepsina alberti*
- Angola Burrowing Skink: *Sepsina angolensis*
- Arnold's Skink: *Proscelotes arnoldi*
- Bloubergstrand Dwarf Burrowing Skink: *Scelotes montispectus*
- Cape Dwarf Burrowing Skink: *Scelotes caffer*
- Dutton's Dwarf Burrowing Skink: *Scelotes duttoni*
- Kasner's Dwarf Burrowing Skink: *Scelotes kasneri* VU
- Limpopo Dwarf Burrowing Skink: *Scelotes limpopoensis*
- Lowveld Dwarf Burrowing Skink: *Scelotes bidigittatus*
- Montane Dwarf Burrowing Skink: *Scelotes mirus*
- Silvery Dwarf Burrowing Skink: *Scelotes bipes*
- Striped Dwarf Burrowing Skink: *Scelotes sexlineatu*
- Western Dwarf Burrowing Skink: *Scelotes capensis*

Writing Skinks

The genus *Lygosoma*
3 species

Description

This is a small group with only three species occurring in southern Africa. The general body shape is cylindrical, robust and muscular. Total length varies from 170 mm to over 280 mm, and width from 8 to 15 mm. The tail makes up about half of the total length, is almost as thick as the body and has a relatively blunt tip. Tails are easily lost when the lizards are handled and only a small proportion of individuals have their original tails. Scales are overlapping and fit tightly together, and are generally highly polished, smooth and shiny in appearance. The limbs are small but well developed, with five short toes on both front and hind limbs. Eyelids are movable and the ear drums are deeply sunk. Ear openings are not very obvious as they are small and are situated low down on the sides of the neck, just below and behind the jawline, with openings that face backwards. The position and size of the ear openings are probably adaptations to a fossorial lifestyle. The snout is wedge-shaped and has a slightly sharpened edge to the upper lip. The snout is also particularly hard and is used for burrowing. Coloration is usually a pale sandy-brown with some speckling, especially on the tail. The Mozambique Writing Skink is usually marked with darker brown and white blotches and streaks.

Biology

Writing Skinks get their name from the muscular side-to-side movement that the lizards make when grasped in the hand. This

Sundevall's Writing Skink is typical of Writing Skinks: it has four short limbs, a robust and muscular body. and a wedge-shaped snout.

In southern Africa, the Mozambique Writhing Skink is restricted to central Mozambique. It also occurs further north.

The Mozambique Writhing Skink is generally darker and more speckled than Sundevall's Writhing Skink.

same movement is used for 'swimming' through loose sand and leaf litter. During 'sand swimming', the legs are held against the body in a way reminiscent of a swimming crocodile, and play no part in locomotion. Writhing Skinks are usually located under rocks or logs and may bury themselves in the sand beneath such retreats. They are most abundant in arid areas where soils are sandy, such as in the Kalahari, but are also found in well-drained alluvium and hillsides in areas of higher rainfall. They appear to be mainly nocturnal and will come to the surface to forage on small arthropods, such as insects and millipedes. Old termitaria also form a favoured retreat on account of the abundant food associated with this microhabitat. When on the surface the legs are used in locomotion, which is a slightly serpentine gait. Writhing Skinks are cryptic and, due to

their fossorial habits, often escape detection for long periods in areas where they are relatively abundant. However, they appear to be fairly rare in much of their range, especially in areas of higher rainfall.

Reproduction

Although Writhing Skinks include species that give birth to live young, the three southern African species lay soft-shelled eggs. Eggs number 2–7 and are laid underground or in old termitaria.

Distribution

Writhing Skinks are limited to the northern half of southern Africa. They are found in southern Angola, Namibia, all but the southern extremes of Botswana, Zimbabwe, central and northern Mozambique, and the northeastern parts of South Africa. Sundevall's Writhing Skink is the most widespread of the three species. The Mozambique Writhing Skink is restricted to central Mozambique and elsewhere further north, and the Bazaruto Writhing Skink is limited to the islands of the Bazaruto archipelago.

Sundevall's Writhing Skink is usually found in sandy areas.

SPECIES IN THE GROUP

- Bazaruto Writhing Skink: *Lygosoma lanceolatum*
- Mozambique Writhing Skink: *Lygosoma afrum*
- Sundevall's Writhing Skink: *Lygosoma sundevallii*

Typical Skinks

The genus *Trachylepis* (previously *Mabuya*)
23 species

Description

This group consists of 23 species that are all very similar in body shape and build. These lizards have fairly shiny scales, well-developed legs and large eyes with movable eyelids. The scales on the body are keeled in most species, the Grass-top Skink being the only exception to this in southern Africa. The largest species have a body length of about 120 mm, and the smallest, around 55 mm. The tail length is about the same as the body length, but this does vary somewhat among species. For example, the Grass-top Skink is unusual for this group as its tail, which is used in locomotion through grass, is over twice the body length.

Coloration varies from one species to the next, but many species have a basic pattern of a brown body with longitudinal light stripes that run from the head or snout to the tail. There may be two, three or even five light stripes, and some species have light or dark speckles on the body. A few species are more brightly coloured, one of the most striking being the Rainbow Skink: dominant males of this species are an attractive coppery brown with white speckling and faint striping, whereas females and juveniles are dark with three prominent light stripes and an electric blue tail. Species within the group can be difficult to differentiate, and the taxonomy is based primarily on scalation, body shape and, to a lesser extent, coloration.

Johan Marais

Typical Skinks, such as this Cape Skink, have well-developed legs and large eyes with movable eyelids.

The Variable Skink is a widespread and common species, and shows geographic variation in its markings.

Red-sided Skinks have highly polished scales and a plain back. Males develop bright red flanks during the breeding season.

Biology

Typical Skinks are conspicuous because they are active by day and are terrestrial, arboreal or rock-living. Although most of the species are habitat generalists, the Wedge-snouted Skink is a sand specialist and is restricted to sand dunes and arid scrublands. Its wedge-shaped snout is probably an adaptation for digging in the loose substrate. The behaviour of Typical Skinks also makes them particularly obvious as they often bask in exposed positions and will allow fairly close approach before fleeing. They will forage actively but will also bask in strategic positions so that they

The Variegated Skink is a slender species that occurs in rocky and sandy areas.

can quickly dart forward and seize passing prey. They will eat a wide variety of insects, such as beetles, flies and grasshoppers, and some, like the Rainbow Skink, are even known to prey on other species of lizards such as young Flat Lizards (*Platysaurus*). Typical Skinks can be habituated to become tolerant of the presence of humans and will feed on non-natural food such a blobs of butter smeared on a tree trunk. Tails are easily shed (and are quickly regenerated) as an anti-predator strategy. The ability to shed tails may be of special importance in species such as the Rainbow Skink where the tail is brightly coloured, the function of the bright colour being to attract the predator's attention away from the lizard's body. The use of a blue tail to distract predators has also evolved in the Angolan Blue-tailed Skink, as well as in several other species of lizards such as the Dwarf Plated Lizard (*Cordylosaurus subtessellatus*), the Blue-tailed Tree Lizard (*Holaspis geuntheri*) and the Blue-tailed Sandveld Lizard (*Nucras caesicaudata*). Typical Skinks often occur in relatively high densities, leading to high levels of social interaction between individuals, with the lizards posturing in an attempt to intimidate each other or fighting for the best retreats and basking sites.

Graham Alexander

Some Cape Skinks lack the typical body patterning.

Johan Marais

Male Rainbow Skinks are iridescent coppery brown, while females and juveniles have an electric blue tail.

TAIL AUTOMOTY

Tails can be shed in response to physical grasping or stress of impending capture. Some species lose tails much more easily than others. A lizard will often return and eat its own tail if it has not been consumed by the predator. In this way, the lizard wins back some of the resources sacrificed in flight. In species where tail autotomy has evolved as a predator escape strategy, muscles, nerves and blood vessels separate easily at cleavage planes in the tail vertebrae.

Johan Marais

As the name suggests, the Ovambo Tree Skink is primarily arboreal, but may also be found in rocky areas.

The Eastern Striped Skink is common in the northeastern parts of southern Africa, and is often found in human dwellings.

The Kalahari Tree Skink is superficially similar to the Striped Skink, but is more speckled on the back.

The Eastern Coastal Skink is found in coastal forest as far south as the northern parts of Durban.

The Karasburg Tree Skink occurs in southern Namibia and adjacent Northern Cape and Botswana.

Reproduction

A minority of the 23 species lay eggs; most produce live young. Reproduction patterns in three of the species are more complicated: some populations of Cape Skink, Variable Skink and Western Three-striped Skink lay eggs, but others of these same species give birth to live young. Growth of juveniles tends to be rapid, and individuals can reproduce within the first year.

Distribution

Many of the species of Typical Skink are habitat generalists and are thus widespread and common, occurring over much of southern Africa. At least one species occurs in any particular area, but more species tend to occur in the northern parts of southern Africa.

Wahlberg's Striped Skink occurs over the northwestern third of southern Africa.

The Montane Speckled Skink is common in gardens in Johannesburg and Pretoria.

SPECIES IN THE GROUP

- Angolan Blue-tailed Skink: *Trachylepis laevis*
- Boulenger's Skink: *Trachylepis boulengeri*
- Bronze Rock Skink: *Trachylepis lacertiformis*
- Cape Skink: *Trachylepis capensis*
- Chimba Skink: *Trachylepis chimbana*
- Eastern Coastal Skink: *Trachylepis depressa*
- Eastern Striped Skink: *Trachylepis striata*
- Grass-top Skink: *Trachylepis megalura*
- Hoesch's Skink: *Trachylepis hoeschi*
- Kalahari Tree Skink: *Trachylepis spilogaster*
- Karasburg Tree Skink: *Trachylepis sparsa*
- Montane Speckled Skink: *Trachylepis punctatissima*
- Ovambo Tree Skink: *Trachylepis binotata*
- Rainbow Skink: *Trachylepis margaritifer*
- Red-sided Skink: *Trachylepis homalocephala*
- Speckle-lipped Skink: *Trachylepis maculilabris*
- Speckled Sand Skink: *Trachylepis punctulata*
- Variable Skink: *Trachylepis varia*
- Variegated Skink: *Trachylepis variegata*
- Wahlberg's Striped Skink: *Trachylepis wahlbergii*
- Wedge-snouted Skink: *Trachylepis acutiblabris*
- Western Rock Skink: *Trachylepis sulcata*
- Western Three-striped Skink: *Trachylepis occidentalis*

CORDYLIDS
Family: Cordylidae

The cordylids are restricted to Africa and have their highest species richness in southern Africa, where a total of four genera and 53 species are currently known to occur, and further discoveries are expected. Cordylids are generally robust lizards with large, distinct heads and stout limbs. Slenderization has occurred in one group of grass specialists (Grass Lizards; *Chamaesaura*) and dorsoventral flattening in a group of rock-living species (Flat Lizards; *Platysaurus*). The majority of species are strictly rock-living, but some are terrestrial or arboreal. All species are diurnal. The eyelids are well developed and movable. The head is usually covered with rugose dermal bony plates above, and large, symmetrical scales below, and the scales on the body are small and granular, or enlarged and plate-like, and arranged in longitudinal and transverse rows (girdles). Many cordylids have a lateral body fold, which runs from the armpit to the back legs. The tail has regular whorls or rings of spinose or strongly keeled scales. Tails are generally only shed when physically grasped, but they do regenerate. The majority of the species are viviparous, but Flat Lizards lay eggs.

Graham Alexander

Cordylids, such the Transvaal Girdled Lizard, are generally large, robust lizards with large, distinct heads and stout limbs.

Sungazer

The species *Cordylus giganteus*
1 species

Description

This group includes only a single species. The Sungazer is a large-bodied Girdled Lizard that differs from other members of the genus in several obvious ways. Apart from its unique habitat requirements and behaviour, the Sungazer is larger and more spiny than any of the other Girdled Lizards. Maximum body length is 170–220 mm, depending from which population the lizard comes. The head is distinct from the body and is triangular in shape. Large occipital scales project backwards from the posterior edge of the head, giving the lizard a dragon-like appearance. These backward-pointing scales are just in front of the ears, partially masking them from view. The eyes are moderate in size and are obvious, with scaly, movable eyelids. The body is stout and robust, and is moderately depressed. Either 10 or 12 longitudinal rows of keeled scales cover the dorsum. Scales on the flanks of the neck and body are strongly spinous, giving the lizard a very rough and armoured appearance. The belly scales are smooth or very slightly keeled and are overlapping. The legs are well developed and muscular, but the feet are relatively small, betraying the fact that Sungazers are not fast sprinters.
The tail is thick and has whorls of large spiny scales, giving the appearance of a medieval weapon. It is as long as, or a little shorter than, the body length and is generally not naturally shed as an anti-predator strategy. The back is yellow to dark brown and the flanks of the body, sides of the head and the belly are a lighter, straw-yellow colour. Juveniles have distinctive coloration, with bars and blotches of yellow to orange, interspersed with blackish brown on the body, and black and yellow bands with orange spots on the tail.

Johan Marais

Sungazers are terrestrial and are found in grasslands.

Biology

Sungazers are diurnal, terrestrial lizards that are restricted exclusively to natural highveld grasslands in South Africa. They usually assume a characteristic posture while basking, with the head and foreparts of the body giving the impression that they are 'gazing' at the world around them. This raised head position allows them an improved view of their immediate surroundings and it is this behaviour that gives these charismatic lizards their common name. Sungazers are ambush foragers and feed almost exclusively on arthropods. In order of importance, prey consists of beetles, millipedes, true bugs, ants, grasshoppers and butterflies. They occasionally consume vertebrates such as small rodents or lizards and there are even reports of adults cannibalizing young. Rather than just feeding on what is on offer, there appears to be a level of prey selection, especially during times when prey is plentiful. Sungazers feed for about eight months of the year, but cease feeding completely during the four coldest winter months. During this time, they remain dormant underground, do not even emerge to bask and lose a significant amount of body mass. When active, they are strongly heliothermic, basking in exposed situations such as on termitaria or on open ground near their burrow entrance. Burrows are self-excavated, single channelled and are usually blind-ended with no terminal chamber.

Burrow length often exceeds 2 m. Although each burrow is typically home to a single individual, up to seven individuals have been recorded in a burrow and juveniles may share burrows with adults. Burrows serve as retreats at night, and to avoid predation, low winter temperatures and high midday temperatures during summer. Individual lizards appear to move between burrows regularly, but adult males may defend particular burrows. Sungazers form loose colonies of several individuals on grassy slopes. Slopes are preferred since this reduces the danger of the burrows flooding during heavy rains. These lizards are slow-growing and have long lifespans.

Conservation

Numbers are declining due to the destruction of habitat from maize, sunflower and wheat farming. Sungazers are also highly prized in the pet trade and muti market. These human-induced conservation threats have resulted in Sungazers being classified by the IUCN as 'Vulnerable'.

Reproduction

Sungazers are live-bearing, usually producing 1 or 2, but occasionally up to 4, young in late summer. The juveniles are slow-growing, and each female probably only gives birth every other year. Ants make up a greater proportion of the diet of juveniles than for adults, but juveniles are still large enough to include millipedes and beetles in their diet.

Distribution

Sungazers are endemic to the highveld grasslands of South Africa and occur in the eastern Free State, the extreme west of KwaZulu-Natal and the southeastern parts of Mpumalanga.

Johan Marais

The Sungazer is the largest and most robust species of cordylid and has rough scales.

SPECIES IN THE GROUP

■ Sungazer: *Cordylus giganteus* **VU**

Girdled Lizards

The genus *Cordylus* excluding *C. giganteus* and
C. coeruleopunctatus
28 species

Description

Girdled Lizards form a large and fairly diverse group of lizards
that have a stout build and spiny, plate-like scales, giving them an
'armoured' appearance. Superficially, they resemble their close
relatives the Crag Lizards (*Pseudocordylus*) most closely, but tend
to be much more spiny and rugose in general appearance. Girdled
Lizards are generally large-bodied, with the body length varying from
60 to 145 mm. The tail is thick at the base and is usually a little longer
than the body, but this varies among species, with the tail being
shorter in some. The head is very distinct from the body, is broad
and triangular in shape, and the posterior edge is lined with a row
of spiny scales. The head is usually relatively depressed, probably
an adaptation for accessing narrow rock crevices. The scales on the
head are usually large, rugose and dull, giving a particularly weather-
beaten appearance. Eyes are well developed and have movable
eyelids. The tympanum is relatively large and is usually visible, but in
some species it may be partially obscured and protected by a row of
protruding scales anterior to the tympanum. The body scales overlap
to an extent, are usually keeled in the majority of species and are
spiny in some. The scales on the body are arranged in regular rows or
girdles, giving the common name for the group. The number of scale
rows on the body varies greatly and is important for distinguishing
among species. Transverse rows of dorsal scales on the body vary
from 16 to 46, and longitudinal rows range from 16 to 26. Ventral
scales are less variable, with 10–18 longitudinal rows. Limbs are

Graham Alexander

*The Black Girdled
Lizard has a build
that's typical of the
genus. The black
colour helps the
lizard absorb heat
in cold conditions.*

sturdy and well developed. Each foot has five toes, and all the toes bear strong, recurved claws for climbing. The tail has whorls of spiny scales. The degree of spinyness is greatest at the tail base, but varies among species. Tails are not easily shed and regenerate slowly.

Generally, Girdled Lizards have a dull coloration, ranging from uniform black in certain species to dark brown, brown or yellow. The Cape Girdled Lizard, Namaqua Girdled Lizard and Karoo Girdled Lizard tend to be a reddish brown. Species such as Warren's Girdled Lizard, Van Dam's Girdled Lizard, Karoo Girdled Lizard, Rooiberg Girdled Lizard and the Zimbabwe Girdled Lizard often have light spots on the body, whereas the Cape Girdled Lizard may have dark spots on the body. The Regal Girdled Lizard has yellow or orange flanks and resembles some of the Crag Lizards in this respect.

Biology

Most Girdled Lizards are strictly rock-living and are restricted to rock outcrops or mountain ranges of particular rock types. Many species rely on rock crevices, using them as sleeping sites and as places in which to take refuge from danger. Rock type is thus an important habitat determinant,

Cape Girdled Lizards form dense colonies of several hundred individuals.

Transvaal Girdled Lizards occur singly or in small groups on scattered rocks.

Limpopo Girdled Lizards are more arboreal than most other Girdled Lizards and are found under the loose bark of dead trees.

Warren's Girdled Lizard occurs on mountain slopes and small rock outcrops in the northeastern parts of South Africa.

because it generally governs crevice size. Some species, such as the Armadillo Girdled Lizard, are known to form dense aggregations or colonies that may number hundreds, and some species appear to have relatively complex social structures including the formation of family units and a degree of kin recognition. Other species, such as the Black Girdled Lizard, are more solitary and are usually only observed in singles or pairs. The Tropical Girdled Lizard, Limpopo Girdled Lizard and Tasman's Girdled Lizard live under the loose bark of dead trees, in hollow logs or between the dead leaves attached to aloe stems. The Large-scaled Girdled Lizard also uses clumps of vegetation for shelter, and is renowned for favouring a succulent, sprawling, ground-hugging Euphorbia (*Euphorbia caput-medusae*) as a retreat; up to a dozen individuals may shelter between the branches of a single plant. Although most Girdled Lizards rely on retreat into rock crevices as their main defence against predation, the Armadillo Girdled Lizard has a unique strategy. As the names suggests,

The Armadillo Girdled Lizard defends itself by rolling into a defensive ball and grasping its tail in its mouth.

they roll into a defensive ball by grasping their tails in their mouths when threatened. The very spiny dorsal scales offer the lizard all-round protection. This quaint behaviour has added to the value of this species in the pet trade.

Karoo Girdled Lizards more typically have a brown, blotched body coloration.

The black body colour of some populations of Karoo Girdled Lizard is an adaptation to cold conditions.

Jordan's Girdled Lizard is very similar to the Karoo Girdled Lizard, but is restricted to the central parts of Namibia.

Girdled Lizards are diurnal heliotherms, using the sun's radiation to warm their bodies to preferred temperatures. Several of the species that occur in the southwest Cape, including the Black Girdled Lizard, Oelofsen's Girdled Lizard, Dwarf Girdled Lizard and Peers Girdled Lizard, are primarily black in coloration. This is probably an adaptation to life in weather that frequently includes mist and fog, and allows the lizards to heat more effectively in conditions that are generally not conducive to basking. Girdled Lizards are typically catholic in their diet and will eat anything they can catch and overpower. Because the lizards are relatively large, almost all invertebrates are fair game. Snails, millipedes, caterpillars, grasshoppers, ants, termites, wasps, bees and beetles have been recorded in the diet, as have vertebrates such as small lizards and frogs. Occasionally, even small amounts of vegetation are eaten.

Conservation

Currently, three species of Girdled Lizard are listed as 'Threatened': the Armadillo Girdled Lizard is listed by the IUCN as 'Vulnerable', mainly as a result of its value in the pet trade. In addition to this species being easy to maintain in captivity, it is attractive and is easily captured. It is currently protected by the Cape Provincial Ordinance and is listed in CITES Appendix II. These measures appear to have been largely successful in reducing the number of lizards being removed from the wild. McLachlan's Girdled Lizard is also listed as 'Vulnerable' on account of its very restricted distribution. Lawrence's Girdled Lizard is listed as 'Near Threatened' due to a restricted distribution. Several other species of Girdled Lizards, such as the Dwarf Girdled Lizard, Dwarf Karoo Girdled Lizard and Large-scaled Girdled Lizard, are probably deserving of a 'Threatened' status and will be listed in the future.

Reproduction

All Girdled Lizards give birth to live young. Litters are usually small, with females of most species producing 1–4 relatively large young in mid- to late summer. Warren's Girdled Lizard and the Gorongosa Girdled Lizard have been recorded having up to 6 babies.

Distribution

The Transvaal Girdled Lizard, Tropical Girdled Lizard, Karoo Girdled Lizard and Cape Girdled Lizard are fairly widespread. The remaining species have restricted distributions and appear to be limited primarily by substrate type. Dependence on substrate means that distributions are probably not constrained by climate. Restricted species are concentrated on the Cape Fold Mountains and up the West Coast of South Africa. Species also occur on the eastern escarpment and the eastern Zimbabwean highlands.

Atherton de Villiers

The Large-scaled Girdled Lizard has very large, strongly keeled dorsal scales.

SPECIES IN THE GROUP

- Armadillo Girdled Lizard: *Cordylus cataphractus* VU
- Black Girdled Lizard: *Cordylus niger*
- Campbell's Girdled Lizard: *Cordylus campbelli*
- Cape Girdled Lizard: *Cordylus cordylus*
- Cloete's Girdled Lizard: *Cordylus cloetei*
- Dwarf Girdled Lizard: *Cordylus minor*
- Dwarf Karoo Girdled Lizard: *Cordylus aridus*
- Gorongosa Girdled Lizard: *Cordylus mossambicus*
- Herero Girdled Lizard: *Cordylus pustulatus*
- Jordan's Girdled Lizard: *Cordylus jordani*
- Karoo Girdled Lizard: *Cordylus polyzonus*
- Large-scaled Girdled Lizard: *Cordylus macropholis*
- Lawrence's Girdled Lizard: *Cordylus lawrenci* NT
- Limpopo Girdled Lizard: *Cordylus jonesii*

- Machodoe's Girdled Lizard: *Cordylus machadoi*
- McLachlan's Girdled Lizard: *Cordylus mclachlani* VU
- Namaqua Girdled Lizard: *Cordylus namaquensis*
- Oelofsen's Girdled Lizard: *Cordylus oelofseni*
- Peers Girdled Lizard: *Cordylus peersi*
- Regal Girdled Lizard: *Cordylus regius*
- Rooiberg Girdled Lizard: *Cordylus imkeae*
- Tasman's Girdled Lizard: *Cordylus tasmani*
- Transvaal Girdled Lizard: *Cordylus vittifer*
- Tropical Girdled Lizard: *Cordylus tropidosternum*
- Van Dam's Girdled Lizard: *Cordylus vandami*
- Warren's Girdled Lizard: *Cordylus warreni*
- Waterberg Girdled Lizard: *Cordylus breyeri*
- Zimbabwe Girdled Lizard: *Cordylus rhodesianus*

Crag Lizards

The genus *Pseudocordylus* and *Cordylus coeruleopunctatus*
8 species

Description

This group of eight species is closely related to, and bears a close resemblance to, the Girdled Lizards (*Cordylus*). One of the Girdled Lizards, the Blue-spotted Girdled Lizard, is included in the Crag Lizard group because it resembles them more closely than it does other Girdled Lizards. Crag Lizards are generally larger, with an adult body length of 76–150 mm. Crag Lizards also differ from Girdled Lizards in that their scales are less spiny and the scales on the neck and back are generally more granular. Although the triangular head shape is similar to that of Girdled Lizards, Crag Lizards have more pronounced, almost bulbous jowls, which are often covered with large, vertically oriented plate-like scales. The scales on the head are noticeably less rugose or spiny than those of Girdled Lizards. The eyes are well developed with movable eyelids, and the tympanum is large and visible but situated far back on the head. Although the scales on the mid-dorsal region of the back are granular, those in the dorsolateral region and those on the flanks are larger, and in the Dwarf Crag Lizard are keeled. The legs are well developed and each foot has five toes. Each toe bears a strong, recurved claw for climbing. The tail has whorls of spiny scales especially near the base, though scales are not as spiny as in Girdled Lizards. Tail length is generally a little longer than the body length, but is much longer in the Graceful Crag Lizard. Tails are not easily shed and regenerate slowly.

Body coloration varies from almost completely black in the Dwarf Crag Lizard, to dark olive, slate grey or yellowish brown. Most Crag Lizards also have bright markings on the body, especially

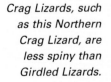

Crag Lizards, such as this Northern Crag Lizard, are less spiny than Girdled Lizards.

Johan Marais

Male Drakensberg Crag Lizards become more brightly coloured during the breeding season.

males during the breeding season. The least flamboyant in this respect is the Dwarf Crag Lizard, which develops only a row of small yellow blotches along the spine. The most ostentatious are the Cape Crag Lizard, Drakensberg Crag Lizard and Northern Crag Lizard. Males of these species develop bright yellow or orange on the flanks of the body, the head and across the throat and chin. Adult females of these species also become more brightly coloured during the breeding season to the extent that, in certain populations, they are difficult to distinguish from the males.

Some male Drakensberg Crag Lizards have turquoise and yellow on their flanks.

Biology

Crag Lizards are all rock specialists and, like the Girdled Lizards, are dependent on certain rock types to provide suitable crevices for protection from predators and the elements. Blue-spotted Girdled Lizards and Drakensberg Crag Lizards sometimes excavate holes under boulders and use these as refuges instead of rock crevices. In general, Crag Lizards are not as gregarious as Girdled Lizards and colonies are diffuse. There may be spatial separation of habitat

use according to the sex and age of the lizards, with adult males commanding the most exposed positions at the top of the rock. Not more than two or three individuals occupy a single crevice. All species are diurnal and are heliothermic, spending early morning and late afternoon basking to regulate body temperature. The Dwarf Crag Lizard follows the trait shown by some Girdled Lizards: it occurs in areas of the southwestern Cape that have frequent

Female Drakensberg Crag Lizards are not as brightly coloured as the males.

Cape Crag Lizards bask while waiting to ambush prey from elevated positions.

mists and fog, and has developed a black coloration that enhances warming. However, Highveld species, such as the Drakensberg Crag Lizard, also experience difficulty in dealing with cold, and cannot prohibit their body temperatures from cooling to levels at which they become comatose during winter nights. They seem to suffer no ill effects from these frequent events as long as they do not freeze, which happens when body temperature drops below -5 °C. Freezing kills the lizards instantly, and those that are forced to use shallow, suboptimal crevices are at risk of not surviving really cold nights.

Crag Lizards are ambush hunters, generally choosing an elevated position on a rock where they bask while waiting for passing prey. When a potential meal moves into range, the lizard darts forward, capturing and dispatching the meal with its powerful jaws. At least some species of Crag Lizards, such as the Drakensberg Crag Lizard, feed very infrequently and appear to be adapted to a low energy lifestyle of low food intake

and low levels of activity. A wide range of invertebrates is eaten, including millipedes, caterpillars, grasshoppers, termites, wasps, bees and beetles. They will also eat small lizards if they can catch them, and at least some Crag Lizard species include leaves, flowers and berries in their diet.

Crag Lizards, such as this Drakensberg Crag Lizard, have pronounced, bulbous jowls.

Blue-spotted Girdled Lizards resemble Crag Lizards more closely than they do other Girdled Lizards.

Juvenile Crag Lizards are dull in coloration and usually have light flecks or spots on the body.

Conservation

The Dwarf Crag Lizard is listed by the IUCN as 'Vulnerable', due mainly to its very restricted distribution and rare occurrence. Research also indicates that this species may be particularly at risk due to climate change. Lang's Crag Lizard and Spiny Crag Lizard are listed as 'Near Threatened' due to their restricted distributions and demand in the pet trade.

Reproduction

All are live-bearing and usually have litters of 2–3 in mid- to late summer, but litters of up to 7 are known. Young are relatively slow-growing and may take two years to reach adulthood. Adults appear to be fairly long-lived, and the Drakensberg Crag Lizard can live in excess of five years, possibly much longer.

Distribution

Crag Lizards are restricted to the southern and eastern parts of southern Africa. As a group, their distribution forms a typical temperate pattern, following the axis of the eastern escarpment and being limited to higher altitudes at lower latitudes. As with the Girdled Lizards, distributions of individual species appear to be limited by substrate, resulting in many of the species having restricted and patchy distributions.

AMBUSH/ACTIVE FORAGERS

Just like snakes, some lizards use ambush as a hunting strategy, while others use active foraging. Some lizards use the two modes at different times, while others use a form of 'slow patrol' that includes both ambush and active components. Ambush foragers (also known as sit-and-wait foragers) feed on mobile prey (which must come to them) and rely on vision for prey detection. Active foragers rely more on chemosensory systems for detecting prey, and are able to find and eat inactive prey. Detection of prey includes the conventional sense of smell, as well as vomerolfaction, which is facilitated by tongue flicking.

SPECIES IN THE GROUP

- Blue-spotted Girdled Lizard: *Cordylus coeruleopunctatus*
- Cape Crag Lizard: *Pseudocordylus microlepidotus*
- Dwarf Crag Lizard: *Pseudocordylus nebulosus* **VU**
- Graceful Crag Lizard: *Pseudocordylus capensis*
- Lang's Crag Lizard: *Pseudocordylus langi* **NT**
- Northern Crag Lizard: *Pseudocordylus transvaalensis*
- Drakensberg Crag Lizard: *Pseudocordylus melanotus*
- Spiny Crag Lizard: *Pseudocordylus spinosus* **NT**

Flat Lizards

The genus *Platysaurus*
13 species

Description

Currently, 13 southern African species are recognized in this group. However, ongoing research suggests that some of the currently defined subspecies are actually full species, and the number of recognized species is thus likely to increase. Flat Lizards are small to medium-sized. Although adult body length can be quite long, from 65–145 mm, the lizards are slimly built and are very agile. Their most noticeable characteristic is a very flattened or depressed body, which allows the lizards into the narrowest of crevices. The body is covered with fine, regular-sized, granular scales on the dorsal parts, giving an almost velvet finish to the skin. The belly scales are large, smooth and rectangular, and are arranged in longitudinal and transverse rows. The head is flattened and is covered with regular, large scales and the snout is acutely pointed. The eyes are well developed and have movable eyelids. The tympanum is large and visible. Limbs are well developed and are held in a widely splayed posture, further accentuating the extreme flatness of the lizards – even the thighs show a degree of flattening. Each foot has five well-developed digits, each with a strong claw that is used for holding onto rock surfaces. The tail is long and slender and is generally much longer than the body. The base of the tail is depressed and may have lateral spines. Although tails are not easily shed, when this occurs, regeneration is fairly rapid.

Johan Marais

Male Flat Lizards are brightly coloured and the females have three prominent lines on the body. These individuals are Dwarf Flat Lizards.

Male Augrabies Flat Lizards have brightly coloured flanks and sides of the head.

Juvenile and female coloration and patterning show very little variation between species: generally the body is blackish brown with three longitudinal white lines. The mid-dorsal line runs from the tip of the snout to the centre of the base of the tail. The two lateral lines run from behind each eye to the sides of the tail base, and are thus parallel to the mid-dorsal line. The tail is light brown, rusty brown, orange or light blue posteriorly, and light flecks or spots occur on the flanks of the body and on the limbs. Males are very colourful, especially during the breeding season. Colours include black, blue, purple, turquoise, emerald green, red, orange and yellow, and the colour mix and patterning depend on the species. In most species, the male's tail is orange, yellow or red, and the dorsal parts of the body are blackish brown with infusions of green, blue, turquoise or orange, in various combinations. The flanks are often more brightly coloured than the dorsum and may also show a stunning array of colours. However, the colours on the ventral surface of the neck and belly are by far the brightest, and usually include rich

The Common Flat Lizard is one of the most widespread species of the genus.

In some populations, male Common Flat Lizards are strikingly marked.

blues, purples, turquoise, orange, yellow or black. Limiting the brightest coloration to the ventral surface means that the colours don't draw the attention of predators, but can be flashed at competitors in a challenge simply by rising up on the forelegs or lifting one side of the body. In some populations of the Common Flat Lizard, females can be almost as colourful as males.

Biology

Flat Lizards are extreme rock specialists and are restricted to exposed expanses of granite, gneiss, rhyolite and certain types of sandstone. Even relatively short stretches of vegetated soil appear to act as barriers to movement, although lizards do travel between nearby outcrops more often than was previously suspected. Flat Lizards are alert, diurnal heliotherms. Their activity period appears to be initiated when direct sunlight hits the entrance to their crevice. Lizards emerge to bask near to the crevice until body temperature approaches preferred levels. Much of the day is spent actively searching for food and interacting with other lizards, interspersed with short periods

Male Waterberg Flat Lizards are usually orange on the flanks, blue on the throat and speckled above.

The Orange-throated Flat Lizard's dorsum is dull in comparison to its belly.

Male Orange-throated Flat Lizards usually have a bright yellow throat and a pale green or blue belly.

The Sekukhune Flat Lizard is found on the Mpumalanga escarpment.

of basking. During summer, these lizards may retreat into their crevices at midday to escape excessive heat but emerge again later in the afternoon when temperatures have cooled. Flat Lizards actively select the crevices in which they spend the night, and they will use the same crevice for many months. The majority of suitable crevices are formed under thin rock flakes which have separated from the bedrock by exfoliation. Of great importance are the internal dimensions of the crevice, but the thickness of the rock flake (the roof) and the crevice temperature all influence the lizard's choice. Adult Common Flat Lizards prefer crevices that are about 7 mm wide: dimensions that allow the lizards easy access, while protecting them from most snakes and other potential predators. At least some species of Flat Lizard are highly social; 30 Common Flat Lizards were found sleeping within a

crevice that was less than a metre in length. Flat Lizards appear to be long-lived for their size and many captive individuals have been known to survive for more than 10 years.

As with many other types of lizards, Flat Lizards consume a wide variety of invertebrates in their diet, including ants, wasps, bees, flies, beetles, butterflies and caterpillars. Prey is actively chased and lizards will often jump into the air to snatch butterflies or flies in flight. Common Flat Lizards have also been observed diving into pools of rainwater to snatch invertebrates from below the water surface. Several species of Flat Lizard also appear to include a significant proportion of vegetable matter in their diet and will eat flowers and ripe berries. This is very unusual, as herbivory is constrained by the physiology of lizards and is usually restricted to much larger species. The Augrabies Flat Lizard is one of the more

Marius Burger

Orange-throated Flat Lizards inhabit large sandstone outcrops on the foothills of the Blowberg in South Africa's Limpopo province.

intensely studied species of Flat Lizard. This species depends heavily on black flies that congregate in their millions along the Orange River, where the species occurs. It also regularly feeds on figs from the Namaqua Fig (*Ficus cordata*).

Conservation

The Soutpansberg Flat Lizard is listed by the IUCN as 'Near Threatened' due to its restricted range. However, this species is common where it occurs and is not under any specific threat at present.

Reproduction

In any population of Flat Lizards, some of the males are territorial and will defend a patch of rock against other males by displaying their bright colours and confronting any intruders. In addition to raising their bodies high on their forelegs to expose their neck and chest, and lifting the side of the body to expose the stomach, males may also arch their backs as they circle their adversary. Usually, this behaviour is sufficient to chase off the intruder, but fights do ensue if the contest is even, and can result in tail loss and bite wounds. In Augrabies Flat Lizard, dominant males command good quality territories that encompass areas with plentiful food resources. They attempt to mate with females entering the territory. Males that are unable to procure or keep territories are known as floaters, and they adopt a 'sneaker' strategy to gain access to females. This mating system is also likely to exist in many of the other, as yet unstudied, Flat Lizard species. Mating generally takes place in September and October. All Flat Lizards are egg-layers and females usually produce a pair of soft-shelled eggs (7–10 x 17–22 mm) per clutch in early summer. These are laid under a rock or in a suitable soil-filled crevice, and nests are often communal in several species. Females may lay multiple clutches in a season. The young hatch in late summer and reach maturity in about a year.

Distribution

Flat Lizards are most species-rich and widespread in Zimbabwe and Mpumalanga province in South Africa. The Cape Flat Lizard and Augrabies Flat Lizard occur in the Northern Cape and southern Namibia, respectively. The remaining species are restricted to the eastern parts of South Africa, eastern extremes of Botswana and western Mozambique. Since the occurrence of Flat Lizards is highly dependent on the substrate type, distributions tend to be either small or patchy.

Martin Whiting

The large Emperor Flat Lizard is easily distinguished from other species by its unique coloration.

SPECIES IN THE GROUP

- Augrabies Flat Lizard: *Platysaurus broadleyi*
- Cape Flat Lizard: *Platysaurus capensis*
- Common Flat Lizard: *Platysaurus intermedius*
- Dwarf Flat Lizard: *Platysaurus guttatus*
- Emperor Flat Lizard: *Platysaurus imperator*
- Lebombo Flat Lizard: *Platysaurus lebomboensis*
- Ocellated Flat Lizard: *Platysaurus ocellatus*
- Orange-throated Flat Lizard: *Platysaurus monotropis*
- Pungwe Flat Lizard: *Platysaurus pungweensis*
- Sekukhune Flat Lizard: *Platysaurus orientalis*
- Soutpansberg Flat Lizard: *Platysaurus relictus* **NT**
- Striped Flat Lizard: *Platysaurus torquatus*
- Waterberg Flat Lizard: *Platysaurus minor*

Grass Lizards

The genus *Chamaesaura*
3 species

Description

The three species in this group bear a close superficial resemblance to one another but can be distinguished by the presence or absence of limbs, and the number of digits on each limb. As the name suggests, Grass Lizards are grassland specialists and show adaptations for 'swimming' through relatively thick grass. They are extremely elongate and serpentine in body form, to the extent that they are easily mistaken for snakes. The body is short relative to the tail and varies from about 130 to 170 mm in adults. The tail is up to three or four times longer than the body, and total length can exceed 500 mm. The head is reasonably distinct from the body and the lizards will often articulate the head to gain a better view, giving the impression of attentiveness. The eyes are obvious and decidedly unsnake-like, with movable, scaly eyelids. Ear openings are moderately sized. All three species have extremely reduced legs, which generally do not exceed 10 mm in length. The Coppery Grass Lizard has four very small legs, each with five digits. The Cape Grass Lizard also has four legs, but these are minute and have only two digits each. The Large-scaled Grass Lizard lacks forelimbs altogether and the hind limbs have only one digit each. The legs are spike-like and may be held perpendicular to the body, especially when the animal is stationary. However, when the lizard is moving the legs are held against the body and play no part in locomotion. Scales on the head, body and tail appear to be very rough and are strongly keeled.

Grass Lizards, such as this Cape Grass Lizard, have an elongate, serpentine body form and as a result are often mistaken for snakes.

Johan Marais

Atherton de Villiers

The Large-scaled Grass Lizard is restricted to grasslands in the eastern extremes of South Africa and the Chimanimani Mountains in Zimbabwe.

Body coloration generally matches dry grass. The dorsum is dark brown or coppery brown, with a white to greyish white or yellow vertebral stripe that runs from behind the head to the tail tip. Regenerated parts of tails do not have vertebral stripes. There are also two dorsolateral, longitudinal, light, black-edged stripes. The flanks are yellow-brown. The Cape Grass Lizard tends to have relatively indistinct patterning and is usually a uniform straw-yellow to olive-brown, often without a vertebral stripe.

Johan Marais

The Cape Grass Lizard has forelimbs and hind limbs, but these have only one or two small digits on each.

Biology

Grass Lizards rely primarily on their long tails for 'grass swimming'. Although tails can be shed easily when grasped by a predator, usually only the smallest possible part is lost, as the loss of larger parts significantly impedes locomotion. Regeneration of lost tails is also very rapid. Grass Lizards do not appear to use holes in the ground as retreats, although they do occasionally shelter under rocks if there is easy access. Although they are capable of fast movement in long grass and use their speed to escape from danger, they appear to use ambush as their primary foraging mode. The elongated

tail is used by the lizards to position themselves in the upper reaches of the grass tufts, which they use as vantage points to scan for passing prey. They appear to feed almost exclusively on small, active, diurnal arthropods, with beetles and grasshoppers being the most common items on the menu. Grass fires are an important conservation threat to Grass Lizard populations in several respects. Fires kill lizards that become trapped in pockets of grassland from which they cannot escape. Transformation of land by humans has exacerbated the negative effects of fire due to the resulting increase in fire frequency, fragmentation of the grasslands and installation of barriers such as roads, walls and channels, over which the lizards cannot easily pass to escape the flames. Fires also change the structure of the grassland habitat making it more difficult for Grass Lizards to locomote. The removal of the grass cover is also likely to increase the risk of predation and reduce the abundance of food. After fires, Grass Lizards typically move into any unburnt patches that remain. It is probably for this reason that populations seem to persist better in grasslands where there are rocky areas – the rocks probably afford some measure of protection from fire and also serve as fire breaks, causing patches of grass to remain unburnt.

Conservation

Currently, none of the Grass Lizards are listed as 'Threatened'. However, populations are fragmented and afforestation poses a significant conservation threat because plantations usually result in the degradation of the grassland.

Reproduction

Grass Lizards are all live bearers, giving birth to 5–12 live young at any time during the summer. Young are about 150 mm in total length at birth, and the tail, which is relatively short in comparison to adults' tails, is only about twice as long as the body.

Distribution

Grass Lizards are very habitat specific and are restricted to montane and highveld grasslands and fynbos on rocky hillsides, mountain slopes and mountain plateaus. They are limited to the eastern and southern parts of southern Africa, occurring along the eastern escarpment and the Cape Fold Mountains. Because of the habitat specificity, Grass Lizard distribution tends to be patchy, and populations are prone to local extinction.

BODY PROPORTIONS

The 'short body, long tail' combination is typical for lizard species that have a slender body as an adaptation for 'grass swimming'. Adaptation to burrowing also usually results in a slender body shape, but this normally results in a 'long body, short tail' combination. Of the two body forms, the 'long body, short tail' form is most similar to that of snakes. This suggests that evolutionary leg loss in snakes may have resulted due to their ancestors being fossorial burrowers.

Unlike other Grass Lizards, the Coppery Grass Lizard has five digits on each of its four feet.

Grass Lizards, such as the Cape Grass Lizard, use their tails for 'swimming' through grass.

SPECIES IN THE GROUP

- Cape Grass Lizard: *Chamaesaura anguina*
- Coppery Grass Lizard: *Chamaesaura aenea*
- Large-scaled Grass Lizard: *Chamaesaura macrolepi*.

PLATED LIZARDS
Family: Gerrhosauridae

Plated lizards are found in Africa south of the Sahara, and in Madagascar. The two subfamilies include a total of five genera and at least 32 species. Of these, three genera and 13 species occur in southern Africa. They are generally large, robust lizards, but some species have undergone extensive slenderization. Slenderization appears to have evolved independently in grass swimmers and sand swimmers. The head is covered with large symmetrical scales, and the body is covered with large rectangular, overlapping plates arranged in longitudinal and transverse rows. A prominent lateral body fold runs from the back of the jaw to the hind legs. The ear is distinct and usually exposed, but it is partially covered with a tympanic scale in some species. All species have prominent eyes and movable eyelids.

Johan Marais

Plated Lizards, such as this Yellow-throated Plated Lizard, have a prominent lateral body fold running down the sides of the body.

Seps

The genus *Tetradactylus*
5 species

Description

These lizards are also known as Plated Snake-lizards due to their serpentine body form and very small legs. The five species found in southern Africa show varying degrees of limb reduction, from fully formed small legs in the Short-legged Seps to minute single-toed limbs that are not very visible in the African Seps. Some African Seps individuals lack forelimbs altogether, and this species is easily misidentified as a snake as it moves rapidly through its grassland habitat. Body length varies from 40 to 80 mm. The tail is long, at least two to three times as long as the body. The distinction between body and tail may not be obvious unless the specimen is in the hand, and it is therefore easy to overestimate the body size. A prominent lateral fold of skin runs along the sides of the body, and the head is moderately distinct. The eyes are well developed and an obvious ear opening lies just above the anterior end of the lateral fold. Dorsal scales are arranged in longitudinal rows and are usually keeled, giving a fairly rough appearance, but not as rough as in Grass Lizards (*Chamaesaura*). However, the dorsal scales of the Short-legged Seps are relatively smooth, giving this species a slightly shiny appearance. All species are coppery brown to dark brown, with faint longitudinal darker brown striping. The head usually has irregular dark spots, and some species have a small area of black-and-white barring on the sides of the neck.

All species of Seps, such as this Common Long-tailed Seps, are snake-like in appearance and have greatly reduced limbs.

Marius Burger

Marius Burger

African Seps sometimes lack forelimbs altogether.

Biology

Seps are highly active, diurnal lizards that are found mainly in grasslands and coastal fynbos. Because all the species are reasonably rare and have restricted distributions, relatively little is known about them. Populations tend to be isolated and patchy, and it is possible that important habitat requirements result in this limited occurrence. Some Seps spend night times and other inactive periods in grass tussocks, whereas others shelter under stones or in old termitaria where they may also get protection from veld fires. These lizards appear to be active foragers and hunt for invertebrates such as grasshoppers and spiders. Although they are highly dependent on their tails for locomotion in grass, they can shed their tails if grasped by a predator. Tail regeneration is rapid.

Conservation

One of the species, Eastwood's Long-tailed Seps, is possibly extinct and listed as such by the IUCN. This species was originally discovered in the Woodbush Forest in Limpopo province in 1913, but has not

been found since. The area is now under extensive pine plantation and it is likely that this modification of habitat has resulted in the demise of the species. Breyer's Long-tailed Seps is also of conservation concern and is listed in the Red Data Book as 'Rare' and by the IUCN as 'Vulnerable', due to its patchy, very limited distribution.

Johan Marais

The Short-legged Seps has relatively well-developed limbs and a short tail when compared to other members of the group.

The Short-legged Seps occurs in the southwestern and southern Cape, the Amatola Mountains and the KwaZulu-Natal midlands.

Reproduction

From the little that is known, it would appear that all species of Seps are egg-layers, with clutches of 1–3 eggs being laid in summer. At least one species, the African Seps, appears to specialize in laying eggs in the colonies of a particular species of ant (*Anochetus faurei*). These ants build mounds of loosely compacted soil around grass tufts and the female Seps burrows into the nest to gain entry to lay her eggs. The eggs from several females may be found in a single ant nest, and it is likely that the eggs gain some protection from the ants, which are able to deliver a painful bite and sting. The ants tolerate the eggs because the eggshell contains pheromones that camouflage their presence in the nest. Hatchlings are about 120 mm in total length and hatch in late summer.

Distribution

Seps are limited to patches of coastal, montane and highveld grasslands, and coastal fynbos in the southern and eastern parts of southern Africa.

Seps have a lateral fold running down the side of the body, as seen in this African Seps.

SPECIES IN THE GROUP

- African Seps: *Tetradactylus africanus*
- Breyer's Long-tailed Seps: *Tetradactylus breyeri* **VU**
- Common Long-tailed Seps: *Tetradactylus tetradactylus*
- Eastwood's Long-tailed Seps: *Tetradactylus eastwoodae* **EX**
- Short-legged Seps: *Tetradactylus seps*

Typical Plated Lizards

The genus *Gerrhosaurus*
6 species

Description

This group consists of six species of large, robust lizards. The largest of these is the Giant Plated Lizard, which is second only to the monitor lizards (*Varanus*) in size and mass, reaching a body length of about 280 mm. Since the tail can be up to twice as long as the body, the maximum total length in this species is not far short of a metre. The other species range from 110–220 mm in body length and have similarly long tails. The body is more or less cylindrical in the Yellow-throated Plated Lizard, Black-lined Plated Lizard and Namaqua Plated Lizard, but is fairly depressed in the other three species. The tail also tends to be cylindrical, but may be depressed in the anterior parts near to where it meets the body. The head is short and fairly indistinct from the neck, and the eyes are well developed and obvious, though not large, and have a scaly lower eyelid. Ear openings are prominent and are situated just behind the jaw. The dorsum of the body is covered with large, rectangular scales arranged in 14–26 regular longitudinal rows, giving these lizards an armoured or 'plated' appearance. Dorsal scales are keeled to strongly keeled in most species, but they are rough rather than keeled in the Rough-scaled Plated Lizard. Ventral scales are smooth in all species and are arranged in 8–18, usually 10, regular longitudinal rows. As is typical for the family, a prominent fold in the skin runs down the sides of the body from the posterior angle of the jaw to where the hind legs articulate with the body. Scales on the skin of the fold are much smaller than those on the rest of the body

Bryan Maritz

Typical Plated Lizards, such as this Yellow-throated Plated Lizard, are generally robust and large, and have well-developed limbs.

and are granular in appearance. Legs are muscular and well developed, but in the two most slender species, the Yellow-throated Plated Lizard and Black-lined Plated Lizard, legs are relatively small.

Body coloration, consisting of browns, reds and greens, tends to match the environment and is probably important in camouflage. Several of the species have

The Black-lined Plated Lizard occurs in the northern parts of southern Africa, extending further south in the east.

Giant Plated Lizards are second only to the monitor lizards in size and mass.

two yellow stripes that run from the sides of the head onto the tail. These stripes may be dark-edged, particularly in the Black-lined Plated Lizard and Yellow-throated Plated Lizard. The flanks may be darker than the dorsum and are often speckled with white spots or have light barring. The belly tends to be a plain, creamy white but the ventral parts of the throat may be brightly coloured. A bright throat is especially common in the Yellow-throated Plated Lizard, which may have a bright yellow, orange, red or even blue throat during the breeding season. At the height of the breeding season, the bright coloration may extend onto the flanks. Juvenile Giant Plated Lizards are distinctively patterned; they are dark brown with yellow speckles over the dorsum and yellow barring on the flanks.

Biology

Typical Plated Lizards are diurnal and most species are mainly terrestrial, living in holes or in termitaria. However, the Giant Plated Lizard is a primarily rock-living species and small family groups typically inhabit rocky outcrops. Recent research suggests that Giant Plated Lizards have a complex social structure, are able to recognize their kin and show a degree of parental care. It is likely that similar social complexities await discovery in other species in this group too. In spite of their large size, the adult Giant Plated Lizards tend to be much more shy and retiring than their young, which can be habituated to human presence with relative ease. At the first signs of danger, adults will usually wedge themselves tightly into rock fissures, from which they are extremely difficult to dislodge. Because of their large size, Plated Lizards are able to include a wide variety of invertebrates in their diet, as well as small lizards and even young tortoises. At least some species appear to include a significant proportion of vegetation in their diet and will eat any soft plant parts, such as flowers and ripe fruit. All species dig holes at the base of bushes or under rocks, or use burrows made by other animals. Giant Plated Lizards and Rough-scaled Plated Lizards also use rock crevices as retreats. In general, Typical Plated Lizards are probably much more common than the frequency of sightings would indicate. The Yellow-throated Plated Lizard can be very common, even in urban areas, and can go undetected in suburban gardens for a considerable time. They evade detection by being very alert and shy, and because they bury themselves in loose sand under rocks. They are able to shed their tails, which are then rapidly regenerated. In general, Typical Plated Lizards appear to be relatively long-lived, slow-growing lizards. Giant Plated Lizards take five years to reach adult size.

Conservation

The Namaqua Plated Lizard is currently listed by the IUCN as 'Near Threatened' on account of its low population numbers. However, it is relatively widespread and more common than encounters suggest and is probably not deserving of this 'Threatened' status.

Reproduction

All the species in this group lay small clutches of 2–8 soft-shelled eggs, which are usually buried under a rock or log. Newly hatched young are recorded throughout summer and the young of the Yellow-throated Plated Lizard can be very abundant in some habitats. Giant Plated Lizards are unusual in that their eggs are usually laid in a crevice and are then covered with soil

The Rough-scaled Plated Lizard has large, obviously keeled scales on the body and big eyes.

Juvenile Giant Plated Lizards are more vividly marked and less retiring than the adults.

The throat of male Yellow-throated Plated Lizards usually becomes bright orange during the breeding season.

by the mother. She guards and cares for the clutch through much of the initial incubation period. The young usually remain in the home range of the parents, forming a family unit with them. Young apparently grow more quickly with the parents than when they are isolated from them, and are often observed using their parents' backs as basking sites.

Distribution

Plated Lizards occur in a wide variety of habitat types, ranging from mountain and highveld grasslands to savanna, bushveld and coastal forest. The Namaqua Plated Lizard occurs in succulent karoo and fynbos. Generally, most of the species are limited to the northern and eastern parts of southern Africa, although the range of the Yellow-throated Plated Lizard extends along the eastern and southern coast to the Western Cape. The Namaqua Plated Lizard is limited to the southern and southwestern parts of the Cape.

The Namaqua Plated Lizard is currently listed by the IUCN as 'Near Threatened'. However, it is widespread and probably does not deserve this status.

SPECIES IN THE GROUP

- Black-lined Plated Lizard: *Gerrhosaurus nigrolineatus*
- Giant Plated Lizard: *Gerrhosaurus validus*
- Kalahari Plated Lizard: *Gerrhosaurus multilineatu*
- Namaqua Plated Lizard: *Gerrhosaurus typicus* **N**
- Rough-scaled Plated Lizard: *Gerrhosaurus major*
- Yellow-throated Plated Lizard: *Gerrhosaurus flavigularis*

Desert Plated Lizard

The species *Gerrhosaurus skoogi*
1 species

Description

This group includes a single, unusual species that appears to be closely related to, and derived from, the typical Plated Lizards. Desert Plated Lizards are relatively large with a maximum body length of about 150 mm. Tail can equal body length, but is usually a little shorter. This species shows many adaptations to burrowing into the loose sand that is characteristic of its habitat. It has a spade-like snout, wedge-shaped head and a robust, cylindrical body with tight fitting scales. The body is widest just in front of the hind legs. The legs are well developed and muscular, and the toes are fringed with rows of scales that project out sideways, giving the lizard excellent grip in loose sand. The tympanum is almost completely covered by an enlarged scale that protects the ear and keeps sand out when the lizard is underground. As with all Plated Lizards, the Desert Plated Lizard has an obvious lateral fold along each side of the body that runs from the angle of the jaw to where the hind legs articulate with the body. Scales in and next to the lateral folds are small and granular but the remaining scales on the body are large and plate-like.

Duncan Mitchell

Female Desert Plated Lizards are usually slightly smaller in body size and have less black on the head and neck than the males.

Coloration matches the substrate on which the lizards live and is generally a very light sandy brown, with a series of evenly spaced pink or orange spots over the dorsal parts. The head is darker and can be a shiny black colour, especially ventrally. The heads of large males in breeding condition become more uniformly black, and the black can extend to partially cover the dorsal parts of the head, chest and belly.

Desert Plated Lizards live mainly on the unstable slipfaces of sand dunes of the northern Namib Desert.

Biology

These diurnal lizards live mainly on the barren slipfaces of sand dunes. They are capable sand-swimmers, using a sinusoidal writhing of the entire body to bury themselves and to move while below the sand surface. They respond to approaching danger either by fleeing with great speed or diving under the loose sand, disappearing from view in an instant. A great proportion of the day is spent buried and inactive, and the lizards emerge in the morning to feed and interact socially, occasionally for up to eight hours in a day. They do not necessarily emerge every day, however, and will often remain buried for several days at a time. On average, individuals will emerge to feed one day in three, and they appear to rely on an endogenously entrained rhythm as a cue for timing bouts of activity.

The infrequency of activity appears to be an energy-saving adaptation and the Desert Plated Lizard has been shown to have a metabolic expenditure of about half that expected of a lizard of its size. Because Desert Plated Lizards occur only in areas of loose, shifting sand, they do not construct permanent burrows and rely on 'sand swimming' to avoid the exceedingly high temperatures that sometimes typify their environment during midday. Like the Shovel-snouted Lizard (*Meroles anchietae*), the Desert Plated Lizard also reduces body contact with the hot dune surface by lifting the tail and hind legs off the surface for short periods. Whether buried or active on the surface, Desert Plated Lizards attempt to maintain body temperatures of about 37 °C. Lizards sometimes precede their surface activity with a period of up to 30 minutes during which they position themselves just below the surface with only their head and shoulders protruding from the sand. This behaviour is probably a form of 'fine-tuned basking', facilitating the careful regulation or raising of body temperature, without exposing the lizard to predators.

Desert Plated Lizards are also unusual among southern African lizards in that they are omnivorous, with about 80% of their diet consisting of plant material. Although

The Desert Plated Lizard has a spade-like snout, wedge-shaped head and a robust, cylindrical body.

the lizards will feed on plant species that grow on the gravel plains between dunes, they depend largely on the Nara plant (*Acanthosicyos horrida*) as a food and water source. Nara is a scrambling thorny, leafless cucurbit creeper that survives in the constantly moving dune sands by having a dense root system and long taproot. Although this plant would hardly seem appetizing to lizards, Desert Plated Lizards appear to be adept at breaking off and swallowing the green, semi-succulent thorns. They also consume the flowers and young shoots of the plant and use Nara plants as a retreat from predators. Young Desert Plated Lizards that do not have the muscle power to handle Nara feed primarily on detritus such as grass seeds, husks and other plant fragments that may be blown into their environment and which accumulate at the bottom of the dune slipface. Desert Plated Lizards will also occasionally consume the abundant Tenebrionid Beetles that occur in their range, but usually only scavenge off the bodies of beetles that have died from other causes. They can form relatively dense colonies and appear to be relatively slow-growing and long-lived.

Reproduction

The mating season is short and extends from mid-January to the end of February. During this period, dominant males establish territories around the perimeter of Nara plants. Males display to females with ritualized shudders and bobs of the body, and actively chase off competitors. Clutches number 2–4 eggs. Hatchlings are about 60 mm in body length.

Distribution

The Desert Plated Lizard is restricted to the dune fields of the northern Namib Desert, occurring from Cape Cross, northwards to the Kunene River, and extending into southern Angola. The remoteness of the Desert Plated Lizard's range and the harshness of the habitat in which it occurs resulted in this species remaining relatively unknown until fairly recently. Captain Skoog collected the first known specimen in southern Angola in 1912, but the occurrence of the species in Namibia was first reported only in 1963. It has been suggested that the Desert Plated Lizard does not occur in the southern Namib because its main food source, Nara, is not as plentiful there.

RARENESS OF HERBIVORES

Vegetable food generally has a lower calorific content than animal protein and plant cells have an indigestible wall of cellulose. Lizards feeding on vegetable matter therefore have to eat more and need to overcome the difficulty of digesting cellulose. The only feasible way of breaking down cellulose is with endosymbiotic bacteria that reside in the gut (as with ruminants such as cattle). Small lizards can therefore not easily meet their energy demands on a purely vegetarian diet.

Shirley Hanrahan

The Nara plant is an important food and water source for the Desert Plated Lizard.

SPECIES IN THE GROUP

■ Desert Plated Lizard: *Gerrhosaurus skoogi*

Dwarf Plated Lizard

The species *Cordylosaurus subtessellatus*
1 species

Description

The single species that makes up this group was previously
believed to constitute two distinct species. However, variation in
the proportions of the head scales and the degree of keeling of the
dorsal scales is now thought to represent little more than regional
variants of a single species. Dwarf Plated Lizards are medium to
small lizards with a maximum body length of 55 mm. The tail is
long, usually about twice the length of the body. The head is short,
slender, depressed and not distinct from the neck. It is covered with
large symmetrical scales, some of which fuse as the lizards mature.
Eyes are well developed with movable eyelids. Ear openings are
semicircular, bordered by granular scales of the lateral fold below,
and partially covered by tympanic shields. The lateral fold runs from
the posterior angle of the jaw to the hind legs. Dorsal scales may be
smooth or keeled and are in 15 longitudinal and 52–55 transverse
rows. Ventral scales are in eight longitudinal rows. Legs are well
developed but are short, with long digits that bear prominent claws.

These lizards are strikingly marked, with a black or dark brown
body and two prominent, cream or yellow, broad, dorsolateral
stripes that run from the snout onto the tail. These stripes become
bright blue on the tail and merge about a third way along its length.
The bright blue tail gives this species a superficial resemblance to
other blue-tailed species such as the Rainbow Skink (*Trachylepis
margitifer*), Angolan Blue-tailed Skink (*Trachylepis laevis*), the Blue-
tailed Tree Lizard (*Holaspis geuntheri*) and the Blue-tailed Sandveld
Lizard (*Nucras caesicaudata*).

*Dwarf Plated Lizards have a slender body and bright blue tail, and
bear a superficial resemblance to blue-tailed skinks.*

Juvenile Dwarf Plated Lizards are more vividly marked than the adults. The tail is easily shed.

Biology

This is a poorly known, diurnal species that is usually found living in sandy areas among rocks. The bright blue tail probably has an anti-predator function, attracting attention away from the body and vital organs of the lizard. As may be expected, the tail is shed very easily.

Reproduction

Two eggs (12–13 x 5–6 mm) are laid during summer. The hatchlings emerge during late summer.

Distribution

The distribution extends from southwestern Angola in the north, southwards through western Namibia, into the Western Cape.

BLUE TAILS

Many species of lizard from many parts of the world have evolved bright blue tails. In all these species, the tail is easily shed, and in several species the tail may actually be waved at potential predators. It would appear that the function of a blue tail is to distract predators away from the vital head of the lizard, thus increasing the chances of escape and survival.

SPECIES IN THE GROUP

- Dwarf Plated Lizard: *Cordylosaurus subtessellatus*

GECKOS
Family: Gekkonidae

Geckos occur throughout the warmer parts of the world, with an impressive 108 genera and more than 1 130 species found worldwide. The family is divided into six subfamilies. This is the most speciose family of lizards in southern Africa, with 15 genera and 111 described species occurring in the subregion. Ongoing research will doubtless raise this number substantially. The gecko assemblage in southern Africa is extremely diverse, and some of the lineages appear to be ancient. Geckos have only small scales on the head, and the teeth are small, numerous and cylindrical. The eyes are usually large, especially in nocturnal species, and are covered with a transparent skin with unmovable eyelids. Since the eyes cannot blink, they are usually cleaned with the tongue. A high proportion of geckos have pads under their digits. These pads are made up of minute hairs that adhere strongly, even to very smooth surfaces such as glass, allowing geckos access to a wide array of microhabitats. The skin is shed periodically and comes off in patches, which are eaten by the gecko. Most geckos are arboreal or rock-living, but some are terrestrial. The majority of geckos are nocturnal. Typically, these reptiles lay clutches of two hard-shelled eggs, with occasionally more than one clutch being laid in a season.

Johan Marais

Like most geckos, the Namib Dune Gecko has large eyes with no movable eyelids. Scales are granular and do not overlap.

Flat Geckos

The genus *Afroedura*
15 species

Description

Currently, Flat Geckos include 15 described species, but many others are known and are in the process of being described in the scientific literature. It is likely that several more species await discovery, and research using genetics to redefine the species in this genus is currently underway. Flat Geckos are medium-sized, typical geckos with a body length of 45–80 mm. The body and head are relatively flat, allowing the geckos to access narrow crevices easily. The head is distinct from the body, and the eyes are large and well developed. Pupils are vertical and slit-like during the day, but become more oval in the dark. The scales on the body are small, smooth and granular, giving a fine texture to the skin. Scales on the belly are slightly larger than those on the dorsal parts. The tail is usually a little longer than the head and body, but may be equal or even shorter, depending on the species and whether the tail has previously been lost and regenerated. Tails are usually thick at the base, especially during times when food is plentiful, as fat reserves are stored there. In some species, such as the African Flat Gecko, the tail may be transversed by 15 or more grooves or constrictions, giving it a segmented appearance. Tails are easily shed, and regenerated tails sometimes have multiple tips and may be almost heart-shaped at the base, especially in species like the Hawequa Flat Gecko. The legs are well developed with five digits on each foot. Digits are dilated at their ends with either two or three pairs of large white pads under each toe, depending on the species. The toes are clawless and have a groove near the tip.

Johan Marais

Flat Geckos, such as this Pondo Flat Gecko, have clawless toes, giving the toes a squared-off appearance.

The Transvaal Flat Gecko is one of the more widespread species of Flat Geckos, occurring from the Limpopo province northwards to the Zambezi.

Juvenile Marley's Flat Geckos have an orange tail.

Marley's Flat Gecko usually occurs on rock outcrops, but is sometimes found on trees.

Flat Geckos usually have a pinkish beige coloration with irregular brown blotches or bars on the head, body and tail. The dorsal parts of the body sometimes have a bluish or pinkish sheen, especially when the skin has recently been shed. Flat Geckos have a limited ability to change colour, and can become almost translucent if they take up residence near security lights that remain on during the night. The belly is white to cream and generally lacks dark blotches.

The Lowveld Flat Gecko has a dark streak from the tip of the nose to the eyes.

Biology

Mainly rock-living and strictly nocturnal, Flat Geckos tend to be restricted to very specific habitat types such as rock outcrops or mountain ranges of granite, sandstone, gneiss or schist. This habitat specificity is probably related to Flat Geckos being selective about the crevices they rest in when inactive. Exfoliating rock flakes that form crevices of just the right dimensions offer Flat Geckos good protection from predators such as snakes and other lizards. Some species of Flat Gecko, such as the Pondo Flat Gecko, Marley's Flat Gecko and occasionally, the African Flat Gecko, may also be found on vegetation, especially trees with loose bark or fluted trunks such as the Fluted Milkwood (*Chrysophyllum viridifolium*). The flutes appear to offer the geckos the same advantages as rock crevices, and allow them to occur more widely in forested areas. The Transvaal Flat Gecko is also found on Baobab trees. The Pondo Flat Gecko and

Woodbush Flat Gecko are also occasionally known to inhabit buildings, but do not appear to thrive in this situation. It has been suggested that populations on buildings are usually displaced over time by the more adaptable Moreau's Tropical House Gecko (*Hemidactylus mabouia*), but this relationship is based on anecdotal evidence that is equivocal. Flat Geckos are accomplished climbers that use their adhesive toe pads to cling to vertical or inclined surfaces. Their gait is more serpentine than that of most other geckos, distinguishing them easily from the superficially similar, but more common, Moreau's Tropical House Gecko. Diet includes most palatable arthropods such as small beetles, moths, flies and spiders that are small enough for the geckos to handle. These are caught at night, either while the gecko moves about on a slow foraging patrol or while it is lying in ambush.

Conservation

One of the subspecies of the Woodbush Flat Gecko (*Afroedura multiporis haackei*), the Woodbush Flat Gecko and the Hawequa Flat Gecko are listed as 'Restricted' in the latest South African Red Data Book due to their restricted distributions. The Hawequa Flat Gecko is also listed by the IUCN as 'Near Threatened'. It is likely that other rare and restricted species of Flat Gecko will soon be added to the list of threatened species as more research highlights the need.

Reproduction

As in many other gecko species, female Flat Geckos lay 2 hard-shelled eggs per clutch. Eggs are laid either in a rock crevice or under loose bark, and vary in size from about 6 x 8 mm in the smallest species, to 14 x 17 mm in the largest. The eggs are slightly soft and sticky when first laid, and may become permanently stuck to one another or to the substrate before hardening. This prevents eggs from being dislodged easily, thus protecting them from being broken. Eggs are usually laid in midsummer, often communally, with up to 60 eggs in a single crevice or suitable rock overhang. It is likely that females are able to lay more than one clutch per season.

Distribution

Flat Geckos are limited in their distribution by their very specific substrate requirements. As a group, they occur over a wide range of altitudes and vegetation types, and usually only one Flat Gecko species occurs in any one locality. This means that populations are fragmented geographically, and many of the species have ranges that may be restricted to a single mountain or mountain range. Generally, Flat Geckos occur only in the more peripheral parts of southern Africa. Some species, such as the Pondo Flat Gecko and Marley's Flat Gecko, occur on the coastal plains of KwaZulu-Natal. However,

The Karoo Flat Gecko occurs in mountainous parts of the Eastern Cape.

The Tembo Flat Gecko occurs in rocky grasslands in the mountains around Queenstown in the Eastern Cape.

most of the remaining species occur in the Cape Fold, Amatola and Drakensberg mountain ranges, on outcrops and inselbergs along the west coast of Namibia and Namaqualand, and along the eastern escarpment in Mpumalanga. Species are also found in the Soutpansberg, Waterberg, and scattered outcrops in Zimbabwe and Mozambique. Currently, no species are known from Botswana.

The Amatola Flat Gecko is restricted to the Amatola and Katberg mountains.

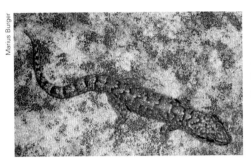

Flat Geckos, such as this Transvaal Flat Gecko, generally have a body coloration that matches the substrate on which they live.

The southern subspecies of the Woodbush Flat Gecko (A. m. haackei) is listed as 'Restricted' in the South African Red Data Book.

The Hawequa Flat Gecko is listed by the IUCN as 'Near Threatened' due to its restricted distribution in the southwestern Cape.

CALCIUM GLANDS

Calcium-storing neck glands are obvious in some gecko species. These are called endolymphatic sacs and are situated on the sides of the neck just behind the jaw, extending backwards from the skull. They are linked to the membranous labyrinth of the inner ear. Geckos are unusual among lizards in laying hard-shelled, calcareous eggs. The stores of calcium are used by the female to produce the eggshell.

SPECIES IN THE GROUP

- African Flat Gecko: *Afroedura africana*
- Amatola Flat Gecko: *Afroedura amatolica*
- Giant Swazi Flat Gecko: *Afroedura major*
- Hall's Flat Gecko: *Afroedura halli*
- Hawequa Flat Gecko: *Afroedura hawequensis* NT
- Kaokoveld Flat Gecko: *Afroedura bogerti*
- Karoo Flat Gecko: *Afroedura karroica*
- Loveridge's Flat Gecko: *Afroedura loveridgei*
- Lowveld Flat Gecko: *Afroedura langi*
- Marley's Flat Gecko: *Afroedura marleyi*
- Mountain Flat Gecko: *Afroedura nivaria*
- Pondo Flat Gecko: *Afroedura pondolia*
- Tembo Flat Gecko: *Afroedura tembulica*
- Transvaal Flat Gecko: *Afroedura transvaalica*
- Woodbush Flat Gecko: *Afroedura multiporis*

Péringuey's Coastal Leaf-toed Gecko

The species *Cryptactites peringueyi*
1 species

Description

This unusual species does not appear to have a close relationship to other southern African species, and its history is enigmatic. It was originally discovered in 1910 when two specimens were collected and described. One of these specimens carried incorrect locality data, while data for the other were vague. For more than 80 years no further specimens were found, and it was assumed that the specimens were actually from another continent. However, in 1992 two populations were discovered in salt marshes, a habitat that would not ordinarily be thought suitable for geckos. Péringuey's Coastal Leaf-toed Gecko has a minute, slim body, with a maximum body length of just 28 mm. The tail is shorter than the body. The head is flattened and is fairly distinct from the body, and the snout is pointed. Eyes are small for a gecko, and in daylight the pupils are slit-like and have a smooth edge. The dorsal parts of the body have tubercles, which are strongly keeled longitudinally. The legs are well developed and each of the digits has a single pair of enlarged leaf-like terminal pads. Males and females differ in coloration: females are plain light brown on the dorsal parts and cream ventrally; males have a similar base colour, but have a longitudinal pale golden dorsal stripe flanked by other stripes.

Marius Burger

Péringuey's Coastal Leaf-toed Gecko is a diminutive species and is restricted to salt marshes in the Eastern Cape.

Hatchling Péringuey's Coastal Leaf-toed Geckos have a total length of approximately 20 mm.

Biology

Little is known about the biology of Péringuey's Coastal Leaf-toed Gecko apart from the fact that it is nocturnal and lives among clumps of salt marsh vegetation. It appears to be rare, even in suitable habitat.

Conservation

This species is currently listed by the IUCN as 'Data Deficient'. However, its highly restricted distribution in a habitat that is prone to human transformation means that it should probably be listed as 'Endangered' or even 'Critically Endangered'.

Reproduction

Two eggs are laid in clumps of vegetation. Hatchlings are little more than 20 mm in total length.

Distribution

It is known only from the lower reaches of the Kromme River and Chelsea Point near Port Elizabeth, where it occurs in the vegetation of salt marshes that border estuaries. It has been suggested that Péringuey's Coastal Leaf-toed Gecko

reached South Africa by oceanic long jump dispersal, possibly on floating pumice, but it remains unclear from where they originated.

Péringuey's Coastal Leaf-toed Gecko occurs exclusively in the salt marshes that border estuaries.

SPECIES IN THE GROUP

■ Péringuey's Coastal Leaf-toed Gecko: *Cryptactites peringueyi* **DD**

Leaf-toed Geckos

The genera *Afrogecko* and *Goggia*
10 species

Description

This group is made up of two species of African Leaf-toed Gecko
and eight species of Dwarf Leaf-toed Gecko. Leaf-toed Geckos
possess a terminal pair of enlarged leaf-like pads on each digit, a
characteristic that is also shown by some distantly related geckos,
such as Péringuey's Coastal Leaf-toed Gecko, and some species on
other continents. Most species of Leaf-toed Gecko are small and
some, such as the Marbled African Leaf-toed Gecko and Richtersveld
Dwarf Leaf-toed Gecko, have a fairly elongate, tubular body form.
Body length in Dwarf Leaf-toed Geckos is 25–35 mm, although the
Small-scaled Dwarf Leaf-toed Gecko is much larger, with a maximum
body length of 68 mm. The African Leaf-toed Geckos are medium-
sized and vary from 50–70 mm in maximum body length. Tail length
varies greatly among species and can be shorter or longer than the
body length. In all species the tail is smooth and tapers evenly to
the tip. It is easily shed and regenerates rapidly. The head is fairly
distinct from the neck and is flattened in most species. However, it
is deeper in the Swartberg African Leaf-toed Gecko, Striped Dwarf
Leaf-toed Gecko and Small-scaled Dwarf Leaf-toed Gecko. The snout
is generally pointed. The eyes are of typical size for geckos and the
pupils have a crennelated or wavy edge in daylight. The tympanum
is small but visible. Females often have large endolymphatic sacs
on the sides of the neck, especially in the breeding season. The body
is covered with small, smooth, granular or flattened scales. The

Johan Marais

*Leaf-toed Geckos
have pairs of
enlarged leaf-like
pads on each digit,
as is apparent in
this Striped Dwarf
Leaf-toed Gecko.*

Swartberg African Leaf-toed Gecko is the only species in the group that has tubercles on the dorsal parts, but these are smooth and flattened. The legs are well developed, and although digits have small claws, these are generally retracted and are not easily visible.

Coloration varies from grey to pinkish, tan, brown or pinkish brown. Often there are wavy lines or irregular scalloped dark bars or dark blotches on the body and tail. Variation in patterning is most extreme

The Marbled African Leaf-toed Gecko occurs over much of the southwestern Cape as far east as Cape St Francis.

The original tails of Namaqualand Dwarf Leaf-toed Geckos are orange in colour. Regenerated tails are dark grey.

The Cedarberg Dwarf Leaf-toed Gecko is found on sandstone outcrops of the Cedarberg and surrounding mountains.

The Swartberg African Leaf-toed Gecko is the largest member of the group. As the name suggests, it is known from the Swartberg, but may occur more widely.

Graham Alexander

The Striped Dwarf Leaf-toed Gecko is the most widespread Leaf-toed Gecko, occurring from southern Namibia south to Saldanha Bay.

in the Marbled African Leaf-toed Gecko. Although most specimens are marbled over the entire body, some have a very prominent vertebral stripe. This variation does not appear to be linked to sex or geography, and individuals with both patterns intermingle in the same populations.

Biology

All Leaf-toed Geckos are nocturnal and most are rock-living. The Marbled African Leaf-toed Gecko is the most adaptable in the group and may be found on rock outcrops, trees and even houses around Cape Town, and along the Southern Cape Coast. They are attracted to outdoor lighting, where they feed on insects that are attracted by the light. The Striped Dwarf Leaf-toed Gecko is terrestrial and shelters under debris during the day. Leaf-toed Geckos include termites and other small insects in their diet.

Conservation

Currently, only the Small-scaled Dwarf Leaf-toed Gecko is listed by the IUCN as 'Near Threatened' on the basis of its restricted distribution. However, the Swartberg African Leaf-toed Gecko is equally restricted and is in need of a conservation evaluation.

Atherton de Villiers

The Small-scaled Dwarf Leaf-toed Gecko is listed by the IUCN as 'Near Threatened' due to its restricted distribution.

Reproduction

All Leaf-toed Geckos lay eggs. Two hard-shelled eggs are laid in each clutch and are deposited in soil-filled crevices or under bark. Marbled African Leaf-toed Geckos lay communally, and more than 30 eggs may be found in a single crevice. It is likely that females lay more than one clutch in a season.

Distribution

All members of this group are restricted to the southern and southwestern parts of southern Africa. Collectively, their distribution extends from the southern extremes of Namibia, southwards and along the Cape Fold Mountains. The Striped Dwarf Leaf-toed Gecko is the most widespread of all members of the group, occurring in low-lying areas along the West Coast from southern Namibia, south to Saldanha Bay. The Marbled Leaf-toed Gecko is also relatively widespread, occurring over much of the southwestern Cape and scattered localities along the south coast as far east as Port Elizabeth. The remaining members of the group are each restricted to particular ranges in the Cape Fold Mountains, Namaqualand or the Richtersveld.

The Richtersveld Dwarf Leaf-toed Gecko has yellow blotches on the body and neck.

Hewitt's Dwarf Leaf-toed Gecko is a small species that is restricted to the western Cape Fold Mountains.

SPECIES IN THE GROUP

- Marbled African Leaf-toed Gecko: *Afrogecko porphyreus*
- Swartberg African Leaf-toed Gecko: *Afrogecko swartbergensis*
- Braack's Dwarf Leaf-toed Gecko: *Goggia braacki*
- Cedarberg Dwarf Leaf-toed Gecko: *Goggia hexapor*
- Essex's Dwarf Leaf-toed Gecko: *Goggia essexi*
- Hewitt's Dwarf Leaf-toed Gecko: *Goggia hewitti*
- Namaqualand Dwarf Leaf-toed Gecko: *Goggia rupicola*
- Richtersveld Dwarf Leaf-toed Gecko: *Goggia gemmula*
- Small-scaled Dwarf Leaf-toed Gecko: *Goggia microlepidota* **NT**
- Striped Dwarf Leaf-toed Gecko: *Goggia lineata*

Tropical House Geckos

The genus *Hemidactylus*
4 species

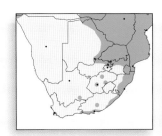

Description

The four species that make up this group are all fairly closely related and similar in appearance. They are medium to large-sized, typical geckos with a body length of 60–90 mm. Scales on the body are granular and interspaced with large tubercles, which are roughly aligned in about 14 rows across the back. Original tails are a little longer than the body length and have six longitudinal rows of enlarged, backward-pointing tubercles. Regenerated tails lack tubercles, are covered only with granular scales and are usually a little shorter than the body. The legs are well developed and toes are obviously dilated at their ends. There are several pads under each toe and these are divided down the middle of the toes into about five pairs. Each toe has an obvious retractable claw. Eyes are large and pupils are vertical with a wavy margin. The belly is usually cream or off-white, and the dorsal parts vary in colour from dark brown or grey to almost white. Usually four or five wavy crossbars made up of spots and blotches cross the back. Tropical House Geckos are able to change colour, and individuals that live around security lights that remain on during the night are usually very pale and may appear to be almost translucent.

Biology

Tropical House Geckos can be locally very abundant and may occur in dense colonies of 20 or more individuals in a single rock crevice. They are nocturnal but are sometimes active during daylight hours,

Moreau's Tropical House Gecko is the most widespread and common species in this group. Scales on the body are granular and are interspaced with large tubercles.

especially on overcast days. Although natural populations occur mainly on large trees and rocky areas, Tropical House Geckos, especially Moreau's Tropical House Gecko, are commensal with man and can be extremely common on buildings, building rubble and other man-made microhabitats. They are especially common on buildings that have security lights that attract insects at night, and the warm microhabitat created by these lights has allowed this species to inhabit areas that would otherwise be too cold. They tend to be very vocal and communicate with each other by making a 'tek-tek-tek' call. When vocalizations do not keep intruders at bay, these geckos will bite to defend their favourite feeding spot from rivals. Moreau's Tropical House Geckos are also regularly found in vehicles, and become inadvertent stowaways that are transported far and wide. This has aided their dispersal to areas far outside of their range. They are also fierce competitors, and they often appear to out-compete other gecko species, especially in localities where human development has made conditions ideal for them.

Reproduction

All species in this group lay 2 hard-shelled eggs in each clutch. Several clutches may be laid by a female in a season. Although eggs are soft when laid, they quickly harden once exposed to air. Eggs are often laid in communal depositories, which may be under bark, rock or debris, or in cracks in rocks. The eggs of Moreau's Tropical House Gecko generally do not adhere to one another or to the substrate on which they are laid. Hatchlings emerge after about 60 days and have a body length of just over 25 mm. Growth is rapid and small young are taken as food by adults. Two species of Tropical House Gecko that occur on Pacific islands are parthenogenetic. In parthenogenetic species, populations are made up entirely of females that are able to produce fertile eggs without mating. This unusual reproductive mode has allowed these species to spread easily from one island to the next, since a single individual is able to found a new population without the need of a mate.

Graham Alexander

Female Moreau's Tropical House Geckos lay clutches of two eggs and may lay several clutches in a season. Here, the two eggs and calcium glands (in the neck region) are obvious.

Distribution

As the name suggests, Tropical House Geckos are most common in warm tropical areas and are thus limited mainly to the northern and eastern parts of southern Africa. They occur in a wide range of habitats, including savanna, coastal bush and miombo woodlands. Moreau's Tropical Gecko is the most common and widespread species in southern Africa and has been expanding its range in South Africa since the early 1960s. Originally, the southern limit for this species was on the east coast, near Lake St Lucia. It has subsequently spread down the south Cape coast and is now found along the coastal strip to Port Elizabeth. This species' distribution has also spread inland in KwaZulu-Natal and it now occurs in many towns where it was previously unknown. It is now also well established in many other parts of the world, including Florida, the West Indies, Trinidad, Tobago, and Central and South America. In southern Africa the Flat-headed Tropical House Gecko and Tasman's Tropical House Gecko are limited to Mozambique and Zimbabwe, respectively, but the Flat-headed Tropical House Gecko also occurs outside of the subregion in Central Africa and in the northwestern parts of Madagascar. The Malagasy population

appears to have been introduced relatively recently. The Long-headed Tropical House Gecko only just enters southern Africa in the western extremes, where it is limited to an area around the mouth of the Kunene River. It occurs much more extensively to the north and extends to Cameroon.

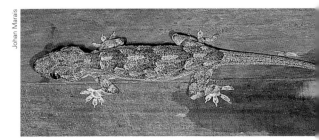

The Flat-headed Tropical House Gecko is the largest species of Tropical House Gecko.

Moreau's Tropical House Geckos are often found near artificial heat and light sources.

PARTHENOGENESIS

Most species reproduce sexually, but several species of lizard and one snake species are able to reproduce without sex. These are all-female species (referred to as parthenoforms) that reproduce without any males in the population, producing offspring that are genetic clones of their mothers. Many, but possibly not all parthenoforms arise as a result of the hybridization between two normal, sexual species. Many parthenoforms have a doubled chromosome number, a condition known as polyploidy.

SPECIES IN THE GROUP

- Flat-headed Tropical House Gecko: *Hemidactylus platycephalus*
- Long-headed Tropical House Gecko: *Hemidactylus longicephalus*
- Moreau's Tropical House Gecko: *Hemidactylus mabouia*
- Tasman's Tropical House Gecko: *Hemidactylus tasmani*

Velvet Geckos

The genus *Homopholis*
2 species

Description

This group includes two species of large, robust, chunky geckos.
Body length ranges from about 75 mm in Muller's Velvet Gecko to
over 120 mm in Wahlberg's Velvet Gecko. The head is very distinct
from the body, and the eyes are large with vertical pupils. Ear
openings are small and oval, and are situated directly behind the
gape of the mouth. The body is covered with small, overlapping
smooth scales that have a characteristic velvety feel. The skin on
the body is generally quite loose and tears easily. The tail is slightly
shorter than the body, is covered with smooth, velvety scales and
sheds easily. The toes are slightly webbed and have large, wide, flat
pads. Each toe has a large claw that forms a pronounced ridge on
the top of the toe. There are 8–12 undivided pads under each toe.
Pads are strongly adhesive, and Velvet Geckos will attempt to clasp
anything within reach when held in the hand.

Coloration is usually slate grey or greyish white, but brown
individuals are also relatively common. Velvet Geckos are able
to change colour to a degree, which aids in camouflage. Usually,
several dark irregular bars cross the body and tail, but some
individuals are almost plain or are slightly mottled, showing little
evidence of crossbars. Some individuals may also have irregular
longitudinal stripes on the dorsolateral parts of the body. The belly
is usually white but often has scattered dark scales, which create an
irregular spotted pattern.

Velvet Geckos, such as this Muller's Velvet Gecko, are large, chunky geckos with a smooth, almost velvety skin.

Johan Marais

Biology

Velvet Geckos are mainly nocturnal, but are sometimes active in the late afternoon. They live in rocky areas or on large trees and are usually slow and deliberate in their movement, but can flee with a burst of speed when under threat. Generally, Wahlberg's Velvet Geckos will position themselves in a favourite ambush site and remain motionless for long periods, waiting for prey to come into range. They often take up permanent residence in the eves of houses and will use security lights as feeding sites. The loose skin tears easily, which may be an escape mechanism. Wahlberg's Velvet Gecko appears to be a habitat generalist and can be found in a wide variety of retreats. The smaller Muller's Velvet Gecko is much more of a specialist and appears to favour holes in larges trees, especially Marula (*Sclerocarya birrea*) and Mopane (*Colophospermum mopane*) trees.

Wahlberg's Velvet Gecko has a head that is very distinct from the body, and large eyes with vertical pupils.

Muller's Velvet Gecko has larger, more prominent scales on the lips than does Wahlberg's Velvet Gecko.

Conservation

Muller's Velvet Gecko is listed by the IUCN as 'Near Threatened' on account of its restricted distribution and rarity. The species was only 'rediscovered' very recently, and its conservation status requires monitoring.

Reproduction

Clutches of 2 hard-shelled eggs are usually deposited under bark or in a rocky crevice. The breeding season appears to be longer in duration than many other southern African geckos and apparently extends into the cooler months.

Distribution

Velvet Geckos are only found in the warmer, northeastern parts of southern Africa, occurring in eastern Botswana, Zimbabwe, Mozambique, and Mpumalanga, Limpopo, northern North West and KwaZulu-Natal provinces in South Africa. Wahlberg's Velvet Gecko occurs widely in savanna and coastal forest, but Muller's Velvet Gecko is restricted, more or less, to Mopane veld.

Wahlberg's Velvet Geckos sometimes have dark blotches or stripes on the back.

SPECIES IN THE GROUP

- Muller's Velvet Gecko: *Homopholis mulleri* **NT**
- Wahlberg's Velvet Gecko: *Homopholis walbergii*

Dwarf Geckos

The genus *Lygodactylus*
12 species

Description

These are small, diurnal geckos that can be locally common. All 12 species look very similar, with small cylindrical bodies and well-developed legs. The body length is usually 35–40 mm, and the tail length is about equal to the body length. The snout is short and pointed, and although the eyes are well developed, they are small in comparison to those of nocturnal geckos. Distinct eyelids lie above the eyes but, as with most geckos, the eyelids are fused and cannot blink. The body is covered with small, granular scales and has no raised tubercles. One digit on each hand and foot is rudimentary, giving the impression that there are only four digits on each. The toes end in an almost heart-shaped widening and the pads under the toes are paired. The longest toe of each foot usually bears four to eight pairs. The four outer toes on each foot have relatively large retractile claws.

Most of the species found in southern Africa are fairly drab in dorsal coloration and are well camouflaged. The dorsum is usually olive-brown, grey-brown or blue-grey and the flanks may bear a series of pale spots, dark-edged pale longitudinal stripes or a series of large dark spots. The belly is usually cream, bluish or yellowish. The throat is either plain white or cream, but may be stippled with grey or brown. In some species, the throat is more colourful; male Chobe Dwarf Geckos have throats that are either all black or pale yellow with two dark chevrons. The tail is either a similar colour to the dorsum or a more orange-brown, especially towards the tip.

Bradfield's Dwarf Gecko is typical of this group. The eyes are small in comparison to those of nocturnal geckos.

Marius Burger

Marius Burger

Johan Marais

The Black-spotted Dwarf Gecko occurs in several isolated populations in the northeastern parts of South Africa.

The Cape Dwarf Gecko is widespread and is plentiful in the suburban parts of cities, such as Pretoria and Durban.

Biology

Dwarf Gecko species are either arboreal, rock-living or both. Some species, such as the Granite Dwarf Gecko, are strictly rock-living and occur only on granite outcrops. This may result in very restricted distributions that are determined by geology rather than climate. The more widespread species, such as the Cape Dwarf Gecko and Bradfield's Dwarf Gecko, are less habitat-specific, occurring in trees, rocky habitats and buildings. Their commensal association with humans has resulted in the Cape Dwarf Gecko extending its distribution to include several cities where it did not previously occur. Although Dwarf Geckos are considered to be strictly diurnal, those living on buildings can extend their activity time into the night where security lighting creates warmer microhabitats that also attract a ready source of food. Night-time security lighting may have facilitated the Cape Dwarf Gecko's range expansion. Their small body size restricts their diet to small insects; ants and termites are important components of their diets, but small moths, flies and other insects are also eaten, often after epic struggles. The tail is unusual in that modified scales at the tip function as an adhesive pad and help the lizard grip on

Johan Marais

The Waterberg Dwarf Gecko is restricted to the Waterberg in Limpopo province.

vertical surfaces. Tails are easily shed and regenerate quickly. The regenerated tail does not have an adhesive pad.

Conservation

Methuen's Dwarf Gecko is of conservation concern and is listed by the IUCN as 'Vulnerable' because of its very restricted range. It is known only from the Woodbush Forest Reserve and surrounding exotic plantations in Limpopo in South Africa.

Reproduction

Two hard-shelled eggs (5 x 7 mm) are laid per clutch. The female may assist the emergence of the eggs from her cloaca with her hind feet, placing the eggs next to one another so that they stick together upon hardening. This prevents them from rolling. Since suitable incubation sites may be limited, eggs are often laid communally, with up to several hundred eggs at various stages of incubation as well as hatched eggs being found in a single cavity. Dwarf Geckos reach sexual maturity about eight months after hatching, and are probably quite short-lived.

Distribution

Most species have restricted ranges and are limited to specific mountain ranges or vegetation types. There are two exceptions: Bradfield's Dwarf Gecko occurs throughout most of Namibia, apart from the coastal areas, and into the northern parts of Namaqualand, while the Cape Dwarf Gecko occurs extensively in the northeastern parts of southern Africa, extending down the east coast to Transkei, and the western parts of the Free State. There is also an introduced population in Port Elizabeth. Dwarf Geckos are not found in the southwestern parts of South Africa.

Johan Marais

Spotted Dwarf Geckos live among rocks on hillsides.

SPECIES IN THE GROUP

- Angola Dwarf Gecko: *Lygodactylus angolensis*
- Bernard's Dwarf Gecko: *Lygodactylus barnardi*
- Black-spotted Dwarf Gecko: *Lygodactylus nigropunctatus*
- Bradfield's Dwarf Gecko: *Lygodactylus bradfieldi*
- Cape Dwarf Gecko: *Lygodactylus capensis*
- Chobe Dwarf Gecko: *Lygodactylus chobiensis*
- Granite Dwarf Gecko: *Lygodactylus graniticolus*
- Lawrence's Dwarf Gecko: *Lygodactylus lawrencei*
- Methuen's Dwarf Gecko: *Lygodactylus methueni* VU
- Spotted Dwarf Gecko: *Lygodactylus ocellatus*
- Stevenson's Dwarf Gecko: *Lygodactylus stevenson*
- Waterberg Dwarf Gecko: *Lygodactylus waterbergensis*

ADHESIVE TOE PADS

Adhesion between a gecko's toes and the substrate is not due to suction, stickiness, electrostatic forces or friction; rather, it is due to intermolecular attractive forces known as Van der Waal's forces. These are weak forces of attraction between molecules and, for the attraction to be sufficiently strong to support the gecko, the pad has to have a very large surface area at a microscopic level and be in very close contact with the substrate.

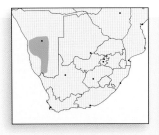

Festive Gecko

The species *Narudasia festiva*
1 species

Description

The single species in this group is not closely related to any other geckos in southern Africa, and it would appear that its nearest relatives are found in the Sahara. Festive Geckos are small, with a maximum body length of just 30 mm. The tail length is usually a little longer than the body. The head is depressed and is not very distinct from the neck. The snout is pointed and the scales on the snout are larger than those on the posterior parts of the head and body. Eyes are large with vertical pupils, and the ear openings are small and round. Dorsal parts of the body are covered with small granular scales and the limbs are well developed. These geckos are distinctive in that they have unusually long, slender digits, which are not dilated at their ends but bear claws. The tail is cylindrical, may be slightly segmented and is easily shed. The scales on the tail are larger than those on the body.

Coloration is varied and the body may be an infusion of purples and browns or greyish, reddish or chestnut-brown. The dorsal parts have a series of narrow, white-edged, black, zigzag crossbars, with cream spots in the angles of the zigzags. Usually, the tail colour differs from that of the dorsal parts and is olive-yellow to yellow or orange, with some black barring. Regenerated tails, however, are uniformly grey.

John Visser

Festive Geckos can be distinguished from other geckos by their unusually long, slender digits, which are not dilated at the ends.

Festive Geckos often have brightly coloured tails. Original tails are barred, but regenerated tails (as pictured here) are uniformly coloured.

Biology

Little is known about the biology of Festive Geckos. They are rock-living and can be found in cracks and crevices of rocks on slopes and ravines. They may also occur in flat areas, where they make use of rocky shelves, sheltering in crevices. Activity follows a mainly crepuscular pattern, with geckos emerging to feed during the early morning and late afternoon. While active, they are agile and swift. The diet consists of a variety of small rock-living insects.

Reproduction

Two hard-shelled eggs (8 x 6 mm) are laid per clutch. These are deposited in rock cracks.

Distribution

Festive Geckos are restricted to arid mountain slopes in central southern Namibia.

SPECIES IN THE GROUP

■ Festive Gecko: *Narudasia festiva*

Giant Ground Gecko

The species *Chondrodactylus angulifer*
1 species

Description

This group includes one unusual species. It is closely related to, and in the same genus as, the Tubercled Geckos, but is quite distinctive, probably as a result of adaptation to different microhabitats. As the name suggests, the Giant Ground Gecko is large with a robust, cylindrical body. Adult body length is about 100 mm, but the tail is shorter than the body. The head is bulbous in shape, is very distinct from the body and has a convex snout. The eyes are large and the pupils are vertical with four small notches. Ear openings are visible and slit-like, but are smaller than the diameter of the eyes. The snout and top of the head are covered with polygonal scales of varying size. Dorsal parts of the body have scattered large tubercles that extend onto the legs and forearms. The tail is cylindrical, tapering and feebly segmented with rings of white tubercles. The legs are well developed, but are fairly slender and are carried under the body in a very characteristic manner, giving the gecko a raised, almost stilt-like gait. The tail is also held high when walking. The digits are unusually short, lacking pads and claws. Instead of pads, the under-surface of the digits is covered with small, spiny scales that are adapted for locomotion on loose sand.

Coloration and patterning are varied, but the basic body colour is usually an orange to reddish brown with white spots of various sizes, becoming white below. Males have more pronounced white

The Giant Ground Gecko is a highly distinctive, large gecko with a body length of about 100 mm.

Johan Marais

spots than females. In some individuals, especially those from the southern parts of the range, a series of four or five large dark-edged white spots runs down each side of the back. Diffuse white lines run from the snout over the head, and in some parts of the distribution the white patterning on

Juvenile Giant Ground Geckos have very large heads in proportion to their bodies.

The Giant Ground Gecko has large eyes with four notches in the slit-like pupils.

the dorsal parts is more extensive, forming several white chevrons that connect the white spots on the dorsal parts. Tails are usually banded.

Biology

These geckos are terrestrial sand dwellers that are especially partial to dry, sandy riverbeds. However, they may be common even in fairly rocky areas in the Karoo. They are strictly nocturnal and spend the day in burrows that they dig, and which may be up to a metre deep, in soft sand. During the night they emerge to feed and will generally move about slowly. Their behaviour of actively searching for food, and the fact that they are relatively slow-moving, makes them especially susceptible to predation and being killed on roads. Diet is made up primarily of termites, moths, beetles and even small lizards. In defence, Giant Ground Geckos will inflate their bodies, stand very erect with tails raised and hiss with an open mouth.

Reproduction

Females lay 1 or 2 hard-shelled, almost spherical eggs (16 x 18 mm). Eggs are laid in a hole dug by the female and are covered once laid. It is likely that more than one clutch of eggs is laid per season. Eggs take about three months to hatch. Hatchlings are 70 mm in total length and reach sexual maturity in one year.

Distribution

The Giant Ground Gecko is restricted to gravel plains and sandy areas between dunes. The species is widespread in the succulent and nama karoo, extending northwards into the Namib Desert, almost to the Kunene River.

SPECIES IN THE GROUP

■ Giant Ground Gecko: *Chondrodactylus angulifer*

Tubercled Geckos

The genus *Chondrodactylus* excluding *C. angulifer*
3 species

Description

The three species that make up this group are closely related and are similar in appearance. All are large, stout geckos that have a robust build. Body length can be up to 100 mm, excluding the tail, which is usually about the same length or a little longer than the body. The head is triangular in shape and the eyes are typical for geckos, with fused eyelids and vertical pupils. The two most widespread species, Turner's Tubercled Gecko and Bibron's Tubercled Gecko, have very obvious, large keeled tubercles over the head, body and tail, giving these lizards a very rough appearance. The tubercles are arranged irregularly and are interspersed with small, granular scales. Tubercles are absent on regenerated tails. Tails are segmented and can become relatively fat at the base, especially during the summer when food is plentiful. Although FitzSimons' Tubercled Gecko has tubercles, they are not keeled and are not interspersed with granular scales. Legs are stout and well developed, and the undivided toe pads are similar to those of the Common Geckos (*Pachydactylus*), to which Tubercled Geckos are closely related. Claws are entirely absent from the fingers and those on the toes are so small that they are only apparent when viewed under magnification.

Body colour is generally brown or grey on the dorsal parts and a creamy white on the belly. Up to six darker-brown, wavy crossbands with infused white spots or flecks pattern the back, but these may not be obvious in individuals that are generally dark. Four dark stripes are sometimes present on the head, running from the snout to the back of the head. Body coloration can vary to a degree over time and generally matches the substrate on which the geckos are living.

Johan Marais

Tubercled Geckos, such as FitzSimons' Tubercled Gecko, are large, stout geckos that have a sturdy build and obvious tubercles on the body.

Tubercled Geckos have large, robust heads and big eyes with vertical pupils.

Biology

Tubercled Geckos are nocturnal and, in natural conditions, occur on rocky outcrops, cliffs or on large trees that have peeling bark. They hide in rock crevices, under large rocks or under bark during the day, emerging to feed at night. All three species are commonly found in close association with human habitation, and individual geckos will often live for long periods of time in the proximity of security lights. They often occur in large aggregations, and more than 100 animals may shelter under a single rock slab. Prey includes a wide variety of invertebrates such as large grasshoppers, mantids and large moths. Tubercled Geckos will even eat small lizards if they can catch them. Typically, the hunting strategy is one of ambush, where prey that comes into range is seized with a rapid and unexpected lunge. However, they will also actively search for prey and will venture onto the ground while hunting. They will not hesitate to bite in self-defence if they are handled.

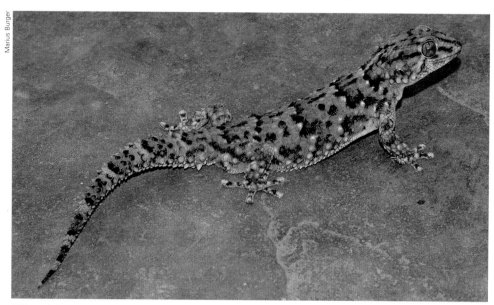

Bibron's Tubercled Gecko is very similar in appearance to Turner's Tubercled Gecko and, until recently, was considered to be the same species.

Johan Marais

Turner's Tubercled Gecko has highly variable body markings. The white spots are limited to the anterior parts of this individual.

Reproduction

Clutches of two hard-shelled eggs are laid under rocks, in rock cracks, under loose bark or in holes dug in sand. Several clutches can be laid by the female during the summer. Eggs are about 13 x 15 mm in size and the young are about 30 mm in body length.

Distribution

Tubercled Geckos occur widely over southern Africa but are absent from the southwestern Cape, southern and eastern coastal regions, all but the northern extremes of KwaZulu-Natal and the Free State. Usually, not more than a single species occurs in any one locality, but Turner's Tubercled Gecko and FitzSimons' Tubercled Gecko may occur together in the northwestern extremes of Namibia, and the distributions of Bibron's and Turner's Tubercled Geckos overlap in southern Namibia. Generally, Turner's Tubercled Gecko is limited to the northern half of southern Africa, whereas Bibron's Tubercled Gecko is the common form in the south.

Marius Burger

Turner's Tubercled Geckos are widespread over the northern parts of southern Africa.

SPECIES IN THE GROUP

- Bibron's Tubercled Gecko: *Chondrodactylus bibronii*
- FitzSimons' Tubercled Gecko: *Chondrodactylus fitzsimonsi*
- Turner's Tubercled Gecko: *Chondrodactylus turneri*

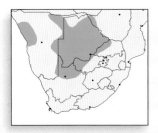

Ground Geckos

The genus *Colopus*
2 species

Description

The two species in this group have a characteristically elongated and slender body shape. They are medium-sized geckos with a maximum body length of about 60 mm and a tail of about the same length. The head is short, convex and fairly distinct from the neck. The eyes are large with vertical pupils that close to leave four pinholes. Ear openings are small and oval. The dorsal parts of the body have granular scales, and the ventral scales overlap to an extent. The limbs are long and slender. The digits are also long and slender in Koch's Ground Gecko, but are short in the Kalahari Ground Gecko. The digits are almost padless and appear to be adapted to a terrestrial lifestyle: in Kalahari Ground Geckos, only females have two small undivided pads on the digits of the hind feet, whereas Koch's Ground Gecko has three pads only on the middle digits. The tail is unsegmented, slender and tapering in Koch's Ground Gecko but relatively stout in Kalahari Ground Geckos.

Koch's Ground Gecko tends to be an anaemic greyish white above and white below. There are several irregular brown crossbars over the dorsal parts of the body and the tail. In the Kalahari Ground Gecko, the body patterning is more conspicuous and attractive, with a complicated pattern of large, dark-edged, pale spots on light orange or brown. In some areas, striped individuals with a dark-edged pale vertebral line on the back are more common.

Ground Geckos have an elongated body shape. This Kalahari Ground Gecko has very vivid markings for the species.

Marius Burger

Johan Marais

Koch's Ground Gecko has anaemic, greyish white body coloration.

Biology

Ground Geckos are strictly nocturnal and rarely encountered. During the day they retreat into short burrows, but they emerge to forage in darkness, especially after rains. Flat, sandy plains are the preferred habitats for both species, where they may be found slowly patrolling for food. Diet consists of small insects such as termites.

Reproduction

Although little is known about the reproduction of Koch's Ground Gecko, the Kalahari Ground Gecko is known to lay 2 hard-shelled eggs, the norm for geckos.

Distribution

The Kalahari Ground Gecko is widespread over the Kalahari region of Botswana and South Africa. Its distribution extends into the eastern parts of Namibia and the western extremes of Zimbabwe. Koch's Ground Gecko has a more restricted distribution, occurring in the northwestern parts of Namibia from Walvis Bay in the south to Cape Cross in the north, extending some distance inland.

Johan Marais

The Kalahari Ground Gecko actively patrols for food on sandy plains.

SPECIES IN THE GROUP

- Kalahari Ground Gecko: *Colopus wahlbergii*
- Koch's Ground Gecko: *Colopus kochii*

Dune Geckos

Selected species from the genus *Pachydactylus*
3 species

Description

Two of the three species in this group, the Namib Dune Gecko and Kaoko Dune Gecko, show a bizarre and remarkable adaptation to life on loose sand: Namib Dune Geckos have extensive webbing between the digits of all four feet, whereas Kaoko Dune Geckos have webbing on their hind feet only. The third species, Austen's Dune Gecko, lacks webbing but is obviously closely related to the other species in the group and is similar in many other characteristics. Dune Geckos are medium-sized lizards with a maximum body length of about 75 mm. Austen's Dune Gecko tends to be a little smaller than the other two species, with a body length of about 45 mm. Tail length is slightly shorter than the body, which is slender in all three species. The head is large and is very distinct from the thin neck. The snout is pointed, especially so in the Kaoko Dune Gecko and Namib Dune Gecko, giving the head an almost triangular shape in these two species. The eyes are very large and distinctive, and although they cannot close, there are prominent eyelids above and in front of the eyes. The ear openings are visible and the Namib Dune Gecko has peculiar, tubular nostrils. The body is covered with fine granular scales, but no tubercles. The legs are thin and stilt-like, especially in the Namib Dune Gecko. In this species the webbing extends almost to the toe tip and each digit has a soft, claw-like scale. The Kaoko Dune Gecko has two small pads under each digit and the digits on all feet also bear claws. In Austen's Dune Gecko, the digits are slightly dilated and there are three pads under each finger and four under each toe. The tail is thin and unsegmented, but may be

Dune Geckos, such as this Namib Dune Gecko, have large, distinctive eyes. Some members of this group have webbed feet.

Johan Marais

The Kaoko Dune Gecko has webbing on the hind feet only and has darker body coloration than the Namib Dune Gecko.

slightly swollen at the base in Austen's Dune Gecko. Males of all three species have a prominent bulge at the base of the tail, which houses the hemipenes.

Coloration is distinctive, but bears some similarities to the anaemic-looking Koch's Ground Gecko (*Colopus kochii*). All three species in this group have an almost translucent appearance. Generally, in the Namib Dune Gecko the body colour is a pinkish brown above and white below. Brown-edged blotches run down the middle of the back and coalesce into a pale, brown-edged line down the tail. The eyes are blood red with a white-edged pupil and white eyelids. The Kaoko Dune Gecko is usually a sandy brown above and chalky white below. Irregular, dark brown spots and bars are scattered over the dorsal parts. Austen's Dune Gecko has a pinkish brown body dorsally, but varies from a light grey to dark brown. There is often yellow on the tail, snout, and back of the head and eyelids. White spots of different sizes cover the body and tail, and the ventral parts are white.

The Namib Dune Gecko has a surprisingly upright posture when patrolling for food. The tail is also carried high.

Austen's Dune Gecko lacks webbing on the feet, but is obviously closely related to the other species in the group.

Biology

All three species in this group are associated with arid, sandy habitats. The Namib Dune Gecko is the most specialized, and is generally found only on wind-blown sands. Although the Kaoko Dune Gecko is also most prevalent on dunes, it also occurs on gravel plains. Austen's Dune Gecko can be locally abundant and is found on sparsely vegetated, stable dunes. All three species are strictly nocturnal and spend the daylight hours in burrows that they construct with almost dogged determination. Burrows may be dug at the base of bushes and rocks, but are sometimes located in open areas. Dune Geckos can be active on cold nights, when temperatures are as low as 15 °C and the wind is strong. They search for food by slowly and deliberately patrolling their turf for small insects and spiders. The posture in all three species is surprisingly upright, and the Namib Dune Gecko carries its tail high. Webbing on the feet gives good purchase on the soft sand.

Reproduction

Two hard-shelled eggs are laid in each clutch and are deposited in a hole dug in soft sand by the female. The eggs take about three months to hatch.

Distribution

Dune Geckos are restricted to a narrow strip along the West Coast of southern Africa. Austen's Dune Gecko occurs from Bloubergstrand in the south, north to just south of the Orange River. The Namib Dune Gecko occurs from just south of the Orange River, north into southern Angola. The Kaoko Dune Gecko is restricted to the northern Namib Desert and coastal regions of southern Angola.

SPECIES IN THE GROUP

- Austen's Dune Gecko: *Pachydactylus austeni*
- Kaoko Dune Gecko: *Pachydactylus vanzyli*
- Namib Dune Gecko: *Pachydactylus rangei*

Common Geckos

Selected species from the genus *Pachydactylus*
5 species

Description

These small to medium-sized geckos have a body length that varies
from 45 to 65 mm. Original tails may be slightly longer than the
body, but regenerated tails are usually shorter. The head is not
depressed and the eyes are large. Ear openings are obliquely oval.
The body is usually a little flattened and has enlarged tubercles,
which are strongly keeled in the Cape Gecko but less so in the other
species. The belly scales are smooth and slightly overlapping. The
legs are well developed, but are stocky and relatively short. Digits
are short with four or five pads below the middle toes. Original tails
are segmented, with each segment consisting of 3–6 scale rows and
a row of tubercles. Tails are very easily shed and regenerate quickly.
The regenerated tails are significantly thicker, especially at the base,
and may be almost carrot-shaped. They lack tubercles entirely and
are similar to the original tails of the Tiger Gecko.

    Colour and patterning vary within and among species. Cape
Geckos and Transvaal Geckos have similar coloration and pattern,
generally a dirty cream, greyish brown, or brown with dark and light
blotches over the head, body and tail that sometimes form diffuse
crossbars. A dark line usually runs from the snout through the eye
on the sides of the head. Cape Geckos tend to have less distinct
patterning and can be almost any earth tone, whereas Transvaal
Geckos are usually redder with bolder patterns. Van Son's Geckos are

Graham Alexander

*Common Geckos,
such as this
Transvaal Gecko,
are generally brown
with dark and light
blotching or barring
on the body. The
tail thickens as a
fat store.*

brown, with up to nine pale crossbars and a pale vertebral stripe, forming a regular geometric pattern on the back and a pale reticulated pattern on the head. Tiger Geckos are either barred with five to six white or yellow crossbars or marked, with many prominent dark spots and a few white spots. O'Shaughnessy's Geckos have striking markings, with five to seven alternating, broad, dark and light bars across the body. The most anterior dark bar circles the head from the tip of the snout, through the eye and across the nape. The top of the head is pale. The belly is uniformly white or dirty white in all species. Juveniles are usually a darker colour and may be purple-brown above with pale crossbands or plain chocolate brown.

Juvenile Van Son's Geckos have fine white spots and lines on the body.

White bars become more prominent in adult Van Son's Geckos, often forming a reticulate pattern on the dorsal parts.

The Cape Gecko occurs extensively over the interior parts of southern Africa. Body tubercles are strongly keeled.

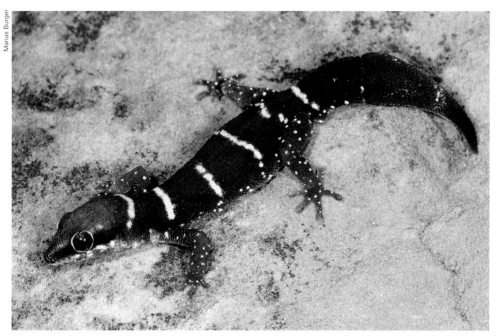

Marius Burger

Tiger Geckos usually have five or six white or yellow crossbars on the body.

Biology

Common Geckos are terrestrial and rock-living. They may often be found in old termitaria, under stones, in rotting logs or in rock crevices where they may be found in groups of two or three. They are strictly nocturnal, emerging to feed on small insects after dark. Tails swell significantly and act as fat storage sites during times of plenty.

Reproduction

Females lay clutches of 2 eggs during summer, and more than one clutch may be laid in a season. Eggs (about 10 x 7 mm) are deposited in old termitaria or under stones. Hatchlings are 30–40 mm in length.

Distribution

Members of this group tend to be widespread in occurrence and collectively range over most of the interior of southern Africa, west of the eastern escarpment. Two species of Common Gecko may occur together in several regions, but it is more usual to find only one in any given area.

Johan Marais

Transvaal Geckos have vertical elliptic pupils that become almost slit-like during the day.

SPECIES IN THE GROUP

- Cape Gecko: *Pachydactylus capensis*
- O'Shaughnessy's Gecko: *Pachydactylus oshaughnessyi*
- Tiger Gecko: *Pachydactylus tigrinus*
- Transvaal Gecko: *Pachydactylus affinis*
- Van Son's Gecko: *Pachydactylus vansoni*

Smooth Geckos

Selected species from the genus *Pachydactylus*
4 species

Description

Geckos in this group are all small-bodied, around 33–40 mm in
length. The tail is about 30% longer than the body, and the head and
body may be slightly or moderately depressed. Eyes are large with
vertical pupils and fairly prominent eyelids that encircle the eyes.
Ears are oval and slightly oblique. Scales on the back are uniform,
granular and may abut or overlap slightly. No enlarged tubercles
are present and, even though there may be feeble keeling of dorsal
scales, the general appearance is one of smooth skin on the back.
Scales on the belly are also smooth and slightly overlapping. Limbs
are well developed and may be slender to fairly stout, depending
on the species. Digits are feebly dilated, with 3–5 pads below the
middle toe. The tail is cylindrical and does not have tubercles. It is
unsegmented in the Speckled Gecko and Schertz's Gecko, slightly
segmented in the Velvety Gecko and obviously segmented in the
Angolan Banded Gecko. Males have an obvious hemipenial pouch.

Coloration and patterning are variable, both within and among
species. The Speckled Gecko is usually mid-brown with tiny white
spots and a pale border around the eyes, but may be pale grey to
purplish brown above with irregular and diffuse patches of dark
brown. Some individuals have scattered, dark-edged, whitish spots
over most of the dorsal parts. Schertz's Gecko is usually dark brown
with dark-edged, pale crossbars, which may be broken along the
vertebral line. The Angolan Banded Gecko has more regular barring,
and juveniles and some adults have five distinct pale bands on
the back. The bands are a very prominent bright lemon yellow in

*Smooth Geckos,
such as this
Velvety Gecko,
have uniform and
granular scales,
giving a general
appearance of
smooth skin.*

Johan Marais

juveniles, becoming white and more diffuse in adults. The bands become wider on the tail, making the tail predominantly pale, especially towards the end. Adults that lose the banding appear speckled. The Velvety Gecko usually has three very broad pale bars: one just behind the head; one in front of the hind legs; and the third over much of

The Speckled Gecko occurs widely in the northern third of southern Africa and over much of Namibia.

Schertz's Gecko is restricted to the coastal parts of northern Namibia.

Sub-adult Velvety Geckos differ markedly in patterning from the adults.

the tail. Boldly marked juveniles mature into adults that have typically diffuse patterns of light and dark spots and blotches on a pale purplish background. This species is capable of colour change and can become very dark purple with tiny white punctuations. All species in this group have white or creamy white bellies.

Biology

Little is known about the biology of these geckos. They are nocturnal and rock-living, inhabiting thin crevices in rocks or gaps under rocks. The Speckled Gecko is more terrestrial and may be found under rocks and stones in open grassy areas. It is slow-moving and may be abundant in certain areas. The species appears to be able to tolerate high temperatures, as it shelters under rocks that become very warm during summer days.

Reproduction

Smooth Geckos appear to have typically gekkonid reproductive characteristics.

Although data for these species are scanty, they all appear to lay 2 hard-shelled eggs per clutch in summer.

Distribution

Three of the species in this group have fairly restricted ranges in southern Africa and are limited to the northwestern parts of Namibia. The Speckled Gecko has a much wider distribution and occurs throughout most of Namibia, extending into the Richtersveld, the northern half of Botswana, Zimbabwe, and the Limpopo and Mpumalanga provinces in the northeastern part of South Africa, across the southern half of Mozambique, and extending into parts of Zambia, Angola and Malawi.

SPECIES IN THE GROUP

- Angolan Banded Gecko: *Pachydactylus caraculic*
- Schertz's Gecko: *Pachydactylus scherzi*
- Speckled Gecko: *Pachydactylus punctatus*
- Velvety Gecko: *Pachydactylus bicolor*

Large-headed Geckos

The species *Pachydactylus gaiasensis* and *P. oreophilus*
2 species

Description

This group includes two species of medium-sized geckos that range in adult body length from 50 to 70 mm. The tail is shorter than the body in the Brandberg Gecko, but is slightly longer in the Kaokoveld Gecko. The head is large and is very distinct from the neck, and the snout is pointed. The eyes are medium to large in relation to the head, and the ear openings are small and horizontally oval. The head and body are fairly depressed. Members of this group have numerous enlarged tubercles separated by granular scales on the back. The legs are well developed, but are reasonably slender. Digits are somewhat dilated at their ends and 6–8 pads underlie each middle toe. The tail is slender and is prominently segmented with transverse rows of strongly keeled tubercles.

Large-headed Geckos tend to have a pink-beige body colour with brown blotches and spots over the body and tail. The belly is mainly white. Kaokoveld Geckos have a poorly-defined collar that circles the back of the head and runs through the eyes. The collar is pale with dark edging. The Brandberg Gecko usually has a pale vertebral line and fine pale spots over the body.

Biology

Large-headed Geckos are nocturnal. Although primarily rock-living, the Brandberg Gecko does forage on the ground.

Conservation

Although neither of the Large-headed Geckos is currently listed as 'Threatened', the Brandberg Gecko has a restricted range and would probably be classified as 'Threatened' if evaluated using IUCN criteria.

Reproduction

Although little is known about reproduction in Large-headed Geckos, it is likely that females lay clutches of 2 eggs under rock flakes.

Johan Marais

As the name suggests, Large-headed Geckos, such as the Brandberg Gecko, have large heads and large eyes.

Kaokoveld Geckos live on rock outcrops and emerge to forage during the night.

Juvenile Kaokoveld Geckos are strikingly marked.

Sub-adult Brandberg Geckos are distinctively marked and usually have a light band around the nape of the neck.

Distribution

This group is limited to the northwestern parts of Namibia. As the name suggests, the Brandberg Gecko is endemic to the Brandberg and surrounding areas. The Kaokoveld Gecko occurs from the Brandberg, north into southwestern Angola.

SPECIES IN THE GROUP

- Brandberg Gecko: *Pachydactylus gaiasensis*
- Kaokoveld Gecko: *Pachydactylus oreophilus*

Large-scaled Geckos

The species *Pachydactylus scutatus* and *P. parascutatus*
2 species

Description

This group consists of two species of small gecko that have an adult body length of about 40 mm. The head is relatively elongate and large, and is distinct from the neck. The eyes have vertical pupils with wavy margins and are relatively small in relation to the size of the head. Ear openings are small and horizontally oval, and the head and body are slightly depressed. Scales on the body are large, rounded and flattened, with an obvious medial keel, and generally in about 14 rows. Although these enlarged tubercles are contiguous, a single small, granular scale is located at each junction between four adjacent tubercles. The belly scales are smooth. The legs are relatively short and stout. Digits are fairly short and somewhat dilated at their ends, and bear 5–7 pads under each middle toe. The tail is slightly longer than the body. It is cylindrical and relatively thick, with distinct whorls of enlarged, keeled tubercles, each separated by two rows of smaller scales.

Body coloration is mainly beige to yellowish brown with a patchwork of darker brown markings. The dark markings are more regularly spaced on the tail and sometimes form transverse bands, especially in the Sesfontein Gecko. A dark stripe extends posteriorly from the tip of the snout through the eye. Common Large-scaled Geckos have a well-defined collar that circles the back of the head and runs through the eyes. The collar is pale with dark edging and is

Johan Marais

Large-scaled Geckos have unusually large, rounded and flattened scales on the body, each with an obvious medial keel, as in this Common Large-scaled Gecko.

Johan Marais

The Sesfontein Gecko was recently discovered, and all known specimens come from the area around Sesfontein in Namibia.

also evident in juvenile Sesfontein Geckos, but without the dark edge. The belly in both species is mainly white.

Biology

Large-scaled Geckos are nocturnal. Although primarily rock-living, the Common Large-scaled Gecko will forage on the ground. Both species in the group have fragile skin that is easily damaged by handling. The fragile skin appears to serve an antipredatory function: predators such as snakes are likely to hold onto a piece of skin, allowing the gecko to rip free and make its escape. This strategy is also seen in Delicate Geckos.

Conservation

Although none of the Large-scaled Geckos are currently listed as 'Threatened', the Sesfontein Gecko has a very restricted range and would probably be classified as 'Threatened' if evaluated using IUCN criteria.

Reproduction

The Common Large-scaled Gecko lays 2 eggs (5–6 x 7–8 mm) under rock flakes. Few other reproduction data are currently known for this group.

Distribution

The Large-scaled Gecko is restricted to the northwestern parts of Namibia. The Common Large-scaled Gecko occurs from south of Sesfontein, northwards over much of Kaokoland into southern Angola. The Sesfontein Gecko has only recently been described, and all known specimens reportedly come from the area around Sesfontein, north of the Hoanib River.

SPECIES IN THE GROUP

- Common Large-scaled Gecko: *Pachydactylus scutatus*
- Sesfontein Gecko: *Pachydactylus parascutatus*

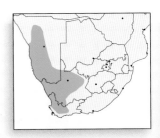

Rough-scaled Geckos

Selected species from the genus *Pachydactylus*
4 species

Description

All members of this group are medium-sized to small geckos with a
very rugose appearance. Body length ranges from 45 to 65 mm. The
tail can be slightly longer than the body in the Western Cape Gecko,
but it is shorter than the body in the other species in the group.
The head is distinct from the neck and is very slightly depressed.
The snout is rounded. Ear openings are small and obliquely oval.
Species in this group have keeled scales over most of their bodies.
Enlarged keeled tubercles occur on the back, head, upper surface
of the hind limbs, and even on the forearms in the Rough Gecko.
Belly scales are keeled in the Rough Gecko but smooth in the other
species. Legs are well developed and are fairly long. Digits are
short and moderately dilated at the tips, with four or five undivided
pads under each. The tail is segmented and covered with irregularly
sized scales that may be keeled or spiny and are at least partially
overlapping. There are two or three enlarged sharp-edged tubercles
on either side of the base of the tail.

Coloration and pattern vary among species: Barnard's Geckos
have a chocolate brown body with a lighter brown head. The
six pale, dark-edged bands on the back may be joined with a
pale vertebral stripe. Karoo Geckos have similar coloration and
patterning, but the bands are not linked with a vertebral stripe.
Rough Geckos are an olive colour with four wavy cream to yellow-
brown cross bands. The side of the head is sometimes also marked
with a white stripe. Western Cape Geckos are generally orange-
brown to dark grey-brown, with large, diffuse paler blotches. The
belly coloration ranges from pale white to dark brown. The eyes are
generally golden brown.

Johan Marais

*The Rough Gecko is
typical of this group
in having a very
rugose appearance,
and enlarged keeled
tubercles on the
head and body.*

Biology

Very little is known about the biology of this group of geckos. They are all nocturnal and different species occupy different microhabitats: the Rough Gecko is partly terrestrial and is often found beneath cover on sandy substrates, but also hides under the bark of trees. Barnard's Gecko is also terrestrial, but is more closely associated with rocky substrates. The Karoo Gecko is strictly rock-living, occupying deep horizontal cracks and crevices in rock outcrops. The Western Cape Gecko is terrestrial and shelters under stones on sandy soil. When threatened, Rough-scaled Geckos arch their tails over their backs and stand high on their legs in a threat display.

Reproduction

No information on reproduction has ever been collected for these species. It is likely that females lay 2 hard-shelled eggs per clutch, as is typical for geckos.

Distribution

Rough-scaled Geckos are restricted to the western parts of southern Africa, occurring from central northern Namibia, through the southern and eastern parts of Namibia, into the Northern Cape and Western Cape provinces of South Africa.

The Rough Gecko is often found beneath cover on sandy substrates and under the loose bark of dead trees.

The Karoo Gecko is strictly rock-living, occupying deep horizontal cracks and crevices in rock outcrops. This individual is a juvenile.

The Western Cape Gecko is terrestrial and shelters under stones on sandy soil.

SPECIES IN THE GROUP

- Barnard's Gecko: *Pachydactylus barnardi*
- Karoo Gecko: *Pachydactylus formosus*
- Rough Gecko: *Pachydactylus rugosus*
- Western Cape Gecko: *Pachydactylus labialis*

Barnard's Gecko is terrestrial, but is often associated with rocky substrates.

Western Geckos

Selected species from the genus *Pachydactylus*
22 species

Description

Currently, this group includes 22 species of medium to small geckos
with depressed heads and bodies. The adults of many of the species
within the group are almost indistinguishable from one another,
and the taxonomy of the group has only recently been resolved
using molecular techniques. Descriptions of two more species are
in the process of being published, and it is likely that several more
species still await discovery. Although San Steyn's Gecko is more
closely related to the Smooth Geckos, the presence of tubercles
on the back and tail gives it a closer superficial resemblance to the
Western Geckos, and it is thus included in this group. The body
length of adults varies from 40 to 60 mm and tails are a little longer.
The head is relatively large and is distinct from the neck. The snout
is pointed, and the eyes are relatively small. The dorsal parts of
the body are covered with granular scales. Enlarged tubercles are
scattered between the granular scales or occur in rows, depending
on the species. Tubercles may be flat, conical or keeled, and are
entirely lacking in one subspecies of the Western Spotted Gecko.
The limbs and digits are moderately stout and 5–7 pads underlie the
middle toe. Tails are relatively thin, but may be moderately swollen
at the base, especially after regeneration. Original tails are obviously
segmented, with transverse rows of tubercles, but regenerated tails
are generally smooth and lack tubercles.

Coloration and patterning are variable, but adults of most
species in the group are a pinkish brown, yellowish brown to brown,
or beige with darker brown spots, blotches or bars on the dorsal
parts. In several species, such as Visser's Gecko and Weber's Gecko,

*Many of the adult Western Geckos, such as this Good's Gecko, are
almost indistinguishable from one another.*

McLachlan's Gecko is restricted to the area around the Karasberge and the Orange River in southeastern Namibia.

black-and-white banding of the tail becomes more vivid posteriorly. In other species, the patterning on the tail is similar to that of the dorsal parts of the body. Individuals of some species, such as the Banded, Waterberg, Robert's, McLachlan's and Good's geckos, also have a well-defined collar that circles the back of the head and runs through the eyes. The belly is usually creamy white. Juveniles are more vividly marked and brightly coloured than the adults, and many have obvious barring, which fades as the geckos grow. In the Western Spotted, McLachlan's and Richtersveld geckos, juveniles have black bodies with various combinations of white bars and saddles and red, black or brown tails.

Biology

Most species of Western Geckos are primarily rock-living, but some are known to venture onto sandy substrates. Werner's Gecko is active in riverine vegetation. All species are nocturnal and spend their inactive periods in rock cracks or under stones or other debris. They feed on a variety of small invertebrates, including spiders, moths, ants, termites and insect larvae. Many of the species appear to be substrate-specific and are found only on particular geological formations or rock types. This specificity has probably been the driving force that has lead to the high rates of speciation and richness within the group.

As with other species in this group, the juveniles of McLachlan's Gecko have striking and distinctive markings.

Monica's Gecko is one of the more terrestrial species in the group. It occurs around the lower Orange River and Fish River Valley.

Johan Marais

Western Spotted Geckos can be locally abundant. They take refuge during the day under exfoliating rock flakes.

Conservation

Although none of the species in this group are currently classified as threatened, Good's Gecko, Griffin's Gecko and the Otavi Gecko have highly restricted ranges that do not fall into any protected areas. Because of previously confused taxonomy, most species are poorly known and are in need of study. Fortunately, the group occurs in areas that have not yet been developed much by humans.

Reproduction

Clutches consist of 2 hard-shelled eggs, which are laid in summer beneath stones or in rock crevices. Eggs vary in size from 9.2–11.5 x 6.5–9 mm. Communal egg laying appears to occur in several of the species.

Johan Marais

Purcell's Gecko is widely distributed in the western parts of the Karoo in South Africa.

Johan Marais

Namaqua Mountain Geckos are common from Kakamas to Vioolsdrif along the Orange River.

Distribution

This group is found over much of western southern Africa, but is excluded from most of the Kalahari, parts of the southwestern Cape and coastal areas. The Tsodilo Gecko is endemic to the Tsodilo Hills in northern Botswana.

The Waterberg Gecko is restricted to the Waterberg Plateau Park and adjacent farms in Namibia.

The Augrabies Gecko is one of the most attractive of the Western Geckos.

Weber's Gecko is strictly rupicolous and occurs in the western Northern Cape and northwestern Western Cape.

SPECIES IN THE GROUP

- Augrabies Gecko: *Pachydactylus atorquatus*
- Banded Gecko: *Pachydactylus fasciatus*
- Baster Gecko: *Pachydactylus kobosensis*
- Cryptic Gecko: *Pachydactylus reconditus*
- Good's Gecko: *Pachydactylus goodi*
- Griffin's Gecko: *Pachydactylus griffini*
- Helmeringhausen Gecko: *Pachydactylus acuminatu*
- Kamaggas Gecko: *Pachydactylus amoenus*
- McLachlan's Gecko: *Pachydactylus mclachlani*
- Monica's Gecko: *Pachydactylus monicae*
- Namaqua Mountain Gecko: *Pachydactylus montanu*
- Otavi Gecko: *Pachydactylus otaviensis*
- Purcell's Gecko: *Pachydactylus purcelli*
- Richtersveld Gecko: *Pachydactylus carinatus*
- Robert's Gecko: *Pachydactylus robertsi*
- San Steyn's Gecko: *Pachydactylus sansteynae*
- Tsodilo Gecko: *Pachydactylus tsodiloensis*
- Visser's Gecko: *Pachydactylus visseri*
- Waterberg Gecko: *Pachydactylus waterbergensis*
- Weber's Gecko: *Pachydactylus weberi*
- Werner's Gecko: *Pachydactylus werneri*
- Western Spotted Gecko: *Pachydactylus serval*

Spotted Geckos

Selected species from the genus *Pachydactylus*
3 species

Description

The three species of geckos in this group have typically short, fat cylindrical bodies. They are small, with a total body length of about 50 mm. Original tails may equal or even slightly exceed this length, but regenerated tails are significantly shorter than the body. The head is not depressed; the snout is bluntly pointed to rounded, and is convex in profile. Eyes are large with vertical pupils and the brow is prominent above and in front of the eye. The ear opening is of moderate size and is horizontally oval. The Golden Spotted Gecko has enlarged tubercles on the back. In the Large-spotted Gecko, tubercles are small and are only slightly larger than the surrounding granular scales. The dorsal scales of the Ocellated Gecko are granular with no tubercles. Scales on the belly are smooth and may overlap slightly. Although the legs are well developed, they are short and stocky. The digits are also short and three or five pads underlie the middle toes. The tail is cylindrical, unsegmented and very easily shed. Tails regenerate rapidly and the regenerated tails are much thicker than original tails. Scales on the tail are larger than the granules on the body, and scales on regenerated tails are of irregular size.

Coloration and patterning are attractive. The Large-spotted Gecko usually has a greyish colour with four rows of elongated

Johan Marais

The Ocellated Gecko is typical of Spotted Geckos in having a short, stout body with spots.

dark brown spots on the back. These may coalesce into bars, and a thick dark bar runs from the snout through the eye to the nape of the neck. The Golden Spotted Gecko is usually pale beige to reddish brown, with four rows of darker reddish brown spots running longitudinally down the back. Spots on the head coalesce to form a broad bar from the snout, through the eye to the nape of the neck, and the brow may be white. The Ocellated Gecko is more variable in coloration, ranging from grey to dark brown. Small, round, white or yellow, dark-edged spots are scattered over the head, body and original tails. The belly is white to off-white in most Spotted Geckos, but may be partially speckled to dark in the Ocellated Gecko. Eyes are generally golden brown.

Biology

Spotted Geckos are timid and inoffensive. They are primarily terrestrial in habit and are usually found under debris, rotting logs, loose bark of dead trees or in moribund termitaria. The Golden Spotted Gecko appears to prefer vertical crevices in rock outcrops, but may also be found under debris in holes. In the Eastern Cape, Large-spotted Geckos frequently hide in the shells of dead land snails and several individuals may be found in a single shell. A very high rate of tail loss suggests high predation pressures, and studies have revealed that some individuals shed their tails several times during their 3–4-year lifespan. Spotted Geckos are nocturnal and feed on small invertebrates, including grasshoppers. Tails become more swollen after periods of plentiful food and serve to store fat for lean periods.

The Golden Spotted Gecko has four rows of darker reddish brown spots running longitudinally down the back.

Large-spotted Geckos frequently take refuge in the empty shells of dead land snails.

Marius Burger

Golden Spotted Geckos prefer to take refuge in vertical crevices in rocks.

Reproduction

Spotted Geckos reach sexual maturity in one year. Females can lay two or three clutches in a season, each consisting of 2 hard-shelled eggs (7–8 x 9–10 mm). Eggs are usually laid in dead logs, under rocks or in crevices, and up to 12 eggs have been found in old land snail shells. Duration of incubation is variable, ranging from two to more than three months. Hatchlings are dark and are about 30 mm in total length.

Distribution

This group is found in the southern and eastern parts of South Africa. The Ocellated Gecko is restricted to the southwestern Cape, extending along the Cape Fold Mountains to Port Elizabeth and the mountains near Cradock. The Golden Spotted Gecko occurs on the inland escarpment in the Western and Eastern Cape, extending into the Free State. The Large-spotted Gecko is more widespread and occurs throughout much of coastal KwaZulu-Natal and Swaziland, south to Knysna, and west, almost to the West Coast on the inland escarpment.

Marius Burger

Juvenile Spotted Geckos are slimmer in build than adults, as is evident in this juvenile Golden Spotted Gecko.

SPECIES IN THE GROUP

- Golden Spotted Gecko: *Pachydactylus oculatus*
- Large-spotted Gecko: *Pachydactylus maculatus*
- Ocellated Gecko: *Pachydactylus geitje*

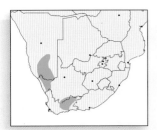

Delicate Geckos

Selected species from the genus *Pachydactylus*
3 species

Description

This is a small group with only three species of large, robust
geckos that all have rough, but fragile skin. Maximum body length
is about 85 mm and the tail is slightly shorter than the body. The
head is depressed and is distinct from the neck. Ear openings are
more or less round in the Namaqua Gecko and Haacke's Gecko, but
are slit-like in the Thin-skinned Gecko. The skin on the head has a
tendency to wrinkle, giving the impression that it is slightly baggy,
and the snout is distinctly convex in profile. The scales on the snout,
chin and throat are small and granular, but are intermixed with
scattered tubercles on the back of the head. The back is covered with
granular scales intermixed with large, longitudinally oval or rounded
tubercles of variable size. These tubercles extend onto the thighs.
The ventral scales are slightly larger than the dorsal scales. Legs are
well developed but relatively short and stocky. Digits are moderate
in length and are noticeably dilated at the tips. Each digit bears 9–13
pads, with the maximum number under the middle digits. The tail
has a thick base and is distinctly segmented, with each segment
consisting of about six transverse rows of regular scales and a row
of tubercles. In the Namaqua Gecko, the tail also bears enlarged
spine-like scales along its sides. Tails are easily lost but regenerate
quickly. Cloacal spines are large in the Namaqua Gecko, but are
small in the other members of the group.

*Like all Delicate
Geckos, Haacke's
Gecko is a large,
robust gecko that
has rough but
fragile skin.*

Johan Marais

Coloration is variable, with dorsal parts ranging from pale pinkish brown to chocolate or olive-brown, with indistinct blotchy markings. There are often five irregular zigzag crossbands on the back, with more regular bands on the tail. The eyes are usually golden to reddish brown and the ventral surface of the body is creamy to yellowish or greyish white. The underside of the thighs is sometimes yellow.

The Namaqua Gecko is found in rock cracks on large outcrops and rocky ravines.

The Thin-skinned Gecko uses its fragile skin to escape from the grasp of predators.

Biology

Delicate Geckos live in rock cracks on large outcrops, rocky ravines, koppies, high mountain slopes and isolated boulders in succulent veld. Although they are mainly nocturnal, they may bask in exposed positions during the day and may be active in the early morning. This group has delicate skin that can easily be ripped. When grasped, the Delicate Geckos twist vigorously, causing pieces of skin to tear off, often facilitating their escape. Apparently, the skin is 'given up' to predators in an escape strategy that is similar to tail loss, and the lost skin is quickly regenerated. This characteristic is not unique to Delicate Geckos and appears to have evolved independently in other groups of geckos – for example, *Elasmodactylus* (not covered in this book), Common Large-scaled Gecko (*Pachydactylus scutatus)*, and Sesfontein Gecko (*P. parascutatus*). Tears in the skin appear to be associated with zones of weakness formed by the presence of the tubercles. The diet of Delicate Geckos consists of beetles, moths, grasshoppers and other appropriately sized invertebrates. Prey is captured mainly by ambush.

FRAGILE SKIN

Tail autotomy is a well-known predator-avoidance mechanism in lizards, where the shed tail either distracts the predator or allows the lizard to escape as the tail is grasped. Less well known is the mechanism whereby pieces of skin are easily torn from the lizard, increasing its ability to struggle free from a predator's grasp. Some species appear to have adaptations that facilitate skin loss under these circumstances: the skin is weak and perforates along lines of tubercles. Only the superficial layers are lost, and they regenerate quickly with apparently little effect on the lizard.

Reproduction

Freshly laid eggs are sticky and soft, and are stuck to rock faces in cracks and crevices where they soon harden. Once hardened, they cannot be removed intact. Eggs are often laid communally, with more than 40 laid by different females in the most favourable crevices. Eggs are more or less round and measure about 16 mm in diameter.

Distribution

Delicate Geckos are restricted to the southwestern parts of southern Africa, from south-central Namibia (where Haacke's Gecko is fairly widespread), south into the Kamiesberge in the Northern Cape in South Africa where the Namaqua Gecko is found. The Thin-skinned Gecko occurs from the inland Cape escarpment on the Nuweveldberg to the southern Cape Fold Mountains.

Johan Marais

The skin on the head and neck of Haacke's Gecko has a tendency to wrinkle, giving the impression that it is slightly baggy.

SPECIES IN THE GROUP

- Haacke's Gecko: *Pachydactylus haackei*
- Namaqua Gecko: *Pachydactylus namaquensis*
- Thin-skinned Gecko: *Pachydactylus kladaroderma*

Marico Gecko

The species *Pachydactylus mariquensis*
1 species

Description

The Marico Gecko appears to be quite distantly related to any other species of geckos. It is a medium-sized gecko with a maximum body length of about 55 mm. The tail is short and usually about 20% shorter than the body. It has a convex head and a short, rounded snout that is not depressed. The eyes are large, with vertical pupils and prominent brows above the eyes. Ear openings are small and are obliquely oval. The dorsal parts of the body are covered with convex granules with no tubercles. Limbs are slender and of moderate length. The digits are also of average length and are slightly dilated at the tips with 3–4 pads under each. The tail is cylindrical, tapering, unsegmented and is covered with slightly overlapping scales that are much larger than those on the back.

Coloration and patterning are varied. Dorsal parts may be greyish, light purplish, yellowish brown or cinnamon. Markings may be variants of the following three patterns: (1) the back of the head, neck, body and tail may have bold, brown, dark-edged, irregular bars; (2) less frequently, a pale, dark-edged broad stripe runs from the nape onto the tail; or (3) small, dark spots may cover the flanks. Some individuals lack any bold markings, having a body covered with fine speckling of brown spots and indistinct barring. The ventral parts are usually uniform creamy white. Coloration usually closely matches the substrate.

Johan Marais

The Marico Gecko has a long body and slender limbs. The tail is slightly shorter than the body length.

Marico Geckos are mainly terrestrial and are found on sandy, flat plains.

Highly variable coloration and markings are typical of Marico Geckos.

Biology

Marico Geckos are terrestrial and are most commonly found on sandy, flat plains. They are nocturnal, spending daylight hours under rocks or stones. In areas where rocks are scarce, the holes of trapdoor spiders or scorpions may be used. Males are able to vocalize with a series of clicks. Generally, Marico Geckos are sluggish. The diet consists of small insects.

Reproduction

Two hard-shelled eggs (10 x 7.5 mm) are laid in a hole excavated under a rock by the female. More than one clutch may be laid in a summer season.

Distribution

Marico Geckos are restricted primarily to the succulent and nama karoo in southern and western South Africa, extending into the western parts of the Free State and Eastern Cape, as well as central Namibia to just south of the Brandberg.

Marico Geckos have large eyes with vertical pupils and prominent brows above the eyes.

SPECIES IN THE GROUP

■ Marico Gecko: *Pachydactylus mariquensis*

Day Gecko

The species *Phelsuma ocellata*
1 species

Description

Namaqua Day Geckos are small, with a maximum body length of about 40 mm and a tail of about the same length or a little longer. The head is depressed and the snout is rounded. Eyes are large and have vertical pupils. As in most species of gecko, the eyes cannot close, but the Namaqua Day Gecko's eyelids form a prominent ring around the eye. The ear openings are relatively large and elliptic in shape. The body is covered with granular scales on the dorsal parts, but scales of the ventral surface are overlapping and larger. All digits are clawless and the inner digit on each hand and foot is rudimentary and much reduced in size. The other digits are obviously dilated at their ends and have seven or eight undivided pads under each. Tails are feebly segmented and are easily shed. The scales on the tail are flattened, occur in regular transverse rows and overlap slightly. Scales on regenerated tails are irregular.

Several of the species of Day Gecko that occur on Indian Ocean islands are among the most brilliantly coloured geckos in the world. However, coloration of the Namaqua Day Gecko is generally cryptic, blending well with the rocks on which it is found. The dorsal parts are light brown to greyish brown or greyish black. A series of pale round spots and smaller dark spots cover the dorsal parts of the body, limbs and tail. Sometimes an inconspicuous, dark stripe runs along the side of the head from the nostril through the eye to the ear opening. The ventral parts of the body are creamy white to bluish white. The throat is usually infused with grey.

Marius Burger

Day Geckos have obviously dilated digits and, in comparison to other geckos, relatively small eyes.

Namaqua Day Geckos are small geckos, with a maximum body length of about 40 mm and a tail of about the same length.

Biology

Namaqua Day Geckos are agile, diurnal, rock-living geckos. Their favoured habitats include boulder-strewn hillsides and rocky outcrops, although they may also be found on trees and bushes. When approached, Namaqua Day Geckos will flee and hide under rock flakes, using their camouflage to good effect. A variety of small spiders and insects – such as beetles, flies, aphids and crickets – have been recorded as being included in their diet.

Conservation

The Namaqua Day Gecko is listed by the IUCN as 'Near Threatened' on account of its restricted distribution.

Reproduction

Two hard-shelled eggs (8.5 x 6.5 mm) are laid in summer. It is likely that females lay more than one clutch per season.

Distribution

In southern Africa, Day Geckos are restricted to the northern parts of Little Namaqualand, the Richtersveld and the southwestern extremes of Namibia. The occurrence of a species of Day Gecko in this area is a biogeographic enigma, since other members of the genus (more than 30 species) are restricted to the east coast of Africa and islands in the Indian Ocean. The direction of prevailing ocean currents makes it difficult to envisage how members of the genus could have dispersed by rafting. At least one species is now feral in Florida, USA, due to their popularity in the pet trade.

Day Geckos bear a superficial resemblance to Dwarf Geckos.

SPECIES IN THE GROUP

■ Namaqua Day Gecko: *Phelsuma ocellata* **NT**

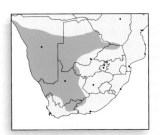

Barking Geckos

The genus *Ptenopus*
3 species

Description

The three species that make up this group are closely related and
share many characteristics that are unusual for geckos. Barking
Geckos do not have pads under the toes, and the toes are not
swollen or dilated as is common in other geckos. The body is stout
and small to medium in size, reaching a length of about 50 mm.
Older individuals can reach 60 mm in body length. The tail is shorter
than the body. The toes have claws and are fringed with scales,
giving good traction on sand. The head is a characteristic bobble
shape with a short, blunt snout and bulging eyes. The pupils are
vertical. The body and tail are cylindrical, and the tail tapers to a fine
point. The body is covered with small, smooth, granular scales.

Coloration is variable, from creamy white to yellow or reddish
brown, mottled with irregular blotches of brown and white speckles.
The tail may be faintly banded. The belly is white but the neck region
has a yellow patch in males. The females of Carp's Barking Gecko
also have a yellow throat during the breeding season. Although
these geckos do not actually bark in the conventional sense, the
males are very vocal, emitting a characteristic 'teck teck teck' that
characterizes areas where Barking Geckos are common. The pitch of
the call is species-specific.

Biology

Barking Geckos are ground-living, active at night and live singly
in burrows that they dig in firm sand. Burrows can be extensive,

Johan Marais

*Barking Geckos
do not have pads
under the toes, and
the toes are not
swollen or dilated
as is common
in other geckos
– illustrated here
by this Common
Barking Gecko.*

up to a metre in length and half a metre below the surface. During the day the burrow is plugged at the surface and is thus camouflaged for protection against predators. This also keeps the burrow cooler on hot days. Males call from the burrow entrance, usually with only their heads protruding. Calling is most intense around sunset on summer nights, but can occur at

As with other species of Barking Gecko, mature male Common Barking Geckos have a yellow throat.

Koch's Barking Gecko is restricted to the northern Namibian coast.

Barking Geckos, such as Koch's Barking Gecko, have large, bulging eyes.

any time on overcast days. Sound appears to be of prime importance in communication between individuals, and calls function in male-male competition, defence of territory and to attract females. Because Barking Geckos are dependent on their burrows, they do not occur on mobile sand dunes where burrows can collapse. They are usually found on sparsely vegetated gravel plains and the compacted silt deposits in dry riverbeds. They are known to occur in fairly dense colonies in places, but can also be widely spaced. Active searching for prey occurs at night after rain, when geckos walk around on the surface. Termites form an important part of the diet when the alates take to the wing after rains. Prey is also ambushed from the burrow entrance.

Reproduction

Females enter the burrows of selected males. Mating takes place in the burrow. The male then leaves the female in the burrow and digs a new burrow nearby. Usually, a single hard-shelled egg is laid in a shallow burrow that is dug by the female.

Distribution

Barking Geckos are limited to the arid western parts of southern Africa. Of the three species, the Common Barking Gecko occurs most widely, ranging through the southern two thirds of Namibia, Northern Cape, central and southern Botswana, the western parts of North West and northern Limpopo. Carp's Barking Gecko is limited to the Namib Desert from the Kuiseb River in the south, north to Rocky Point. Koch's Barking Gecko occurs between the Kuiseb River mouth and Lüderitz.

SPECIES IN THE GROUP

- Carp's Barking Gecko: *Ptenopus carpi*
- Common Barking Gecko: *Ptenopus garrulus*
- Koch's Barking Gecko: *Ptenopus kochi*

Namib Day Geckos

The genus *Rhoptropus*
6 species

Description

Six species of Namib Day Gecko occur in southern Africa. Species are superficially similar in appearance and are distinguished from one another by some differences in coloration and minor differences in scalation, that can only be discerned with the lizard in hand. However, since these diagnostic characteristics also appear to vary widely within each species, the taxonomy within the group has been unstable until recently, when species boundaries were defined using genetics. Namib Day Geckos are small to medium-sized, ranging in body length from 40 to 75 mm, with a torpedo-shaped body, long slender legs and well-developed toes on each foot. The body form and widely splayed legs give these geckos the appearance of being fairly flat and allows them to hug the rock surfaces on which they live, making them difficult to spot in their natural habitat. The tail is about the same length as the body, but may be a little shorter or longer, depending on the species. The nasal scales around the nostrils are raised, forming peculiar nasal swellings. Eyes are large with vertical pupils. As with most other species of gecko, the eyelids are fused. The snout tapers acutely in front of the eyes and is concave between the eyes and the tip of the pointed snout. The scales on the back are usually small, granular and smooth, but may be very feebly keeled or very weakly tubercular. Scales on the snout and head are slightly larger than those on the back and may also be slightly keeled or tubercular. Ear openings are relatively large and may be partly covered with a flap of skin. The group is unusual in having several elongated chin scales, which run from the front edge of the jaw to

Johan Marais

Namib Day Geckos, such as this Kaokoveld Namib Day Gecko, have long, slender legs and well-developed toes on each foot.

under the jaw. Toes on the forelegs are all relatively similar to each other in length, but there are usually three long and two short toes on the hind legs. Toes are slender and obviously enlarged at the ends, but do not have claws. The pads under the toes are not divided and number from 5 to 13.

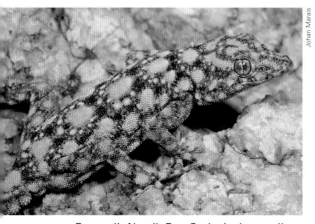

Barnard's Namib Day Gecko is the smallest species of the genus.

Coloration is varied and tends to match the substrate on which the geckos occur. It may vary from light olive-grey, greyish brown, sooty brown or blackish to black. There may be scattered spots of white, yellow, pink, brown or dark-edged brick red. Some individuals show little evidence of spots. Legs are generally slightly lighter than the body coloration and may be yellowish brown above. The tail may be partially banded. The ventral coloration is usually lighter than the dorsal parts and may be whitish, bright yellow or even bluish slate. Some of the species appear to have the ability to change their coloration to match the substrate on which they live.

Biology

Namib Day Geckos may be locally abundant and are the dominant group of lizards in areas where the habitat is suitable. They are extremely active, quick-moving and appear to have more stamina than other lizards

Boulton's Namib Day Gecko occurs from the southwestern parts of Angola through most of Damaraland in Namibia.

Bradfield's Namib Day Gecko is restricted to the coastal parts of central Namibia.

of similar size. Most species of Namib Day Gecko are primarily rock-living and are restricted to rocky outcrops, large boulders and cliffs. However, the Common Namib Day Gecko is confined mainly to open flats and gravel plains with scattered rocks. Namib Day Geckos favour arid to hyper-arid environments, although Barnard's Namib Day Gecko appears to be restricted to areas with a slightly higher rainfall. Ants form an important component of the diet, but other small insects are also eaten.

Reproduction

Eggs are laid in pairs under stones or rock flakes, or are glued onto the rock surface in crevices, making them impossible to remove intact. Females usually lay 2 eggs in a clutch and may lay more than one clutch in a season.

Distribution

Namib Day Geckos are extreme arid specialists that are restricted to the coastal regions of the West Coast of southern Africa, from the Kuiseb River in the south, north into southern Angola. Up to three species may occur in the same area.

Like other Namib Day Geckos, Bradfield's Namib Day Gecko has large eyes and obvious, immobile eyelids.

SPECIES IN THE GROUP

- Barnard's Namib Day Gecko: *Rhoptropus barnardi*
- Boulton's Namib Day Gecko: *Rhoptropus boultoni*
- Bradfield's Namib Day Gecko: *Rhoptropus bradfieldi*
- Brandberg Namib Day Gecko: *Rhoptropus diporus*
- Common Namib Day Gecko: *Rhoptropus afer*
- Kaokoveld Namib Day Gecko: *Rhoptropus biporosus*

ORDER: CROCODYLIA

Currently, the order Crocodylia consists of 24 living species, divided into three families: the Alligatoridae (alligators), Crocodylidae (crocodiles) and Gavialidae (gharials). This species number is only a small fraction of the number that is recorded in the fossil record. The order is confined mainly to the tropics, but the distributions of the American Alligator (*Alligator mississippiensis*) and the Chinese Alligator (*A. sinensis*) do extend to areas where winter temperatures fall below freezing. Crocodylians and birds are the only living representatives of an ancient group, the Archosauria, which includes the dinosaurs, pterosaurs and thecodontians that arose more than 220 millions years ago. All living species of Crocodylians are aquatic, but some of the extinct forms were terrestrial. The New Caledonian Crocodile (*Mekosuchus inexpectatus*) was a 2-m terrestrial species that is thought to have fed on molluscs, as its posterior teeth were rounded. This species became extinct as recently as 1 600 years ago, possibly as a result of the arrival of humans on the island.

Members of the Crocodylia typically have elongated bodies with robust skulls, a long snout and strongly toothed jaws. The neck is short and the body is relatively depressed, especially in large individuals. The limbs are generally short and sturdy. The tail is thick and laterally compressed. The body, head and tail are heavily armoured with tough keratinous scales and osteoderms. The cloacal opening is longitudinal. All species are egg-layers and most species have a degree of parental care of the eggs and young.

Johan Marais

The Nile Crocodile is the only southern African reptile belonging to the order Crocodylia. All living species are strictly aquatic.

CROCODILES
Family: Crocodylidae

The Crocodylidae is the most speciose family in the Crocodylia, consisting of three genera and 16 species. They occur in the New World tropics and throughout the more tropical parts of Africa, India, Southeast Asia and northern Australia. They differ from other Crocodylia in that the fourth mandibular tooth lies externally on each side of the mouth when the mouth is closed.

All living species of crocodilians are exclusively aquatic, but some of the extinct forms were terrestrial.

Nile Crocodile

The species *Crocodylus niloticus*
1 species

Description

The Nile Crocodile is the only crocodile species that occurs in southern Africa. This iconic animal is instantly recognizable; it is very large and robust, with adults averaging 2.8–3.5 m in length, reaching a maximum length of around 5.5 m in southern Africa. Nile Crocodiles in East Africa reportedly grow even larger, and there are many reports of specimens exceeding 7 m. Although it is likely that these are exaggerations of the truth, the Nile Crocodile is second only to the Indopacific Crocodile (*Crocodylus porosus*) as the largest living reptile. By today's standards, even a 5-m crocodile is regarded as exceptionally large, and crocodiles of this size can weigh more than a ton. However, it is estimated that fewer than 2% of the crocodiles in the wild in southern Africa exceed 3 m. Males grow much larger than females and are far more robust. The Nile Crocodile has a long snout with large teeth that are visible even when the jaws are closed. Its eyes and nostrils are situated high on the head so that they protrude from the water when the crocodile floats just beneath the surface. The ears are located just behind the eyes and have slit-like openings. Plates on the head are fused to the skull, whereas most of the skin on the back and tail is covered in horny scales, each containing a bony plate called an osteoderm. The tail is laterally compressed and has two rows of projecting scales anteriorly, which join to form a single row along the posterior third of the tail.

The Nile Crocodile is the only crocodile species that occurs in southern Africa and is instantly recognizable.

Johan Marais

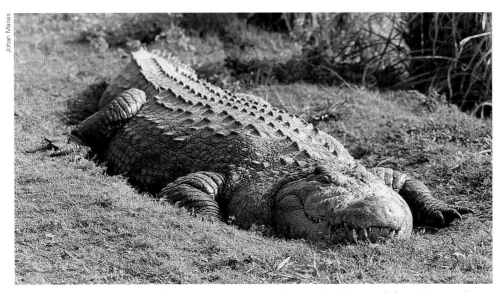

The Nile Crocodile is one of the largest extant reptile species. Large adults can exceed a ton in mass.

Adult Nile Crocodiles are dark olive-green or brown above with darker markings on the back, sides and tail. The underside of the body and the inside of the mouth are pale yellow or cream. Juveniles are more vividly marked and are greenish to light brown with darker markings on the back, sides and tail, and pale yellow to whitish below.

Biology

Nile Crocodiles inhabit rivers, lakes, swamps, estuaries and mangroves. They may be active during the day and at night, but usually spend much of the daytime basking, often with the mouth agape. It is unclear why crocodiles gape in this manner. Nights are usually spent in the water, since this prevents body temperature from dropping too low, and this is also when they do most of their hunting. As juveniles are more vulnerable to predation, they are secretive in comparison to adults and tend to favour more heavily vegetated backwaters, where they are known to dig shelters into the banks with their mouths. Crocodiles are easily located at night using a spotlight, as their eyes are reflective. They

are efficient and fast swimmers, propelling their bodies through the water using their tails. The legs play little part in swimming and are generally held against the body. Crocodiles are also comfortable on land and, despite their short limbs, can run with surprising speed over short distances.

Nile Crocodiles are consummate divers and can remain underwater without breathing for a considerable time. Crocodiles show many adaptations in this regard, and have a unique circulatory system that allows for great flexibility and control of blood flow. Heart rate can be slowed during dives so that oxygenated blood is directed only to the organs, such as the brain and heart, which cannot function without it. Ear openings and nostrils can be closed to keep water out during dives, and the nasal passages are separated from the mouth by a secondary palate, facilitating the opening of the mouth and feeding underwater. Stones of varying sizes are found in the stomachs of most adults, and these may function as ballast, increasing the specific gravity of the crocodile so that it can dive more easily. The increased specific gravity conferred by the stones allows diving crocodiles to take about 12% more air in their lungs during dives.

Hatchling crocodiles feed on insects, tadpoles, frogs and fish. As they grow, they broaden their diet to include terrapins, water birds and small mammals – virtually anything that they can overpower. Adults feed on fish (especially catfish), large mammals and birds. In some areas zebra, wildebeest and other antelope are favourite prey items. Nile Crocodiles have even been known to take rhinos, young elephants and hippo. Prey is generally ambushed at a water hole or river edge, seized by the snout, dragged into the water and killed by drowning. Crocodiles are not able to bite

Johan Marais

Nile Crocodiles inhabit a wide variety of wetlands, including rivers, lakes, swamps, estuaries and mangroves.

mouthfuls off their prey, and so rip chunks of meat off by grabbing onto their prey and rolling their bodies, or by shaking smaller prey items vigorously so that they break apart. Several crocodiles will feed off the same carcass if it is large enough, and they are even known to co-operate by herding fish into shallow water in a co-ordinated manner in order to trap them.

Reproduction

Nile Crocodiles reach sexual maturity when they are about 12–15 years old and in excess of 2.3 m in length. Large males are very territorial and will defend a harem of between 6 and 10 females from other males. Fighting among males is common and can occasionally end in death for one of them. A female indicates willingness to mate by partially lifting her head out of the water to expose her throat. The male then rubs his chin on the female's back, neck and head, and will twist his tail beneath hers in order to copulate. Actual mating takes only a few minutes, but may occur several times a day over many days. Mating season is between July and September, and egg laying takes place from October to December.

Prior to laying, the female selects a suitable nesting site on a dry, sunny patch of sand well above the flood line. She excavates a 300–450 mm-deep hole with her hind limbs and lays her eggs over a period of 1–4 hours. Most females lay eggs between the hours of 16h00 and 22h00. She then fills the hole, using the sand that she excavated, and carefully compresses the nest with her hind feet. Females generally protect their nests from predators such as Monitor Lizards (*Varanus*), baboons and even hyaenas. The female will remain in the water or bask on land close to the nest and dash forward quickly with mouth agape should any predator or person approach. Despite these efforts, more than half (in some areas up to 90%) of nests are destroyed by predators, largely Monitor Lizards.

Females larger than 3 m lay 34–75 eggs measuring 78 x 51 mm and weighing as much as 120 g each. Smaller, younger females produce fewer eggs, a high proportion of which may be infertile. These small clutches range from 20 to 60 eggs that measure 65 x 44 mm and weigh approximately 80 g each. The eggs are white and hard-shelled. Incubation takes between 73 and 95 days, depending on temperature. The incubation temperature, and other factors such as humidity, also determines the sex of the young. Eggs incubated between 31 and 34° C develop into males, whereas eggs incubated above or below this temperature develop into females. When ready to break free from their eggs, the hatchlings call from within the eggs and attract the attention of the mother. She will usually then dig open the nest, pick the young up in her mouth and carry a few hatchlings at a time to the water. The female may even pick up eggs in her mouth and gently crack them to assist the youngsters in the hatching process. Hatchlings measure 250–320 mm in total length.

Conservation

In southern Africa, Nile Crocodiles are restricted largely to game and nature reserves, and it is estimated that there are fewer than 12 000 individuals remaining in the wild. Nile Crocodiles are farmed for their skins and meat, and in some countries, such as Zimbabwe, farmers are permitted to harvest a limited number of crocodile eggs from the wild. The skin industry is well regulated, and the Nile Crocodile is listed in Appendix II of CITES, but is not listed by the IUCN as 'Threatened'. The greatest threat to the Nile Crocodile is the reduction in habitat resulting from extraction of water for human usage. Water pollution is also a potential threat; all rivers flowing through the Kruger National Park flow from industrial areas, and it has been suggested that some deaths among adult crocodiles in the park are due to contamination.

Johan Marais

It is unclear why crocodiles gape. It has been suggested that gaping serves a thermoregulatory function; however, it also occurs in cold conditions.

Distribution

Historically, Nile Crocodiles occurred as far south as East London, but today they extend only as far south as the Tugela River in KwaZulu-Natal. They occur north of the Tugela into northern Zululand, Mpumalanga, North West, Limpopo, and into Mozambique, Zimbabwe, eastern and northern Botswana, and northern Namibia. They also occur extensively north of southern Africa.

Danger to man

Nile Crocodiles are extremely dangerous to humans, and many people are killed by them in southern Africa every year. A 3-m Nile Crocodile can easily overpower an adult human, and smaller crocodiles have caused extensive injuries in attacks. Rural people who depend on river water for drinking and washing are most at risk, as are fishermen.

SPECIES IN THE GROUP

■ Nile Crocodile: *Crocodylus niloticus*

ORDER: TESTUDINES

The Testudines is an ancient reptile order that comprises more than 295 species of turtle, tortoise and terrapin, which are distributed worldwide in tropical and temperate oceans and continents. They are grouped into 14 families, and 100 genera. Five families, 14 genera and 27 species occur in southern Africa or off its coast. The order is divided into two well-defined suborders: the Pleurodira, which typically withdraw their heads into their shells by horizontal bending; and the Cryptodira, which withdraw their heads into their shells directly backwards, with a vertical flexure of the neck. Testudines are unique in having a shell built into their skeleton that provides protection from physical harm. The shell has an inner bony layer and an outer layer of horny plates. It consists of an upper half, the carapace, and a lower half, the plastron. In some groups, the shell has been secondarily reduced to the extent that horny plates are entirely lacking and there is a thick leathery covering instead. All members of this order lack teeth. Food is sliced by sharp horny ridges that cover the jaws. All species lay eggs.

Johan Marais

The members of the order Testudines are unique in having a shell built into their skeleton. The species pictured here is a Leopard Tortoise.

SIDE-NECKED TERRAPINS
Family: Pelomedusidae

This is a primitive family of medium-sized terrapins that is restricted to Africa, Madagascar and the granitic Seychelles. The family contains two genera and at least 18 species, but further research is needed to resolve several taxonomic issues. Both genera and six species occur in southern Africa, but neither is endemic to the sub-region. Species that belong to the Pelomedusidae family are able to withdraw the head into the shell, but do so by turning the head to one side, rather than retracting it straight back. The carapace lacks nuchal and supracaudal scutes, and the plastron has an intergular shield. Musk glands (stink glands) are located on the ventral surface next to the fourth and eighth marginal scutes. The hind feet are webbed and are used for propulsion in water. All species are aquatic and lay soft-shelled eggs.

The Side-necked Terrapins, such as this Serrated Hinged Terrapin, are restricted to Africa, Madagascar and the granitic Seychelles.

Marsh Terrapin

The species *Pelomedusa subrufa*
1 species

Description

This group contains a single distinctive species of freshwater terrapin.
Maximum shell length is about 325 mm; mass around 2.5 kg. Males
grow larger than females. The shell is robust, unhinged and relatively
flat in profile. Viewed from above, the shell has an oval shape. There
are five vertebral scutes, four pairs of costals and 11 marginal scutes
on each side. Marsh Terrapins lack a nuchal scute. In males, the
plastron has upturned femoral shields near the hind legs, thought to
facilitate mounting the female. Musk glands are located on the ventral
surface in soft skin next to the fourth and eighth marginal scutes.
These glands produce a foul-smelling secretion when the terrapin is
stressed. The head is relatively large, especially in juveniles, and the
chin bears a pair of short tentacles. The eyes are well developed and
have round pupils. The nostrils open at the tip of the snout, giving the
head an almost pig-like appearance. The neck is long and muscular,
and can be sufficiently extended by the terrapin for it to right itself
if it is turned onto its back. When withdrawn into the shell, the head
is turned to one side so that one eye remains visible. The forelimbs
and hind limbs are about the same size and carry five robust claws
each. The hind limbs are webbed and are used to propel the terrapin
through water.

Body coloration is generally dark, and the dorsal parts of the
body appear to be a dirty black when wet. When dry, however, the

*Marsh Terrapins
have a robust,
unhinged shell.
The shell is much
flatter than that of
Hinged Terrapins.*

Richard Boycott

Richard Boycott

Juvenile Marsh Terrapins have a relatively large head.

carapace can be dark brown, grey or dark olive-green. The marginal shields are paler on the ventral surface, but the plastron can be completely black, brown, or have a pattern with a pale centre. The head is dark olive or grey above, sometimes with a fine vermiculated pattern. Below, the head and neck are a pale, off-white colour. The tail is significantly longer in males.

Biology

The Marsh Terrapin is a highly adaptable, aquatic species that is active during the day or night. It inhabits a wide variety of temporary and permanent water bodies, and will even take up residence in artificial farm dams and sewage treatment plants; it has become more common as a result of human development. Marsh Terrapins will move overland during wet weather and have been known to move considerable distances from one water body to the next. Juveniles are often found in the small pools formed by tyre tracks on dirt roads. During dry periods, they will dig into mud or bury themselves into soil to aestivate, where they will remain in a torpid state until conditions improve. They will, however, stay active throughout the year if there is access to permanent water and winter temperatures do not drop too low. Usually, Marsh Terrapins can be observed basking with necks extended, on rocks, logs or at the water's edge. They may even use the back of a hippo as a basking site. In situations where they are not harassed, they rapidly become habituated to human presence and learn to beg for food by swimming at the surface near human activity. However, when molested or cornered in shallow water, they will intentionally stir up the mud to provide themselves with cover. If seized, Marsh Terrapins produce a noxious secretion from their stink glands, leaving a foul smell that will linger on the hand for days. They are long-lived, and individuals have been kept in captivity for more than 16 years.

Marsh Terrapins are active hunters that will generally consume anything they can catch. They have been recorded feeding on aquatic animals such as insects, fish, tadpoles, crabs and frogs. Birds are ambushed while drinking at the water's edge, and ducklings are caught from

Marsh Terrapins occur over much of southern Africa and are excluded only from very arid and cold parts.

below. Carrion, such as that resulting from crocodile kills, also provides a ready meal for the adaptable Marsh Terrapin. A significant amount of vegetable matter, mainly water plants, is also consumed.

Reproduction

Mating occurs during spring and summer, and takes place in water. The male mounts the female and attaches himself to her shell by hooking the claws of all four limbs over her marginal scutes. The male courts the female by rubbing his chin tentacles on the back of her head, and expelling a stream

Marsh Terrapins have well-developed eyes with round pupils, and nostrils at the tip of the snout.

of water from his nostrils into her face. Clutches of 10–30 soft-shelled, elliptical eggs (about 30 x 20 mm) are laid in a hole that is excavated by the female during summer. Before digging, the female will usually soften the ground by emptying the fluid from her cloaca. Incubation lasts about three months and hatchlings, each about 30 mm in length, dig themselves out of the nest cavity over a period of days.

Distribution

This is the most widespread and common species of terrapin found in southern Africa. It occurs wherever suitable water bodies are present, but is absent from the most arid parts of the Northern Cape province, the southern half of Namibia and the southeastern parts of Botswana. It may also be absent from the cold, higher-lying parts of Lesotho, but occurs extensively outside of southern Africa, north to the Sudan and Egypt, and is found on Madagascar.

SPECIES IN THE GROUP

■ Marsh Terrapin: *Pelomedusa subrufa*

Hinged Terrapins

The genus *Pelusios*
5 species

Description

This group includes five medium-sized, freshwater terrapins, ranging in adult weight from 700 g to 7 kg, with shell length ranging from 200–400 mm. The Serrated Hinged Terrapin is easily the largest species in the group. Females are larger than males. The shell is robust, and is more convex or domed in profile in comparison to the shell of Marsh Terrapins (*Pelomedusa subrufa*). Viewed from above, the shell has an oval shape and may be slightly wider posteriorly. The plastron has a well-developed hinge just behind the front legs, which allows the anterior third of the plastron to be raised when the head and forelimbs are withdrawn into the shell, concealing them completely. There are five vertebral scutes, four pairs of costals and 11 marginal scutes on each side. The nuchal scute is lacking. Musk glands are located on the ventral surface in soft skin next to the fourth and eighth marginal scutes. These glands produce a foul-smelling secretion when the terrapin is stressed. The eyes are well developed with round pupils. The nostrils are round and open at the very tip of the snout. The head is broad and relatively flattened, and the snout is more rounded than that of the Marsh Terrapin. There are two or three short tentacles on the chin. The beak is unicuspid in the Okavango Hinged Terrapin and Pan Hinged Terrapin, but bicuspid in the other three species. The forelimbs and hind limbs each carry five robust claws and are about the same size. The hind limbs are webbed and are used to propel the terrapin through water.

When observed in their natural habitat, Hinged Terrapins generally appear to be dark in coloration with little patterning, since any patterning is usually obscured by algal growth on the shell and

Richard Boycott

Hinged Terrapins, such as this Serrated Hinged Terrapin, have a shell that is more domed in profile than that of the Marsh Terrapin.

body. Although the shells of all five species are dark brown, dark olive or black on the dorsal parts, the marginal scutes often bear lighter blotching of brown, yellow or orange. Younger specimens may also show a degree of stippling on the costal shields. The plastron tends to be more strikingly marked, and varies from being entirely black in some individuals of the Mashona Hinged Terrapin, to having a yellow centre. This is especially evident in the Yellow-bellied Hinged Terrapin, which may have a plastron with a light yellow centre, darkening to black on the periphery. The Okavango Hinged Terrapin may also have white edging to the plastral scutes, and the yellow of the Pan Hinged Terrapin is blotched with dark brown patches. Head coloration tends to be dark brown to black above and lighter below, often with yellow or light brown on the flanks. The Pan Hinged Terrapin and Serrated Hinged Terrapin often have vermiculations on the dorsal parts of the head, and the Okavango Hinged Terrapin has reticulate yellow patterning on the dorsal parts of the head. The neck and limbs are either yellow, pale brown or black.

Biology

All species of Hinged Terrapin are aquatic and are found in temporary and permanent water bodies. When water bodies dry up, they burrow into mud or soil to aestivate, and will remain in a torpid state until the next rains. Dispersal occurs during the wet season, and individuals may be found some distance from the nearest water. Hinged Terrapins are typically observed while they bask on exposed rocks, logs or at the water's edge. They are long-lived, and individuals have been kept in captivity for more than 29 years. Mainly carnivorous, they feed

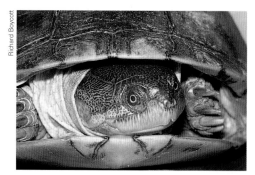

The Yellow-bellied Hinged Terrapin derives its name from its yellow plastron.

The Serrated Hinged Terrapin is the largest species of Hinged Terrapin and can attain a mass of 7 kg.

on aquatic insects, tadpoles, frogs, crabs, worms, snails and fish. These terrapins have also been recorded picking ticks off the skin of wallowing animals, and are partial to carrion. They also consume a significant amount of plant material such as ripe fruit and the roots and stems of aquatic species.

Reproduction

Hinged Terrapins breed throughout the summer months. All species lay soft-shelled eggs and clutches of between 8 and 48 eggs (35 x 22 mm) are laid between October and March. Females of some species may lay more than one clutch per season. Incubation may be as brief as two months, but is dependent on the temperature.

Distribution

Hinged Terrapins are much more restricted in their range, and of rarer occurrence, than Marsh Terrapins. All species are limited primarily to the northern and northeastern parts of southern Africa. Four also occur more extensively to the north of southern Africa, but the Okavango Hinged Terrapin is restricted to the Okavango Swamps and the Zambezi River above the Victoria Falls. The Yellow-bellied Hinged Terrapin and Pan Hinged Terrapin also occur on Madagascar; the Yellow-bellied Hinged Terrapin occurs on the Seychelles.

The Okavango Hinged Terrapin is restricted to the Okavango Swamps and the Zambezi River above the Victoria Falls.

The Serrated Hinged Terrapin is widespread in the northeastern parts of southern Africa.

Hinged Terrapins, such as this Okavango Hinged Terrapin, are highly aquatic, spending most of their active time in water.

SPECIES IN THE GROUP

- Mashona Hinged Terrapin: *Pelusios rhodesianus*
- Okavango Hinged Terrapin: *Pelusios bechuanicus*
- Pan Hinged Terrapin: *Pelusios subniger*
- Serrated Hinged Terrapin: *Pelusios sinuatus*
- Yellow-bellied Hinged Terrapin: *Pelusios castanoides*

SOFT-SHELLED TERRAPINS
Family: Trionychidae

This family is widely distributed in the northern hemisphere, and species richness is highest in North America and Southeast Asia. There are 14 genera comprising at least 26 species. Two of the genera just enter southern Africa, each represented by a single species. Soft-shelled Terrapins have no horny shields or scutes on their carapace or plastron. The bones of the shell are reduced and are embedded in thick, leathery-textured dermal tissue. The shell is relatively flat, disc-like and flexible. In some species, flaps to the outer margin of the shell allow the tail and hind limbs to be withdrawn and completely concealed. The neck is usually long and extendable, and the head can be completely withdrawn into the shell. Unlike the Side-necked Terrapins, which have hard beaks, the lips of Soft-shelled Terrapins are fleshy, but are still able to inflict very painful bites. The snout is drawn into an extended proboscis that acts as a short snorkel. There are three claws on each foot.

Steve Spawls

Soft-shelled Terrapins, such as this Nile Soft-shelled Terrapin, have no horny shields or scutes on their carapace or plastron.

Soft-shelled Terrapins

The genera *Trionyx* and *Cycloderma*
2 species

Description

This group contains two species of highly unusual, distinctive, large
terrapins that have round disc-like shells that lack horny shields.
The Zambezi Soft-shelled Terrapin can attain a carapace length of
560 mm and a mass of up to 14 kg, whereas the Nile Soft-shelled
Terrapin is much larger, with a carapace length of up to 950 mm and
a mass of 40 kg. Females grow larger than males. The shell is tough,
leathery and slightly flexible. It is generally smooth in adults but has
an indistinct vertebral ridge and tubercles in juveniles. The Zambezi
Soft-shelled Terrapin has flexible flaps on the posterior half of the
shell that cover the hind limbs and tail. The head is elongate and
the snout is drawn into a proboscis, giving the head an almost pig-
like appearance. Fore- and hind limbs are about equal in size and
are obviously webbed, and each foot has three prominent claws.
The upper side of each front foot bears 3–5 peculiar, sharp-edged,
crescent-shaped skin folds, and the heel of each foot bears one. The
tail is small, especially in females.

The body colour is usually uniform pale to dark olive above,
sometimes with indistinct blotching. Juveniles are generally more
vividly patterned and are pale green or grey with a white edge to
the carapace in the Zambezi Soft-shelled Terrapin, and spotted in
the Nile Soft-shelled Terrapin. The plastron and ventral parts of the
limbs are generally lighter than the carapace, and can be pinkish

*In southern Africa,
the Zambezi Soft-
shelled Terrapin is
restricted to eastern
Zimbabwe and
the Mozambique
floodplain.*

The Nile Soft-shelled Terrapin may occasionally venture into the marine environment.

The Nile Soft-shelled Terrapin only enters southern Africa in the northwestern extremes and is restricted to the Cunene River.

or pale grey. The head and neck are usually dark dorsally and pale laterally. The top of the head and neck bear five longitudinal dark lines. The Nile Soft-shelled Terrapin may be speckled with small spots, especially on the head, where the spots may form vermiculations.

Biology

Soft-shelled Terrapins occur primarily in fresh water, and can be found in rivers, lakes and pools. However, Nile Soft-shelled Terrapins may also venture into marine or estuarine habitats, and some populations outside of southern Africa appear to remain exclusively in salt water. Tolerance of saltwater allows dispersal from one river mouth to the next and is probably how this species colonized the Cunene River, since it does not occur above the Ruacana Falls. High densities of Nile Soft-shelled Terrapins occur in the Cunene estuary, where their snorkel-like snouts can be seen protruding from the water whenever the terrapins take a breath. Soft-shelled Terrapins are highly mobile both in water and on land. They tend to be shy and will conceal themselves in the soft mud substrate when harassed. However, they also defend themselves by biting and scratching when handled. The

Nile Soft-shelled Terrapin is renowned for its viciousness, and is capable of inflicting serious injury when not treated with due caution. Both species appear to be long-lived and individuals have been kept in captivity for more than 30 years. Molluscs are the most important component of the diet for both species, and they have been observed digging for buried mussels with their forelimbs. Aquatic insects, frogs and fish are also eaten, and the Nile Soft-shelled Terrapin includes palm nuts and other fruits in its diet.

Conservation

The Zambezi Soft-shelled Terrapin is listed by the IUCN as 'Near Threatened' due to harvesting of turtles and eggs. However, harvesting is limited, and the listing is probably due to the species being cryptic and poorly known.

Reproduction

Nesting occurs in late summer. Clutches of 15–60 eggs are laid in cavities dug by the female in exposed sand banks near the water's edge. The eggs are almost spherical and are about 30 mm in diameter. Unlike those of Side-necked Terrapins, the eggs of Soft-shelled Terrapins have hard calcareous

Wulf Haacke

The Zambezi Soft-shelled Terrapin is listed by the IUCN as 'Near Threatened' on account of harvesting of terrapins and their eggs for human consumption.

shells. Incubation in the Nile Soft-shelled Terrapin is 2–3 months, but appears to be much longer in the Zambezi Soft-shelled Terrapin, with hatchlings emerging early the following season. Although little detailed information is known about the reproductive history of soft-shelled terrapins, it would appear that females lay several clutches during each breeding season.

Distribution

Soft-shelled Terrapins have a very restricted distribution in southern Africa. The Nile Soft-shelled Terrapin is found only in the northwest of the subregion and is restricted to the Cunene River, below the Ruacana Falls. However, it occurs in most of the major rivers to the north and throughout much of tropical Africa, extending to the Nile. The Zambezi Soft-shelled Terrapin occurs from Tanzania, parts of Malawi and Eastern Zimbabwe to the Save River on the Mozambique floodplain.

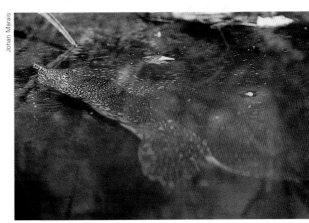

Johan Marais

Soft-shelled Terrapins, such as this Nile Soft-shelled Terrapin, use their proboscis-like snout as a snorkel.

SPECIES IN THE GROUP

- Nile Soft-shelled Terrapin: *Trionyx triunguis*
- Zambezi Soft-shelled Terrapin: *Cycloderma frenatum* **NT**

LEATHERBACK TURTLES
Family: Dermochelyidae

This family consists of a single, unique species of turtle that has a cosmopolitan distribution. The head, which can only be partially withdrawn into the shell, lacks enlarged shields and the limbs are clawless. The family is defined by a number of unique attributes to the bones of the skull.

Warren Schmidt

Leatherback Turtles are able to maintain relatively high body temperatures, even in cool water. This allows them to range into temperate seas.

Leatherback

The genus *Dermochelys*
1 species

Description

The Leatherback Turtle is the largest species of turtle, and the only living reptiles heavier than it are the Nile Crocodile (*Crocodylus niloticus*) and Indopacific Crocodile (*Crocodylus porosus*). The maximum carapace length is usually about 1.67 m, but the largest on record is 2.5 m, weighing 860 kg. The shell is broad and streamlined. Unlike the other sea turtles, whose shells are covered with horny plates, the Leatherback Turtle's shell lacks epidermal scutes and is covered only with leathery skin. There are seven very prominent ridges that run the length of the carapace and meet at the posterior tip of the shell. The head is massive and the beak is bicuspid. The eye opening has a near-vertical orientation and the nostrils open at the tip of the snout. Forelimbs are modified into large flippers that may exceed 3 m from one tip to the other. The hind limbs are strongly webbed and paddle-like, but are much smaller than the forelimbs. The body colour is usually a uniform dark grey or black, but the throat and neck may be blotched with pink or white. The plastron is usually paler than the dorsal parts.

Biology

Leatherback Turtles are found exclusively in marine habitats and are highly specialized for a pelagic lifestyle. After entering the water shortly after hatching, males spend their entire lives in water and females only come ashore to lay eggs. Leatherback Turtles routinely travel distances of several thousand kilometres per year, and different individuals follow widely divergent paths across the ocean.

The Leatherback Turtle is the largest species of turtle in the world and can reach a mass of 860 kg.

Their main food consists of gelatinous plankton such as jellyfish, but they also feed on molluscs, echinoderms and crustaceans. These turtles are fast-growing and may live for more than 30 years.

The Leatherback Turtles are the most accomplished reptile divers, spending about 60% of their time at depths of between 10 and 250 m. Occasionally, they undertake very deep dives. The deepest dive on record is 1 230 m, but it is likely that even deeper dives are undertaken, because only a few individuals have ever been monitored. Leatherback Turtles can stay submerged for more than 40 minutes on a single breath. They store oxygen supplies in their blood system and tissue, and do not appear to rely on air in their lungs during dives. The blood has high concentrations of haemoglobin and thus a high oxygen carrying capacity. The lungs collapse at great depths due to the hydrostatic pressure and are thus unable to supply oxygen to the body at this time.

Leatherback Turtles can maintain a significantly higher body temperature than the water in which they swim due to several anatomical adaptations. Their large size, small surface area to volume ratio, layers of subdermal fat and an efficient counter-current heat exchange system in the flippers all serve to conserve heat that is produced by metabolism. Temperature differences of up to 18 °C between body and water have been recorded, and the ability to remain warmer than the water allows Leatherback Turtles to range into cool, temperate waters. Although it has previously been suggested that high body temperatures are indicative of an endothermic metabolism more similar to that of mammals than other reptiles, Leatherbacks are simply efficient at retaining the small amounts of heat generated by their typical reptilian metabolic processes.

Hatchling Leatherback Turtles fall prey to many predators when emerging from their nests.

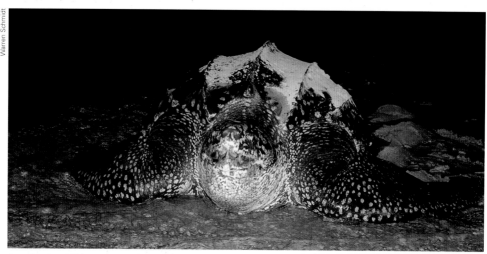

Leatherback Turtles have no horny plates on the carapace or plastron. Instead, the scutes are covered with a leathery skin.

Female Leatherback Turtles come ashore to nest on the Maputoland and Mozambique coast during summer.

Conservation

The Leatherback Turtle is listed by the IUCN as 'Critically Endangered'. This ranking means that the species is 'facing a very high risk of extinction in the wild in the near future'. It is also listed in Appendix I of CITES. There have been dramatic worldwide declines in populations of Leatherback Turtles since the 1980s, which appear to be primarily due to the high numbers of turtles being caught as by-catch during pelagic long-line fishery operations. Leatherback Turtles forage along oceanic fronts, where warm and cold water meet, which is also where pelagic fishery operations concentrate. Research on population trends and mortality rates indicate that the Leatherback Turtle population in the Indo-Pacific is likely to become extinct soon, and has already reached critically low numbers. Populations that bred on Indian shores died out before 1930, and those from Sri Lanka and Malaysia have recently become effectively extinct. At least 1 500 female

Leatherbacks were killed per year by long-line and gill-net fisheries during the 1990s, representing a 23% annual mortality rate. Research indicates that mortality rates of less than 1% per annum are needed for populations to be sustainable. Data collected by conservation authorities in South Africa during the 1980s indicated that, to an extent, the population nesting on the northern KwaZulu-Natal and Mozambique coasts has recovered from past exploitation of nesting females and eggs. However, although the number of nesting females has increased, it is unlikely that protection of nesting beaches alone will suffice in the longer term. Ominous reports of Leatherbacks being caught by long-line fishing off Madagascar suggest that this population may soon follow trends shown by other Indo-Pacific populations. Immediate worldwide action is needed to drastically reduce the Leatherback Turtle mortality due to long-line fishing if the imminent extinction of this iconic species is to be prevented.

Reproduction

In southern African waters, mating takes place offshore in early spring, and nesting occurs from October to late January. Females have a multi-year reproductive pattern, returning to the same beach to nest every 1–5 years. Up to 1 000 eggs may be laid in a nesting year, in clutches of about 100 at about 10-day intervals. The females drag themselves onto the nesting beach at night and dig nest cavities above the high-water mark using their hind flippers. The eggs hatch after about 70 days. The hatchlings dig themselves out of the nest cavity at night, the timing of which is probably an adaptation to reduce the risk of predation. Maturity is reached at 5–14 years of age.

Like all marine turtles, Leatherback Turtles have temperature-dependent sex determination, whereby the sex of the hatchling is dependent on the incubation temperature of the egg. The pivotal temperature (temperature at which incubation results in a sex ratio of 1:1 for a clutch) is 29.4 °C, with eggs incubated above this temperature all developing into females. In some instances, prevailing environmental conditions have resulted in extremely biased sex ratios of hatchlings for a given year, and some nesting beaches have produced only a single sex in some years.

Distribution

Leatherback Turtles are distributed worldwide in tropical and temperate waters, including most of the Atlantic and Indo-Pacific oceans. They appear to prefer open water, and turtles are highly mobile, with individuals ranging over entire ocean basins every year. In southern Africa they are more frequently recorded off the east coast and females come ashore to nest on the Maputoland and Mozambique coasts. Genetic research indicates that individuals from the various ocean basins are very closely related to each other, indicating that there is genetic mixing on a worldwide scale, and that all individuals belong to a single species.

Research indicates that populations of Leatherback Turtles are declining rapidly worldwide.

On occasion, Leatherback Turtles have been recorded diving to depths exceeding 1 km. They can also remain under water for a considerable length of time.

SPECIES IN THE GROUP

■ Leatherback Turtle: *Dermochelys coriacea* **CR**

SEA TURTLES
Family: Cheloniidae

This family consists of five genera and six species of large Sea Turtle. It has a world-wide distribution in tropical and temperate seas, with four of the species occurring throughout the Atlantic and Pacific oceans. The shells are flattened and streamlined, and are covered with horny shields. The forelimbs are modified into large flippers. The carapace has 11 or more pairs of marginal scutes around the periphery. The neck withdraws vertically into the shell, but cannot be hidden completely.

Sea Turtles are large, ocean-going turtles that only come ashore to lay eggs.

Sea Turtles

The family Cheloniidae
4 species

Description

Four species of sea turtle occur off the southern African coastline.
All are relatively large, with a maximum carapace length ranging
from 750 mm in the Olive Ridley Turtle to 1.4 m in the Green Turtle.
Maximum carapace length in Hawksbill and Loggerhead turtles is
just over a metre. Females grow larger than males. Olive Ridley
Turtles reach a maximum mass of 45 kg, whereas the other species
can easily exceed 100 kg. The shell is generally heart-shaped, is most
elongate in Hawksbill Turtles and broadest in Olive Ridley Turtles.
Olive Ridley Turtles have six to eight vertebral shields. The other
species generally have five vertebral shields, although occasionally
individuals with four, six or even as many as nine are found in
Green and Loggerhead turtles. Green and Hawksbill turtles have
four pairs of costals, Loggerhead Turtles have five, and Olive Ridley
Turtles have 6–8 pairs. A nuchal scute is present, which may rarely
be divided. The scutes on the carapace of Hawksbill Turtles overlap,
but do not in the other species. Marginal scutes generally number
12 or 13 on each side of the carapace in the Loggerhead, Green and
Hawksbill turtles, and 13 or 14 in the Olive Ridley Turtle, but aberrant
counts are not uncommon. The posterior marginals are strongly
serrated in the Hawksbill Turtle. The upper jaw is flush with the
lower jaw in Green Turtles, projects forward weakly in Loggerhead
and Olive Ridley turtles, and does so strongly in Hawksbill Turtles,

*Sea Turtles, such
as this Loggerhead
Turtle, are large
with flattened and
streamlined shells
that are covered
with horny shields.*

Richard Boycott

Orty Bourquin

The Hawksbill Turtle has been listed by the IUCN as 'Critically Endangered' as its shell is used to produce tortoiseshell products.

forming a hooked beak. There are enlarged scales on the head, and those of the Green Turtle each have a pale border. The forelimbs are modified into large flippers, which are relatively rigid and provide the thrust needed to propel the turtles in water. The hind limbs are shorter than the forelimbs, are strongly webbed and are used primarily as rudders during swimming. Green Turtles have a single claw, and the other species each have two claws on each foot. Claws tend to be more pronounced in juveniles and males. Males have much longer tails than females.

Dorsal coloration varies from dark olive-green, olive-grey, brown or orange-brown. There is often mottling of orange, yellow, brown or black infusions, especially in younger animals. Sea Turtles are paler below, which probably provides them with some degree of camouflage when viewed from below.

Biology

Sea Turtles are great travellers and can cover distances of several thousand kilometres each year. Juveniles are more pelagic than adults, drifting in the ocean currents. They can spend several years in deep water before returning to inhabit shallow coastal waters as they mature. Green Turtles may remain resident in an area for a considerable time, regularly entering estuaries to feed or to escape the cold. High densities of this species have been recorded in the Cunene River estuary on the northern Namibian border, and it is likely that the warm waters of this estuary offer some respite from the cold waters of the Benguela Current that sweeps the west coast of southern Africa. 'Cold-stunning', due to abnormally cold weather conditions, can kill young and adult turtles when body temperatures are forced below 15 °C, immobilizing and eventually drowning them.

Although not as proficient as the Leatherback Turtle, Sea Turtles are able to maintain body temperature above water temperature. For example, Loggerhead Turtles have been recorded maintaining differentials of up to 8 °C between body and water temperature. These turtles bask while floating, with the carapace exposed to the sun's rays. Heat is efficiently conducted through the shell to the blood in the alveoli of the lungs, which are situated just below the highest point of the carapace. This heat is then transported to the internal parts of the body by the circulatory system. When the turtles dive, the 'thermal window' that allowed heat into the body so effectively is closed by dramatic changes in the circulatory system. These changes limit the blood flow to the lungs while maintaining blood flow to rest of the body. The flexibility and versatility of the circulatory system

of Sea Turtles is made possible by the incomplete ventricular septum in the heart, which allows blood to be shunted from the pulmonary to the systemic systems, or vice versa. Green Turtles have also been recorded basking out of water on the Hawaiian Islands and on the secluded beaches on the west coast of southern Africa. It is possible that these animals are forced onto land by low water temperatures.

Sea Turtles spend the major portion of their lives diving. Loggerhead Turtles, for example, spend about 85% of their time submerged, and dives can last up to 40 minutes, although most are of shorter duration. They have a high aerobic capacity, which allows prolonged exercise without fatigue, a characteristic that is usually only associated with the endothermic birds and mammals. Occasional deep dives to avoid predators, or for feeding, may extend well beyond 40 minutes and can reach several hundred metres in depth. Such dives are facilitated by a high tolerance to anaerobic metabolism in the brain. The main oxygen store carried by the turtles during diving appears to be in the large lungs; there is little specialization of the blood or lungs, as is seen in the Leatherback Turtle. However, Sea Turtles' lungs cannot completely resist the hydrostatic pressure, and begin to collapse at 80–160 m below the surface. Air is forced from the alveoli of the lungs into the main, non-respiratory airways. This limits oxygen exchange at the lung surface during deep dives, but is probably important in preventing damage of the delicate cells in the alveoli due to high oxygen partial pressure under these conditions, and also prevents turtles from experiencing the bends when they surface. During deep dives, the heart rate slows and blood supply to the peripheral parts of the body is reduced drastically, resulting in energy saving.

There are several reports of turtles 'hibernating' on the ocean floor without ready access to air. Loggerhead Turtles have

Richard Boycott

Female Loggerhead Turtles lay 4 or 5 clutches of about 100 eggs each during a breeding season.

been observed hibernating while partially buried in the walls of submarine canyons, and Green Turtles have been seen resting in a state of dormancy on the ocean floor. This peculiar behaviour suggests that these turtles can survive without breathing for weeks or even longer, but the phenomenon has not yet been investigated.

Sea Turtles are long-lived and take many years to reach maturity. Hawksbill and Olive Ridley turtles become sexually active at 6–10 years of age, Loggerhead Turtles take 15–20 years, and Green Turtles are particularly slow in maturing, taking 20–50 years. Evidence suggests that Green Turtles can live for more than 100 years.

The diet of Sea Turtles is varied and specialized, and changes as the turtles mature. Juvenile Green Turtles feed on jellyfish and other planktonic creatures, but become vegetarian as they mature, feeding almost exclusively on sea grass, algae, and mangrove tree leaves and cotyledons. Juvenile Hawksbill Turtles eat floating seaweed, but switch to benthic invertebrates such as corals, sea urchins and sponges when adult. Juvenile Loggerhead Turtles feed on jellyfish and other planktonic creatures, but adults turn primarily to molluscs, sea urchins and crustaceans as their main prey items. Olive Ridley Turtles feed on crustaceans, fish and squid.

Conservation

The Hawksbill Turtle is listed by the IUCN as 'Critically Endangered' on account of exploitation for tortoiseshell. The other three species of Sea Turtle that occur in southern African waters are listed by the IUCN as 'Endangered' and all appear in CITES Appendix I. Threats include high levels of harvesting of beaching females and clutches of eggs for human consumption, exploitation for the curio trade, by-catch by pelagic fisheries, pollution and degradation of nesting habitat. Also, night lights from urban areas disorientate emerging hatchlings, making them move away from, rather than to, the water. Conservation measures appear to be effective, and the level of threat is under control in South Africa and Namibia, with

Ezemvelo KZN Wildlife

Green Turtles are slow-growing and can take as long as 50 years to mature. Evidence suggests that they can live for more than 100 years.

numbers of nesting Loggerhead Turtles on the South African coastline appearing to have recovered since the 1980s. However, the levels of exploitation are largely unmonitored in Mozambique.

Reproduction

Of the four species in this group, only Loggerhead Turtles nest regularly on the southern African coastline in any numbers. Several hundred females lay eggs each year on the Maputoland coast, between Cape Vidal and the Mozambique border, in KwaZulu-Natal. An unknown number of these turtles nest along the Mozambique coast, and a small number nest on the Bazaruto Archipelago. Mating takes place in coastal waters between September and October, and females are able to lay several batches of fertile eggs after a single mating. Each female lays 4–5 clutches at 15-day intervals, but may only return to lay every second or third year. Females come ashore at night to dig nests above the high tide mark. The eggs are about 45 mm in diameter, and an average clutch numbers just over 100. Nesting occurs from the end of October to January, incubation takes about two months, and hatching takes place from January to mid-April.

Although hatching may occur at any time of day or night, hatchlings only emerge from the nest at night. They begin digging immediately after hatching, but their emergence is synchronized with darkness, as digging is inhibited by high temperatures and ceases when the sand reaches 30 °C. They will therefore wait for the cool surface sand at night before emerging. Once they have emerged, the hatchlings make a frenetic rush to the sea. Females return to their natal beaches to nest. A few Green Turtles also nest on the Bazaruto Archipelago off the Mozambique coast. Their reproductive biology is similar to that of Loggerhead Turtles, but females usually lay 2–3 clutches per season.

Sea Turtles have temperature-dependent sex determination, where the sex of the hatchling is dependent on the incubation temperature of the egg. The pivotal temperature (temperature at which 50% of the clutch will be female) is 28.6–29.7 °C for Loggerhead Turtles, with eggs incubated above this temperature developing into females. In Green Turtles, the pivotal temperature is 28.7 °C.

Distribution

Sea Turtles are wide ranging, and all species in the group occur in tropical and temperate seas throughout the world. In southern Africa, all four species occur along the east coast, especially in the northern parts, but only the Green Turtle occurs on the West Coast, probably extending as far south as Walvis Bay on the Namibian coast.

Richard Boycott

The upper jaw of Loggerhead Turtles projects slightly forwards. This characteristic distinguishes them from Green Turtles.

SPECIES IN THE GROUP

- Green Turtle: *Chelonia mydas* **EN**
- Hawksbill Turtle: *Eretmochelys imbricata* **CR**
- Loggerhead Turtle: *Caretta caretta* **EN**
- Olive Ridley Turtle: *Lepidochelys olivacea* **EN**

TORTOISES
Family: Testudinidae

This family contains at least 45 species of terrestrial tortoise, which are grouped into 11 genera. Species occur on several Indian Ocean and Galapagos islands, and on all the continents except Australia and Antarctica. They reach their highest species richness in southern Africa, where 14 species, grouped into five genera, occur. Tortoises are diurnal herbivores that have well-developed bony shells that serve to protect the body. The shell is covered with horny shields or scutes. Eyes are well developed, and large scales cover the head. The head is characteristically withdrawn straight back into the shell by a vertical, S-shaped bending of the neck. In all southern African species the head can withdraw completely so that that it is entirely hidden by the forelimbs, which are also withdrawn and are closed over the head. The legs are well developed and the rear legs are columnar in structure. They are generally covered with large tubercles, which serve to armour the legs and provide added protection when the head is withdrawn into the shell. The feet are never webbed and usually carry stout claws. Males have an obviously longer tail than do females, and their plastron tends to be concave to facilitate mounting the female. All species lay eggs, which have hard, calcareous shells.

Marius Burger

Tortoises are unmistakable. They reach their highest species richness in southern Africa, where 14 species occur.

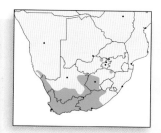

Padlopers

The genus *Homopus*
5 species

Description

This group consists of five species of very small tortoise. Carapace length ranges from 60–165 mm, and females generally attain a slightly larger size than males. Body mass in adults can vary from less than 70 g to 650 g. One member of the group, the Speckled Padloper, is the smallest species of tortoise in the world. The carapace is not hinged, is relatively flat in profile and almost rectangular when viewed from above. The shields on the carapace are never raised into pyramids and are usually depressed in the centre, giving an almost 'garage door' appearance. The gulars are paired and a nuchal shield is present. Marginal shields usually number 11 or 12 on each side, although deviations in scute counts and pattern are relatively common in the group. There are usually five vertebrals and four pairs of costal shields. The beak varies from being obviously hooked in the Parrot-beaked Tortoise, to weakly hooked or completely unhooked in the other species. Viewed from the front, the beak is usually tricuspid, but may be unicuspid or straight in the Speckled Padloper. The edge of the beak is obviously serrated in the Greater Padloper, less so in the Parrot-beaked Padloper and Karoo Padloper, and may be smooth in the Speckled Padloper and Nama Padloper. Forelimbs have either four (Greater Padloper and Parrot-beaked Padloper) or five nails and are covered with large overlapping scales. Hind limbs always have four nails. Buttock tubercles are present in the Greater Padloper and Speckled Padloper, but are generally absent in the other species. The tail lacks a terminal spike in all species.

The Parrot-beaked Padloper is found in coastal fynbos and is restricted to the southern Cape. This specimen is unusual in having five, rather than the typical four, pairs of costal shields.

Marius Burger

Coloration is variable, both within and among species, and often appears to match the dominant colours of the rock or soil in the natural habitat. The primary carapace colour varies from a yellowish, reddish or toffee brown to dark brown. The Karoo Padloper is always plain and is usually toffee brown in colour, whereas the other species have some degree of patterning or speckling on the carapace. The Greater Padloper usually has dark brown scutes with pale yellow edges, although the pale edges are faded in most large individuals. The Nama Padloper and Parrot-beaked Padloper normally have dark edging to the scutes. As the name suggests, most Speckled Padlopers have dark speckling on the carapace, which sometimes forms a regular star-like pattern. Generally, skin colour on the head and legs matches, or may be a little darker than, the colour of the carapace.

Biology

Padlopers are normally associated with rocky or stony areas, and often occur on ridges or plateaus. Horizontal rock crevices appear to be a very important habitat component as tortoises use them for protection from predators and from very hot and cold conditions. These tortoises are good climbers and can negotiate rocky terrain and steep climbs with remarkable ease. Their small size and flat profile make it possible for them to access crevices that would exclude other species. The Nama

The nasal scales of male Parrot-beaked Padlopers become orange during the breeding season.

Padloper's shell is thin and flexible as well, further facilitating access. In some parts, Padlopers hibernate in deep burrows in winter, but in warmer parts they may be active through the winter period. Although they appear to be relatively fast-growing, and may even reach sexual maturity in just over a year, they are probably long-lived and there are records of individuals living for up to 30 years in captive conditions. Little is known about the natural diet of Padlopers, but they are known to feed on grasses, herbs and shrubs. Succulents are included in the diet of species that occur in arid regions, and provide much of the water requirements of the tortoises. Insects are also consumed on occasion.

The Karoo Padloper occurs widely in the southern parts of the nama karoo.

The Nama Padloper has a restricted distribution and is listed by the IUCN as 'Vulnerable'.

Conservation

The Nama Padloper has a restricted distribution and is listed by the IUCN as 'Vulnerable'. This species was only recently rediscovered and described in the scientific literature The Speckled Padloper is listed by the IUCN as 'Near Threatened', and one of its subspecies, the Southern Speckled Padloper (*Homopus signatus cafer*), is listed as 'Restricted' in the latest Red Data Book on South African reptiles due to its limited range. It was recently also rated as one of the 25 most endangered tortoises in the world by the International Turtle Conservation Fund. All species of Padloper are listed in CITES Appendix II on account of their demand in the pet trade. Generally, this is a poorly known group and research on population demographics and distribution are needed to better evaluate the conservation status of all species.

Reproduction

Both the mating and laying seasons appear to extend from late winter to late summer. During the mating season, combat between males appears to be common and animated, at least in some of the species, and aggressive males may even target females. Parts of the head of Parrot-beaked Padloper males may change colour to a deep red-orange during the breeding season. Mating is preceded by males following females and by head bobbing from both sexes. Clutches are small, and 1–4 eggs are laid in small excavations dug by the female, usually about 70 mm below the substrate surface. The hole is often dug under overhanging rock slabs, which may offer additional protection to the clutch. The smaller species appear to lay only one egg per clutch, but several clutches may

The Parrot-beaked Padloper is one of the smallest tortoises.

The smaller species of Padloper, such as this Southern Speckled Padloper, generally lay a single egg in a clutch.

Padlopers, such as this Speckled Padloper, have an unhinged, relatively flat carapace that is almost rectangular when viewed from above.

be laid per season. Although eggs can take as little as three months to hatch, those laid late in summer can have delayed incubation and may take more than 300 days to hatch.

Distribution

All species of Padloper are endemic to southern Africa and are generally distributed in the southern and southwestern parts of the subregion. Several of the species appear to be restricted to relatively arid areas, but the Parrot-beaked Padloper is found in the more moist coastal regions of the south coast, from the Cape Peninsula, eastwards to East London, and inland to Cradock and Middlepos. The Greater Padloper is found in the grasslands and bushveld of mountain plateaus up to an altitude of 1 800 m in the south and south-central parts of South Africa and southern Lesotho. Its range overlaps with that of the Karoo Padloper, which is restricted to the Karoo, from Montagu to Britstown, and Somerset East to Vanwyksvlei. The Speckled Padloper is restricted to the West Coast of South Africa and the southern extremes of Namibia, and the Nama Padloper is found only in southern Namibia, from Lüderitz, south to the Orange River.

The Greater Padloper is the largest Padloper and usually has a plain shell.

SPECIES IN THE GROUP

- Greater Padloper: *Homopus femoralis*
- Karoo Padloper: *Homopus boulengeri*
- Nama Padloper: *Homopus solus* **VU**
- Parrot-beaked Padloper: *Homopus areolatus*
- Speckled Padloper: *Homopus signatus* **NT**

Angulate Tortoise

The genus *Chersina*
1 species

Description

The single, unique species of medium-sized tortoise that makes up this group is the sole member of the genus and is endemic to southern Africa. It is unusual in that it has only a single projecting gular shield; all other land tortoises have a pair. This shield protrudes forward in males and is used in male-male contests as a battering ram. In exceptional cases, total shell length may reach 300 mm and mass can exceed 2 kg, but maximum lengths of 250 mm and masses of about 1.5 kg are more usual. Males grow larger than females. The carapace is not hinged and has a pronounced dome and steep sides. Viewed from above, the shell has a narrow, oval shape, which is more elongate and rectangular in mature males. A small nuchal scute is present as well as five vertebral scutes, four pairs of costals, and 10–12 marginal shields on each side. There are five claws on the front feet and four on each of the hind feet. The beak may be bicuspid or tricuspid, and is sometimes serrated. There are no tubercles on the buttock and the tail has no terminal spike.

This is a strikingly marked species. The vertebral and costal shields are dark grey or black with a yellow centre that encircles a dark areola. Yellow lines of varying width connect the centres of the costals to the marginal scutes. The marginal scutes are patterned with alternating triangles of black and yellow, forming a regular zigzag around the margin of the carapace. Old individuals may become darker and plainer in coloration. Uniform pale individuals are also known.

Angulate Tortoises have striking markings; there is a regular zigzag around the margin of the carapace.

Marius Burger

Biology

The Angulate Tortoise is a hardy generalist that is found in a wide variety of vegetation types, ranging from semi-desert to fynbos, succulent karoo to thicket. It can occur at densities in excess of 15 individuals per hectare, but appears to be sensitive to veld fires: aseasonal wildfires can have an important negative impact on population numbers. In many of the warmer parts of its range, this species can remain active year-round. Home ranges are relatively small, at around 2.5 ha. The species has been recorded to live more than 32 years in captivity, and appears to be a generalist feeder. It has been recorded consuming a wide variety of plant species, including grasses, annuals and succulents. Like several other species of tortoise, it has been recorded drinking water by sucking it into the nostrils.

Reproduction

Male Angulate Tortoises exhibit intensive male-male combat during the mating season, which lasts from September to April. They use their enlarged gular shields as levers to overturn and repeatedly ram rivals. The intention to mate is signalled with head-bobbing and nudging, and the male will persistently trail the female until successful. Adult females are gravid for much of the year and have a cyclical pattern whereby several single or, very occasionally,

Angulate Tortoises can occur at densities above 15 individuals per hectare.

2-egg clutches are laid between March and December. The time between laying is variable (23–212 days) and ovulation occurs immediately after an egg has been laid, except during a brief resting period in January, when the females are not gravid. On average, females produce 4 hard-shelled eggs (25 x 35 mm) per year, but this can vary from 1–6. Females usually lay shortly after rain has softened the ground, but will also urinate to facilitate digging of the 120-mm-deep nest cavity. The period of incubation is variable, ranging from 3–7 months, depending to some extent on the temperature. Hatchlings are about 35 mm long and emerge after the first winter rains.

Distribution

This species is endemic to the southern and Western Cape coast, occurring from East London in the east, and extending just into the southwestern extremes of Namibia. Although it is typically a coastal species, the range does extend inland significantly in the southeastern parts, occurring as far inland as Cradock. However, population densities are much lower inland.

Angulate Tortoises can drink by sucking water through their nostrils.

SPECIES IN THE GROUP

- Angulate Tortoise: *Chersina angulata*

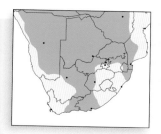

Leopard Tortoise

The genus *Stigmochelys pardalis*
1 species

Description

The single species included in this group is easily the largest tortoise species in southern Africa. It can exceed 40 kg and has a carapace length of 750 mm in exceptional cases. However, most adults range from 300–450 mm and weigh 8–12 kg. Females usually grow larger than males. In addition to Leopard Tortoises varying markedly in adult size, there is also a great deal of variation in the shape of the carapace, coloration and degree of patterning. Although most individuals have a relatively smooth, highly domed carapace, the dorsal scutes of some are each raised like small pyramids, possibly as a result of diet. The shell is not hinged. There are usually five vertebrals, four pairs of costals and 10–12 marginals on each side. The posterior four marginals on either side are usually serrated, at least to some extent, and the posterior-most two are often upturned, especially in old individuals. There is no nuchal shield. The plastron is obviously concave in adult males. The eyes are well developed, and the head is rectangular in profile. The beak is usually unicuspid and may be strongly serrated, but is entirely smooth in some individuals. The legs are well developed and there are five claws on each of the front feet and four on each hind foot. The forelimbs are armoured with large tubercles and there are tubercles on the buttock. The tail is much longer in males and does not have a terminal spine.

The Leopard Tortoise is easily the largest species of tortoise in southern Africa. It derives its name from the dark spots on the carapace.

Johan Marais

Coloration varies geographically, especially in adults. Juveniles tend to be pale yellow with a large dark spot in the centre of each vertebral and costal scute. All scutes on the carapace are usually dark-edged. In adults the carapace tends to become a dull brown, with irregular dark brown or black flecks radiating from the centre of the vertebrals and costals. Some individuals are irregularly blotched, giving a spotted appearance. Very large, old individuals may become almost completely plain dull brown.

Biology

Like most species of tortoise, Leopard Tortoises are diurnal, emerging to bask in the morning before commencing feeding. Inactive and dormant periods are spent under thick vegetation or in appropriately sized crevices, where the tortoise may dig a shallow 'scrape' that it can use for extended periods. Individuals will remain in such retreats, without emerging, for weeks during cold periods. Leopard Tortoises appear to have home ranges that can exceed 80 ha in extent, and in some situations, much larger. Growth is slow during the first years, probably because small tortoises are more prone to predation and are thus restricted in their feeding activity as a result of their need to remain under cover. However, when body size has increased to the point of providing a measure of protection, growth accelerates, and sexual maturity is reached at about 10 years of age. Data on captive specimens indicate that Leopard Tortoises are probably long-lived, as some individuals have been known to survive for more than 30 years.

The diet includes a wide variety of plants, including succulents, grass shoots and fallen fruits. Short, tender grass that grows on path edges or ungulate grazing lawns appears to be an important food source. Fungi, carnivore faeces and bones are also consumed, possibly as a source of calcium. The sense of smell appears to be

important for locating food. Under captive conditions, phosphorus-rich or calcium-poor foods that result in diets of low calcium-phosphorus ratios tend to result in scute pyramiding. In the same way, excess protein or the lack of ultraviolet light exposure can cause carapace deformation, especially in the first five years.

Reproduction

Leopard Tortoises have an extended breeding season. Mating has been recorded from September to April, during which

Leopard Tortoises have a varied diet, including succulents, grass shoots and fruits.

time the male's forthright and animated approach to procreation includes bouts of competitor ramming and boisterous butting of prospective mates. Several clutches of 6–18 hard-shelled eggs (diameter about 45 mm) are laid between October and May. Prior to laying, the female uses her keen sense of smell to select the appropriate soil conditions for a nesting site. She then urinates to soften the ground and digs a hole about 250 mm deep with her hind feet. After laying is complete the cavity is carefully filled with the excavated soil, which is patted firmly in place with the hind feet. Incubation is generally slow and can exceed a year, but the majority of eggs appear to hatch in March and April. After hatching, juveniles may be trapped in the nest cavity for an extended time and may have to wait for the softening effects of soaking rain before being able to dig themselves free. The hatchlings usually dig an exit tunnel with a 45° inclination to the surface. Average hatchling mass is about 35 g.

Leopard Tortoises have home ranges that can exceed 80 ha in extent.

Leopard Tortoises often have a serrated beak, but some individuals, such as this one, have smooth beaks.

Distribution

The Leopard Tortoise has an atypical distribution pattern in southern Africa. It is widespread over most of the northern parts of the subregion, extending through the central parts of South Africa to the south Cape coast, from Montagu in the west, almost as far east as East London. In Namibia, it is excluded only from the western coastal parts, and it occurs throughout Botswana, Zimbabwe, and through much of the Limpopo, North West and Mpumalanga provinces in South Africa. It is found in the northern parts of Gauteng and the northern parts of KwaZulu-Natal. It also occurs widely north of southern Africa, extending to Ethiopia and the Sudan. The Leopard Tortoise's popularity as a pet has resulted in it being introduced to many areas in South Africa where it did not previously occur, especially around towns and cities. Intriguingly, several feral populations have been established in this way, but it is uncertain if these will be self-sustaining in the long-term.

SPECIES IN THE GROUP

■ Leopard Tortoise: *Stigmochelys pardalis*

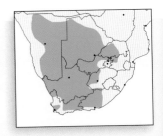

Tent Tortoises

The genus *Psammobates*
3 species

Description

This group includes three species of small tortoise that have characteristically raised scutes on the carapace and striking geometric patterns on the shell. The taxonomy of the group is not yet fully resolved, and ongoing genetic research is likely to reveal the presence of cryptic species. This is especially likely in one of the currently defined species, the Karoo Tent Tortoise, which has three recognized subspecies and a significant amount of variation in colour, patterning and morphology. Adult carapace length ranges from 80–150 mm and body mass from 200–600 g. Females grow larger than males. Tent Tortoises normally have a strongly domed carapace, but some populations of Karoo Tent Tortoise have a relatively flat carapace. The shell is not hinged. A nuchal scute is present and, in the Kalahari Tent Tortoise, is sometimes divided in two. The gulars are paired and are longer than they are broad. There are five vertebrals, four pairs of costal scutes and usually 11 marginal scutes on each side, but individuals with 10 or 12 are known. The anterior and posterior marginal scutes are strongly serrated in the Kalahari Tent Tortoise, but are relatively smooth in the other species. The eyes are well developed and relatively large. The snout is often bulbous and there are enlarged scales on the head. The beak is

Marius Burger

Tent Tortoises, such as this Karoo Tent Tortoise, typically have striking geometric patterns on the shell.

The Kalahari Tent Tortoise has serrated marginal scutes, a feature that distinguishes it from other Tent Tortoises.

The Geometric Tortoise is restricted to the coastal renosterveld of the Western Cape. It is listed by the IUCN as 'Endangered'.

Young Geometric Tortoises hatch after rain and emerge from their nests between March and May.

usually hooked and can have 1–3 cusps. Forelimbs have five claws and enlarged scales, which may be arranged in rows or cover the anterior surface completely. The hind limbs have four claws. Buttock tubercles are present in the Kalahari Tent Tortoise and Karoo Tent Tortoise, but absent in the Geometric Tortoise. The tail does not have a terminal spine.

Most Tent Tortoises are brightly coloured, with striking markings, making them the most attractive group of tortoises in southern Africa. The Geometric Tortoise has a carapace that is shiny black with bright yellow rays radiating from the centres of the scutes. The plastron can be pale yellow with a black centre, or dark with a yellow margin. The Kalahari Tent Tortoise has similar shell markings to the Geometric Tortoise, but the colours tend to be less vivid. Colours and markings in the Karoo Tent Tortoise are variable, ranging from vivid black and yellow geometric patterns similar to the Geometric Tortoise, to uniform russet or dark brown without any evidence of rays. Where rays are evident, they can vary from pale yellow to brown or orange. The head and legs are generally yellow or orange with black bars or blotches.

Biology

Little is known about the biology of Kalahari and Karoo Tent Tortoises as both species typically occur in low densities, making research difficult. Conservation threats to the Geometric Tortoise have focused attention on this species, and it is thus better known despite its extreme rarity. Geometric Tortoises can occur at densities of more than 2.5 tortoises per hectare in prime habitat, but populations are susceptible to veld fires, especially when the veld is burnt frequently because of human intervention. Mortality rates of up to 80% have been recorded after fires, and the recovery of populations is dependent on the successful emergence of hatchlings after the fire. Since Geometric

Tortoises take 5–8 years to mature, veld fires that occur more frequently do not allow these young tortoises to reach sexual maturity and can, therefore, threaten the survival of entire populations. The Kalahari and Karoo Tent Tortoises tend to become more dormant during the dry winter and may partially bury themselves in sand or retreat into animal burrows. The Geometric Tortoise is active throughout the year, but does become less active during the colder months. Tent Tortoises are particularly active after rain. Like most tortoises, they are long-lived and have been kept for more than 19 years in captivity.

Some populations of Karoo Tent Tortoise exhibit a peculiar behavioural adaptation that allows them to drink rainwater that runs off their shells. The posterior parts of the body are raised by fully extending the hind limbs, and the forelimbs are pressed firmly along the anterior margin of the shell. Rain falling on the anterior parts of the shell runs forwards into the furrow formed by the forelimbs and shell, and is channelled to the mouth. Little is known about the preferred diet of Tent Tortoises, as they do not thrive in captivity. They have been observed eating succulents, herbs and grasses.

The Karoo Tent Tortoise occurs at low densities throughout its range and is generally difficult to find.

Conservation

Although the Kalahari Tent Tortoise and Karoo Tent Tortoise are widespread, they tend to occur at low densities over most of their range and are listed in CITES Appendix II. The Geometric Tortoise is more threatened. It is listed in CITES Appendix I and classified by the IUCN as 'Endangered', indicating that it is facing a very high risk of extinction in the wild in the near future. Populations have declined due to the destruction of its natural habitat for farming, the encroachment of urban sprawl, the establishment of invasive alien vegetation, pollution, poor veld management and increased frequency of veld fires. Only small pockets of suitable habitat remain and these fragments are isolated, leaving populations 'marooned' as if on islands. These small, isolated populations are prone to extinction through random population fluctuations, and the survival of the species is now reliant on active conservation management. Survival of the Geometric Tortoise is also dependent on protection of the remaining suitable habitat. More than 90% of the original renosterveld, on which the species depends, has already been transformed by human activity.

Reproduction

The reproductive pattern of Tent Tortoises is typified by extended breeding cycles and low rates of egg production. Mating occurs from July to December. The Kalahari Tent Tortoise male may butt and nudge the female as a prelude to mating. Kalahari Tent Tortoises lay single-egg clutches, whereas Karoo Tent Tortoises lay clutches of 1–3 eggs. Geometric Tortoises can lay 1–5 eggs, although 5-egg clutches are rare. Eggs are oval and generally about 30 x 36 mm in size. Laying can occur any time from August to June, and incubation can be anything from 120 to 220 days. Geometric Tortoises

Johan Marais

Karoo Tent Tortoises are found in areas of rocky sandveld.

have been recorded laying two clutches in a season, and it is likely that the other species can also lay more than one clutch per year. Young hatch after rain and emerge between March and May. They have a shell length of about 25–30 mm.

Distribution

The Geometric Tortoise has a very restricted distribution and is limited to renosterveld in the Western Cape coastal area, extending from Gordon's Bay, northwards to the vicinity of Eendekuil. The Karoo Tent Tortoise is much more widespread, occurring throughout the nama karoo and into the succulent karoo. The Kalahari Tent Tortoise is also widespread and occurs over much of the eastern and northern parts of Namibia, Botswana, the western parts of the Free State and North West provinces, and the northern parts of the Northern Cape province of South Africa.

Richard Boycott

Three subspecies of the Karoo Tent Tortoise are currently recognized. Some of these may prove to be different species.

SPECIES IN THE GROUP

- Geometric Tortoise: *Psammobates geometricus* **EN**
- Kalahari Tent Tortoise: *Psammobates oculiferus*
- Karoo Tent Tortoise: *Psammobates tentorius*

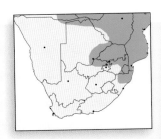

Hinged Tortoises

The genus *Kinixys*
4 species

Description

This group includes four species of medium-sized tortoise that have an elongated shell and a well-developed hinge between the seventh and eighth marginal scutes on the posterior half of the carapace. The hinge is poorly developed or completely absent in juveniles. Maximum shell length varies from 155 to 210 mm and adult body mass varies from 600 g to nearly 2 kg. Females grow larger than males. The carapace is generally convex, but may be depressed so that the middle of the back is relatively flat. There are five (sometimes six) vertebral scutes, four pairs of costals and 11 (occasionally 12) marginals on each side. A nuchal shield is usually present and may be divided. The prominent beak is tricuspid in the Natal Hinged Tortoise and unicuspid in the other species. There are five claws on the forelimbs and four on each hind limb. The forelimbs have enlarged tubercles, which are arranged in rows and interspersed with smaller scales. The tail has a terminal spine, which is more prominent in males, and the buttocks lack turbercles.

Coloration and markings are variable. Some individuals of each species are uniform brown, whereas others have vivid concentric rings of yellow and dark brown on the dorsal scutes. Other individuals have a broken, rayed pattern on a dark brown and yellow background. Usually, the areola has a dark centre and yellow rim, and the dark and light rays radiate from this rim. The head and legs are usually yellow or brown with dark brown or black blotches.

Richard Boycott

Hinged Tortoises, such as this Lobatse Hinged Tortoise, have a hinge between the seventh and eighth marginal scutes on the carapace.

Biology

Hinged Tortoises generally occur in relatively low densities. A study on Speke's Hinged Tortoise reported a density of just over two individuals per hectare. However, they appear to be quite mobile and have home ranges of several hectares. They are diurnal and active from early morning to late afternoon. Activity is stimulated by rainfall. Lobatse Hinged Tortoises appear to return to a familiar retreat site such as a shallow burrow, termitarium or an appropriately sized rock crevice in which they shelter, and this is likely to provide some protection from fire and low night-time temperatures. Veld fires can be a major cause of mortality in Hinged Tortoises, and Lobatse Hinged Tortoises often bear evidence of healed burns. Hinged Tortoises become dormant during the dry season, sheltering in mammal burrows or partially burying themselves under bushes. Speke's Hinged Tortoise has been shown to exhibit metabolic depression during this time, with a metabolic rate only half the expected level. Specimens have lived for up to 22 years in captivity. Diet is varied and includes grasses, succulent and semi-succulent shrubs, forbs and a variety of indigenous fruits. Millipedes, insects, snails, mushrooms and carrion are also eaten.

Conservation

The Natal Hinged Tortoise is listed by the IUCN as 'Near Threatened'. Threats include extensive habitat destruction in the restricted range of the species. All Hinged Tortoises are listed in CITES Appendix II.

Reproduction

Most observations report mating from September to November, but mating behaviour has also been recorded in the Natal Hinged Tortoise during February. Laying takes place from November to April, with clutches numbering 2–10 hard-shelled eggs (approximately 35 x 45 mm). Bell's Hinged Tortoise lays several clutches

Speke's Hinged Tortoise occurs in the savannas of northeastern southern Africa.

Graham Alexander

Richard Boycott

Habitat transformation has resulted in the Natal Hinged Tortoise being listed by the IUCN as 'Near Threatened'.

throughout the breeding season at 40-day intervals, and it is likely that other species in the group show similar laying patterns. Reported incubation times vary from three to more than 10 months, and hatchlings have been recorded from September to April.

Distribution

Hinged Tortoises are restricted to the northern and eastern parts of southern Africa. Bell's Hinged Tortoises and Speke's Hinged Tortoises are widespread, occurring north into east and central Africa. The remaining two species have more restricted ranges and are endemic to southern Africa. The Lobatse Hinged Tortoise occurs in parts of North West and Limpopo provinces of South Africa, extending marginally into Botswana, and the Natal Hinged Tortoise is restricted to parts of the KwaZulu-Natal lowlands, extending into Swaziland and the southeastern parts of Mpumalanga. Hinged Tortoises occur in a wide range of habitat types, including bushveld, thornveld, savanna woodland, forest and grassland.

Richard Boycott

Bell's Hinged Tortoise is restricted to the eastern parts of southern Africa, but occurs widely in other parts of Africa.

SPECIES IN THE GROUP

- Bell's Hinged Tortoise: *Kinixys belliana*
- Lobatse Hinged Tortoise: *Kinixys lobatsiana*
- Natal Hinged Tortoise: *Kinixys natalensis* **NT**
- Speke's Hinged Tortoise: *Kinixys spekii*

GLOSSARY

The definitions provided here pertain specifically to their usage and meaning in this guide – they may also have other meanings.

Aeolian: Relating to the wind; produced or carried by the wind. Aeolian sands have been transported and deposited by wind.

Aestivate: To become dormant in response to dry conditions.

Alate: The winged, sexual stage of a termite.

Anterior: The front.

Antivenom (also antivenin): An antidote to venom. Antivenom for treatment of southern African venomous snakes is produced by immunization of horses.

Aquatic: Living in water.

Arboreal: Living in trees.

Biogeography: The study of distributions of organisms.

Biome: A major biological community defined by its structure and process (eg savanna).

Body temperature: The core body temperature.

Carapace: The dorsal (upper) half of a tortoise or turtle shell.

CITES: An acronym for the Convention on International Trade in Endangered Species of Wild Fauna and Flora, an international agreement between governments.

Cladogram: A diagram that shows the evolutionary relationships between taxa.

Cloaca: The chamber into which the urinary, digestive and reproductive systems discharge their contents, and which opens to the exterior. Found in amphibians, reptiles and birds.

Crepuscular: Active at dusk and dawn.

Critically Endangered: A specific threat level for a 'Threatened' species, defined by the IUCN as 'facing an extremely high risk of extinction in the wild'.

Cryptic: Hidden or difficult to see.

Cytotoxic: Damaging to tissue.

Data Deficient: A category defined by the IUCN for a species where inadequate information exists to make an assessment of its threat status.

Diurnal: Active during the day.

Dorsal: Pertaining to the upper surface.

Dorsolateral: Pertaining to the sides of the upper surface.

Dorsum: The back of an animal.

Ecoregion: A broad level of habitat type, equivalent to a biome.

Endangered: A specific threat level for a 'Threatened' species, defined by the IUCN as 'facing a very high risk of extinction in the wild'.

Endemic: Limited in distribution to a particular area.

Endogenous: From within – the timing of an endogenously entrained rhythm is controlled from within the body.

Endotherm: An organism that produces enough metabolic heat to raise body temperature significantly. Endotherms increase metabolic heat production in response to low temperatures.

Extinct: A specific category defined by the IUCN for a species where 'no reasonable doubt exists that the last individual has died'.

Fang: A modified hollow or grooved tooth that conducts venom.

Forb: A herbaceous plant that is not a grass.

Fossorial: Living underground.

Gular: Relating to the throat.

Haemotoxic: Adversely affecting the blood.

Heliotherm: An organism that uses the sun's rays to raise body temperature.

Hemipenes: The paired copulatory organs of male squamate reptiles.

IUCN: The World Conservation Union.

Keratinous: Consisting largely of keratin, a fibrous protein.

Lateral fold: A fold of skin along the sides of certain lizards.

Loreal scale: A scale between the nasal and preocular scales.

Maxillary bone: A bone in the upper jaw, which carries the fangs in venomous snakes.

Metabolism: The sum total of all chemical reactions in the body. The metabolic rate refers to the rate of these reactions.

Monophyletic: (of a group of species) Evolved from a common ancestor.

Myotoxic: Adversely affecting the muscles.

Near Threatened: A category defined by the IUCN for a species that does not qualify as Threatened, but is close to qualifying or is likely to qualify in the future.

Neurotoxic: Adversely affecting the nerves.

Nocturnal: Active during the night.

Osteoderm: A small bone in the skin of some reptiles.

Oviparous: Egg-laying.

Paraphyletic: (of a group of species) Containing an ancestral species together with some, but not all, of its descendants.

Parthenogenetic: The ability to develop fertile eggs without mating.

Pelagic: Living in the water column of the open ocean, usually away from the coastline.

Phylogeny: The evolutionary relationships between organisms.

Physiology: The bodily function of organisms or the study thereof.

Placenta: The organ of exchange between maternal and foetal blood.

Plastron: The ventral (lower) surface of a tortoise or turtle shell.

Poisonous: Toxic when ingested; for example, some mushrooms are poisonous.

Posterior: The rear part.

Prehensile: Capable of grasping.

Quadrate: A jaw bone in all vertebrates except mammals. The quadrate is highly modified in certain snakes, allowing for a wider gape.

Red Data Book (RDB): A book that specifically assesses the conservation status of a particular group of species.

Robust: Strongly built or having a strong physique.

Rudimentary: Vestigial and having no function.

Rugose: Wrinkled or rough.

Rupicolous: Rock-living.

Scalation: The pattern that scales form.

Scute: A scale; a thin, flattened, plate-like structure that forms part of the epidermis in reptiles, fish and on birds' legs.

Selected body temperature: The core body temperature 'chosen' by an animal through physiological or behavioural means. This temperature is set in the hypothalamus.

Sidewinding: A mode of locomotion used by certain snakes when on smooth or friable surfaces. Progression is achieved by throwing successive undulations of the body forward to gain purchase.

Species richness: The number of species in a given area.

Speciose: (of a taxonomic group) Having many species.

Spinous: Spiny.

Subcaudal: A scale on the ventral part of the tail.

Systematics: Biological classification and the study of relationships between organisms.

Taxon: A taxonomic group at any level of the systematic hierarchy. (Plural = taxa)

Taxonomy: The study of classification, including the delineation and description of species.

Tenebrionid beetle: A beetle belonging to the family Tenebrionidae, a speciose family that includes many species that occur in the Namib Desert.

Termitarium: A termite nest. (Plural = termitaria)

Terrestrial: Living on the ground surface.

Thignotherm: An organism whose body temperature is affected by conduction with the substratum. Fossorial reptiles tend to be thignothermic because much of their surface is in contact with the substratum (*see also heliotherm*).

Threatened: A category defined by the IUCN that includes the 'Critically Endangered', 'Endangered' and 'Vulnerable' threat levels. Also used more generally to denote species that are of conservation concern.

Torpor: A state of dormancy.

Tubercle: A small, rounded protuberance.

Tympanum: The eardrum.

Vasoconstriction: A reduction in the diameter of vessels in the arterial system.

Vasodilation: An increase in the diameter of the vessels in the arterial system.

Venom Clade: The group of related species that have all descended from the same venomous ancestor; includes snakes, Agamas, Monitors and Chameleons.

Venomous: Toxic when injected into the tissue of the body.

Ventral: Relating to the underside.

Ventricular septum: A muscular wall that divides the ventricular region of the heart into two or more chambers.

Vertebral: Pertaining to the region of the backbone.

Vertebrates: Animals that have backbones (includes fish, amphibians, reptiles, birds and mammals).

Vestigial: Reduced in size due to evolution.

Viviparity: Producing live young.

Vulnerable: A specific threat level for a 'Threatened' species, defined by the IUCN as 'facing a high risk of extinction in the wild'.

INDEX TO SCIENTIFIC NAMES

INDEX TO COMMON NAMES

Numbers in **bold** refer to photographs.

Left: Wahlberg's Snake-eyed Skink

TERRAPINS
Terrapin